DATE DUE

Globalization and Human Rights

Globalization
and Human Rights

EDITED BY

Alison Brysk

UNIVERSITY OF CALIFORNIA PRESS

Berkeley   Los Angeles   London

8971745

A portion of the royalties from this book will be donated to Human
Rights Watch University, an electronic educational project under
construction by Human Rights Watch. For more information,
contact:

Pamela Bruns, Executive Director
Human Rights Watch, California
11500 West Olympic Blvd.
Los Angeles, CA 90064

University of California Press
Berkeley and Los Angeles, California

University of California Press, Ltd.
London, England

© 2002 by
The Regents of the University of California

Library of Congress Cataloging-in-Publication Data

Globalization and human rights / edited by Alison Brysk.
      p.   cm.
    Includes bibliographical references and index.
    ISBN 0-520-23237-2 (cloth : alk. paper)—ISBN 0-520-23238-0
(paper : alk. paper)
    1. Human rights.   2. Globalization.
    I. Brysk, Alison.
    JC571.G584   2002
    323'.09'0511—dc21

                                        2002002825

Manufactured in the United States of America

10   09   08   07   06   05   04   03   02
10   9   8   7   6   5   4   3   2   1

The paper used in this publication is both acid-free and totally
chlorine-free (TCF). It meets the minimum requirements of
ANSI/NISO Z39.48–1992 (R 1997) (*Permanence of Paper*).♾

CONTENTS

LIST OF ILLUSTRATIONS / *vii*

ACKNOWLEDGMENTS / *ix*

Introduction: Transnational Threats and Opportunities
Alison Brysk / *1*

I. CITIZENSHIP

1. Who Has a Right to Rights?
Citizenship's Exclusions in an Age of Migration
Kristen Hill Maher / *19*

2. Tourism, Sex Work, and Women's Rights in the Dominican Republic
Amalia Lucia Cabezas / *44*

II. COMMODIFICATION

3. Interpreting the Interaction of Global Markets and Human Rights
Richard Falk / *61*

4. Economic Globalization and Rights: An Empirical Analysis
Wesley T. Milner / *77*

5. Sweatshops and International Labor Standards: Globalizing Markets,
Localizing Norms
Raul C. Pangalangan / *98*

III. COMMUNICATION

6. The Ironies of Information Technology
Shane Weyker / *115*

7. Globalization and the Social Construction of Human Rights Campaigns
Clifford Bob / *133*

8. The Drama of Human Rights in a Turbulent, Globalized World
James N. Rosenau / *148*

IV. COOPERATION

9. Transnational Civil Society Campaigns and the World Bank Inspection Panel
Jonathan Fox / *171*

10. Humanitarian Intervention: Global Enforcement of Human Rights?
Wayne Sandholtz / *201*

11. Human Rights, Globalizing Flows, and State Power
Jack Donnelly / *226*

Conclusion: From Rights to Realities
Alison Brysk / *242*

WORKS CITED / *257*
CONTRIBUTORS / *301*
INDEX / *303*

ILLUSTRATIONS

FIGURES

4.1. Increase in Security Rights Due to Increase in Trade Openness / *91*

9.1. The Political Dynamics of the World Bank's "Sustainable Development" Reforms / *194*

TABLES

1. Streams of Globalization and the Effect on Rights / *8*

4.1. Summary Statistics / *86*

4.2. General Subsistence Rights Model / *87*

4.3. Subsistence Rights Model with Economic Freedom / *88*

4.4. General Security Rights Model / *89*

4.5. Security Rights Model with Economic Freedom / *90*

5.1. Standards, Markets, and Norms / *102*

6.1. Opportunities and Pitfalls of New Technology for Human Rights NGOs / *129*

8.1. The Impact of Turbulence and Globalization on the Conduct of Most Obstreperous Actors in Four Domains of Human Rights / *162*

9.1. World Bank Safeguard Policies / *178*

9.2. World Bank Inspection Panel Claims Filed, 1994–1998 / *182*

9.3. Official Responses to World Bank Inspection Panel Claims Filed, 1994–1998 / *183*

9.4. World Bank Board Votes on the Itaparica Dam Resettlement Claim, September 1997 / *190*

ACKNOWLEDGMENTS

This book was made possible by the support of many people, who share in its merits, while I remain responsible for its shortcomings. It originated as an individual research initiative, generously supported by the Global Peace and Conflict Studies program of the University of California, Irvine. I received helpful suggestions when I presented versions of this research at the UCLA conference "Transnationalism in the Americas," convened by Raymond Rocco, and in the University of Southern California Political Science Department Colloquium series. Next came a 1999 American Political Science Association panel presentation, with Richard Falk, Andrew Moravcsik, James Rosenau, and Kathryn Sikkink, whose contributions are much appreciated.

The January 2000 conference at UC Irvine that produced these essays was generously funded by the University of California's Institute for Global Conflict and Cooperation. Besides the authors of the chapters that follow, thanks are due also to Helen Ingram, George Lopez, Cecilia Lynch, Richard Matthew, Sharon McConnell, David Meyer, William Meyer, Alison Renteln, and David Smith for their useful presentations and commentary.

Neither the conference nor this book would have been possible without the help of Lykke Anderson of the UC Irvine staff and a dedicated band of doctoral students: Suzanne Cornwell, Stephanie Di Alto, Rebecca Griffin, Celine Jacquemin, and Sharon McConnell, whom I would like to single out for her logistical aplomb and thoughtful input. Celine Jacquemin excelled at every phase, with amazing dedication, resourceful research, stellar technical support and first-rate editorial assistance.

I was also blessed with a team of insightful, responsible contributors. Jack Donnelly made a range of important intellectual contributions beyond those reflected in his chapter, including leading the concluding discussion at the conference and detailed thoughtful correspondence now reflected in my concluding chapter. Richard Falk and James Rosenau also provided valuable editorial support in addition to their individual scholarly contributions.

Many thanks also to the University of California Press and Reed Malcolm for their support and to two anonymous reviewers for suggestions that strengthened the final text. I greatly appreciate, too, the permission granted by Lynne Rienner Publishers to reprint Jonathan Fox's chapter and by the United Nations photo archive for the cover image.

Finally, always, all my works grow from the support of my family. My husband and partner, Mark Freeman, helps me to think globally and acts locally to keep the world turning. The love of my daughters Miriam and Ana constantly teaches me what is important.

Miriam asked the fundamental question about this volume: "Who's this one for?" This one's for you and your sister, and for all the brothers and sisters you've never met—the next generation struggling to grow up with human dignity in a globalizing world.

Introduction

Transnational Threats and Opportunities

Alison Brysk

Globalization—the growing interpenetration of states, markets, communications, and ideas across borders—is one of the leading characteristics of the contemporary world. International norms and institutions for the protection of human rights are more developed than at any previous point in history, while global civil society fosters growing avenues of appeal for citizens repressed by their own states. But assaults on fundamental human dignity continue, and the very blurring of borders and rise of transnational actors that facilitated the development of a global human rights regime may also be generating *new* sources of human rights abuse. Even as they are more broadly articulated and accepted, the rights of individuals have come to depend ever more on a broad array of global actors and forces, from ministries to multinationals to missionaries.

What are the patterns of the human rights impact of globalization? Are new problems replacing, intensifying, or mitigating state-sponsored repression? Are some dynamics of globalization generating both problems and opportunities? How can new opportunities be used to offset new problems? And how has the idea and practice of human rights influenced the process of globalization?

How does globalization—which liberals claim will promote development, democracy, personal empowerment, and global governance—instead present new challenges for human rights? Globalization is a package of transnational flows of people, production, investment, information, ideas, and authority (not new, but stronger and faster).[1] Human rights are a set of claims and entitlements to human dignity, which the existing international regime assumes will be provided (or threatened) by the state. A more cosmopolitan and open international system should free individuals to pursue their rights, but large numbers of people seem to be suffering from both long-standing state repression and new denials of rights linked to transnational forces. The essays in this volume show that the challenge of globalization is that unaccountable flows of migration and open markets present new threats, which are not amenable to state-based human rights regimes, while the new opportunities of global information and institutions are insufficiently accessible and distorted by persistent state intervention.

The emergence of an "international regime" for human rights (Donnelly 1986), growing transnational social movement networks, increasing consciousness (Willetts 1996), and information politics have the potential to address both traditional and emerging forms of human rights violations. The United Nations has supervised human rights reform in El Salvador, Cambodia, and Haiti, while creating a new high commissioner for human rights. The first international tribunals since Nuremberg are prosecuting genocide in the former Yugoslavia and Rwanda. Transnational legal accountability (Stephens and Ratner 1996) and humanitarian intervention promote universal norms and link them to the enforcement power of states. Thousands of nongovernmental organizations monitor and lobby for human rights from Tibet to East Timor (Boli and Thomas 1999). Alongside principled proponents such as Amnesty International, globalization has generated new forms of advocacy such as transnational professional networks (Doctors without Borders), global groups for conflict monitoring, and coalitions across transnational issues (Sierra Club–Amnesty International). New forms of communication allow victims to videotape their plight, advocates to flood governments with faxes, Web sites to mobilize urgent action alerts. But the effectiveness of global consciousness and pressure on the states, paramilitaries, and insurgents responsible for long-standing human rights violations varies tremendously. And access to the new global mechanisms is distributed unevenly, so that some of the neediest victims—such as the illiterate rural poor and refugee women—are the least likely to receive either global or domestic redress.

Beyond this interaction of new solutions with old problems, *new* human rights problems may result from the integration of markets, the shrinking of states, increased transnational flows such as migration, the spread of cultures of intolerance, and the decision-making processes of new or growing global institutions (Kofman and Youngs 1996; Mittelman 1996; Held 2000). The increasing presence of multinational corporations has challenged labor rights throughout Southeast Asia, along the Mexican border, and beyond. Increasing levels of migration worldwide make growing numbers of refugees and undocumented laborers vulnerable to abuse by sending and receiving states, as well as transnational criminal networks. Hundreds of Mexican nationals die *each year* crossing the U.S. border; in contrast, 450 German migrants were killed during forty years of Europeans crossing the Berlin Wall. International economic adjustment and the growth of tourism are linked to a rise in prostitution and trafficking in women and children, affecting millions in the Caribbean, Southeast Asia, the post-Soviet states and even the United States. The U.S. State Department estimates that one to two million persons each year are trafficked for various forms of forced labor and "modern-day slavery"—including almost 50,000 annually to the United States (Richard 1999). The same Internet that empowers human rights activists increases government monitoring, instructs neo-Nazis, and carries transnational death threats against dissenters. Unelected global institutions like the World Bank, international peacekeepers, and environmental NGOs administering protected areas increasingly control the lives of the most powerless citizens of weak states.

In this volume, we attempt to map new territory, bring together diverse perspectives, challenge conventional wisdom, and begin to cumulate research to address these questions and contradictions. Our aim is not to introduce a new theory of globalization, but rather to identify generalizable patterns from diverse developments. In order to make sense of these developments, we must first consider the general trends of human rights and globalization. Then we can map patterns in the globalized development of human rights threats and opportunities.

HUMAN RIGHTS IN A GLOBAL ARENA

Human rights are a set of universal claims to safeguard human dignity from illegitimate coercion, typically enacted by state agents. These norms are codified in a widely endorsed set of international undertakings: the "International Bill of Human Rights" (Universal Declaration of Human Rights, International Covenant on Civil and Political Rights, and International Covenant on Social and Economic Rights); phenomenon-specific treaties on war crimes (Geneva Conventions), genocide, and torture; and protections for vulnerable groups such as the UN Convention on the Rights of the Child and the Convention on the Elimination of Discrimination against Women. International dialogue on human rights has produced a distinction between three "generations" of human rights, labeled for their historical emergence. Security rights encompass life, bodily integrity, liberty, and sometimes associated rights of political participation and democratic governance. Social and economic rights, highlighted in the eponymous International Covenant, comprise both negative and positive freedoms, enacted by states and others: prominently, rights to food, health care, education, and free labor. More recently discussed collective rights may include rights such as membership in a cultural community and access to a healthy environment (Chris Brown 1997). These "generations" of rights often involve different sets of actors and different levels of state accountability.

While the origins of the international human rights regime, U.S. foreign policy, NGO monitoring, and much previous scholarship have focused on security rights, this project will entertain a broader conception of linked political, social, and cultural rights grounded in the Universal Declaration. A focus on security rights may be desirable for clarity and manageability, as well as because security rights of life and freedom are "basic" or enabling rights that make the pursuit of other rights possible (Shue 1980). However, human rights claims have an inherently expanding character, which requires the consideration of every type of threat to human dignity under a range of changing social conditions. Thus, both liberty and survival may involve social issues, such as the right to free labor and to organize for better labor conditions. Some vulnerable groups, notably women and indigenous peoples, may face linked threats that emanate from public and private actors, and seek cultural freedoms to meaningfully participate in civic life. Furthermore, the very process of globalization blurs distinctions among categories of rights: humanitarian intervention seeks to rescue ethnic groups, women working as prostitutes are beaten by police for "bothering tourists" to feed their children, and rights to privacy and expression collide on the Internet (also see McCorquodale and Fairbrother 1999). In this volume, these linked rights can be delineated by granting priority to those rights that enable others and those violations that present the greatest harm to victims.

Human rights values derive from and are justified by reference to philosophical constructions of human nature, cultural and religious traditions, demands from civil society, and international influence. In practical importance, the latter two political factors are the most important source of human rights in the contemporary world (Perry 1998; Montgomery 1998). Accordingly, despite frequent violations in practice, international consensus has implanted human rights as a nearly universal vocabulary of debate, aspiration, and civic challenges to state legitimacy.

Analysts of human rights have identified a variety of psychological, social, economic, and political patterns that put societies "at risk" of human rights violations. These generally include authoritarian government, civil war, strong ethnic cleavages, weak civil society, power vacuums, critical junctures in economic development, and military dominance (Mitchell and McCormick 1988; Haas 1994; Donnelly 1998b). Above all, the study of human rights teaches us that human rights violations usually reflect a calculated (or manipulated) pursuit of political power, not inherent evil or ungovernable passions (Gurr 1984; Human Rights Watch 1995b). One of our first tasks is to analyze the effect of globalization on these risk factors.

The effect of globalization on state-based human rights violations will depend on the type of state and its history. In newly democratizing countries with weak institutions and elite-controlled economies (Russia, Latin America, Southeast Asia), the growth of global markets and economic flows tends to destabilize coercive forces but increase crime, police abuse, and corruption. Global mobility and information flows generally stimulate ethnic mobilization, which may promote self-determination in responsive states but more often produces collective abuses in defense of dominant-group hegemony. On the other hand, the same forces have produced slow institutional openings by less fragmented single-party states (like China and Mexico). In much of Africa, globalization has ironically increased power vacuums, by both empowering substate challengers and providing sporadic intervention, which displaces old regimes without consolidating new ones. Some of the most horrifying abuses of all have occurred in the transnationalized, Hobbesian civil wars of Sierra Leone, Angola, and the Congo.

But the literature on human rights has also moved beyond the conventional wisdom that situated human rights violations and remediation predominantly within the state, to suggest ways in which globalization creates new opportunities to challenge the state "from above and below" (Brysk 1993; Risse et al. 1999). Human rights research has produced both evidence of new capabilities for monitoring, pressure, and sanctions (Alston and Steiner 1996; Keck and Sikkink 1998), along with reports of new types and venues of abuse (Human Rights Watch 1996; Fields 1998; Rickard 1998; Peters and Wolper 1995). In general, analysts of globalization find that states' international integration improves security rights, but increases inequality and threatens the social rights of citizens (Crossette 2000; Milner 1998). However, neither economic development nor economic growth in and of themselves improve human rights performance (Montgomery 1998: 325; Amartya Sen 1999; Tan 1999). In addition to globalization and growth, findings on the effectiveness of international pressure on state human rights policy suggest that target states must be structurally accessible, internationally sensitive, and contain local human rights activists for linkage (Burgerman 1998; Sikkink 1993).

There is little systematic evidence available on the overall human rights impact of *global* flows and actors, and that which does exist is often contradictory. For example, quantitative studies that demonstrate improved security rights where MNCs (multinational corporations) are present (Meyer 1998) contrast with case studies documenting multinational reinforcement of state coercion and labor suppression (Arregui 1996; Ho et al. 1996). Other scholars suggest that the impact of multinationals depends more on their type of production, customer base, or sending country than their globalizing nature (Spar 1998). Similarly, some studies indicate that even within "economic globalization," different types of global economic flows at different times will have different impacts on democracy and human rights (for example, for Li and Reuveny 2000, trade is negative but foreign direct investment is positive). There is some basis for believing that new global human rights mechanisms, such as transnational NGO campaigns, may be particularly effective against transnational actors like multinationals. Analysts argue that transnational human rights threats can be most easily met by transnational human rights campaigns, since it is easier to access transnational actors than repressive states, transnationals cannot cloak their abuses in sovereignty rationales, global elites are increasingly amenable to "rights talk," and global civil society can provide local linkages for transnational networks (Rodman 1998; Brysk 2000a). The research in this volume suggests that the human rights impact of globalization depends on three types of factors: the type of globalization involved, the level of analysis addressed, and the type of state that is filtering globalizing flows.

GLOBALIZATION: RIGHTS AND WRONGS

What do we mean by globalization? While some analysts treat globalization as a predominantly economic process or even a synonym for global capitalism (Greider 1997; Korten 1995), others focus on the growth of international institutions and organizations (Ruggie 1998). Some scholars emphasize the impact of transnational demographic, environmental, and cultural flows (Kearney 1995; Sassen 1998, 1996), while others plot the emergence of cross-border networks that may constitute a "global civil society" (Kaldor 1999; Lipschutz 1996; Wapner 1996). In this project, these developments are seen as facets of a linked, albeit uneven, process. In an extension of Jan Aart Scholte's definition, globalization is an ensemble of developments that make the world a single place, changing the meaning and importance of distance and national identity in world affairs (Scholte 1996b: 44).[2] Nevertheless, aspects of globalization that occur simultaneously may have very different logics and impact for human rights—as the sections of this book reflect.[3]

In order to analyze globalization as a comprehensive process, it must be recognized as a dynamic process, that is, a change over time. One of the biggest challenges to analyzing the current era of globalization is the observation of historical periods with similar elements and very different political results (Hirst and Thompson 1996). However, globalization need not be entirely new to be significant, and significant in new ways. Some suggest that globalization has occurred in waves, with the current wave linked to U.S. hegemony and the emergence of a "democratic peace" in the core of the world economy.[4] The current wave of globalization does surpass previous eras in the breadth, scope, and intensity of the combination of connection, cosmopolitanism, commodification, and communication. It is this combination of norms, flows, institutions, and markets that has particular political consequences for human rights.

A more globalized world is simultaneously more *connected, cosmopolitan, commodified,* and influenced by *communication. Connection* is a functional parameter of globalization, involving increasing numbers, volumes, and salience of transnational flows of bodies, business, information, and norms. The sections of this volume are organized around these flows: transnational migration and citizenship, global markets and commodification, international uses of information and communication, and transnational norms embodied in attempts at governance. The *cosmopolitan* dimension is structural; the evolution of multiple, linked, and overlapping centers of power above and below the state. This is closely related to James N. Rosenau's analysis of a "multi-centric" turbulent world. *Commodification* highlights distinctive characteristics of expanding world markets and their relationship to other flows, institutions, and states. As Richard Falk's contribution details, globalization as commodification means that increasing spheres of social relationship are based on exchange value, including citizenship. The underlying causal dynamic that has catalyzed and intensified each of these dimensions of globalization is *communication*, which combines an increase in technical capacity and volume, a shift in the distribution of capabilities, a diversification of channels, and an expansion of content (Deibert 1997). As Shayne Weyker and Clifford Bob discuss, communication carries both information and norms, affective images and transnational identities. Both terrorism and the international response also reflect these characteristics.

What are the effects of globalization? Optimists suggest that transnational integration will empower citizen challenges to state power (Falk 1995; Rosenau 1997), while revisionists assert that globalization reiterates national and/or market exploitation (Bhabha 1998a; Burbach et al. 1997; Brecher and Costello 1994; Mander and Goldsmith 1996). One attempt to resolve this debate delineates good and bad forms of globalization; "globalization from above" versus "globalization from below." (Hunter 1995; Falk 1994) Another set of scholars contend that a deeper process of globalization has transformed the fundamental forms of world politics through changing identities, evolving social forms such as networks, and the diffusion of an increasingly influential world institutional culture that includes support for human rights or at least democracy (Robertson 1992; Castells 1997; Meyer et al. 1997). This project suggests, instead, that different elements and levels of globalization may produce distinct effects of empowerment, exploitation, and evolution; also Friedman 1999).

But these diverse effects are not random or wholly ambiguous. Previous research suggests that world politics is clustered in three streams, with distinctive logics: the interstate realm, global markets, and transnational civil society. These domains are differentially accessible and responsive to human rights appeals, with civic actors most amenable and states most resistant to a reconstruction of existing relationships. Furthermore, the appeals of target groups are facilitated when markets, states, and transnational social forces are separable rather than working in tandem (Brysk 2000a). Globalization is most positive for human rights when it enables the exchange of informa-

TABLE 1. Streams of Globalization and the Effect on Rights

	Mobility (Maher, Cabezas)*	Markets (Milner, Pangalangan)*	Information (Wekyer, Bob)*	Governance (Sandholz, Fox)*
Security rights	refuge, abusive policing	monitoring, abusive policing	HR regime campaigns	intervention, legal action
Social rights	exploitation	exploitation	campaigns	sanctions
Collective rights (see Brysk 2000b)	diasporas	homogenization	empowerment	alternatives

*Chapters in this volume.

tion and the formation of new identities, and most negative when it reinscribes borders and props up repressive states. Global markets, on the other hand, generate systematically contradictory effects that depend heavily on the type of state and sector involved. Meanwhile, global civil society introduces new norms, which sometimes become institutionalized as evolving human rights standards, and, ultimately, objects of interstate enforcement. Recent events suggest that a fourth realm of transnational violence may have its own patterns and effects.

We can thus begin to map the effects of different forms of globalization on different kinds of rights (see table 1). Increased mobility provides refuge to some but also opportunities for abusive policing and economic exploitation. Global markets also increase economic exploitation, but may provide increased monitoring of social and security conditions. Information facilitates campaigns for all types of rights, as well as the formation of transnational networks and reporting to the emergent "international human rights regime." And governance provides a new array of enforcement tools, from intervention to law to economic sanctions.

Meanwhile, these streams of globalization are unfolding at different levels of analysis—the second key factor suggested by our approach. Rosenau's contribution examines the human rights impact of globalization *across* states and concludes that transnational flows and institutions are constructing evolving responses to "the most obstreperous actor" (still usually a state). By contrast, Richard Falk distinguishes globalization *above* and *below* the state, attributing threats mainly to unaccountable transnational market forces and institutions, partly combated by the struggles of grassroots global civil society. Donnelly introduces the missing element of globalization *through* the state, which he finds highly problematic for social rights, in ways that also reiterate the distinction between different streams of globalization and their differential effect on rights.

These levels of analysis overlap with the streams of globalization. Global mobility operates across and through the state, and the rights impact is generally more positive across and more negative through—both Kristen Maher and Amalia Lucia Cabezas suggest that policing creates more violations than migration itself. Global markets may be across (financial flows), above (multilateral trade and financial institutions), through (economic adjustment), or below (grassroots protests, shifts in local production or consumption). This is part of the problem in assessing the contradictory effects of markets on rights (Wesley Milner's analysis is across and above, while Raul Pangalangan's is through and below). Global information is predominantly across and below the state, hence it tends to facilitate rights unless bottlenecks develop through (Weyker) or above (Bob) the state. Finally, global governance appears as the paradigm of globalization from above. But Fox explores a trilateral struggle between a multilateral institution above, a transnational campaign below, and recalcitrant states in the middle, while Wayne Sandholtz shows that globalization from above can partially supersede the state level—when states have lost legitimacy across the international system. The latter has wider implications for the study of global governance, as it suggests that the development of global norms and institutions is actually a three- or four-level game, not just an interstate coordination problem (Evans et al. 1993; Smith et al. 1997).

Finally, our analysis shows that the human rights impact of globalization is filtered through the type of receiving state (Holm and Sorensen 1995). Much of the literature on globalization has overlooked the effect of globalization on the state; globalization has produced a new "globalized state"—changing rather than eroding sovereignty (Ian Clark 1999). As some scholars have argued, power is moving from weak states to strong states, from all states to markets, and away from state authority entirely in certain domains and functions (Strange 1998; Schmidt 2000). At the same time, the state is the main administrator of globalization. As one partisan of globalization puts it, globalization means that the quality of the state matters *more*, since the state is "the operating system for global capitalism" (Friedman 1999: 134). Thus, the struggle for human rights in a global era is now from above, from below—and still through the middle.

THE GLOBALIZED STATE AS THREAT

In the security sphere, states respond with increased repression to fragmentation, transnationalized civil war, and uncontrolled global flows such as migrants and drug trafficking. Transborder ethnic diasporas help inspire civil conflict, while the global arms trade provides its tools. Even extreme civil conflicts where states deteriorate into warlordism are often financed if not abetted by foreign trade: diamonds in the Congo and Sierra Leone, cocaine in Colombia. While nonstate actors like insurgents and paramilitaries pose increasing threats to human rights, state response is a crucial multiplier for the effect on citizens. Since all but the most beleaguered states possess more resources and authority than rebels, they can generally cause more damage—and human rights monitoring in a wide variety of settings from Rwanda to Haiti attributes the bulk of abuses to state (or state-supported) forces. States also differ in their ability and will to provide protection from insurgent terror campaigns (like that in Algeria).

Global economic relationships can produce state policies that directly violate social and labor rights and indirectly produce social conflict that leads to state violations of civil and security rights. While globally induced economic adjustment may cut state services and intensify poverty and protest, global windfalls of wealth may also underwrite repressive and predatory states, as in Angola, where oil revenues have fueled repression and civil war (Harden 2000). It is states that largely determine labor rights and security response to labor dissidence; states also regulate multinationals, certify unions, and form joint ventures with global investors.

GLOBALIZATION AND THE CITIZENSHIP GAP

Just as globalized states may present new threats alongside long-standing patterns of repression, globalization offers states declining opportunities to serve as a source of human rights protection. Increasing numbers of residents of increasing numbers of states are less than full citizens. Over 25 million people are international refugees, while an estimated similar number are economic migrants—mostly undocumented and generally lacking civil rights (Mills 1998: 97–124). Refugee camps can also become sites or sources of human rights violations, as in Rwanda, Lebanon, Guatemala, and Indonesia. Within many countries, internally displaced persons, rural-urban migrants, and isolated peasants (often illiterate) are also undocumented and lack rights and civil status. In China alone, an estimated 100 million people are unregistered domestic migrant workers (Solinger 1995). Many millions around the world live in occupied territories or emergency zones where citizenship was never granted or has been suspended. A number of the states hosting the world's 300 million indigenous people assign them special juridical status—often tutelary—which may fall short of conventional citizenship. Similarly, a significant number of states (especially in the Middle East) circumscribe the rights of the female half of their populations—and personal status codes contravene international human rights standards and sometimes directly deny citizenship or nationality (Chinkin 1999). Analysts of globalization speak of variable levels and configurations of citizenship within the same state, depending on the triangulation between a given sector, state power, and transnational forces, and even regional zones of limited citizenship (such as limitations on movement, speech, and assembly in export-processing zones) (Ong 1999).

Meanwhile, alongside people who are not citizens, states have diminished capacity to control the conditions of citizenship—even for those securely inscribed within the juridical and social status. Observers of states undergoing both political and economic liberalization decry the emergence of "delegative democracy," which is characterized by "low-intensity citizenship" (O'Donnell 1994; Stahler-Sholk 1994). More and more legal citizens lack effective accountability for power relationships; their lives depend on distant investment decisions, organizational resolutions, religious edicts, and information campaigns. "Economic liberalization is exacerbating the gap between rich and poor within virtually all developing regions. At the same time, other elements of globalization are increasing the inequalities of political power and influence, as well as highlighting new dimensions of inequality. For one group of countries globalization is eroding the cohesion and viability of the state" (Hurrell and Woods 1999: 1). These global forces are often translated into local conditions in opaque ways, which deepens the gap of information, knowledge, and control further. Since migration is the transnational flow with the strongest claim to state control, it is interesting that Maher and Cabezas each note a "citizenship gap" both for aliens to developed countries and citizens of developing countries (vis-à-vis tourists).[5]

TYPES OF STATES AND THE IMPACT OF GLOBALIZATION

Beyond these general trends of accelerating threats and declining opportunities, the impact of globalization on human rights conditions differs in different types of states. Many analyses of transnationalism suggest that the impact of global forces on various issue-areas is filtered by domestic characteristics (Risse-Kappen 1995; Keohane and Milner 1996)—even straightforward economic effects depend on a state's factor endowments, economic institutions, and policies (Stewart and Berry 1999).[6] One scholar outlines a general pattern of types of states with different patterns of international interaction: premodern, Westphalian modern nation-states, and postmodern, with the former and latter departing significantly from standard scholarly assumptions of sovereignty, anarchy, and self-help (Sorenson 2000).

We can further develop these distinctions, and the tendencies of different types of globalizing states for human rights performance and the citizenship gap. First, in collapsing and "failed" states such as large sectors of Africa, foreign aid and international organizations often simultaneously prop up power vacuums and assist victims (Ignatieff 1998). Globalization brings increased market flows and weak intervention, but little accountability and no definitive governance. Here, the citizenship gap is most severe, as victims lack control at the community, state, and international level. In second place, aspiring theocracies like Afghanistan—which make war on women—are less a return to tradition than a reaction against foreign penetration sustained by international identity politics. Victims lack both state citizenship and voice in the religious/ethnic community, which engenders "private" violations. Similarly, ethnocracies are both inspired by and reactive to international forces. Sometimes international organizations intervene, as in Kosovo. However, interveners, ethnocratic and emerging states, and ethnic communities all violate rights (the way ethnic Albanians in Kosovo are now persecuting Serbs), and none are subject to citizen accountability. Next, the few remaining "hard states"—such as China—seem to be evolving toward what has been labeled "market Leninism," in which centralized political control coexists with (and indeed may depend upon) opening to global markets. But in such states, growing international influence does seem to foster some partial increase in transparency, the rule of law, and international cooperation—although it has not yet produced systematic improvement in human rights. The citizenship gap here is predominantly democratizing the state, and secondarily accessing market pressures. Most of Latin America, parts of Southeast Asia, and many post-Soviet states are now "low-intensity democracies," with globalizing electoral regimes systematically skewed by social inequalities and weak states. Residents of these areas have low-quality citizenship and no access to the market forces that dominate their states. Even postmodern, liberal capitalist democracies experience human rights impacts from globalization, becoming more connected and aware but simultaneously overloaded in state capacity to process diverse and complex issues. We too lack full control over global markets, although we are more insulated from their effects than citizens of weak or authoritarian states. We are also more dependent on the opportunity of the globalization of information, but thus more vulnerable in those situations where information is a threat: as surveillance, ideology, or terror.

GLOBALIZATION, HUMAN RIGHTS, AND THE NEW WORLD ORDER

These essays were written during 2000, before the September 11th terrorist attacks on New York and Washington ushered in a new world order framed by renewed security threats, directly targeting globalization, along with an international military response. While in some ways these events go beyond the scope of issues considered in this volume, in others they strengthen the relevance and urgency of this analysis.

The nature of the threat, its targets and impact, and the response all indicate the growing power of globalization as a parameter of political action. The emergence of transnational civil networks capable of state-level crimes against humanity depends upon the globalizing patterns of connection, communication, and even commodification (via financial networks). It is inspired by a transnational ideology of a radical, extremist version of Islamic fundamentalism that is largely reactive to economic and cultural globalization, and thus targets sites and symbols of both cosmopolitanism and hegemony. The shattering impact of threats to globalizing flows such as air travel on the world economy and daily life demonstrate how deeply dependent we have become on these connections. And even the U.S.-sponsored response has gone beyond the historical standard reaction of a great power under direct attack; it is more internationalist, multisectoral in its treatment of areas like migration and finance, and much more conscious of human rights issues such as laws of war, refugees, and humanitarian assistance.

While the crisis of 2001–2002 has diminished global levels of migration and economic exchange, it has increased flows of communication and governance. And the new world order has not diminished the salience or fundamentally altered the pattern of the human rights impact of any of the forms of globalization. Indeed, the impact on human rights of the new global threat of terrorism itself largely follows the logic suggested by this volume, with the most deleterious spillovers linked to state-regulated migration and governance (intervention), mixed results of markets, and enduring avenues of appeal via global communications. Our second factor, the type of state, is also relevant, as liberal democracies are most vulnerable to the new threat, while failed states suffer disproportionately from the response. The final element—level of analysis—matters in a new way that will require further study, as international authorities above and through the state struggle to respond to unaccountable forces across and below state boundaries.

The first global conflict of the new millennium marks a new phase in the development of human rights, which should heighten our attention to the issues examined in this volume. The persistence of human rights as a focus of legislative and public debates on security measures in the United States and Germany, as well as the widespread efforts to foster tolerance and support for Muslim minorities, show that liberal human rights standards have shifted the agenda beyond those of previous conflicts. Although such standards are not always achieved, and new security policies sometimes do violate civil liberties, human rights norms and networks remain legitimate and incorporated in international policymaking and the politics of the dominant international powers.

Yet the background and supporters of the terrorists demonstrate the limitations of liberal conceptions, and the connections between chronic denials of economic, social, and political rights and a climate of dysfunctional political violence. Without excusing or justifying the moral responsibility of terrorists, we must understand the conditions that make perpetrators more likely to arise and gain credence. The emergence of new human rights threats from the ashes of Cold War struggles, at the haunting edges of the globalizing world economy, should remind us to broaden our attention beyond the core conflict of each era—to consider those at the peripheries, whose pain or pathology may well become the theme of the next epoch. In this new world order, it is ever more urgent to deepen our understanding of the new global threats to human rights, even beyond the normative and cosmopolitan connections charted below—for our own survival.

MAP OF THE VOLUME

In this volume, we try to assess the impact of globalization on human rights and the impact of human rights on globalization. The chapters cannot possibly encompass the full range of either globalization or human rights, but they do sample across the spectrum of threats and opportunities. Although most of the chapters are global in focus, those that concentrate on a place or region include the United States (Maher), Latin America (Cabezas), Asia (Pangalangan), and Africa (Bob). Similarly, the contributors bring a variety of methodologies to bear on common questions: theoretical deduction (Falk, Rosenau, Donnelly), cross-national quantitative study (Milner), policy analysis (Maher, Fox, Sandholtz), and case studies (Cabezas, Bob).

The first section, "Citizenship," analyzes the effect on rights as people cross borders and states shift capabilities and goals. This essay has identified a broader "citizenship gap," as globalized states introduce new threats and provide declining opportunities to citizens, while increasing numbers of residents lack citizenship claims. Illustrating the latter dynamic, Kristen Maher deconstructs the immigration policy of the largest receiving nation, the United States, in relation to labor flows from Latin America and the rights ideology of liberalism. In a complementary geography and analysis, Amalia Lucia Cabezas shows how prostitution in the Dominican Republic is constituted by global economic adjustment and northern tourism. However, her contribution also emphasizes both the role of the state as an intervening actor in economic development and policing and sex workers' transnational mobilization for labor and security rights.

In "Commodification," the book turns to the globalization of markets. Richard Falk highlights the political impact of economic globalization, and the contradictions between economic and political liberalism for social rights. Wesley Milner's comprehensive study of economic liberalization establishes the differential impact of structural integration on different types of rights. By contrast, Raul Pangalangan documents and analyzes mobilization against the deleterious effects of multinational labor exploitation in Asia.

"Communication" examines the influence of information flows and global civil society on human rights. Shane Weyker provides an overview of the inherent potential and pitfalls of the new information technologies for human rights activists. Clifford Bob documents the power and distortions of transnational communications and network appeals, through a comparative case study of Nigeria's Ogoni. Both authors emphasize the social context of information and the organizational politics of NGOs. James Rosenau applies his pioneering analysis of global turbulence to the cosmopolitan governance of "most obstreperous actors."

The next section, "Cooperation," explores the emerging exercise of institutional authority across borders on behalf of human rights. Jonathan Fox explores an increasing mechanism of international accountability: transnational mobilization against a global institution. Then, his chapter outlines the limitations of institutional reform, seeking largely social and collective rights. Wayne Sandholtz chronicles the emergence and limitations of a norm and practice of humanitarian intervention—when global human rights standards trump state sovereignty. Finally, Jack Donnelly analyzes the evolving role of state power in filtering the impact of globalization on human rights.

CONCLUSION

This introduction has begun to lay out some of the patterns of the human rights impact of globalization. Taken together, the essays in this volume help to answer the other questions that frame the inquiry. The contributors show how globalization generates both threats and opportunities for human rights, and many assess new forms of human rights accountability.

Like so many other studies of human rights, this one must conclude that the effectiveness of both new and old human rights mechanisms is "half full." Transnational advocacy, international law, sanctions, intervention, media campaigns, lobbying states, and empowering victims does make a difference across borders as within them. Migrants' rights may improve, markets can be better monitored, international organizations may become more accountable, intervention can restrain or remove abusive power holders or combatants. But these improvements are uneven, and the new range of global threats is not matched by the new global opportunities.

We argue that these differences in threat and response can be better understood in terms of the type of globalization, the kind of rights affected, and the filtering role of the state. Ultimately, this differentiated approach should allow a more differentiated response to new challenges. It may also move analysis of globalization beyond reflexive condemnation or enthusiasm, largely rooted in preexisting perspectives, toward a theoretical appreciation of a multivalent social process in its own terms.

The improvement of human rights requires strengthening existing mechanisms to confront new challenges, but also addressing the second half of our mandate: increasing the influence of human rights on globalization. Among other things, this means improving awareness and analysis of the connections between different kinds of rights, the distinct facets and implications of globalization, and the new forms of communication and governance necessary to meet the new challenges. The essays in this volume point the way toward that goal. The concluding analysis will attempt to sketch the implications of such a program for the theory and the practice of globalization.

NOTES

Versions of this chapter have been presented at the American Political Science Association's 1999 meeting and the January 2000 conference on Globalization and Human Rights at University of California Irvine, funded by the Institute for Global Conflict and Cooperation. The author wishes to thank participants in both conferences, and especially Jack Donnelly, for constructive comments that have influenced the concepts and analysis presented here.

1. While the terrorist attacks on 11 September 2001 have slowed certain globalization flows in the short run, the shape and long-term trend of globalization remain significant.

2. Scholte 1996b also reminds us that recognition of globalization does not require it to have touched all actors, replaced the state, become the primary motor of international relations, unfolded in a linear fashion, or guaranteed equal access to new world orders (45).

3. Kudrle 1999, which also postulates communications, market, and "direct" (mainly global governance) forms of globalization, labels human rights a "globalism-enhanced psychological externality" (18).

4. I am grateful to Gerson Shafir for this suggestion.

5. Thanks to Sharon McConnell for this observation.

6. This is not an inevitable or structural phenomenon but a contingent development of historical legacy with state strategies and identities. For example, while Singapore and Taiwan have pursued similar paths of political economy based on initial authoritarianism, Taiwan has opted to expand social consensus and the rule of law to full democratization and position itself as a beacon of democracy (Tan 1999).

I

Citizenship

1

Who Has a Right to Rights?

Citizenship's Exclusions in an Age of Migration

Kristen Hill Maher

Transnational migration—or the flow of "bodies across borders"—presents a range of potential threats to human rights. The most politicized and visible among these threats are those posed to migrants by exploitative trafficking networks that profit from migrants' vulnerabilities, coercing them into circumstances that include life-threatening dangers, slave-labor conditions, or forced prostitution. These circumstances violate migrants' most fundamental rights and certainly deserve international attention. However, globalizing processes have also produced less visible but more numerous rights vulnerabilities among migrants who live as noncitizen residents in foreign states. Noncitizen populations pose a quandary for the administration of human rights because human rights norms have generally been enacted within the nation-state system and administered as the rights of citizens. That is, while the human rights regime is international, its greatest influence has been to establish standards for states' obligations vis-à-vis their own citizenries. Hence, even in Western states that are vocal champions of human rights, policymakers debate the extent to which they are responsible for protecting the full range of human rights for noncitizen migrants, particularly migrants lacking state authorization.

In the United States—the primary case examined in this chapter—policies and practices toward noncitizens often fail to uphold international human rights standards as outlined in the Universal Declaration or in later conventions regarding the rights of migrants. Human rights organizations have documented violations at the hand of Immigration and Naturalization Service (INS) and Border Patrol agents such as the excessive use of force[1] (at times resulting in death), sexual abuse, and the denial of food and water.[2] In the past several years, the Border Patrol has become much more careful about its public image, but it continues to adopt enforcement strategies that place border-crossing migrants at risk. For instance, San Diego's Operation Gatekeeper has adopted a conscious strategy of channeling crossing attempts east of the city, where apprehensions are easier but the terrain and weather conditions are much more dangerous. Following the implementation of this strategy, hundreds of migrants have died during border crossing from heat exposure, cold exposure, drowning, and dehydration.[3] While the Border Patrol is less directly culpable for these deaths than in circumstances of violent confrontation, the current enforcement policy clearly prioritizes successful border control over the lives of migrants. Nonstate actors have reproduced these priorities in self-appointed citizen patrols that "arrest" migrants in border regions in confrontations that have sometimes turned violent, such as in the May 2000 Arizona incident in which ranchers on horseback shot at undocumented migrants with high-powered rifles.[4]

Noncitizen migrants in the United States are also vulnerable to violations of political and social rights. Most prevalent among these are the violations of labor rights that regularly occur, with state agencies either cooperating or failing to intervene. There is ample evidence of employers who use threats of reporting workers to the INS in order to preempt organized demands, who report undocumented workers in retaliation for refusals to accept poor working conditions, or who call the INS to collect workers once production or harvest demands end (e.g., Bacon 1999: 161, 165; Calavita 1992). While individual workers hypothetically have the right to legally challenge unpaid salaries, poor working conditions, or abuses at the workplace, few have the resources to do so, and those who are undocumented risk not only the loss of a job but also deportation once they bring their plight to the attention of the courts. The relative priority of labor law in relation to immigration law has been ambiguous and often subordinated in practice.

Recent policies have also left open potential for rights violations in deportation, detention, and asylum procedures. Two acts passed in 1996—the Anti-Terrorism Act and the Illegal Immigration Reform and Immigrant Responsibility Act (IIRAIRA)—struck a blow against the right of appeal in summary deportations of undocumented immigrants, a particular concern for those claiming asylum. The current expedited review process risks violating the international human rights principle of *non-refoulement*,[5] as it undercuts asylum-seekers' capacity to demonstrate their credible fear of persecution upon return (Langenfeld 1999). The IIRAIRA also included a very controversial statute broadening the definition of a deportable crime, which has resulted in the deportations of even naturalized citizens who were earlier convicted of crimes that now constitute deportable offenses. In cases in which a return to the country of origin is not possible, such as to Cuba or Vietnam, these "criminal aliens" face indefinite detention, in violation of due process rights.

While the above policy shifts might be perceived to be *anti-immigration* in orientation, much of the policy in the 1990s would more fairly be represented as *anti-immigrant,* focused on limiting immigrants' rights (Jonas 1999: viii). California's infamous Proposition 187, which would have denied undocumented migrants access to even primary education or health care,[6] represents the kinds of issues that continue to be debated at a national level. Should noncitizen immigrants have the same rights as citizens to Medicaid, Social Security, Supplemental Security Income (SSI), food stamps, Temporary Assistance to Needy Families (TANF), educational loans and grants, unemployment compensation, or housing assistance? The policy response to date has been mixed, but there has been movement in the direction of denying all noncitizens social services, as in the case of the 1996 federal welfare reform (H.R. 3734), which made most noncitizens ineligible for most forms of assistance.[7] Additionally, there have been recurring proposals to limit the access of the undocumented to citizenship (and hence to the economic and political benefits of citizenship), for instance, by changing the Fourteenth Amendment to the Constitution in order to eliminate birthright citizenship for the children of undocumented immigrants.

What we see in these examples is a political culture in which universal personhood continues to be subordinated to citizenship as a basis for rights. That is, the violations and vulnerabilities of migrant rights enumerated in these examples can all be understood as extensions of a cultural logic in which even human rights are framed as entitlements exclusive to citizens. My analysis suggests that popular and political discourse in this context conceptualizes citizenship less in objective terms (as a legal status) than as a relational identity defined in opposition to "aliens," particularly in reference to labor migrants from less developed states. This constructed opposition— positioning migrants as lacking a legitimate claim to rights—has two dimensions, which I address below. The first dimension of the citizen-alien opposition rests on logics grounded in liberal notions of contract and property that position migrants as criminals, trespassers, and usurpers who have forfeited claims to rights by virtue of individual breaches of contract or law. The second reflects a neocolonial logic that legitimates differential claims to rights in accordance with an individual's position in a racialized international division of labor, equating the privileges that accompany First World status with a greater entitlement to rights.

These oppositions between citizens and aliens pose obstacles for migrants' claims to rights based on universal personhood, even within a state that formally supports international human rights norms.[8] The nature of these obstacles is largely cultural—that is, they have to do with how rights, citizenship, and belonging are popularly conceived, and how popular conceptions shape policy and law. In making this claim, I am assuming a close connection between public policy and the hegemonic norms of political culture in civil society.[9] This linkage is most overt in policies enacted through popular referenda, such as California's Proposition 187. However, it also exists in policy enacted through the legislative process, insofar as cultural norms limit what policymakers find imaginable and politically feasible. Cultural norms and constructions also undergird arguments in policy debates and inform the assumptions made about population groups (cf. Ingram and Schneider 1997; Stone 1997).

While this essay is written in a primarily theoretical mode, its argument is informed by empirical studies conducted in Europe and the United States, as well as by my own research on immigrant labor in southern California.[10] It begins by reviewing why there has been so much recent migration into industrialized states and what consequences this migration has had for conceptions of membership and rights. It then elaborates how liberal and neocolonial logics are commonly used in U.S. political culture (and particularly in the Southwest) to frame citizenship in opposition to the migrant "alien" in ways that have consequences for migrants' claims to rights.

MIGRATION TRENDS AND MIGRANT RIGHTS
IN INDUSTRIALIZED WESTERN STATES

Industrialized states have all experienced growth in immigration in the past twenty years, particularly from less developed regions. In the United States, immigration levels in the 1990s have been higher in proportion to its population than in any other period besides the turn of the century; in raw numbers, current immigration flows are the largest in history (Castles and Miller 1998). Why is this migration occurring? Many residents and policymakers of immigrant-receiving states share a common misperception that migration flows are the "rational" consequence of inequalities of wealth between states, that endless numbers of people from poor regions are clamoring to enter richer economies. The migration literature largely debunks this perception as a myth, explaining migration patterns as systemic rather than the product of individual aspirations for greater prosperity.

Most generally, this literature asserts that migrations are patterned rather than random flows of people from poverty to wealth. They occur within relatively predictable geographies, they are limited in their scope and endurance, and they are often stimulated by established relationships between the sending and receiving states, such as quasi-colonial bonds or a history of active labor recruitment (Sassen 1999; Castles and Miller 1998). In a globalizing economy, migration to industrialized states is also spurred by economic links formed through international investment and production. As borders open to flows of goods, services, information, and capital, there will also be cross-border movement of labor (Sassen 1996, 1988).

Finally, contemporary migration patterns reflect a shift in the structure of economies in receiving states. Given the turn from Fordist to post-Fordist production and toward flexible accumulation (Harvey 1989), industrialized economies have developed labor markets that have a shrinking number of primary sector jobs and a growing number of informal, part-time, or minimum wage jobs. The latter jobs—whether in the service sector, agricultural production and processing, construction, or high tech manufacturing—are increasingly performed by immigrant or migrant workers. This pattern exists not only in traditional countries of immigration, such as Canada, the United States, and Australia, but also in states that claim no significant history of immigration. A recent comparative study of immigrant labor in San Diego, California, and Hamamatsu, Japan, found that both economies have come to incorporate significant numbers of immigrant workers and exhibit similar patterns in the kinds of jobs in which immigrants predominate (Cornelius 1998).

What these trends indicate is that immigrant or migrant labor from less-developed states is becoming structurally embedded in the economies of industrialized states. Additionally, once immigrants predominate in given job categories, these jobs tend to become perceived as "immigrant jobs" (cf. Cornelius 1998; Ortiz 1996; Hossfeld 1988), or even as jobs only fit for immigrants, such that a division of labor that depends upon immigrant labor also is socially or culturally reinforced (Maher 1999). For all these reasons, migration into industrialized states does not appear to constitute a temporary or random flow easily stanched through stricter border regulation. Rather, it is an indelible part of the new political geography in a globalizing economy.

This migration poses serious challenges to the international nation-state system and to a state-centered administration of rights. The nation-state system presumes the territorial basis of each citizen community (Malkki 1994), the "national" basis of the citizenry (Anderson 1991), mutually exclusive political memberships (Brubaker 1989), and legal equality among all community residents (Fiss 1999). In contrast, international migration creates deterritorialized, transnational communities (Basch et al. 1994; Rouse 1995; Appadurai 1990), dual citizens with multiple political memberships (Hammar 1990), ethnically or "nationally" diverse populations, and internal distinctions in terms of legal statuses and rights (Bauböck 1991, 1994). In regard to this last effect of migration, consider the range of possible legal statuses, which include native-born citizens; naturalized citizens; permanent residents (or "denizens"); temporary residents, such as students or short-term workers; guests, such as tourists; and undocumented residents who have overstayed a short-term visa or entered the country without authorization. These multiple statuses are accompanied by differences in state-defined rights that, over time, can serve as the basis for a "class" or castelike social structure (Fiss 1998, 1999).

The inequalities in rights between residents of democracies has been identified as particularly problematic in countries like Germany, which until recently has made full citizenship status largely inaccessible to large numbers of Turkish guest workers, even through the third generation of their residence in the territorial state, given a definition of membership based on "blood" or heritage (Brubaker 1998). But even when there is relative institutional openness to mobility between statuses, as there is in the United States, transnational migration and the remaining institutional regulations produce social and legal inequalities between those of different legal statuses in relation to the state. While there is hypothetical mobility at the individual level, at a collective level, the residential community in the United States at any given point in time incorporates groups with differing rights and social stature, differences understood as ensuing from different legal statuses.

One political and scholarly response[11] to migration's challenges to the administration of rights has been to turn to international law to establish and protect a more equal and universal basis for rights than membership of the territorial nation-state. At the end of World War II, international law regarding the rights of migrants focused primarily on refugees and rights to asylum. However, after widespread foreign labor recruitment to Europe and North America during the 1950s and 1960s and a rising swell of anti-immigrant sentiment since the 1970s, labor migrants have also become the focus of a series of international charters establishing a growing range of rights. The International Labor Office (ILO) Conventions of 1949 and 1975 provided for nondiscrimination in employment and some degree of cultural autonomy for migrants within the contracting states. United Nations charters such as the UNESCO Declaration on Race and Racial Prejudice (1978) and the UN convention on the Protection of Rights of All Migrant Workers and Their Families (1990) collectively address a considerable range of economic, civil, and social rights of individuals as well as the cultural rights of migrant groups, such that migrants now claim rights to "employment, education, health care, nourishment, and housing [as well as] [t]he collective rights of nations and peoples to culture, language, and development" (Soysal 1994: 157).

Yasemin Soysal (1994) argues that migration and international law have together produced a shift in the basis of individual rights from those rooted in the nation-state and citizenship to those rooted in international law. This shift comprises a "reconfiguration of the institution of citizenship" (163): the dawn of a "postnational" age in which the rights once reserved solely for citizens of territorial nation-states are expanded on the basis of universal personhood. The "two elements of modern citizenship"—identity and rights—have thus been decoupled, and the national order of things transgressed (159). Nation-states do not disappear in this postnational age, nor does identity become irrelevant. In fact, states retrench in new and creative ways, and nationalism still flourishes. Soysal explains: "As an identity, national citizenship—as it is promoted, reinvented, and reified by states and other societal actors—still prevails. But in terms of its translation into rights and privileges, it is no longer a significant construction" (159). The postnational order does not signal the end of the nation-state, but it does make it less autonomous and sovereign in matters concerning the rights of migrants, with boundaries that are more fluid. It also makes identity largely irrelevant to claims to rights.

Soysal is not the only scholar making this argument. Several years earlier, James Hollifield (1992) observed that contractarian notions of citizenship were being supplanted by internationalist human rights norms, particularly in Europe. Similarly, David Jacobson claims that "the basis of (nation)-state legitimacy is eroding" and that international human rights norms have become more salient in both the United States and Europe (1997: 72). These authors all correctly note the rise of human rights discourses as a significant development for nation-states and citizenship. However, they share a tendency to overgeneralize developments in Europe to other regions such as North America, and to assume a *unidirectional process* in which rights are becoming disentangled from traditional notions of contract, identity, and the nation-state. In the United States, it is far from obvious that international human rights norms have pervaded popular or political culture, or that identity-based notions of citizenship are in retreat. A review of the abundant legislation in the past decade regarding the basic civil, social, and economic rights of noncitizens reveals only that these rights are greatly disputed.

Even looking at Europe, there is plenty of evidence that identities still matter to rights claims and that human rights are not hegemonic norms, given persistent racial violence against those identified as foreign, discriminatory police action, and differences between migrants' and "natives'" access to a full range of civil rights (Bhabha 1998a, 1998b, 1999; Stolcke 1999). Jacqueline Bhabha has also observed that while globalization and universal human rights norms clearly constrain the autonomy of nation-states, citizenship has simultaneously gained salience: "There is a noticeable resurgence of attention paid to the question of who is part of the collective, what the criteria for membership or exclusion should be, and what the benefits and duties of citizenship might entail" (1999: 12). These trends are not entirely contradictory. The new standards for EU citizenship are crafted along postnational lines insofar as they provide free movement and civil and economic rights across state borders within the European region. They are designed to promote uniform access to fundamental human rights. At the same time, by granting a full range of rights only to nationals of member states, European citizenship standards reinforce national belonging as a prerequisite for human rights, indirectly affirming the sovereignty of nation-states to make decisions about criteria for exclusion. On this basis, even long-term permanent residents in EU member states are excluded from the right to free movement within the EC region; they have no formal political representation; and they are vulnerable to deportation, despite human rights to family life. Similarly, the evaluation of asylum cases in European states has often prioritized immigration statutes over the applicants' right to asylum (Bhabha 1999).

These exclusions occur, says Bhabha, because "nondiscrimination conflicts with the project of delineating Europe. . . . [D]rawing the territorial and cultural boundaries of Europe requires discrimination, exclusion, and the adoption of criteria that marginalize and dichotomize" (1998b: 601). In effect, European citizenship has no positive content and is defined primarily by its exclusions (i.e., those whom member states exclude), which are informed in part by issues of identity. This tendency has led some to identify the project of regional integration in Europe as the creation of a "fortress Europe," in which not only territory and rights but also European-ness is fortified against the incursion of those who are not imagined to be part of the European tradition.[12]

The trends in the United States largely parallel those in Europe, apart from dimensions specific to the regional integration of the EU. As Jacobson (1996) observes, there is some evidence that human rights norms occasionally influence policy in the United States. However, there is simultaneously renewed emphasis on citizenship, both in terms of who properly "belongs" to the citizen community and in terms of the rights to which one is thereby entitled. While human rights norms have not gained hegemony in political discourse or practice in the United States, they have arguably destabilized traditional assumptions about rights being grounded in nation-state membership. Therefore, what we see in contemporary political culture is a proliferation of discourses about citizenship, or alternative ways of framing belonging and rights. Some of these discourses are genuinely more inclusive and posit new ways of conceiving of migrant membership in the political community—for instance, by conceiving of the relevant rights-bearing "citizen" community as comprising all those who are socially or economically embedded in society or simply those with long-term residency (see note 11). Others are sharply at odds with the extension of rights to migrants. This is particularly true of those who define citizenship and entitlement to rights *in opposition to migrants.*

THE CITIZEN AND ALIEN
AS RELATIONAL IDENTITIES IN THE UNITED STATES

Much like the emerging definition of the "European citizen," citizenship in the United States is defined largely in terms of those it excludes. More than just a legal status in relation to the state, citizenship marks belonging and entitlement to rights, qualities defined as much by cultural norms and practices as by legal statutes.[13] "The citizen" who is a full member of the political community and who is entitled to a full range of rights is therefore a constructed identity, subject to regular contestation and gradual change. What I argue here is that a key shift in the construction of citizen identity in the United States (and especially in California) in the past decade has been a renewed tendency[14] to define it in opposition to "aliens," and particularly to migrant and immigrant workers performing low-skilled or subordinated labor. This opposition between citizens and aliens is therefore not only about membership in the political community, but about the extent to which a person is imagined to have legitimate claims to rights.

While this dichotomy between citizens and aliens might seem like the most obvious possible opposition, it has not always been key to the definition of citizenship. For instance, Judith Shklar (1991) has written a very influential analysis of American citizenship history that instead focuses on the opposition of citizens to those excluded from voting or earning: those restricted from participating in public affairs or markets on the basis of their race or gender. She argues that the practice of slavery and the exclusions of women from public life helped produce the substance and status of the citizenship of white men. If Shklar is right, we might best understand the current opposition of citizens and aliens as a new dichotomy through which the substance and status of citizenship is being produced.

THE CITIZEN AS LEGAL AGENT AND CONTRACT MAKER

One of the conceptual bases for denying rights to migrants comes directly out of the liberal tradition, and particularly out of notions of contract and consent. Given the cultural hegemony of the liberal tradition in the United States,[15] it is not surprising to find that it underlies dominant conceptual understandings of political community, citizenship, and rights.

American liberalism—which has been specified as "contractarianism" by some (e.g., Pateman 1988) and as "consensualism" by others (Schuck and Smith 1985)—centers contract and consent as the bases for human relations. Membership in political community is therefore imagined to be the result of rational individual decisions to entrust innate authority to a governing body. Law—the statement of the will of the majority—applies to all citizens equally, and rational citizens agree to its regulation because their interests are served by having these same policies regulate the behavior of other citizens. Lawbreaking in this case would be a breach of contract; a failure to respect the authority of the political body (and the will of the majority) to which each citizen has entrusted her "natural" sovereignty.

What are the implications of a liberal political logic for the position of migrants? In contrast to models of political membership that presume an organic, functional, or identity-based definition of community,[16] a liberal definition of membership focuses on the individual (apart from social or economic contexts), legal provisions for admission to the body politic, and the consent of the governed. The inclusion or exclusion of the migrant, then, rests on her own will and consent as well as that of the body politic, as expressed through policy.

Peter Schuck and Rogers Smith (1985) note that John Locke (whose writings strongly influenced the design of the U.S. Constitution) focused his attention on the consent of the individual joining society and failed to address the issue of whether a citizen body could refuse a new member. They argue that *mutual* consent should be the logical extension of Lockean liberal democracy, and that, in fact, this principle has undergirded much of the approach to citizenship in the United States.[17] If membership in political community requires the mutual consent of the governed, then immigration statutes become not just the state's regulatory mechanism for in-migration but also an indirect statement of the will of the people. This formulation has a number of critical consequences.[18]

Most critically for our focus here, the emphasis on contract and consent has consequences for the social construction and human rights claims of undocumented immigrants. Within the frame of liberal or consensual thought, immigrants who enter U.S. territory without documentation commit more than a misdemeanor[19]—they also commit an affront to the principle of consent and the popular will.[20] What this means in practice is that it has been possible to imagine undocumented immigrants as *outside civil society*, outside the bounds of civil law, since the polity has never approved their presence. Given a position which is "always already illegal," they can be imagined as having no claims to the civil or social rights allocated and protected by the state. And given the liberal assumption of rational, autonomous action by all individuals, migrants who have "chosen" to cross state borders without authorization are imagined to have consented to the conditions of "rightslessness." Their border crossing involves a "knowing defiance" of American law, a "calculated risk" (Schuck and Smith 1985) in which migrants exchange their right to rights for economic opportunity.

This liberal frame for the relationship between the individual and society (and hence for legitimate claims to rights) differs considerably from that of international human rights, which is also liberal in orientation but universalist rather than state- and contract-centered. International human rights norms, in contrast, locate rights in the individual in a manner that permits stateless persons, migrants, and refugees to make claims to rights even while they are outside the jurisdiction of a state that recognizes them as members.

The former, state-centered conceptualization of immigrant rightslessness has arguably become more prevalent in American popular and legal cultures in the 1990s, as evidenced by claims such as those of Proposition 187 authors that the undocumented have "no rights" (Jonas 1999: 106) and by the plethora of policy proposals and new legislation that undercut immigrants' social and economic rights. Legislation and INS practices related to border control have also reinforced this trend: in the late 1990s, enforcement efforts have particularly targeted "criminal aliens" for deportation, based on IIRAIRA's expanded range of "deportable" crimes and reasons for detention. In popular media, these efforts have been reported haphazardly as targeting "criminal aliens," "criminal illegal aliens," and "illegal aliens," representing what is arguably a discursive blurring between a "criminal" status and an "illegal" status. What is interesting here is that while INS policy officially differentiates between the categories of "criminal" and "illegal," media representations suggest that in popular consciousness, undocumented immigrants are often represented as people who have "broken the law," with little differentiation between those who have simply crossed the border and those who have committed much more serious offenses. And with the increased criminalization of border crossing, in fact, the INS has begun putting those who have been caught in unauthorized border crossing more than once in detention with drug dealers and violent criminals. These detention practices contribute to blurring the distinction between criminal and undocumented aliens.[21] Immigrants who have been understood as "always already illegal," are simultaneously coming to be defined as "always already criminal," a process with complex repercussions in terms of popular sentiment, future public policy, and the potential for migrants to make human rights claims.[22]

Consider the oft-made claim that American resources should be reserved for "tax-paying citizens." This phrase alternately suggests that those who do not pay taxes or those who do not hold legal citizenship (or both) cannot make legitimate claims upon public resources. The conception of citizens as exclusive proprietors of public resources arguably has some basis in the liberal tradition outlined above, as well as in the contemporary cultural trend toward privatization.[23] Residents who are excluded from proprietorship are then positioned as illicit usurpers of privately owned resources. Proposition 187 and the 1996 welfare reforms certainly reflect this logic: when citizens are imagined as the exclusive proprietors of public goods, migrants are positioned as ineligible for even the limited social rights provided in the United States.

This might also extend the criminality of migrants from just the undocumented to all those who are excluded from citizen proprietorship, given that the presence of those who do not "own" public spaces or goods might be understood as a criminal act of trespassing. Imagining citizens as exclusive proprietors of the public sphere makes the presence of "nonowners" suspect even when they are in public spaces in which legal citizenship status is hypothetically irrelevant: schools, parks, beaches, city halls, public roadways, the DMV, bus stops, pools, libraries, hospitals.[24] The actual legal status of the "intruders" is not known in most such interactions, and many claims of an illicit appropriation of public spaces or goods by noncitizens presume a noncitizen or undocumented status on the basis of race or ethnicity. Pat Buchanan recently repeated an oft-told story about someone rushing a family member to the emergency room, only to find what he considered a disproportionate number of patients who "clearly were recent arrivals from south of the border." He concludes the story with its moral: "Illegal aliens to the front of the line, American citizens to the rear."[25] This story not only presumes that the proper place of citizens is in the front of the line when it comes to rights to emergency care but also that the "usurpers" of this right were "illegals," a determination based on their appearance and perhaps on the language they spoke. This kind of assumption—unfortunately a common one in California[26]—links rights based on legal status to those based on racial or ethnic identity, an overlapping of liberal and racist discourses further discussed below.

To sum up, liberal thought permits an opposition between contract makers who have legitimate claims to the resources and spaces of the public sphere in "their" state and migrants, who, in contrast, are perceived as having forfeited any claims to rights, as criminal invaders,[27] trespassers, or usurpers of "privately held" resources. This opposition functions to undercut migrants' claims to fundamental civil and economic rights; it leaves little space for rights claimed on the basis of universal personhood. While international human rights norms are also grounded in liberal notions of the individual and rights, they are not as compatible with the popular versions of liberalism that focus on contract and property.

THE CITIZEN AS A FIRST WORLD SUBJECT

So far, this analysis has focused on the ways that migrants are imagined to fall outside the legally defined citizen community and therefore to lack a right to rights. However, this liberal discourse is not the only basis for the common cultural perception of migrants as less entitled to rights. The illustration discussed above, in which Buchanan identified Latino-looking, Spanish-speaking peoples as less entitled to emergency room care than "citizens" involves further assumptions about race, citizen identity, and entitlement to rights. And because Buchanan's story is not uncommon—I have personally heard this same kind of story told about "illegals" taking over public beaches, retail shops, public health clinics, and public school classrooms—its underlying premises are worth exploring. The primary difference between a liberal discourse about rights and the Buchanan story is that particular racial identities matter in the latter. "Liberal subjects" are empty of identity: they are interchangeable vessels of rights and obligations, distinguishable only in terms of the contracts they have made. If the citizens or the alien usurpers of public resources in Buchanan's story were identified only on the basis of documented legal status in relation to the state, it would have been strictly liberal in orientation. However, both citizens and illegal aliens in this story were identified by race. We might conclude that race was simply used as a shorthand indicator of legal status. But I would also like to suggest that Buchanan and others who tell similar stories consider Latinos (and particularly Latino immigrants) to properly belong in back of the line when it comes to eligibility for rights and resources. The underlying logic is not only liberal but also neocolonial in orientation. That is, the common perception of "alien" Latinos as having a lesser entitlement to rights than "citizens" is based in part on their racial identity[28] and their "Third World" position within the global economy. Elaborating this argument requires turning first to the historical context of citizenship, immigration, and labor recruitment in the United States.

Scholars of U.S. citizenship history have noted that—much as the United States is a liberal society with hypothetical equality among all its members— its practices have frequently been illiberal and exclusionary. Rogers Smith (1993, 1997) argues that there have been multiple traditions underlying historical citizenship practice in the United States, including a tradition he identifies as "ethnocentrism" or "ascriptive inegalitarianism," which defines membership according to ascriptive identities such as gender, race, ethnicity, and national origin. He notes that not only exclusions from citizenship but also inequalities within the citizen body have been justified through a logic that rested on elaborate arguments about proper or natural biological hierarchies. While others have tried to reconcile these exclusions and hierarchies with the egalitarianism of liberal ideals,[29] Smith suggests that ethnocentrism and liberalism have coexisted throughout U.S. history, and that they have been freely combined by actors more concerned with the political effectiveness of ideas than with their logical consistency.

Similarly, the aforementioned work by Judith Shklar (1991) identifies illiberal practices and exclusions as definitive in the American citizenship tradition. She argues that the meanings and status of American citizenship have historically been defined in relation to those who have been denied full membership or rights. For this reason, she adopts the notion of "standing"— meaning roughly social status or public presence—as the defining characteristic of citizenship. Understanding citizenship as a matter of relational "standing" takes the focus away from formal legal statuses or the formal possession of liberal citizenship rights and instead permits us to consider *degrees of membership* and the ensuing relative claims to rights by different groups resident in the territorial state.[30]

Although the population in the United States today descends almost entirely from settler or immigrant groups, historically, not all immigrants have been considered equally "alien." Beginning with the constitutional exclusion of slaves and continuing with immigration and citizenship laws in the late nineteenth and twentieth centuries, different ethnic and racial groups were legally excluded from citizenship rights. The Chinese Exclusion Act of 1882, for instance, made Chinese residents ineligible for citizenship, a law that was not fully retracted until 1943 (Reimers 1998: 12). And even in cases in which nonwhite minorities have been eligible for citizenship, the United States has a recurring and well-documented history of the exclusion of minority groups from the exercise of equal rights. Racial segregation, political disenfranchisement, internment camps, intimidation, vigilante justice, and the appropriation of property have all produced a pervasive racial stratification in social relations throughout most of U.S. history.

To a certain extent, these exclusionary practices reflected racial ideologies produced during colonialism—the early phases of globalization—with its legitimating rhetoric that contrasted degraded or savage peoples with more evolved, "civilized" Europeans. For instance, Americanization campaigns in the Southwest that schooled Chicana/o and Mexican immigrant youth in middle-class moralities represented these efforts as uplifting a savage and inferior people, while in fact preparing them for a subordinate place in society as domestic servants and manual laborers (cf. Gonzalez 1990; Romero 1992). The United States did not have a formal colonial relationship with all the population groups that were racially subordinated,[31] but its racial ideologies reflected and reproduced those that undergirded the colonial project.[32] For this reason, I represent them here as "neocolonial" in nature.

The history of rights exclusions in the United States also reflects the circumstances under which many African, Asian, and Latino migrants originally came to the United States That is, there have been particular tensions over "who has a right to rights," given that many of those who have come to the United States as laborers have not been understood to be potential citizens in a community of equals. The United States has long relied on the undervalued labor of foreign or internally subordinated workers to support its economic growth and development. Originally, these workers were imported as slaves or indentured servants, who undergirded prosperity in the cities of the Northeast and in agricultural plantations in the South. Later, western states began importing workers to construct transportation infrastructure and to work in mining and agricultural production. The rapidly industrializing economy in the nineteenth and early twentieth centuries was hungry for low-skilled labor, much of which was supplied by immigrants. But while foreign workers were welcomed and in many cases recruited to supply labor, they were not generally invited to become social and political equals. In fact, the demand for foreign labor was largely a demand for socially subordinated labor. Their relative powerlessness and exclusion from the rights due to other workers constituted a large part of their appeal.[33] European immigrants helped satiate this labor demand, particularly in the early twentieth century; however, they were much more likely than non-European immigrants to achieve some mobility and hence inclusion by the second generation.[34]

In the Southwest, labor demands during early industrialization were filled largely with Japanese, Chinese, and Mexican workers. The annexation of this territory by the United States with the Treaty of Guadalupe Hidalgo in 1848 began a process by which Mexican citizens who had been resident in this territory lost their property and found themselves positioned as unskilled labor. This population was fairly small, however, until the early twentieth century, when industrialization in Mexico and the Mexican Revolution generated substantial migration north, a migrant flow that substantially increased the proportion of Mexicans and Chicanos among the ranks of those performing the least skilled and least valued jobs in the Southwest.[35] By the 1930s, this reliance upon subordinated Chicano and Mexican labor had become structurally embedded in the Southwestern economy, a de facto "internal colonial" labor system marked by significant occupational stratification between races, a dual wage system that paid Mexican workers less than others for equivalent jobs, and effective systems of labor repression (Barrera 1979; Montejano 1987).

In the postwar economic boom, Southwestern agriculture formalized this reliance on Mexican labor by developing the Bracero Program, a guest-worker program with Mexico intended to maintain a legal supply of undervalued labor with no obligation to incorporate the workers into the citizen community. This program was widely criticized for failing to replace undocumented labor flows with braceros,[36] as well as for failing to supply labor that remained temporary. While this program was discontinued in 1964, it has had a number of long-lasting effects: first, it set into motion a continuing pattern of migration from Mexico to the United States,[37] and, second, it continues to serve as a rough model for the immigrant worker ideal. The notion of contract workers—who labor in necessary but undesirable jobs on a temporary basis without becoming incorporated into society, bringing family members with them, or making demands for rights beyond the terms of the contract—continues to appear in popular and policy discourse. It underlies the repeated proposal before Congress during the 1990s to reenact a guest-worker program with Mexico and seems to inform popular hopes for an immigrant workforce that will labor without settling and without making demands for social or political rights (cf. Maher 1999; Chavez 1997; Hondagneu-Sotelo 1995). As noted earlier, many of these workers labor in conditions that violate domestic labor laws as well as international human rights standards. While these violations are legitimated in part through the liberal logics elaborated in the previous section, there are a number of additional legitimating arguments at work in popular and policy discourse that deserve brief mention.

First, we see an argument that workers are only here on a temporary basis, so that their home states rather than the host state should be primarily responsible for the protection of their rights. This line of logic essentially conceives of all labor migrants as guest workers, even when they have not migrated under the rubric of a guest-worker contract. This conception makes a number of unrealistic assumptions. For instance, while some sending states do work to promote better working conditions for their citizens abroad,[38] their capacity to do so is quite limited, given that many sending states lack political leverage in relation to receiving states, and that the migrants are geographically removed from the infrastructure such as legal support, health care systems, and education systems that could help provide political or social rights. Additionally, as Phil Martin points out, "there is nothing more permanent than temporary workers" (1994: 96). That is, even migration that is intended to be short-term often turns into long-term or even permanent, given the incorporation of these "temporary" migrants into families, communities, and economies in the receiving state and the difficulty of reincorporating into home communities and economies. The international human rights regime has also come to constrain state enforcement of temporary labor migration, insofar as measures like Operation Wetback in 1954, in which undocumented migrants (as well as some Latino permanent residents and citizens) were rounded up en masse and deported, are no longer politically feasible (cf. Hollifield 1992). For these reasons, labor migration is often less temporary than is popularly imagined, such that a host state's abdication of responsibility for migrant rights leaves migrants in the vulnerable nether-space between states for long periods of time.

Second, the labor relationship is often construed as a strictly private arrangement between workers and employers that takes place in the economic realm rather than the political realm. If workers' rights are being violated, it is therefore economic actors rather than state actors who are primarily responsible. Insofar as this is true, it poses a serious problem for human rights protection in a globalizing era: it is notoriously difficult to enforce rights among economic actors who have not agreed to international treaties. However, it is not entirely true that labor relationships are not political or subject to law, because the state has domestic labor laws that to some extent reflect international human rights standards. Part of the problem in the United States is that the state has not consistently applied these labor laws to immigrant populations, and that labor organizations have historically organized in opposition to undocumented workers. The good news in this regard is that the Equal Economic Opportunity Commission (EEOC) and the AFL-CIO both in the past year endorsed the enforcement of the labor rights of all migrant workers, an indicator that the state and employers in industries with unionized labor may both become more accountable for migrant labor rights in the coming years.

Finally, and most critically to the argument about the neocolonial logic underlying rights exclusions, migrant workers' relative lack of rights is legitimated in terms of comparisons with the imagined conditions in the workers' home countries. That is, it is argued: no matter how bad the conditions are for migrants in the United States, they must be better than those to which these migrants are accustomed. This argument, which shows up often in policy debates, in news coverage, and in interviews with employers, such as in my own research in southern California (Maher 1999), seems to be informed by stereotypes about the uniform poverty and political tyranny assumed to characterize sending states.[39] It suggests that workers migrating from less developed states must be in desperate circumstances in which they do not or should not expect the human rights to which those from the First World are entitled.

While it is true that the availability of work and higher salaries in the United States contributes to workers' decisions to migrate (at times by means that risk their lives), the assumption of migrant workers' desperation is in some cases overstated. Demographic studies of labor migration demonstrate that those who migrate tend *not* to be those who are most economically destitute (Castles and Miller 1998; Cornelius 1998). Transnational migration requires some combination of financial, human, and social capital[40] in order to cover the costs of the trip, to secure housing, and to gain access to employers. Instead, a number of studies suggest that the assertion of workers' desperation serves to legitimate the inequalities of the labor relationship, including subordination and low wages. For instance, my own 1997 fieldwork among employers of immigrant workers revealed that many employers either rejected workers who appeared to have resources or willfully ignored their training and education. Workers who had college degrees or had previously worked as teachers, nurses, or small business owners were treated (and paid) exactly like those without any education or skills (Maher 1999). Migrant workers in this context and in others (cf. Constable 1997: 75–77) reported needing to act out an economic desperation and inferiority that they did not actually feel, at times obscuring their family resources, their education, or their ambitions in order to keep their jobs.[41]

While the representation of migrant workers as uniformly poor and needy helps employers legitimate labor relations in which workers are poorly paid and subordinated, the more general cultural representation of migrants as people who have fled unthinkable conditions also serves to legitimate their lesser entitlement to rights. That is, it appeals to structural disparities in the global economy in order to explain why Third World "aliens" should be grateful for the opportunities available to them in a First World economy rather than expecting the full range of human rights available to those who properly "belong" in the First World. Insofar as the division between First and Third Worlders is a racialized one, this neocolonial logic also reproduces the racial hierarchies that have characterized so much of U.S. and global colonial history. In effect, it translates racial and economic privilege into a greater entitlement to rights. In doing so, it obscures the universal nature of human rights, which do not in theory vary according to race, legal status, national origin, or economic position.

CONCLUSION

The patterns evident above suggest that there are a number of discourses in the United States that define citizenship in ways that rest on an implicit contrast with "Third World" immigrants, and particularly the undocumented. The conceptual and social contrast between "the citizen" and "the alien" both informs the substance and status of American citizenship and simultaneously constructs the immigrant worker as an outsider, a trespasser, and a social inferior with fewer claims to rights. This contrast rests in part on liberal notions of contract, consent, and property, but also on racial or neocolonial ideologies that underlie the continuing divisions between the First and Third Worlds. Together, these philosophical strains produce a discursive distinction between citizens and alien workers as mutually exclusive categories and as legally or "legitimately" unequal in their entitlement to rights. While these are not exhaustive of the possible discourses about citizenship in the United States, discourses such as these help make possible some of the systematic rights violations we see occurring in relation to migrant workers. To some extent, the 1996 videotaped beating of immigrants in Riverside was not an anomaly in INS agent behavior but a phenomenon consistent with Proposition 187 and labor abuses—all logical extensions of the cultural construction of immigrants having a lesser claim to rights (cf. Jonas 1999: 106).

These legitimations of migrant rightslessness are not trivial in an economy that increasingly relies upon imported, and particularly Third World, labor for unskilled manufacturing and service sector jobs. In California, for instance, the proportion of restaurant cooks who were foreign-born increased from 29 percent to 69 percent between 1980 and 1996. During this same period, the proportion of foreign-born gardeners almost doubled, and that of construction laborers more than tripled (Cornelius 1998). The demand for immigrant labor in California and in the United States at large appears not to be a temporary phenomenon; rather, it appears to be an increasingly structurally embedded part of an economy that is producing the greatest job growth in low-skilled, part-time and "flexible" labor sectors. Now more than ever, the United States is taking advantage of the "extraordinary economic and job growth that can be achieved with a First World infrastructure and a Third World labor force" (Martin 1994; cf. Muller and Espenshade 1985). Insofar as this trend continues, the ways in which citizenship and rights are conceived will become increasingly critical in coming years.

Fortunately, the logics I examine here are not the only ones present. Studies claiming a growing commitment to human rights norms in the United States are not entirely mistaken. For instance, the recent commitment by the EEOC and the AFL-CIO to the labor rights of immigrants is a stance more consistent with human rights norms than the discourses discussed above. We are also seeing the growth of NGO activity committed to protecting the rights of immigrants,[42] as well as activism among migrants who lobby for human rights protection via hometown associations (cf. Rivera-Salgado 1999). Mobilization at subnational and transnational levels for migrant rights has the potential to destabilize the construction of rights as derivative of one's legal citizenship in the nation-state or of First World privilege. Certainly, too, there is commensurate activity among scholars working to reconceptualize citizenship in ways that do not exclude migrants from rights claims. While human rights norms are not yet hegemonic, U.S. political culture is increasingly marked by contestation about the nature of political membership and the basis for rights claims.

As discussed earlier, the United States is not alone in its reliance upon foreign labor or in its violations of migrant rights. Given a growing reliance upon labor from less-developed economies in all industrialized and many industrializing states, the U.S. case should be understood in a global context. The processes of globalization pose a number of challenges to human rights. Most simply, the transnational labor migration that is a critical feature of the globalizing economy leaves many migrants in an ambiguous and vulnerable position in which it is not clear which state is accountable for their protection of their rights. Internationally, migrant workers from less-developed economies constitute a large and growing population that falls outside the traditional human rights focus on the relationship between states and citizens.[43] These migrants are vulnerable to rights violations by the state apparatus dedicated to regulating immigration. And even when state actors are not themselves the ones violating migrant rights, states have often been reticent to intervene in cases of violations by market actors. That is, a complication of labor migration in a global economy is that rights violations occur increasingly in the market sphere—a more diffuse source of violations than those by tyrannical leaders and more difficult to monitor and regulate in a state-centered human rights regime.

Finally, we have some reason to expect that globalization may spread or at least reinforce neocolonial ideologies that undercut migrant rights. The transnational flow of labor from less developed economies to high-growth or high-tech economies reproduces a social order and division of labor in receiving states that is stratified by race and global class position. This division of labor will almost certainly reproduce neocolonial ideologies such as those evident in the U.S. case.[44] While international human rights norms assume universality, the transnational flow of labor in the globalizing economy is likely to produce discourses that presume that one's identity and position matter to one's proper claims to rights. One of the most critical sites for conflict in a globalizing era regarding the rights of migrants will therefore be the realm of ideas, between alternative conceptions of who has a right to rights.

NOTES

1. These violations include some that occur in places other than right at the border, such as the well-publicized 1996 videotaped beating of undocumented immigrants who had fled from immigration officers in Riverside, California, east of Los Angeles. A week later, seven immigrants died at the end of a similar chase (Bacon 1999).

2. For instance, see the report of the American Friends Service Committee on human and civil rights violations along the U.S.-Mexican border between 1995 and 1997 (Huspek et al. 1998) and that of Americas Watch (1992). Watchdog groups have also made record of rights violations against Latino/a U.S. citizens or permanent residents apprehended by immigration enforcement personnel.

3. Eschbach et al. 1999 estimates that more than 1,600 migrants died in crossing during the years 1993–97 borderwide, but the actual number was probably higher, given that these represent only those deaths in which bodies were found and reported. José Luis Soberanes Fernandez, head of the independent Mexican National Commission for Human Rights (CNDH), estimates 450 deaths.

4. This incident allegedly followed an open invitation on the Internet to come to Arizona to "hunt illegals" ("Mexico Group Seeks UN Help with U.S. Border Abuse," Reuters, 14 May 2000).

5. Defined as requiring "that a country not return (in French, *refouler*) a refugee to his home country when the refugee would be persecuted or killed upon return" (Langenfeld 1999).

6. Placed on the ballot in the 1994 elections, Proposition 187 was passed by 58.8 percent of California voters. In 1998, a district judge found all but one provision of this proposition (that to raise the penalty for fraudulent immigration documents) to be unconstitutional, and it was never legally put into practice. However, many Latino Californians reported instances of discrimination and civil rights violations after Proposition 187's passage, for instance, being asked for proof of citizenship in the grocery store or by landlords. The reputation of Proposition 187 in retrospect is that it was particularly mean-spirited, and efforts to put a similar measure on the 2000 ballot failed. However, the kinds of issues it raised about the rights of immigrants continue to constitute a serious debate in public discourse and in the policy arena.

7. Originally, this legislation made *all* noncitizens—including permanent, temporary, and undocumented residents—ineligible for social benefits. It later was amended to restore benefits to disabled or elderly legal residents who had been present prior to the enactment of this legislation in 1996. However, no new noncitizen immigrants are eligible.

8. Others have observed how the greatest champions of human rights have failed

to fulfill their own ideals in other ways. Robert Justin Goldstein (1987), for instance, notes that the U.S. definition of human rights is "curiously narrow," focusing almost exclusively on political rights, almost completely ignoring the social and economic rights outlined in the Universal Declaration.

9. This approach differs significantly from one that considers "political culture" to operate only in a nonstate realm, such that one might discuss the mutual effects of policy on culture or vice versa. Instead, I assume that policy and popular discourses both operate in roughly the same cultural milieu of values, meanings, constructions, and symbols.

10. The latter focused particularly on the household service sector, one of the fastest-growing markets for migrant labor both in the United States and internationally.

11. There has also been growing pressure to adopt different criteria for membership and hence eligibility for the full rights of citizens. Rather than distinguishing between residents in a given political community in terms of their legal status in relation to the state, some scholars advocate considering: how long a migrant has been resident in a community, the extent to which she is embedded in substate systems and institutions, whether she has family and social networks in the community, what kinds of contributions she has made to collective well-being or resources, whether she fulfills a necessary social or economic function, and whether she is politically active in extra-electoral ways, such as in social movements or lobbying. For studies that discuss one or more of these alternative criteria for citizenship rights, see Carens 1989; Hammar 1990; Walzer 1983; Bauböck 1991, 1994; Rivera-Salgado 1999; Pincetl 1994; and Flores and Benmayor 1997. I return to this topic in the conclusion.

12. See, e.g., Lutz 1997; Kofman 1995; and King 1997.

13. Of course, law and culture are not entirely separate, as cultural norms are frequently reproduced in law, and legal change (such as civil rights legislation) can initiate cultural transformations.

14. The widespread nativism and focus on the immigrant "alien" as a threat during the 1990s has in many ways reflected the nativism of the turn of the century. See Feagin 1997 and Higham 1988.

15. Liberalism provides not only a frame for government and citizenship but also the principles underlying much of cultural and economic life in the United States. Louis Hartz (1955) stated this case most strongly, arguing that Lockean liberalism in America constitutes a dogmatic set of principles for a way of life that has achieved "moral unanimity," a near-tyrannical commitment to "irrational Lockeanism," against which there is no space for argument. Paradoxically, this unreflective devotion has not identified its own substance as liberalism but rather as "Americanism": "There has never been a 'liberal movement' or a real 'liberal party' in America: we have only had the American Way of Life, a nationalist articulation of Locke which usually does not know that Locke himself is involved. . . . This is why even critics who have noticed America's moral unity have usually missed its substance" (11).

16. As mentioned in note 11.

17. Schuck and Smith regard the principle of ascription that informs the Fourteenth Amendment (which grants birthright citizenship in an effort to avoid the discrimination to which consensualism might give rise) as an inappropriate relic of medieval custom. Acquiring citizenship simply by virtue of the place of one's birth

circumvents consent altogether, they observe, aside perhaps from the tacit consent of the parents and later of the grown child. They argue that granting citizenship status to the children of undocumented immigrants is a particular affront to consensual principles, because immigration law (and by extension, popular will) has explicitly *not* granted the parents entrance to U.S. territory. However, others have used the consensual frame to turn this argument on its head, noting that the native-born children of undocumented immigrants have not themselves consented to growing up as perpetual outsiders with fewer rights.

18. In addition to criminalizing the undocumented, the statutory ethos permits and legitimates discriminatory exclusions of particular groups of people to whom the citizen body (or their representatives) do not wish to extend an equal membership. As Rogers Smith (1997) illustrates, strategic exclusions based on racial, ethnic, or other ascriptive identities have been the norm more than the exception in U.S. history. In contemporary political culture, with public rhetoric committed to "equal opportunity," nondiscrimination, and an end to racism, few public figures are willing to say that citizenship should be restricted along racial or ethnic lines. However, it is much more common to claim that the citizen body has the right to decide its own future, to determine the shape, color, and culture of its own polity—a claim that mixes notions of self-determination with those of contract and consent, and that essentially legitimates whatever discriminations in admission suit the majority.

19. At the time of this writing, unauthorized border crossing into the United States is still categorized as a mere misdemeanor (8 U.S.C. § 1325), while subsequent illegal entry is a felony (8 U.S.C. §§ 1325, 1326).

20. I am grateful to Jack Donnelly for pointing out that this particular logic resembles a sort of democratic populism, closer perhaps to the philosophy of Michael Walzer than of the social contract tradition, which tends to assume limits (e.g., of justice) to the law that can be imposed by popular will. While I have not conducted an extensive philosophical analysis of American political culture, it appears to contain strains of multiple philosophical traditions, including multiple versions of liberalism.

21. See, e.g., Michel Foucault's (1977: 27) argument that practices of detention construct criminalities, including equivalent crimes.

22. The trend toward the criminalization of migration is not unique to the United States. Bhabha also notes that the 1985 and 1990 Schengen agreements in Europe "cast immigration as a subcategory of criminal activity, along with drug smuggling and antiterrorist measures" (1998b: 609).

23. Private property played a critical role in the Lockean story about the original creation of political communities, as well as in early definitions of the citizen community in the United States. The exclusion of the unpropertied from full membership or rights was based in part on the argument that those without property would have no permanent interest or stake in civil society, and hence should not be entrusted with its decision making. While formal citizenship is no longer restricted to the propertied, the past two decades have witnessed a resurgence of the notion of citizens as proprietors—and, in this case, as the rightful "owners" of public goods and public spaces. I argue elsewhere (Maher 1999) that the emerging notion of the citizen-proprietor reflects the logic of privatization, in which all notions of "the public" are eroding (cf. McKenzie 1994; Reich 1991a, 1991b).

24. See Marchevsky 1996 on protectionism with respect to public spaces as evi-

dence of a desire to further segregate highly segregated cities. See Maher 2000 on the emergence of this proprietary logic and the relations of citizen-owner/migrant-trespasser in privatized, often gated, communities in the suburbs. Actual legal statuses are not known in most of the interactions in public spaces and "race" is used as an indicator of legal versus "illegal" status.

25. From a speech given in San Diego on 28 April 2000. See "Buchanan Fears Mexico to Seize Southwest," *San Diego Union Tribune*, 29 April 2000, A11.The quoted text can be found at the Buchanan Reform website, http://www.gopatgo2000.com/new/speeches/trouble_in_neighborhood.htm.

26. Anti-immigrant or restrictionist fervor has often identified anyone who looks Latino as a suspected "illegal." When a self-appointed Citizen Patrol approached Latinos at San Diego's airport in 1996 asking for documentation, it was on the basis of such overgeneralization of undocumented status to all Latinos, which likewise lies behind incidents in which the INS or Border Patrol have apprehended, detained, and even killed U.S. citizens in the border region. One of the primary reasons Proposition 187 earned a reputation for being racist was that both citizens and permanent residents found themselves subject to discrimination after its passage (Bacon 1999: 169–70).

27. While I have not pursued it here, there is also a common discourse in the border region that undercuts the rights of undocumented migrant rights by likening them to an invading army, an enemy force with respect to whom basic human rights are suspended, as in wartime. The dichotomy is generally that between "citizens" and "enemies," or even "friends" and "foes." The construction of undocumented migrants as an invading army also appears to be part of the justification for vigilante violence against migrants on the border.

28. I am assuming here that races are socially constructed categories that differ across time and between societies. In Latin America, of course, "Latino" does not exist as a racial category. In the United States, this category began with the Census invention of "Hispanic" identity, a clustering together of many ethnic, national, and racial groups based on geography and language. While the Census no longer includes "Hispanic" in its race question (but rather in a separate question about "Hispanic origin"), in most other contexts "Hispanic" or "Latino" is coded as a "race" equivalent to "White" or "Asian." I am adopting this informal categorization in my discussion about race above, given that this is closest to the cultural "common sense" that seems to inform the practices of rights exclusion I am examining.

29. For instance, some authors treat historical inequalities as more or less significant exceptions to liberal egalitarianism (e.g., Myrdal 1944; Huntington 1981). Others see inequalities as not only tolerated but produced by Lockean liberalism (e.g., Macpherson 1962; Pateman 1988).

30. This understanding of citizenship also suggests that there might be a number of ways to frame the meaning and boundaries of citizenship at any given place and time, and that their relative appeal will depend upon available philosophical traditions, cultural constructions, and political contingencies.

31. Of course, as a settler state that expanded its borders through conquest in relation to both Native American and Mexican populations, the United States was certainly imperial. It has also had (and continues to have) an imperial presence globally, including in Latin America, the Caribbean, and the Philippines. My claim here

is simply that not all instances of racial subordination in the United States were produced during the age of empire with clear spatial boundaries between colony and metropole.

32. See Balibar 1991 regarding how racisms in different times and places have learned from each other, such that they reflect a common (il)logic, even while arising from historically specific social relations. Also see literatures that elaborate the "internal colonial" relations in the Southwest (e.g., Montejano 1987; Barrera 1979) and those that define nonwhite minorities in the United States as Third World peoples, given the common colonial history that produced racial inequalities both in the United States and in the international arena (e.g., Mohanty 1991).

33. See, e.g., McWilliams 1939.

34. Assimilation and hence mobility in the United States depended in part on gaining admittance to the category of whiteness, as Ignatiev argues in *How the Irish Became White* (1995).

35. The proportion of Mexican and Chicano workers was also affected by legislation that stanched the flow of workers of other nationalities, including the Chinese Exclusion Act of 1882 and the "Gentleman's Agreement" with Japan in 1907.

36. Calavita 1992 argues that employers continued to use both the threat and the actual employment of undocumented labor during the Bracero Program in order to maintain leverage against labor demands. In effect, agricultural employers and the INS worked together to exert labor control, with bracero workers "contracting" into a position that was little more than indentured servitude.

37. There are a number of reasons why the initiation of migrant flows tends to produce continued migration, including the formation of transnational social networks and communities that produce migration for family reunification and provide social capital, easing the costs of migrating, finding housing, and finding work. Additionally, labor migration tends to restructure the economy and social structure of sending communities, making continued migration more likely and more necessary. See Massey 1999 and Glick Schiller 1999.

38. Most also continue to offer limited citizen rights to those who are not resident in the home country, such as the right of return, to own property, and—in some cases—to vote.

39. It may also be a deduction from liberal conceptions of migration as a rational individual choice. That is, if migrants choose to work in poor conditions in the United States, this choice must still be one that optimizes, meaning that conditions must be worse in their home countries. This assumption oversimplifies the family, economic, and political contexts for why migration occurs.

40. Social capital here refers to the social networks that can provide information, financial support, housing, and access to employers. Migrants without these social networks are much more likely to need money and education or skills in order to successfully make the move.

41. This performance of inferiority and neediness not only affirms the devaluation of the worker but reinforces and reproduces the inequalities in the international division of labor. The assumed uniform poverty among imported workers positions them as distinctly Third World in relation to employers, who are by contrast positioned as members of the First World, who enjoy not only a better class position but also greater privilege and entitlement. The contrast in relative class position and priv-

ilege produced by the importation of foreign workers to do devalued and subordinated labor may help explain the growing employment of foreign workers even in industrializing states such as Malaysia, Hong Kong, and Pakistan. Employers of foreign workers (particularly as household servants) may be working to distance themselves from the stigma of Third-Worldness, to mark a greater status and even modernity. A number of studies suggest that the class and racial status that attends the hiring of Third World women as domestic workers may help explain the proliferation of the international "maid trade" (cf. Chin 1998; Constable 1997; Heyzer et al. 1994).

42. For instance, the National Network for Immigrant and Refugee Rights (NNIRR) is an umbrella organization for local immigrant and refugee rights affiliates such as the Coalition for Humane Immigrant Rights of Los Angeles (CHIRLA) and the United Network for Immigrant and Refugee Rights (UNIRR) in Chicago.

43. A critical dimension of contemporary migration and rights vulnerabilities that I have not touched upon here is that transnational labor migration is becoming increasingly feminized (Morokvasik 1984; Cornelius 1998). That is, more women are migrating internationally for work—particularly in jobs that have been "traditional" women's work like domestic service and prostitution—and constitute a growing proportion of those that are vulnerable to migrant rightslessness.

44. All structural inequalities that are not enforced by violence rely upon legitimating ideologies. But we might also expect that people who live in economies strongly stratified by race and global class position "learn" from their daily experience. For instance, when almost all of the household service workers in white southern Californian suburbs are Latina immigrants, children in these suburbs grow up with firsthand "knowledge" of their relative privilege, which includes not only the power to command and the right to be served, but also perhaps a greater entitlement to resources and rights.

2

Tourism, Sex Work, and Women's Rights in the Dominican Republic

Amalia Lucia Cabezas

Making women, rather than men, the focal point of inquiry profoundly alters the concepts of human rights and globalization. In truth, the spectacle of young women wearing tight miniskirts and stiletto heels rarely comes to mind when thinking of human rights violations and the impact of globalization. But it is one of the effects of globalization in the Caribbean region. Consider, for example, the following account: a young woman leaving a disco at a tourist resort in the Dominican Republic is arrested by the police, who are rounding up all Dominican women as they leave the premises. Nightly police sweeps are customary. The young women arrested are verbally abused, beaten, and sometimes even raped by the police. Charged with "bothering tourists," they are thrown in prison and are not released until they have paid a hefty fine.[1] This is one form of state-inflicted violence rendered invisible by the normal registers and conceptualizations of human rights abuses.[2]

In this essay, I discuss how the forces of globalization, as experienced in tourism development, generate new problems, reconfigure old ones, and create unprecedented opportunities for women in the Dominican Republic. I examine how the human rights language is empowering sex workers to form collective, politicized identities and transnational networks and alliances. Notwithstanding the many battles waged on their bodies, female sex workers have found a language in which to articulate their complaints and challenge the state in the public sphere.

HUMAN RIGHTS AS WOMEN'S RIGHTS

Most of the human rights violations that poor women face are gender- and class-specific. Men who participate in prostitution, whether as clients, as prostitutes, or as intermediaries, are seldom penalized.[3] Middle-class "call girls," usually university students and office workers, operate under covert conditions that provide protection denied their more visible working-class counterparts.[4] Working-class women negotiate directly with their clients in public places, which excludes them from the more ambiguous transactions that take place under more "romantic" and less obviously commercial courtship scenarios.

The growth of tourism in the Dominican Republic has facilitated international migration for tourism workers and concomitant increases in crime, police abuse, corruption, and the deterioration of women's rights. The mass arrests of women that take place outside discos, on beaches, and in restaurants—any public place where women congregate—have created new forms of violence against "public" women. Women are subject to arbitrary arrest and detention; they are subject to indiscriminate roundups and taken to jails, where they are confined with the general criminal population.[5] According to Yolanda, one of thirty-five women whom I interviewed for my study of sex work and tourism, "I have been arrested many times, not for stealing but for being in the street. They tell me that it's for bothering the *gringos,* and I have to pay a fine and spend up to five days in jail. Sometimes up to eight days in jail. They push you and hit you and throw you in their trucks all the time calling you names. It's so bad here that now there are many women, many housewives, who go out at night to eat a pizza or something, and they get arrested. The police think that they are 'of the street.' Now all *Dominican women* are suspect" (Cabezas 1999).

All women are stigmatized and criminalized as potential sex workers. Ultimately, all women face restrictions on their freedom of movement. The police officers and the state profit from these arrests. Women are arrested to regulate the number of prostitutes in the streets and discos, to discipline and exact bribes and sexual favors from them, and to control the businesses that do not pay bribes to the police.

Commercial sex workers seldom receive police protection when they are raped, beaten, or robbed by their clients or intermediaries. In many countries of Latin America, the legal framework does not even recognize the rape of prostitutes as a crime (Acosta 1996). In a tourist setting, complaints against the police exist in a context in which citizens already feel like outsiders in their own land. Citizens are disempowered by the social arrangements that constitute the hosts as subservient to the guests. Furthermore, sex workers are perceived as guilty and not entitled to equal protection under the law. They are not seen as victims. "The more women deviate from this framework [the monogamous heterosexual reproductive relationship] of acceptable gendered behavior, the more they risk being disciplined, either directly by the rules criminalizing prostitution or indirectly through the law's failure to protect them from abuse," Dan Danielsen and Karen Engle note (1995: 4).

Although violence against women has held an important position in the conception of women's rights as human rights, the "public" and "private" forms of abuse that sex workers face have not been part of the discourse.[6] Global and local campaigns to raise awareness of violence against women fail to recognize the injustices against sex workers. When female prostitutes enter into human rights discourse, they usually do so only if they clearly are victims, either of trafficking or of forced prostitution. The lack of juridical protection, and criminalization by the state, renders female prostitutes particularly vulnerable to gender-based violence and abuse. Women who willingly work in prostitution are without the explicit protection of victimhood as defined by the language and conventions of human rights. Sex workers are at best invisible and at worst deserving of abuse. It is ironic, therefore, that they have gained agency and political opportunity in applying the human rights discourse to their mobilization efforts. In fact, human rights discourses serve as a framework for organizing their struggle against the state's monopoly in regulating the practices and politics of sexual commerce and for vindicating the rights of sex workers.

TOURISM DEVELOPMENT

The Dominican Republic has a population of 8 million people, with an unemployment rate that hovers above 20 percent. Its market-oriented economy focuses on export-processing manufacturing (free-trade zones), nontraditional agricultural and agroindustrial production, and tourism (Raynolds 1998; Safa 1995). Tourism is by far the largest and fastest-growing sector of the national economy.

Many young Dominicans travel from the capital or rural areas to sell services and goods to tourists in the resorts. They feed their families by combining a number of income-generating activities in both the formal and informal sectors of the economy. The high demand for sexual services in the tourist marketplace (sex trade zones) constructs opportunities for men and women to develop liaisons with foreigners and to travel, marry, migrate, or at least make enough money to support themselves and their families. This link to the global economy is known as sex tourism, the term used to delineate sex work connected to tourism. It is specifically tied into the travel and leisure sector's demand for racialized and sexualized encounters with the "natives" (Enloe 1989; Kempadoo 1999).

The growth of tourism in the Dominican Republic is tied to the dynamics of a globalized economy and facilitated by the development of international systems of communications and transportation. With the closure of Cuba's tourist industry in the 1960s, the United Nations, the World Bank, and the Organization of American States urged the Dominican Republic to build its tourist infrastructure (Barry et al. 1984; Lladó 1996). Through loans and development packages, the Dominican Republic transformed the structure of its economy and redirected its economic strategy to capture the surplus income and foreign investments of developed nations. By the 1980s the country was well on its way to replacing its sugar plantation economy with a tourist economy.[7]

The technological revolution experienced in the tourist-generating countries of the North has helped to further the growth, development, and integration of the travel and tourism industry. The global mass tourism industry is vertically and horizontally integrated through its transnational operations to encompass travel agents, tour operators, hotel, and air travel in a worldwide system. Marketing campaigns generated in Western countries ensure the flow of visitors. Tour operators in western Europe and North America successfully market tourist packages consisting of many different components. For example, the increasingly popular all-inclusive package can be prearranged to fulfill all of a tourist's wants and needs for a single price. The package is paid for in the location of origin, guaranteeing that the bulk of tourist expenditures remain in the generating countries.[8] These packages discourage tips, forcing tourism workers to supplement their low wages in other ways. In essence, this economic strategy incorporates poor countries into an essentially consolidated global system under conditions established by the wealthier nations.

By definition, international tourism is dominated by outside interests and only minimally open to the exercise of local control. Not only does the organizational structure of the industry maintain the profits within the wealthy tourist-sending nations but, as hosts of a conglomerate service industry, Dominicans must accommodate their "guests" with a low-cost labor force, favorable political climate, tax exemptions, and lax environmental restrictions.[9] Furthermore, since transnational corporations rarely invest large amounts of their own capital, the country must incur further debt to develop luxury beach resorts and airports (Lea 1988). Infrastructure development for tourist resorts such as new roads and power supplies is funded via local sources and foreign loans (Truong 1990). Redirecting its resources to activities that appeal to foreigners has generated new inequality within the nation. While the tourists enjoy potable water, paved roads, electric energy, and thirty-six airports, Dominicans experience daily blackouts, lack of clean water, lack of public transportation, and shortages and deficiencies in all forms of infrastructure.[10]

Since mass tourism offers jobs that are seasonal, low-skilled, and low-paid, many of the people who work in the tourist economy must also provide for themselves through work in the informal sector of the economy. The organization of the tourism industry, with its dependence on the informal sector, responds to the dynamics of global restructuring (Sassen 1998; Portes and Schauffler 1996). Research on global restructuring points to the use of nonstandard employment, flexible reorganization of the labor process, and increases in informal market arrangements (Mullings 1999; Poon 1990). Part-time work, seasonal work, subcontracting, work intensification, and the changing boundaries of work are easily recognizable in the tourism and sex trade of the Caribbean.

Economic restructuring has generated new possibilities for women's economic independence, whether through wage labor or international migration. But these opportunities have appeared in conjunction with increases in male unemployment, female-headed households, and egregious violations of human rights connected with labor migrations to western Europe (Deere et al. 1990; International Organization for Migration 1996; König 1998; Safa 1995). Slaverylike tendencies in the labor practices of export-processing zones and the migration of women to western Europe, particularly connected to marriage, sex work, and domestic work, are now more prevalent in the Caribbean and Latin American regions than they were before the push to develop tourism (Azize Vargas 1996; McAfee 1991).[11]

SEX WORK AND TOURISM

In the Dominican Republic, and in many other parts of the world, sex work is an economic strategy that provides a form of temporary subsistence for many poor women and men. There are no distinct boundaries between sex workers and other women. Instead, a woman's entry into the sex trade is mediated by political, economic, social, and psychological factors. Sex workers are neither passive nor dependent and have strong beliefs about familial responsibility and obligations. Their work constitutes an important form of family labor that sustains their siblings, children, parents, and other relatives.

The sale of sexual services in a tourist economy operates in shifting, provisional, and unstable categories of work and romance. A recent study of tourism workers highlights the occurrence of sexual relations between hotel employees and guests. The study, conducted in 1996, discloses that 38.5 percent of male sex workers also have jobs as waiters, porters, and security guards in the hotels, and 36.8 percent work as *motoconchos*—motorcycle taxi drivers (CESDEM 1996). Many of the hotel workers who provide tourists with food and beverage service, maintenance, administration, entertainment, and reception also provide sex.

The typical worker in the Dominican hotel industry is young: 62 percent are between the ages of seventeen and twenty-nine (CEPROSH 1997). Indeed, age, appearance, and sexuality are important social characteristics in the service economy of hospitality jobs (Adkins 1995). Sexuality pervades the organization of work, impinging on the design of jobs and motivating workers in various occupations. For some jobs, such as those that coordinate entertainment and recreational activities for tourists in the resorts, the only requirement is that the employee appear young and "sexy." These workers, laboring simultaneously in the formal and informal economies, suggest new patterns in the organization of labor. In fact, my research indicates that the boundaries between paid work and unpaid work, leisure and labor, romance and work are increasingly difficult to discern in a tourist economy.

In my study of sex work and tourism, I interviewed thirty-five women in the resort of Sosúa.[12] Most of these young women, between the ages of twenty-one and thirty-five, had been working for more than five years in transitional forms of sexual commerce connected to the mass tourism market. They negotiated directly with men from western Europe and Canada, with an age range between twenty and eighty years. Their clients were married or single, accompanied by their wives, family, and friends, or traveling alone.

The women I interviewed were usually unemployed or employed in jobs that did not pay them sufficiently. They entered into the sex trade voluntarily, being informed and initiated by their friends as to the availability of work. When I asked the women what motivated them to pursue sex work, they typically responded, "La situación económica [The economic situation]." Other forms of wage labor, such as work in export-processing zones and domestic work, offer a lot less pay and less flexible work schedules. For women with minimal education, no other accessible alternatives provide a family wage commensurate with sex tourism.

Many women perceive sex work as a transitional stage to a stable relationship. The majority of men and women who work with foreigners hope to attain what is commonly termed "La Gloria [The Glory]." Women, in particular, hope that marriage to a foreigner will provide them with a house, a livelihood, opportunities for migration, and care and protection for their families and children.[13] Despite the social stigma of the activity itself, sex work is not solely a business arrangement; it is also a means to attain socially acceptable arrangements, values, and behaviors.

This hope is not irrational in the context of the internationalization of the sex trade. The Swiss consulate asserts that on the average there are six marriages per week between Swiss men and Dominican women (International Organization for Migration 1996). Some of the young women whom I interviewed had traveled to Europe and elsewhere in the Caribbean to work in the sex trade. Many Latin American women travel to work in the European sex industry, not only because it affords them more money but also because it provides them with some distance from the shame associated with prostitution.[14] However, once in Europe, Dominican women are vulnerable to the many human rights violations that immigrants confront, including inability to obtain a working visa, xenophobia, criminality, racism, and labor abuses.[15]

However, sex workers' connection to transnational economies, cultures, and organizations has demystified their social position and politicized them as to their rights. Opportunities now exist to organize locally, regionally, and across national boundaries to challenge the politics of prostitution in the public sphere, internationally as well as locally.

SEX WORKER ORGANIZATIONS

Since the 1970s, sex workers have organized themselves as political activists, demanding equal protection under the law, improved working conditions, and the right to pay taxes, travel, and receive social benefits. In Latin America, and many parts of the Third World, sex worker organizations have sought to redefine and transform prostitution into a new political subjectivity promoting social, political, and judicial change (Bell 1987; Delacoste and Alexander 1987; Kempadoo and Doezema 1998; Pheterson 1989). During the 1980s, sex worker organizations became visible in South America, and sex worker unions and organizations now exist in most countries of Latin America and the Caribbean. Venezuela has the Asociación de Mujeres por el Bienestar y Asistencia Recíproca (AMBAR), Chile has the Asociación Pro-Derechos de la Mujer, "Angela Lina" (APRODEM), and Mexico has the Unión Unica, with more than 20,000 members, including bar owners, bartenders, and taxi drivers in addition to sex workers and their families (Azize Vargas 1996; Cabezas 1998). There are also sex worker organizations in Argentina, Brazil, Colombia, Costa Rica, Nicaragua, and Surinam.

Because sex workers confront both sexual and labor discrimination and abuse, many of the new organizations use the term "worker" to legitimize prostitution as labor and thereby distance themselves from the social stigma and religious mores that have traditionally shrouded prostitution. The sex worker movement has shifted the debate to the conditions of their work and the social and economic circumstances of their existence.

The United Nations and other international bodies have competing discourses on prostitution. The ideological range is quite wide but encompasses the abolitionist, regulationist, and those that seek to distinguish between forced and voluntary forms of prostitution (Bindman 1997; Kempadoo and Ghuma 1999). These positions are reflected in numerous international conventions and instruments. Some, such as the United Nations Educational, Scientific, and Cultural Organization (UNESCO) and the Working Group on Contemporary Forms of Slavery, argue that prostitution in all of its forms constitutes a human rights violation. There has been a strong ideological stance, particularly on the part of the highly influential Coalition against Trafficking in Women, to treat all modalities of prostitution and trafficking as sexual exploitation. Other conventions, such as statements of Anti-Slavery International and the International Labor Organization, have more nuanced views of prostitution. Some organizations advocate distinguishing between forced and voluntary forms of prostitution. Sex worker activists claim that the distinction between forced and voluntary prostitution signals a dangerous split among sex workers—that the forced prostitute is a victim to be protected and exonerated from sexual wrongdoing, while the voluntary prostitute is a deviant and a whore who is not entitled to protection (Kempadoo and Doezema 1998).

Various international organizations have legitimized the conceptualization of prostitution as a form of labor. Anti-Slavery International, formed in 1839 and now the world's oldest human rights organization, acknowledges that most men and women working as prostitutes are subject to abuses similar to those experienced by others working in low-status jobs in the informal sector of the economy. They propose the application of existing human rights and labor standards to the sex industry, asserting that the "marginal position of sex workers in society excludes them from the international, national, and customary protection afforded to others as citizens, workers, or women" (Bindman 1997: iii). Likewise, the International Labor Organization, while failing to recognize prostitution explicitly as work, recognizes that where prostitutes are considered workers with rights under standard labor legislation, they are entitled to proper working conditions and to protection from exploitation and discrimination (Lim 1998; Kempadoo and Ghuma 1999).

Fueled by the dynamics of globalization itself, the sex worker movement has become increasingly global as a result of electronic communication, media coverage, and the alliances, networks, and circuits of information created by transnational nongovernmental organizations (NGOs), international conferences, the UN focus on violence against women, and the AIDS pandemic.[16] No longer limited by state politics, transnational NGOs provide an important bridge to dispossessed and exploited people in authoritarian countries, who use transnational social movements as a means to expand local political participation (Cohen 1998). The transnational advocacy networks of the sex worker movement have linked activists across international boundaries to produce political mobilization and informational exchanges (Kempadoo and Doezema 1998; Keck and Sikkink 1998).

Women working in prostitution confront problems that are inherently transboundary in nature, and sex workers in many parts of the world face similar social stigma, criminalization, working conditions, human rights violations, and lack of health and safety protection, among other things. Sharing information, organizing strategies, and support across national borders proves crucial.[17] For instance, in Venezuela in 1997, AMBAR mobilized global support against an illegal office search by the local police. They staged an Internet call for action, requesting and receiving worldwide support opposing the abuses perpetuated against them by agents of the state. As a result of their efforts, a routine violation of law became an affair of international concern.

HUMAN RIGHTS AS SEX WORKER RIGHTS

The movement to politicize women's rights as human rights was probably not meant to apply to sexual outlaws.[18] In the realm of the sex trade, working women are readily protected as victims of trafficking or sexual exploitation, but support is more difficult for women who insist on the right to possess their own bodies. At the Fourth World Conference on Women in Beijing in 1995, language to define women's sexual rights was debated, but ultimately rejected. The Platform for Action, which outlined the human rights of women in twelve critical areas, also rejected the rights of lesbians and excluded the term "sexual orientation" from the platform (Bunch and Fried 1996). Only in the health section of the platform does it state, "The human rights of women include their right to have control over and decide freely and responsibly on matters related to their sexuality, including sexual and reproductive health, free of coercion, discrimination, and violence" (Bunch and Fried 1996; Wallace 1997).

In furthering the ambiguity and confusion, the platform addresses prostitution in its definition of violence against women in paragraph 113 (b) as: "Physical, sexual and psychological violence occurring within the general community, including rape, sexual abuse, sexual harassment and intimidation at work, in educational institutions and elsewhere, trafficking in women and forced prostitution" (Wallace 1997). This formulation, by exclusion, creates a category of noncitizens who are not entitled to the same rights. A closer reading of the platform reveals the lexicon of the abolitionist stance. The terms of the debate, such as "sexual slavery," "sexual exploitation," "traffic in women" are prevalent throughout the document. Here the platform colludes with the position shared by UNESCO and the Coalition against Trafficking in Women, ignores women's sexual agency and the lived experiences of the vast majority of migrant women who enter into the sex trade and labor migrations without coercion. The less sensational, but more prevalent realities, is the global demand for cheap labor that entangles women and girls from the South and the East in networks that comprise family and friends, as well as "traffickers" and mafialike organizations. The "illegal" status of migrant women in the receiving country is what permits their exploitation by agents and middlemen. Nation-states are implicated because they facilitate and benefit this traffic through immigration policies, economic development schemes, and the billions of dollars sent home by migrant women (Azize Vargas 1996; Wijers and Lap-Chew 1997).

Nevertheless, since the early 1990s, the Dominican sex worker organization Movimiento de Mujeres Unidas (MODEMU) has employed the human rights framework to articulate sex workers' demand for recognition of their rights and for social respect. In appropriating the human rights discourse, sex worker organizations have occupied a space and adopted a language that provide them with legitimacy and the imperative for fair treatment to bring about social change.

The rhetoric of human rights serves as a vehicle for direct social and political action. Indeed, the sex workers' movement has reformulated the concept of prostitution as work and linked it to a human rights discourse for organizing and consciousness-raising. This position was articulated at MODEMU's first national conference:

> What does the term "prostitute" mean to sex workers? We unanimously reject the term "prostitute" for being pejorative and referring to us as devalued women and human beings. We have been identifying with the term ["sex worker"] because it at least recognizes that we do a job. We can do this with the name that we want, and we can make society listen to our dreams: of being women with dignified work and with the same opportunities as all Dominicans, to an education, a job, and with the opportunity of walking the same streets during night or day, without a mask. We demand of the Dominican state, and of all society, that they stop rejecting us, and that they understand us. The Dominican government has the obligation to guarantee us the right to a life of dignity and that is what we want, as a right guaranteed in the Universal Charter of Human Rights.[19]

The language of human rights—particularly women's human rights—addresses the forms of violent exclusion, discrimination, and abuses that sex workers face. In using a rights-based discourse, sex workers claim their rights as women, as workers, and as citizens.

In its newsletters and other educational materials, MODEMU approaches the empowerment of sex workers using a rights-based feminist discourse. In *fotonovelas,* the organization enumerates sex workers' social and civil rights and their obligations as citizens:

> We have [the right] not to be seen as criminals. Not to be abused, persecuted, or mistreated. Not to be exploited; by persons or groups in the business of trafficking in women; to have the opportunity to form labor unions and alternative forms of employment. Respect for our right to decide over our bodies and our lives. The right to raise our children. That our children are not discriminated for being the children of sex workers. That authorities rightly attend to our complaints when our rights are violated. *(Nosotras tambien tenemos derechos* 1997)

The consumption of sex across international boundaries has generated increased global concern, and NGOs, sex worker organizations, feminist groups, and others are constructing sex as a topic of global politics. Sex is a political issue that is being contested, monitored, and disciplined across the boundaries of nation-states.

The UN special commissioner's report on the forms of violence against women is a case in point. The special rapporteur commissioned a global study of violence against women, including forced prostitution and traffic in women, for the 1997 human rights meetings of the United Nations. This UN-sponsored conference brought together sex workers from all over Latin America, the Caribbean, and elsewhere, sex worker advocacy organizations, migrant women's advocacy organizations in Europe, and feminist and women's organizations from western Europe and the Americas.[20] Representatives from seven sex worker organizations shared information about the practices of the sex trade, organizing strategies, and gains in obtaining social acceptance in their respective countries.

Sex as a topic of international surveillance is capturing the attention of the international media as well. The Dominican Republic, along with many other Third World countries, is scrutinized by the transnational media, the United Nations, and transnational NGOs for its contribution to sex tourism, transnational sex workers, and child prostitution (O'Connell Davidson and Sánchez Taylor 1996; Silvestre et al. 1994). In 1997, for example, the international media condemned the Dominican Republic for sex tourism and child prostitution with a scandalous report in the Miami *Herald*'s Spanish-language edition, *El Nuevo Herald,* and a British Broadcasting Corporation report on sex tourism in the Dominican Republic (Moya 1997; Tamayo 1997; Velásquez 1997).

The account of this scandal and the responses by the Ministry of Tourism and MODEMU suggest that the human rights framework has solidified the position of sex workers in challenging public policy. On hearing of the reports by the BBC and the *Herald,* an embarrassed Félix Jiménez, the new secretary of tourism, attempted to deal with the bad publicity by resurrecting legislation to concentrate sexual commerce geographically through zoning laws (Bonilla 1997). In other words, he proposed a red light district to contain all forms of prostitution. He indicated in a press conference that the majority of tourist arrivals were "families and married couples" and denied that tourism to the Dominican Republic was composed principally of men seeking sexual pleasure and adventure. He recognized, albeit reluctantly, the reality of sex tourism. However, he disclaimed any systematic effort on the part of the Ministry of Tourism or the transnational conglomerates of the tourism industry to promote this activity. Instead, he blamed it on the immorality of certain travelers and of some Dominicans. Unlike his predecessor, who conceptualized sex tourism as the work of organized criminals (the "deviancy" approach to prostitution), Félix Jiménez explained the incidence of sex tourism in his country as the work of pathological individuals.

MODEMU, in conjunction with advocacy NGOs such as the Centro de

Orientación e Investigación Integral (COIN), responded rapidly to the new secretary of tourism. In their press release, they pointed out that this situation would victimize women working in prostitution, and a sex worker advocate argued that because the problem of prostitution is a global phenomenon that affects all nations in social and economic crisis, "its solution cannot be based in the condemnation of our women to discriminatory policies and violations of rights" (Placencia 1997). They called for a meeting with the secretary of tourism and sent him a list of issues to discuss, including alternative solutions to sex work and tourist-oriented prostitution. MODEMU asked for the creation of educational programs for women sex workers in the Dominican Republic and for Dominican women working in the sex trade overseas. They requested literacy and job training programs, funding for micro-enterprises, and medical, legal and psychological services for sex workers (Placencia 1997). Finally, MODEMU demanded that tourism and migration officials be trained so as not to violate the human rights of "our" women. The secretary of tourism did not respond to their challenge (Ferreira 1997). Nevertheless, the government's response to international surveillance and MODEMU's retaliation illuminate how the state is being challenged on various fronts in its effort to control and regulate the sex trade. Sex workers won a political victory by using the language of human rights to articulate their demands.

CONCLUSION

To visit the telecommunications center in Sosúa is to witness the everyday networks and patterns of social relationships that emerge as the countervailing structures of globalization. Most tourist-oriented sex workers create and maintain transnational communications through faxes, wire transfers, telephone, and electronic mail. These relationships link them to a global economy that otherwise circumscribes their participation. While the World Bank, the International Monetary Fund, and international capital dictate development strategies that target them as a low-cost labor force in export processing and service industries, Dominican women counteract this exploitation and domination by refashioning a different reality for themselves.

The economic strategies of working-class Dominicans are grounded in the differentials of profit established by multinational enterprises. The new social and cultural shifts created by the globalization of the tourism and sex industries have generated for women new forms of race, gender and class inequality. Women utilize the processes and logic of globalization to secure opportunities for economic mobility through the tourist trade, including sex work and marriage to tourists. They appropriate the human rights rhetoric to craft a language and space of empowerment in a discourse that otherwise disregards their needs. Sex workers challenge being categorized as criminally deviant subjects and disrupt the human rights policies that render them victims. Instead, they insist on generating public discussions of their identities as "mothers, sisters, friends" and as workers.

NOTES

1. These are specific laws enacted to protect the rights of visitors. There is also a special police unit to protect tourists. The mass arrests target all Dominican women, regardless of whether they are soliciting tourists. All working-class women in "public" geographic spaces are particularly vulnerable to such arrests.

2. In the Dominican Republic, prostitution operates in a gray area of the law. No laws precisely prohibit a woman's sale of her sexuality. The laws that speak most directly to prostitution deal with the practices of intermediaries and pimps who profit from prostitution. See Articles 334, 334–1, and 335 of the Dominican penal code (Law 24–97: 21; Señor 1989).

3. For a discussion of the relationship between prostitution laws and the female body, see Frug 1995: "[The] sexualization of the female body explains an experience many women have: an insistent concern that this outfit, this pose, this gesture, may send the wrong signal—a fear of looking like a whore" (14).

4. These young women are usually found in the casinos, drinking, gambling, and having friendly chats with foreigners. They appeal to the male tourists who refuse to negotiate directly with professional sex workers (Moya et al. 1992).

5. Prison conditions are extremely poor. Women complain of overcrowded jails and unhealthy and unsanitary conditions. Women and girls are incarcerated with murderers, rapists, and other hardened criminals.

6. See Donna Sullivan (1995) for an incisive discussion of the effects of the private/public demarcations in international law.

7. "The across-the-board claim made by World Bank and other international organizations that the expansion of tourism will bring structural improvement to many countries proves rash on closer inspection," Albrecht Iwersen and Susanne Iwersen-Sioltsidis note, however (1996: 306).

8. The all-inclusive package has increased the instability for workers in the tourism industry. It has raised their salaries a little, but not enough to compensate for the loss of gratuities. These workers, vulnerable to seasonality in an industry characterized by unstable, low-paying positions, are subsidizing the low cost of the all-inclusive packages with their loss of wages.

9. A ten-year tax exemption is in effect for hotels in the Dominican Republic; other tax incentives include the exemption on the repatriation of profits, including the exoneration of taxes and the procurement of financing resources (Miolan 1994; Lladó 1996).

10. This situation is also the outcome of policies imposed by the International Monetary Fund and the World Bank (Deere et al. 1990; McAfee 1991; Raynolds 1998).

11. Many women in Latin America use networks of family and friendship to travel to western Europe, the Middle East, and Asia to work in the sex industry. The num-

ber of Dominican sex workers currently abroad is estimated at more than 50,000 women (International Organization for Migration 1996). Many hope that their work will procure them enough money to send remittances home to support their families, send their siblings to school, and build a home or a small business on their return (König 1998).

12. Sosúa is a resort town in the northeast corner of the Dominican Republic. Sosúa and its adjacent tourist enclave constitute the largest and oldest tourist node of the country.

13. This appears to be a commonality that working-class women, whether employed as domestics or sex workers, share. Studies on the characteristics common to household workers in Santo Domingo during the 1980s found that the majority of domestic workers hoped "to marry a good man and not have to work" (Duarte 1989: 213). Certainly, unlike sex workers, domestic workers do not target their employers as potential marriage partners. For working-class women who have to provide a livelihood for themselves and their children, marriage appears as a refuge from the constant struggle for survival.

14. Various investigations found that Dominican women utilize trafficking agents to obtain job contacts, visas, and other travel arrangements. Most of these women go into debt to pay for their travel and end up in forms of indentured servitude to the traffickers. For those in the sex industry, studies indicate that the majority of women knew what they were going to do but were unprepared for the discrimination and other forms of abuses that they encountered (Azize Vargas and Kempadoo 1996; Kempadoo 1999; Wijers and Lap-Chew 1997).

15. Immigration laws in western Europe impose further vulnerability. "All countries impose a probationary period raging from a year to five years, during which the spouse's status is linked to the husband and the dissolution of marriage constitutes grounds for the revocation of the residence permit," Eleonore Kofman explains (1999: 133). This situation forces many women to remain in violent relationships for fear of deportation.

16. Homosexuals and sex workers were targeted at the inception of the AIDS pandemic for outreach educational programs sponsored by U.S. Agency for International Development and the Pan American Health Organization. As Steve Epstein reminds us, "the stigma of disease has been linked with the stigma of deviant sexuality" (1996: 21). And as Donna Guy points out in *Sex and Danger in Buenos Aires,* prostitutes have a long history of being defined as medically dangerous in the gendered constructions of disease (Guy 1990: 209).

17. Sex worker organizations face numerous challenges. Many of the organizations, especially those that receive support from NGOs or HIV/AIDS-related groups can more easily take advantage of global communication networks to facilitate transnational support and cooperation and to share information and resources. But many of the organizations face precarious financial conditions and limited access to technological resources. It is also difficult to organize women in the commercial sex trade because, for many women, it is work that they undertake sporadically, between marriages, jobs, or when there is a family emergency. Long-term organizing proves difficult because many of the forms of prostitution are provisional, fluid, and shrouded in fear, shame, and secrecy.

18. The issue of prostitution is seen primarily through the prism of sexual exploitation or forced prostitution and trafficking in women. See Peters and Wolper 1995.

19. Salas 1996: 58–59. The conference took place in 1996 at the Instituto Internacional de Investigaciones y Capacitación de las Naciones Unidas para la Promoción de la Mujer (United Nations International Institute for Research and Training for the Advancement of Women) in Santo Domingo.

20. See "Prostitutas piden mayor participacion social," and "Conferencia acusa a paises complicidad trafico mujeres" (both 1996).

II

Commodification

3

Interpreting the Interaction of Global Markets and Human Rights

Richard Falk

A CONTEXT FOR INQUIRY

"The battle of Seattle" posed the first *political* crisis of globalization, just as the Asian financial crisis of mid 1997 posed the first *economic* crisis. Those protesters on the streets were potent in their impact because their grievances were aligned and resonant with a high level of discontent among the intergovernmental officialdom gathered in Seattle for the meetings of the World Trade Organization. At its core, the encounter was between an economistic view of the future, premised upon technological innovation, economic growth, and profits, and a normative view, or more accurately, a clash of normative views of the future, based on the well-being of society and its citizenry, including the economically disadvantaged. In effect, it was not globalization that was at issue, but what kind of globalization.[1]

Although overly simple, it seems clarifying to associate the WTO hierarchy and its ideological and political support with "globalization-from-above," and the protesters in the streets and their governmental allies with "globalization-from-below."[2] Most enthusiasts for globalization-from-above tended to echo the sentiment expressed by Thomas Friedman's phrase "senseless in Seattle," namely, the irrationality of challenging the extraordinary engines of globalization that had produced the greatest surge of economic growth in human history.[3] Such apologists for globalization regard its more radical critics as failing to comprehend the degree to which world trade and investment are improving the life prospects of most people on the planet, including many of those in the South who had previously been consigned to subsistence, or worse. Their social argument is that neoliberal implementation of economic policy on a global scale, given accelerating technological innovation, is creating conditions for spreading "the good life" further than ever before in history.

The detractors, who created the headlines in Seattle, leaving to one side the capricious and diversionary anarchists who vandalized symbolic sites of capitalist enterprise, had an entirely different agenda. They were above all challenging their image of the WTO (and globalization more generally) from a bewildering variety of directions.[4] Their main target was a set of market-driven ideas and practices that they alleged was being administered and imposed by a managerial oligarchy that subordinated human dignity and evaded democratic control and accountability. The WTO was a particularly significant arena that appeared to epitomize these broader concerns about the way in which global economic policy was being shaped. The WTO's Green Room decision-making procedures seemed designed to deny policymaking influence to dissident perspectives from the South. Furthermore, the secretive operating procedures relied upon also seemed calculated to override normative and functional concerns about such competing national policy priorities as environmental protection and human rights.[5] At least from the outside, it seemed as if the WTO was evolving into a powerful and hierarchical instrument of global economic governance that was unaccountable, opaque, and exclusive.[6] From the outset, there were concerns about transfers of sovereignty to the WTO without adequate deliberation in accordance with constitutional procedures. Ralph Nader was particularly agitated by his conviction that the rights of Americans had been compromised by the hasty manner in which Congress lent its approval to the WTO.[7]

Beyond these process issues, the WTO was accused, especially by activists and official representatives from the South, of fashioning, in the name of "free trade," arrangements that were of benefit mainly to the most developed countries of the North. For non-Western delegations to Seattle, "free trade" was an alarming instance of Orwellian language, in reality, a code phrase for "unfair trade," that is, trade that discriminated against the commodity-oriented production of many countries in the South. And there were concerns that moves within the upper echelons of WTO to extend protection to "intellectual property rights" and services would perpetuate poverty and backwardness in the South and inhibit the dynamics of technology transfer and the sharing of knowledge.

On this primary level, the scope and intensity of discontent exhibited inside and outside meeting halls in Seattle converged to raise deep questions about the political viability of globalization. As the MIT economist Paul Krugman argued, unless the managers of globalization can broaden their constituency far beyond the elites that gather each year for the World Economic Forum in Davos, their days of ascendancy are numbered. Seattle above all raised the first formidable challenge to the *legitimacy* of globalization-from-above as currently constituted.[8] Meeting that challenge involves several simultaneous axes of response: democratization, human rights, and global equity (as between rich and poor countries, regions, and economic sectors). It also involves an educational and cognitive set of questions relating to a better understanding of the net benefits and detriments that can be fairly attributed to globalization-from-above, and the consequences of moving its operations in more democratically and socially accountable directions. Normative issues are also at stake, especially whether high degrees of inequality (with widening disparities) and pockets of marginalization are intrinsic to sustaining aggregate growth for the world economy as a whole.[9] In effect, can neoliberal globalization be reformed without undermining its beneficial effects?

In this essay, the focus is upon human rights and their relationship to the prevailing structures and processes of globalization. My attempt here is to articulate the relationship between human rights and the global market under changing contemporary conditions and perceptions. First of all, it is necessary to challenge the traditional, ideologically driven position in much anti-imperialist literature to the effect that there is an inherent contradiction between the promotion of human rights and the goals of global market forces. Secondly, I argue that to enhance the legitimacy of globalization-from-above, global corporations and banks are growing increasingly responsive to human rights narrowly conceived. Thirdly, I seek to show that globalization-from-below activists are becoming more committed to a different, broader idea of human rights, which directly challenges globalization-from-above. And, fourthly, I suggest that this challenge can only be successfully met by a radical extension of democracy that goes well beyond state/society electoral relationships and brings democratic procedures and values to global arenas of authority. In effect, democracy must be deepened at the level of the state and extended effectively to cover international institutions and transnational market forces. Such an agenda does have the effect of creating a series of strong ideological tensions between advocates of a neoliberal market-managed world order and the proponents of world order resting on the foundations of global democracy.[10]

One form of this encounter is purely discursive. It results from the differing images of both "democracy" and "human rights" held by governments and global market forces, on the one side, and by most activists, on the other. The U.S. government is at the forefront of encouraging democracy and adherence to human rights in the conduct of its foreign policy and in the enactment of its global leadership role. Yet Washington is also leading the opposition to extending democracy to global arenas like the UN and WTO and is opposed to conceiving of human rights as encompassing economic, social, and cultural issues.

CHALLENGING THE TRADITIONAL UNDERSTANDING

A presumed antagonism between creating optimal conditions for capitalist operations and human well being has existed since the earliest period of the industrial age. The Marxist/Leninist tradition has given the strongest expression to the inherent nature of this antagonism. For instance, in Lenin's famous essay "Imperialism, the Highest Stage of Capitalism," there is this typical passage: "[B]oth uneven development and a semi-starvation level of existence of the masses are fundamental and inevitable conditions and constitute premises of this mode of production. As long as it remains what it is, surplus capital will be utilized not for the purpose of raising the standard of living of the masses in a given country, for this would mean a decline in the profits for the capitalists, but for the purpose of increasing profits by exporting capital abroad to the backward countries." Any effort to use capital surpluses, that is, profits, for the sake of human betterment, rather than for either enrichment of the capitalist class or reinvestment to achieve even greater profits, is doomed, Lenin argues. In his words, "if capitalism did these things it would not be capitalism."[11] Some of that view lingers as an ideological overhang that prevents a more empirically grounded inquiry into the actual and differential impacts of capital upon human well being.

It should be acknowledged, at the same time, that apologists for capitalism, with their facile assumptions of an "invisible hand" and "trickle down" benefits of economic growth, are ideologically removed from the existential reality of human suffering. There is a refusal to admit the extent to which profit-making modes of enterprise override more compassionate approaches to economic activity. A related set of distortions arises when aggregate growth figures are relied upon to establish benevolent impacts on human well-being without examining the distribution of income, the persistence of poverty, and the unequal effects of economic growth.

In the international setting of business and finance, there seemed to be a clear bias in the decades of the Cold War for authoritarian government in the countries of the South,[12] which overlapped with and was concealed beneath the view that anti-capitalist political tendencies were overtly, or at least covertly, Marxist, and hence geopolitically aligned with the Soviet adversary. What seemed clear in a series of countries was that any effort to challenge the privileges of foreign investment would be met by American-led intervention and the restoration of anti-labor, oppressive governments that were hostile to human rights. The CIA interventions in 1953 and 1954 against the Mossadegh government in Iran that had nationalized the oil industry and a year later against the economic populism of the Arbenz reformist government of Guatemala remain paradigmatic. Similarly, the sharp American turn against Castro's Cuba in the early 1960s and the intervention in Chile that produced the Pinochet dictatorship in 1976 were promoted by influential foreign investors in the United States. In response to these patterns of intervention, many writers of a progressive identity insisted that the best interests of international capital were served by governments that controlled labor rigidly and offered stability and favorable conditions to foreign investors. Such reasoning meant a preference for political leadership that denied elemental human rights to their citizenry. This ingrained antagonism between human rights and global market forces has frequently been rearticulated in relation to the dynamics of economic globalization.[13]

This view of overseas capitalist operations was generally correct in its assessments of the driving logic to maximize profits, and its collaboration with colonial and imperially oriented governments from which investment capital emanated. It was substantially validated by three sets of fundamental conditions. First of all, the nature of foreign investment was concentrated on the extraction of raw materials and somewhat later on industrial operations of subsidiaries. In both settings, reduced labor costs translate into higher profits, and there is no commitment to the improvement of the territorial society. And, secondly, the geopolitical setting of the Cold War fostered an impression that economically and socially progressive tendencies on a domestic level were likely to correlate with pro-Soviet sympathies, thereby representing a setback for the West on the zero-sum chessboard of political alignment. Such underlying conditions did tend to convince both government policymakers and their critics that what was good for business was bad for people. This orientation was established before globalization and has been somewhat uncritically perpetuated in much of the subsequent literature.[14]

The third set of conditions was the relative insulation of foreign investment activity from transnational activist and media scrutiny. Such relationships were treated generally within state/society settings unless prompting an intervention to protect foreign economic interests, and then it was the intervention that attracted notice and produced controversy.

RECONSIDERING THE INDICTMENT OF GLOBALIZATION-FROM-ABOVE

At a cognitive level, there are substantial grounds for challenging the view that globalization-from-above has had detrimental cumulative effects on human well-being generally and human rights in particular. Recent, more empirically grounded work has argued the reverse proposition: the more receptive to foreign investment and the operation of MNCs a country is, the better its human rights record is likely to be. In William Meyer's words, "[t]he implications from the combined studies suggest that the engines of development school is correct in its assertions that MNCs promote both civil-political rights and socioeconomic welfare at the international level."[15]

Clearly, the mood and global climate leads global corporations to be perceived as actively promoting such a correlation. One of the more notorious of these corporations, Shell, has been running a series of prominent advertisements proclaiming its commitment to human rights. The text of a series of ads that appeared in *The Economist* during 1999 ran the following text under the logo of Shell and a question, "Is there a choice?": "At Shell, we are committed to support fundamental human rights and have made this commitment in our published Statement of General Business Principles. It begins with our own people, respecting their rights as employees wherever they work in the world. We invest in the communities around us to create new opportunities and growth. And we've spoken out on the rights of individuals—even if the situation has been beyond our control. It's part of our commitment to sustainable development, balancing economic progress with environmental care and social responsibility."[16]

It is natural to wonder about the sincerity and depth of such sentiments. Corporate performance is still predominantly measured by bottom-line profits as recorded in quarterly reports to stockholders. The incentive to maximize profits, regardless of human and environmental consequences, remains high. Overwhelmingly, as well, MNCs seek to insist on the sufficiency of their own efforts, that is, self-implementation of human rights standards, and are strongly resistant to the establishment of enforcement or even accountability and transparency procedures. Such resistance is partly an ideological expression of the neoliberal dislike of public sector regulation, but it also fuels the impression that when MNCs start preaching on behalf of human rights and environmental quality, it is time to cast a suspicious eye.

At the same time, there are some objective factors that may be making true believers out of even the most cynical practitioners of public relations hype. First of all, even during the latter stages of the Cold War, there was mounting skepticism as to the benefits of authoritarian rule for profitable foreign investment. The experience with military government in Latin America during the early 1980s, even when the generals embraced the economics of "the Chicago boys," was generally disappointing. It turned out that economic performance in these countries was enhanced by the restoration of moderate constitutionalism, although it is true, with a neoliberal outlook. But beyond this, since 1989, the Cold War has ended, and with it "the cover" given to unseemly coalitions between foreign investors and authoritarian government has been stripped away. Without this cover, some of the more notorious examples of geopolitically supported repressive governments have collapsed, such as in Indonesia and Zaire. In retrospect, these governments are derided by establishment critics as instances of "crony capitalism," hotbeds of nepotism, corruption, and elite kleptocracy. IMF and World Bank support, which was sustained for such regimes without blinking in the past, is now conditioned by demands associated with democratization and heightened social sensitivity.

The end of the Cold War has also pushed the United States, as global leader, to associate its foreign policy more explicitly with such objectives as the promotion of human rights and constitutional democracy. Indeed, it has proclaimed "an end of history" consensus to the effect that only market-oriented constitutionalism is a legitimate foundation for state/society relations. In interpreting the outcome of the Cold War, stress is also laid on the bureaucratic rigidities of a command economy and an authoritarian state, depriving the society of the creativity needed for success under postindustrial conditions. Against such a background, without geopolitical rationalizations available to overlook abusive human rights records, the political pressure to combine participation in the world economy with democracy and human rights has increased markedly. It is doubtful whether the Suharto regime in Indonesia would have been driven out of power without such a change in the imperatives of global leadership in the conditions of the 1990s.

Perhaps, most important of all factors has been the effectiveness of campaigns mounted by the transnational and local social forces encompassed in the terminology of globalization-from-below. The campaigns of civil resistance and consumer boycott mounted by activists and NGOs have demonstrated considerable capacity to induce changes in corporate and banking behavior. Debora Spar, like Meyer, uses quantitative studies to bolster the counterintuitive conclusion that "foreign investment tends . . . to improve the conditions of human rights in developing countries, either as a direct result of the firms' activity or because investment creates other conditions that enable human rights to improve."[17] Spar's analysis is partly shaped by her view of a changing calculus of interests facing MNCs "and particularly the calculus that surrounds their treatment of human rights issues." She explains this shift by reference to "the advent of the Internet," which "has dramatically increased the reach and scope of even marginal activist groups."

These groups have achieved effectiveness by relying on their own forms of "soft power," working in conjunction with the global media, to create what Spar calls "the spotlight phenomenon." This capacity to publicize repressive practices is particularly effective, given the shifts in the character of much multinational enterprise in the direction of consumers, and the overall rise of consumer-oriented "franchise capitalism." When Nike or Gap rely on sweatshops to produce the goods sold on the world market, they invite scrutiny, as well as costly and dismaying consumer boycotts and demonstrations. In such a fish bowl, a positive reputation in relation to human rights and social responsibility is an invaluable corporate asset.

The Davos perspective has also been shaken in recent years by a series of developments in the final decade of the twentieth century. The first of these was the series of European populist reactions to the perceived social harm being caused by neoliberal global economic policies. These European reactions ranged from a surge of right-wing politics that reaffirmed territorial nationalism to the series of widely supported truckers' strikes in France at the end of 1995. Even as strong an advocate of globalization-from-above as French President Jacques Chirac relented by calling for the achievement of "a social Europe." The second development was the social and political fallout from the Asian financial crisis of 1997, and the perception that the IMF medicine of "structural adjustment" had been a heartless response that plunged masses of people below the poverty line, while largely insulating the richest strata of society. Increasingly, calls were heard from leading voices of global capitalism, particularly George Soros, for a less economistic orientation toward the world economy. At Davos in 1998 and 1999, there were calls for "globalization with a human face," and even the theme of the last session of the World Economic Forum was "responsible globality."[18] In this regard, the idea of the world economy as self-organizing was challenged, and proposals for "a new financial architecture," became commonplace. The IMF and World Bank engaged in highly publicized exercises of self-criticism and organized dialogues with their fiercest critics from the ranks of globalization-from-below. And, thirdly, came the protests in Seattle, with a combined agenda, quietly reinforced by governments that felt excluded from the authority structures of the world economy. In essence, this call from Seattle is for the democratization of the emergent system of global economic governance, most clearly symbolized by the existence and operations of the WTO. And by democratization is implied a series of adjustments in the interface between constitutional order and human rights that can be identified by such labels as participation, transparency, accountability, and equity or fairness.

In effect, there are several factors that seem to be encouraging a convergence between the orientations of leaders of globalization-from-above and the normative demands of most representatives of globalization-from-below. Whether these developments produce a sufficiently substantive, as distinct from a rhetorical or nominal, reorientation of institutional practices remains problematic at this point.

To illustrate this point, it is also far from clear how to interpret such crucial questions in relation to China, regarded as both a major trading and investment partner and a prime human rights violator. Critics of China's authoritarian practices argue for its admission to the WTO in terms of the engine-of-development thesis, which holds that capitalist growth will enhance human rights. Some ideologically conservative opponents of a normal relationship with China believe, however, that it is possible to combine a repressive state with a successful economic performance, and that despite the large mutual benefits to be expected, China should not be allowed to participate fully in the world economy until its human rights record improves.

For its part, China justifies its claim to entry into the WTO partly on non-economic grounds, as a means of exerting leverage on behalf of developing countries. Both China and India have called on developing countries to band together within the WTO to ensure that it better reflects "the interests and demands of developing countries." Echoing the anxieties of activists in the North, India's minister of commerce and industry has been officially quoted as saying in the aftermath of Seattle that "the WTO cannot be allowed to become another world government."[19]

Globalization-from-above, as a framework of ideas and activities that together constituted the world economy is definitely under a series of normative clouds and is facing its most serious political challenge. There are three main arenas of contestation: the adaptation of the private sector to calls for more deference to the social and humanitarian implications of business and financial operations; the democratization of policymaking procedures of international economic institutions; the mediating role that leading states, especially the United States, and various coalitions of states play in balancing the claims of capital-driven globalization and people-oriented globalization.

William Meyer makes a useful distinction between the aggregate positive effects of increasing foreign economic presence on overall human rights and specific instances of exploitative operations that are characteristic of a particular firm or sectoral activity, such as textile manufacturing. The willingness of corporations and banks to subordinate profit-making opportunities to human rights considerations is still very much in doubt within state/society settings. An uncertainty about the scope and foundation of human rights norms shapes an analysis of whether the normative agenda of the protesters at Seattle is likely to be substantially accommodated or not.

GLOBALIZATION-FROM-BELOW
AND THE SUBALTERN DISCOURSE ON HUMAN RIGHTS

From the perspectives of globalization-from-above, including its main governmental supporters among the leading highly developed countries in the North, human rights are conceived narrowly as pertaining mainly, if not exclusively, to civil and political rights. And even these rights are minimally conceived as compared to the coverage that seems to be implied by a simple textual reading of the main human rights treaty instruments. In essence, what is encompassed is a constitutional form of government based on periodic multiparty elections, whose outcome is respected, and protection of the individual against such direct forms of abuse as torture. In contrast, the social forces engaged in globalization-from-below insist upon a far broader conception of human rights, extending to, if not focusing upon, economic, social, and cultural concerns. Also, folded into "human rights" is an idea of democracy that is more substantive in its modes of operation than the constitutional model with respect to such matters as inclusion, participation, openness, and rule-of-law accountability and its applicability to global arenas of policymaking and authority.[20]

The conceptual differences in these two prevailing discourses on human rights are of fundamental importance. The primary discourse, reflecting the hegemonic global position and ideology of the U.S. government, as well as dominating the activity of voluntary human rights organizations (Human

Rights Watch, Amnesty International), media treatment, and academic approaches, reduces the international law reality of human rights to its endorsement of a constitutional electoral process and protection for the individual against government abuse.[21] The main point here is that this primary discourse is generally treated as if it is the authoritative and preferred conception of human rights.[22]

Such a view is misleading and confusing, overlooking the extent to which, in the setting of globalization, the scope of human rights, including the right to development, is at the center of contestation. The position being taken by those here identified with globalization-from-below is that neoliberal globalization has contributed to wider income and wealth disparities without addressing the persistence of poverty and unemployment in a serious fashion. This pattern of widening disparities applies within societies in both North and South, and also as among regions, with the deteriorating circumstances of sub-Saharan Africa and the Caribbean being generally identified as leading examples of regional victimization. Furthermore, they argue that this failure is unacceptable and needs to be corrected by way of altered policies and reformed institutions. Without such adjustments, the economic and social rights of billions of people in the world are being persistently violated.

The narrow discourse does not generally even bother to refute the wider claims of human rights. It ignores such claims, and has been able to control the discourse in such a manner that it is presupposed that "human rights" refer only to a limited conception of civil and political rights. As might be expected, challenges to this subaltern view of human rights tended to be mounted, at first, mainly in developing countries.[23] In these settings, the assumption was that an expanded scope of human rights was legally and morally justified and politically necessary. Such views themselves generate rebuttals that argue that the inclusion of economic and social rights generates duties that are vague, controversial, and would, if accepted, dilute the authority and impact of human rights as behavioral norms. Along similar lines, there is a liberal line of argument that views the universality of human rights as only upheld by the narrower conception.

In my view, the universality of human rights cannot be achieved by the dominant discourse, as the scope of rights protected will not resonate with the peoples and intellectual representatives of many non-Western countries. Nor will an inversion of the dominant discourse that subordinates political and civil rights to the priorities of economic and social rights, along with the imperative of development. I believe that it is becoming increasingly clear that only the subaltern discourse that encompasses the full panoply of human rights can establish the moral, political, and cultural ground for the genuine embrace of human rights on a universal foundation.[24]

The Universal Declaration of Human Rights lays the foundation for superseding the dominant discourse by adoption of the subaltern discourse in two of its "sleeping provisions," Articles 25 and 28. Article 25 (1) provides a normative response to the failures of neoliberal globalization to take seriously the challenge of persisting poverty.[25] The text of Article 25 (1) is as follows: "Everyone has the right to a standard of well-being of himself and of his family, including food, clothing, housing and medical care and necessary social services, and the right to security in the event of unemployment, sickness, disability, widowhood, old age or other lack of livelihood in circumstances beyond his control."[26] Although the gendered language of this provision is now a matter of embarrassment, the substantive commitments express the essence of subaltern concerns about the substance and priorities of human rights. What a different globalization it would be and become if the economic policymakers at Davos and at the annual economic summits of the Group of Seven (G-7) were to prescribe concrete steps to ensure phased realization of the Article 25 (1) commitment. From a strictly materialistic perspective, this is one of the two core demands of the subaltern discourse on human rights.

The second core demand is delimited by Article 28, which frames the entire undertaking of human rights: "Everyone is entitled to a social and international order in which the rights and freedoms set forth in this Declaration can be fully realized."[27] Such an entitlement links the subject matter of human rights to the quest for humane governance, and more modestly with demands for global reform.[28] Reflecting the background of economic concerns in the 1940s, Article 28 refers to "a social and international order," omitting a direct reference to its economic dimension. As the protests in Seattle made evident, one central preoccupation of civil society perspectives was drastic reform of global economic governance, with specific attention to the manner in which the WTO and Bretton Woods institutions operate and affect the well-being of people, especially the poor and marginalized.

There is another strand to this struggle to promote the subaltern discourse on human rights, and this concerns the efforts to implement the Program of Action adopted at the Copenhagen UN Social Summit of 1995 and, more generally, the implementation of recommendations arising from the UN conferences of the early 1990s on environment and development, human rights, population, and women. In an important respect, these UN conference arenas were settings in which the subaltern agenda achieved salience and influence as a result of transnational militancy on the part of resisters to globalization-from-above.

GLOBALIZATION AND THE INCLUSION OF SUBSTANTIVE DEMOCRACY

The mainstream human rights discourse emphasizes a bundle of rights associated with the effective enactment of electoral or formal democracy, that is, the holding of periodic, free, multiparty elections. This conception of democracy is underpinned by the protection of civil and political rights and seems to coincide with the precepts of liberal democracy as developed by the countries of western Europe and North America. It is also the meaning of "democracy" that is embedded in "the democratic peace" literature.

The subaltern perspective associated with counterhegemonic practices, and with the implementation of the right of development, has moved by stages toward a less electorally based and state-centric conception of democracy.[29] This extended view of democracy has two main dimensions: a rethinking of citizen participation in state/society relations and an extension of the spirit and practice of democracy to all arenas of decision, including those situated beyond the reach of the territorial sovereign government. Such an enlargement of democracy is responsive to the distinctive challenges being posed by neoliberal globalization. The neoliberal ideological climate of opinion induces the social disempowerment of the state, shifting responsibility for human betterment increasingly to the private sector. The globalization of business, finance, and informatics, along with a support set of international institutions operating in accordance with neoliberal logic, has fashioned a system of global economic governance that is at once far more powerful than the United Nations and organized in a manner that is even less representative of the peoples of the world and their diversities of civilization and religion. As a result, there is a convergent call for democratization in relation to regional and global undertaking that is tending to unify the outlook of various tendencies present in global civil society.

The emphasis on substantive or normative democracy reflects a shift in emphasis from party politics and formal institutions of government to grassroots and local initiatives. Its concerns overlap the entitlements provided by economic and social rights, the right to development, and assurances that government and business operate in a manner that is fair, noncorrupt, and accountable. One important priority of this new democracy movement is a challenge to "cultures of impunity," and strong support for the establishment of an international criminal court that would hold public officials accountable for crimes of state, including severe abuses of human rights, as well as crimes against humanity (and genocide), in which citizens and minorities were the target of abuse.

The construction of global democracy is a direct response to globalization, with its dual tendency to evade state controls by penetrating them at will or by situating key activities beyond territorial control. Flags of convenience on the high seas and offshore banking are illustrative of how difficult it is to achieve effective regulation on behalf of the global public interest in a system that continues to be premised on ideas of territorial sovereignty. The Seattle/Washington, D.C., protests of 1999–2000 were mainly directed against various anti-democratic features of the WTO/IMF/World Bank network of linked institutions.[30] Both the non-Western delegations from many countries and most street protesters agreed on the importance of democratizing the structure and procedures of the WTO and other international institutions. This call meant more representativeness in decisional protocols, greater transparency internally and externally, meaningful access and voice opportunities for civil society organizations, mechanisms to ensure accountability, and action in accordance with the rule of law.

Putting this emphasis on global democracy in an analytical frame of rights, such a struggle for "a new political architecture," amounts to an effort by transnational social forces to implement the promise of Article 28. In effect, given the structures and ideology of neoliberal globalization, it has become impossible to realize many distinct human rights without a series of substantial modifications in the character of the existing international order. The challenge is less to circumvent the state so as to achieve a cosmopolitan order than it is to exert sufficient countervailing pressures to achieve the social reempowerment of the state. Such reempowerment would then convert the state into an agent for the achievement of equity and compassion toward those people and regions being hurt by the impact of globalization-from-above. At present, the G-7 group of states that set global economic policy are agents of neoliberal market-oriented policies that assess performance by economistic measures such as growth and profitability, with the premium placed on efficient uses of capital. The human effects are seen as incidental and temporary, eventually overcome by robust aggregate growth.

Additionally, the push for global democratization looks toward the UN system as the basis for global governance. Its agenda is diverse, involving especially a reduced dependence on geopolitical management and greater participation by global civil society. Two important "fixes" for this aspect of the global democratic deficit are some form of "Tobin tax" on global financial transactions to weaken the leverage presently exercised by the main financial contributor states and the establishment of a Global Peoples Assembly to provide a direct participatory vehicle for the social forces of global civil society.[31]

CONCLUSION

There are many shifting realities associated with human rights and globalization. There are significant reasons to reconsider the presumed contradiction between market forces and human rights, but there are also grounds for skepticism about how far such reconciliation can go. This skepticism is intensified if human rights are understood from the perspective of the subaltern discourse, which combines a critique of hegemonic structures with a commitment to a just world order enabling all peoples to achieve material, social, and spiritual dignity.

There exists a positive law foundation for extending the full sweep of the subaltern discourse to human rights in "the sleeping provisions" of Articles 25 (1) and 28 in the Universal Declaration of Human Rights. Such a discourse also corresponds to the orientation of many non-Western civil society organizations, and, through the pedagogy of the UN global conferences of the 1990s, a consensus on such an outlook dominates the outlook of global civil society. Such an orientation provides a counterpoint to the view from Davos, the neoliberal thinking that has moved to incorporate the narrow or mainstream view of human rights.

Finally, there is the parallel divergence with regard to the common affirmation of "democracy." The narrow discourse associates democracy with elections and constitutional moderation in state/society relations. The subaltern discourse accepts this Western view of democracy, but extends it vertically (to include political action that is not associated with the state but extends to the grassroots, the workplace, and the family) and horizontally (to embrace the emergent governance structures and practices that are shaping transnational behavior in all domains). Globalization from above and below must be supplemented by democracy and the full spectrum of human rights, so that global markets can truly meet human needs.

NOTES

1. A fragment of the opposition is also primarily statist, and even localist, that is, hostile to any form of globalization, either championing a territorialist and chauvinistic agenda, eventuating in rightist forms of populism, or embracing some neo-Luddite variant of ecological fundamentalism. Ross Perot and Patrick Buchanan express backlash political reactions to globalization, whereas a range of thinkers and activists, especially in the United States and Europe, represent the ecological backlash.

2. Falk 1999b; see also Smith and Guarnizo 1998; Keck and Sikkink 1998.

3. For background, see Friedman 1999; and see also "The Real Losers" and "Global Disaster," *Economist,* 11 December 1999, 15, 19–22.

4. For background on this negative profile of globalization, see Grieder 1997; John Gray 1998.

5. See Martin Khor, "Developing Countries Decry WTO's Secretive Talks," Third World Network Features, November 1999.

6. See full-page newspaper ads by coalition of anti-WTO activists on the menace of "invisible government" behind the mask of the WTO, e.g., *New York Times,* 29 November 1999, A15.

7. See Nader and Wallach 1996.

8. Krugman 2000. Krugman suggests that current modalities of economic integration are the second attempt at globalization, the first failing due to a lack of political support, producing the economic balkanization of the 1930s that produced the Great Depression. For an analysis along similar lines, Gilpin 2000: esp. 293–357.

9. For insightful discussion of these issues, see Baudot 1999: 27–36.

10. For a volume of essays exploring many of these themes, see Archibugi et al. 1998.

11. "Imperialism, the Highest Stage of Capitalism," in Lenin 1975: 204–74; quotations from 226.

12. This preference pattern is most trenchantly depicted in Chomsky and Herman 1979.

13. See, e.g., Grieder 1997; Barnet and Cavanagh 1994; Korten 1995; and John Gray 1998.

14. There is in the literature of globalization a historical view that situates globalization further back, commencing no later than the late nineteenth century. See Hirst and Thompson 1996; see also Krugman 1999 on the idea that economic balkanization associated with protectionism temporarily destroyed the earlier phase of globalization. In effect, economic nationalism induced the Great Depression. Krugman's important point is that unless the architects of globalization convince the citizenry that it is beneficial, a democratic society will support backlash policies that could result in a global economic meltdown. From this perspective, Seattle was an urgent alarm bell signaling the emergence of significant resistance to globalization-from-above as currently practiced. Given the postulates of political democracy, even narrowly conceived, globalization-from-above will be repudiated, even if its economic performance is beneficial, unless it can command sufficient political support.

15. See Meyer 1998, 108; on the basis of sophisticated quantitative assessments of MNC impacts, Meyer also writes that "[a]ll tests . . . show that with increased economic development comes improvement in human rights" (136).

16. See also the ad in the *Economist*, 10 June 2000, between 50–51, on Shell's environmentalism; and see in a similar vein the Philip Morris two-page spread in the same issue, between 23–24, on the company's efforts to end hunger under the human rights slogan, "Dignity . . . is life without hunger." The point here is the impulse by global corporations is to overcome their bad normative images rather than to flaunt their products or boast about market successes.

17. Spar 1999; see also Spar 1998.

18. Kofi Annan made an appeal to MNCs at Davos in 1999 to apply international environmental and human rights standards in their overseas operations on a voluntary basis, even when not pressed to do so by territorial governments, and pledged UN cooperation with any efforts undertaken.

19. STRATFOR.COM Weekly Global Intelligence Update, 11 January 2000, http://www.stratfor.com/p.1.

20. On scope of "democracy," see Held 1995; and see also Archibugi et al. 1998.

21. There are some exceptions. For instance, the Center for Economic and Social Rights in New York City has been doing excellent work since it was founded a few years ago.

22. For a well-reasoned argument to this effect, see Ignatieff 1999: esp. 43–54.

23. For some useful non-Western, subaltern thinking on human rights, see Muzaffar 1993; Kothari and Sethi 1989. For balanced, diverse perspectives, see Bauer and Bell 1999. And see also An-Na'im 1992.

24. For a critique of the provincial Western liberal claims of universality as related to Islam, see Falk 1997: 7–23.

25. The magnitude of poverty in the world is dramatically understated by using the World Bank subsistence yardstick of $1 per day; even with this standard, there are more than one billion poor people in the world at this time, but if the yardstick

were more realistically fixed at $2 or $3 per day, or even $5, the scale of poverty would be more appropriately gauged. Also, given income/wealth disparities and trends, the maldistribution of material benefits for work would be more easily understood to be a fundamental global social issue.

26. For text of UDHR, see Weston et al. 1997: 375–79, at 378.

27. Ibid.: 379.

28. For broad assessment, see Falk 1995; Commission on Global Governance 1995.

29. For insight into the subaltern discourse, see Guha, 1982, 1986. For a range of subaltern perspectives, see Williams and Chrisman 1994; Spivak 1999.

30. The protesters were also concerned about child labor and working standards of safety, that is, about the protection of human rights for vulnerable categories of people. Arguably, labor union protests in the United States and elsewhere against such deprivations are motivated by selfish concerns relating to jobs and wages.

31. Falk and Strauss 2001.

4

Economic Globalization and Rights

An Empirical Analysis

Wesley T. Milner

As we enter the twenty-first century, many scholars, media commentators, and citizens alike are attempting to grapple with the ever-increasing rate at which our world is becoming more integrated. Numerous components of "civilization" (e.g., capital, labor, goods, services, information, disease) that were once relatively fixed from a geographical standpoint are now hurled around the planet at previously unthinkable speeds. This notion of "globalization" has been seen as the solution to some contemporary problems, including underdevelopment, malnutrition, and perhaps human rights violations.

However, some have argued that this latest "wave" of globalization is no different from previous periods of increased trade and integration. Paul Hirst and Grahame Thompson (1996) argue that the global economy is no more open now than at the beginning of the industrial revolution in the 1870s. They argue that much of the so-called "globalization" affects only the global North (primarily Europe, Japan, and North America) and continues to ignore the global South. While it is true that the Group of Seven (G-7) still commands extreme power throughout the world, I argue that this latest round of globalization is distinct in both quantitative and qualitative terms. As Alison Brysk's introduction indicates, the current wave of globalization indeed surpasses previous eras in its breadth, scope, and intensity. International trade, for instance, increased twice as fast as global gross domestic product in the 1990s. While still not a majority of that growth, developing countries' share rose from 23 to 29 percent. The speed and volume of financial flows has also soared in the past decade. With overall foreign direct investment at over $3,455 billion (in 1997), the industrial world accounts for approximately 68 percent, leaving the developing countries with over 30 percent (World Bank 2000: 33–38).

This same period has witnessed the creation and implementation of important human rights instruments that have been incorporated into a so-

called international human rights regime that connects international organizations and networks to each other, as well as victims and violators to global
institutions. As a result of new communications technologies and increasing
interdependence, governments are finding it increasingly difficult to violate
their citizens' human rights without attracting the attention and ire of interested individuals, governments, and international organizations around
the world.

Indeed, overall human rights practices have improved worldwide in the
present generation. However, this improvement has not been universal or
linear (Milner et al. 1999). The technological advances allowing human
rights advocates to become more active can also be used by those who are
intent on violating basic human rights. For this current project, the task then
is to determine what effect (if any) this movement toward greater global integration and economic liberalization is having on basic human rights over
time. This cross-national study attempts to trace the impact of economic globalization on basic human rights in order to shed some light on these contradictory trends.

DEFINING BASIC HUMAN RIGHTS
Security Rights

The most widely accepted notion of human rights addresses the "integrity
of the person," or "physical integrity."[1] Abuses that violate the integrity of
the person are commonly seen to include execution, torture, forced disap-
pearance, and the imprisonment/detention of persons, either arbitrarily or
for their political and/or religious beliefs.

Moving beyond the definitional stage, the choice of measurement tech-
nique is more difficult. Thomas Jabine and Richard Claude's *Human Rights
and Statistics: Getting the Record Straight* (1992), which examines numerous
quantitative approaches to human rights research, is one of the earliest and
better guides in this endeavor. In choosing between the typical events-based
and standards-based approaches, I have decided to utilize the standards-
based framework.[2] The measure I employ is the five-point political terror
scale, or PTS, created from the annually published human rights reports of
Amnesty International, in which a 5 represents a country where these rights
are not abused, while the lowest score, 1, is assigned to countries that are
the worst human rights disasters.[3]

Subsistence Rights

In keeping with the comprehensive nature of this volume, I go beyond the
traditional focus of integrity-of-the-person rights and also consider the more

controversial subsistence rights, which include unpolluted air and water; sufficient food, clothing, and shelter; and minimal public health care. The acceptance of these rights was illustrated in U.S. foreign policy by the unveiling of the "New Directions," or "Basic Needs," mandate by Congress in 1973. This marked a major departure in foreign aid from the development assistance policies of the 1960s to the proposed goal of meeting the needs of the poorest people in the poorest countries. This was to be accomplished by concentrating assistance on food production, nutrition, health care, and education. In addressing this aspect of human rights, Bruce Moon argues that the provision of these needs requires few compromises concerning competing policy goals.[4] Furthermore, numerous international human rights instruments also call for the protection of these specific rights by all signatory countries.

From a measurement standpoint, economists and political scientists have traditionally relied upon gross national product as gauge of development or basic human needs. While it is a widely available measure, it is hampered by many weaknesses (Milner et al. 1999). An alternative composite measure and indeed one of the most popular approaches was proposed by David Morris (1979). This "Physical Quality of Life Index" (PQLI) combines infant mortality, life expectancy, and literacy.[5] The performance of each country is ranked on a scale of 0 to 100 (for each of the components), where 0 indicates the worst performance (since 1950) and 100 represents the optimum performance (i.e., expected this century).[6] Though this approach has its critics, Morris (1979, 1996) and Moon (1991) persuasively discount the potential weaknesses.[7]

DETERMINANTS OF HUMAN RIGHTS PRACTICES

Global Integration

Hypothesis: The greater the extent to which a country is integrated into the international political economy, the more likely it is to guarantee basic human rights.

This hypothesis is the focus of a long-standing theoretical debate. As illustrated by K. J. Holsti (1985), globalism predicts that growing interdependence of nations will result in a global society or community, in contrast to traditional realist assumptions of a perpetual struggle for power. Independence involves trade, technology, communication, and the "vast network of transnational relationships between private citizens, associations and companies" (52). Indeed, in the past twenty years, the increasing speed of technological developments has transformed the way in which governments and individuals conduct their affairs. The onslaught of the computer has revolutionized the financial and trade markets into a worldwide marketplace. Since the 1970s, global trade has risen dramatically relative to previous levels and gross domestic product. As a result of this increase in trade and investment (along with technological innovation and deregulation of capital markets by governments), gross international capital flows rose to $3,500 billion annually (World Bank 2000). Indeed, as large as the growth in trade has been, the increased volume in international finance has dwarfed progress in trade. Even in developing countries, international flows doubled from $52 billion in 1977 to $110 billion in 1987 to $1,043 billion in 1997 (Keohane and Milner 1996; World Bank 2000). Furthermore, in the aftermath of Latin American nations' debt problems in the 1980s and the more recent Asian and Russian financial crises, the influence of the International Monetary Fund and World Bank on developing countries' domestic economic policies (and, indeed, the developed world's need to remedy the crises) strengthens the argument that interdependence is increasing.

To my knowledge, there are only two scholars who have linked the level of incorporation into the global system with variations in human rights practices. Ted Robert Gurr (1986) contends that since nations on the periphery of the system are not subject to retribution, they can engage in state terrorism against their citizens. Indeed, it appears that the most egregious violators have been those countries with little (or no) connection to the outside world (e.g., Cambodia under Pol Pot, Albania during the Cold War, North Korea until very recently) because sanctions placed on them would have little effect. In employing an empirical test of Gurr's initial work, Craig Webster (1994) finds marginal support for the hypothesis that linkages with the international system have a positive impact on states' respect for human rights.

The incorporation of a state into the international community should, therefore, have a positive effect upon a regime's treatment of its citizenry. With the advances in worldwide communication, this argument makes intuitive sense. Further integration into the world community would result in information concerning domestic human rights abuses being dispersed more quickly to the outside world and therefore bringing pressure on the offending government (Webster 1994: 95). Continuing this line of reasoning, we could expect improvements in human rights practices as a result of expanded integration. As stipulated in the numerous international human rights instruments (e.g., the International Bill of Human Rights), the world community has agreed upon certain human rights standards.[8] If governments choose to contradict these accepted standards, they run the risk of bad publicity (which could indirectly injure them economically by way of reductions in foreign investment) and perhaps economic sanctions, which would be directly deleterious. Robert Keohane and Helen Milner (1996: 19) argue that in an age of increasing capital mobility, internationalization should even affect those countries not integrated into the global system (i.e., those countries whose economies are not open).

As illustrated in Brysk's introduction, there are numerous definitions of globalization. In keeping with the overall focus of this project, I conceptualize it as a multifaceted process, defined as the degree to which nations are economically and politically incorporated into the overall international system. In measuring global integration, I examine three separate but associated components. These are integration into the postwar Bretton Woods system, trade openness, and financial openness.

For my measure of Bretton Woods regime integration, I look to Webster's (1994) measurement of membership in the World Bank, the GATT, and the IMF. A simple dichotomous rating is applied where a country is coded a "one" if it is a member and "zero" if it is not in any given year. Membership is then totaled so that the highest possible score for a nation is three and the lowest is zero. The data indicating membership come from various issues of *The Political Handbook of the World*.

Trade openness is simply measured as exports plus imports as a percentage of gross national product (Heston and Summers 1991). Unfortunately, there has been little success in accurately estimating financial openness for the vast majority of countries throughout the world. Data on gross financial inflows and outflows as a percentage of gross national product simply are not available during this time. Until very recently, studies of capital controls were limited to indirect measures such as covered interest differentials (Kasman and Pigott 1988; Frankel and McArthur 1988; Ito 1986; Dooley and Isard 1980) or a dichotomous indicator of whether or not nations imposed restrictions on capital flows (Alesina et al. 1994).

By improving on the simple dichotomous discussion of whether countries impose restrictions on capital, I have tracked the trends for each of the various capital controls for both the OECD and non-OECD nations as reported by the IMF. Ultimately, I have chosen to combine these measures of capital controls into one overall indication of international financial openness. This variable ranges from zero to six (according to how many individual capital restrictions were imposed for a given country in a given year). In order to simplify interpretation, I have recoded this measure where zero indicates the least open economy and the value six indicates the most open international market.[9]

Economic Freedom

Hypothesis: The higher the level of economic freedom in a country, the more likely the government is to guarantee basic human rights.

Before I address the issue of how to operationalize economic freedom, it is important for us to make the linkage between economic choice and basic human needs. Tying in with the literature on economic development, it can be argued that economic freedom is indeed related to GNP. Economic theory suggests that higher incomes and increasing living standards are dependent on increases in the production of goods and services that are valued by society. James Gwartney, Robert Lawson, and Walter Block (1997) suggest that as a nation reaches high levels of economic freedom, it will enjoy swift growth.[10] Because economic growth can be seen in part as a process of discovery, nations with greater economic freedom should tend to have higher rates of growth than those with low levels of freedom. Therefore, higher levels of economic freedom should result in higher levels of per capita GNP, resulting in higher levels of economic rights as compared to lower levels of freedom.

Gerald Scully (1988) supports this position in his analysis of 115 market economies for the period 1960–80. He found that politically open societies that guarantee private property rights and the market allocation of resources grow at three times the rate and are two and one-half times as efficient as societies in which these freedoms are not guaranteed. Gwartney, Lawson, and Block (1997: 92–93) empirically show that, on average, countries with more economic freedom have a higher per capita GDP. If the argument holds that increased levels of GNP result in higher physical quality of life, then economic freedom should (at least indirectly) have an effect on basic human needs.

In defining economic freedom, it is perhaps easier to begin with an identification of losses in freedom. Ronald Jones and Alan Stockman (1992) point out that constraints imposed by a third party on voluntary transactions will result in a loss of economic freedom, which is the sum of the losses in consumer and producer surplus in those constrained transactions. From a positive framework, I can say that individuals possess economic freedom when (a) property they acquire without the use of force, fraud, or theft is protected from physical invasions by others and (b) they are free to use, exchange, or give their property to others as long as these actions do not violate the identical rights of others (Gwartney et al. 1997: 12).[11] In choosing an appropriate measure of economic freedom, I am faced with essentially three choices— the Fraser Institute, Freedom House, and Heritage Foundation rating systems. The Fraser Institute system provides the most comprehensive index, incorporating seventeen components that cover four areas of economic freedom: (1) money and inflation, (2) government operations and regulations, (3) takings and discriminatory taxation, and (4) international exchange. A 0–10 rating scale is used for each component. Details of the ten-point Fraser index are shown in Appendix A. While there is a striking degree of similarity between the rating systems of Freedom House, Fraser Institute, and Heritage Foundation, I have chosen to use the Fraser measure, which I find superior overall, for my analysis. Not only is it more comprehensive, both in its combined indicators and its historical coverage of the period from 1975 to 1995, but it better addresses a number of very complex methodological issues that arise in creating an index such as this.[12]

Democracy

Hypothesis: The more democratic a government, the more likely it is to guarantee basic human rights.

Recent literature on human rights has found a relatively strong relationship between democratic forms of government and protection of human rights. It appears that there are a number of theoretical justifications for this conclusion. Conway Henderson (1991) was one of the first to empirically test this hypothesis that the more democratic the government, the less likely it is that it will oppress its citizens. Because the democratic process is built on bargaining and compromise, it provides a substantive alternative for dealing with conflict. We are also warned by Henderson that democracy must truly be legitimate, in the sense that functional institutions ensure the participation of various interests. Steven Poe and C. Neal Tate (1994) in their pooled cross-sectional study of integrity-of-the-person rights substantially extended the findings of Henderson (1991, 1993) with different measures of democracy. In his investigation of democracy and international conflict, Dixon (1994: 15–17) continues the argument that "bounded competition," with its rules, procedures, and guidelines, socializes democratic leaders to the effect that bargaining and compromise are the only avenues to dispute resolution.

A second theoretical basis for expecting greater human rights guarantees with greater democratization is that democracies offer their citizens the ability to remove potentially abusive leaders before violations have become too severe. This usually includes not only the right to vote but also the capability to oust officials for unconstitutional behavior. This obviously assumes that a country will have constitutional guarantees of human rights—which most indeed have. Thirdly, the civil liberties usually associated with democracies (such as freedom of speech, press, assembly, etc.) enable citizens and opposition groups to publicize government abuses. These freedoms could also result in publicity about potential abuses being exported to the international community (e.g., the UN, EU, Organization for Security and Cooperation in Europe, and nongovernmental organizations such as Amnesty International), which could lead to further pressure on the government in question.

Turning more specifically to democracy and its effect on basic human needs, a number of scholars have proposed that democracies are better equipped to provide their citizens with these rights. Moon and Dixon 1985, Rosh 1986, Spalding 1985, and Moon 1991 find that political democracy is associated with higher levels of basic needs satisfaction, even when controlling for wealth (i.e., GNP). These conclusions are bolstered by the fact that they utilize different measures of democracy. Spalding 1985 and Rosh 1986 offer the definition provided by Arat 1991 and Moon and Dixon 1985 and Moon 1991 use that of Bollen 1990.[13]

The measure that most closely meets my definitional and practical means is Keith Jaggers and Ted Robert Gurr's Polity III democracy measure, which covers 161 nations from 1946 through 1994. Jaggers and Gurr (1995) argue that there are three essential, interdependent components of democracy in the context of Western liberal philosophy. First, there must be institutions and procedures through which individuals can voice their preferences about alternative political policies and leaders. Second, it is vital that there be adequate constraints on the power of the executive. Finally, the state must guarantee civil liberties (e.g., freedom from slavery/servitude, torture, arbitrary arrest and imprisonment, and inhuman punishment). Operationally, their democratic indicator is drawn from subjective codings of the openness and competitiveness of executive recruitment, the competitiveness of political participation, and the level of constraints on the chief executive.[14]

Control Variables

This essay focuses on international political economy variables associated with increasing globalization, but there are a number of other factors that have garnered much interest in the development literature, as well as in human rights studies. In my desire for the most comprehensive (as well as most parsimonious) model of international political economy and basic human rights, I therefore control for a number of these variables. These include economic development, economic growth, international war, civil war, and population growth.[15]

From an operationalization standpoint, I follow a number of authors (McKinlay and Cohan 1975, 1976; Mitchell and McCormick 1988; Poe and Tate 1994) in using gross national product per capita for level of economic development, and percentage growth in GNP per capita for economic growth.[16] To operationalize both international war and civil war, I utilize the scales proposed by Small and Singer 1982. In measuring the population variable, I incorporate the natural logarithm of total national population. The log is employed to overcome the skewed distribution of total population, which would otherwise hamper the statistical assumptions. In measuring population growth, I utilize the average percentage increase in national population from year to year.

RESEARCH DESIGN

One criterion for judging empirical research is to what extent a particular study is generalizable to the greater population (in this case, the almost 200 countries of the world). But aside from a few exceptions (e.g., Poe and Tate 1994; Heinish 1994; Henderson 1993; Park 1987), the vast majority of work in the field utilizes a less than comprehensive sample of countries. This obviously restricts the generalizability of any results. In addition, the study of integrity-of-the-person violations has typically involved cross-national, cross-sectional samples that do not allow for any change that might occur within countries. Finally, only a few scholars (Poe and Tate 1994; Heinish 1994; Webster 1994; Henderson 1991, 1993) move beyond simple bivariate studies and utilize multivariate analysis. Therefore, in order to test my multivariate model of human rights variation, I have chosen to employ pooled cross-sectional time-series (PCT) analysis or time-series cross-section (TSCS) as it is sometimes called. Empirical analysis was performed for 176 countries for the years 1980–93.[17] Furthermore, I use the increasingly common Beck and Katz procedure that provides "panel-corrected standard errors" (PCSEs). The models that I develop of subsistence rights and security rights are as follows.

Subsistence Rights

$$\text{subsistence rights}_{tj} = a + B_1 \text{ subsistence rights}_{(t-1)} + B_2 \text{ Bretton Woods}$$
$$\text{membership}_{tj} + B_3 \text{ trade openness}_{tj} + B_4 \text{ financial}$$
$$\text{openness}_{tj} + B_5 \text{ economic freedom}_{tj} + B_6 \text{ democracy}_{tj} +$$
$$B_7 \text{ economic development}_{tj} + B_8 \text{ economic growth}_{tj} +$$
$$B_9 \text{ international war}_{tj} + B_{10} \text{ civil war}_{tj} + B_{11} \text{ population}$$
$$\text{growth}_{tj}$$

Security Rights

$$\text{security rights}_{tj} = a + B_1 \text{ security rights}_{(t-1)} + B_2 \text{ Bretton Woods}$$
$$\text{membership}_{tj} + B_3 \text{ trade openness}_{tj} + B_4 \text{ financial}$$
$$\text{openness}_{tj} + B_5 \text{ economic freedom}_{tj} + B_6 \text{ democracy}_{tj} +$$
$$B_9 \text{ economic development}_{tj} + B_7 \text{ economic growth}_{tj} +$$
$$B_8 \text{ international war}_{tj} + B_9 \text{ civil war}_{tj} + B_{10} \text{ population}$$
$$\text{growth}_{tj}$$

Preliminary correlation analyses revealed associations among the independent variables that might indicate multicollinearity. This problem of a linear or near linear relationship among independent variables is common with time series and cross-sectional data.[18] Initially, it was suspected that the measures for globalization, while theoretically separate aspects of integration, might exhibit collinear relationships. Luckily, there is no sign of multicollinearity among these globalization indicators.[19] Having said that, there are indications that incorporating population level and the lagged value for subsistence rights could be problematic. Physical Quality of Life at $_{t-1}$ is collinear with economic development and democracy.[20] I also decided to refrain from drawing inferences from models utilizing the subsistence rights at $_{t-1}$.[21]

TABLE 4.1. Summary Statistics

Variable	N	Mean	Median	St. Dev.	Min.	Max.
Subsistence rights	2,217	67.66	73.2	20.56	14	99
Security rights	2,208	3.56	4	1.15	1	5
Bretton Woods	2,099	2.46	3	.80	0	3
Trade openness	1,704	72.21	61.45	47.49	6.32	423.41
Financial openness	1,662	3.05	3	1.63	0	6
Economic freedom	420	4.57	4.4	1.48	0.6	9.3
Democracy	1,900	3.86	1	4.36	0	10
Economic development	2,185	3,908	1190	6,086.60	53	36,670
Economic growth	2,160	3.16	3.01	12.89	−95.5	128.57
International war	2,240	.08	0	.27	0	1
Civil war	2,221	.10	0	.30	0	1
Population growth	2,440	2.19	2.19	4.35	−48.45	126.01

ANALYSIS AND RESULTS

To summarize the hypotheses of the model, it is expected that global integration, economic freedom, and democracy will have a positive effect on basic human rights (both subsistence and security) as measured by the Physical Quality of Life Index and Political Terror Scale, respectively. Furthermore, the analysis controls for the effects of economic development, economic growth, presence of civil and/or international war, and population growth. It is assumed that economic development will have a positive effect on basic human rights while each of the other controls is expected to have a negative effect. Table 4.1 contains descriptive statistics for all the variables used in the analysis. The results of the pooled cross-sectional time-series (PCT) procedure are illustrated in tables 4.1–4.5. Because of the reduction in cases resulting from limited data for economic freedom, I first report the general model and then add economic freedom.[22]

Subsistence Rights Models

Based on my proposed hypotheses, the analysis presents some very interesting, if not surprising results. I find that global integration as measured by regime membership and trade openness has a positive effect on subsistence rights (table 4.1). Financial openness, however, has a negative impact on basic human needs. As expected, democracy and economic development are highly significant and in a positive direction.[23] Civil war and population growth influence our dependent variable in a negative fashion as hypothesized. Conversely, international war has a somewhat positive effect on subsistence rights. In terms of overall goodness of fit, the χ^2 indicates that the

TABLE 4.2. General Subsistence Rights Model

Independent Variable	Coefficient	Panel Corrected Standard Errors	Z
Constant	51.97***	2.39	21.67
Bretton Woods	2.13**	.76	2.80
Trade openness	.04***	.008	4.91
Financial openness	−.72***	.23	−3.10
Democracy	1.14***	.10	11.46
Economic development	.001***	.00007	16.73
Economic growth	−.02	.03	−.88
International war	2.52*	1.16	2.16
Civil war	−4.46***	1.07	−4.13
Population growth	−.35***	.10	−3.38
Number of cases	1,084	Adjusted R^2	.56
χ^2	802.47***	F	154.94***
Probability > χ^2	0.00	Probability > F	0.00

*$p \leq .05$
**$p \leq .01$
***$p \leq .001$

overall model is significant. The adjusted R^2 is also reported from the basic OLS regression and shows that the model can explain some 56 percent of the variance in subsistence rights. Finally, the high F statistic attests to an overall statistical significance of the regression. The probability > F reported in each table tells us the probability of a greater F statistic if we draw samples randomly from a population in which the null hypothesis is true (Hamilton 1998: 132).

If economic freedom is added to this general model (table 4.2), the results are slightly altered. First, economic freedom is found to have little significance. While financial openness is influential above, it loses any impact when combined with economic freedom. Trade openness remains robust and in a positive direction as do democracy and economic development. The χ^2, F statistic, and R^2 again indicate a good fit. With the inclusion of economic freedom, the reader must be mindful that the sample is greatly reduced (here, only seventy-one countries for three years). This could explain some of the inconsistencies with the general model.

Security Rights

In the general model (table 4.3), we find that eight out of our ten independent variables exhibit statistically significant effects on security rights. Not

TABLE 4.3 Subsistence Rights Model with Economic Freedom

Independent Variable	Coefficient	Panel Corrected Standard Errors	Z
Constant	65.20***	5.12	12.72
Bretton Woods	−3.38**	1.43	−2.70
Trade openness	.05**	.01	2.86
Financial openness	.20	.49	.40
Economic freedom	−.18	.73	−.25
Democracy	1.97***	.22	8.73
Economic development	.0009***	.0001	5.24
Economic growth	−.07	.07	−1.05
International war	2.85	2.54	1.12
Civil war	−3.07	3.21	−.95
Population growth	−.15	.11	−1.39
Number of cases	199	Adjusted R^2	.61
χ^2	232.22***	F	32.22***
Probability $> \chi^2$	0.00	Probability $>$ F	0.00

*$p \leq .05$
**$p \leq .01$
***$p \leq .001$

surprisingly, previous security rights practices in a country have a tremendous impact on current policies. Concerning our issue of global integration, trade openness and financial openness positively influence these rights. Our third measure of globalization (Bretton Woods membership) has no discernible effects. As expected, and as we have seen before, democracy and economic development are quite influential in explaining levels of human rights abuse. Looking at domestic and international war, these exhibit negative effects that would support the findings of Rasler 1986 and Poe and Tate 1994. Population growth also has a negative effect in support of my hypothesis. In terms of overall goodness of fit, the χ^2 indicates that the overall model is significant. The adjusted R^2 is also reported from the basic OLS regression and shows that the model can explain almost 75 percent of the variance in security rights. Finally, the high F statistic attests to an overall significance of the regression.

While adding economic freedom (table 4.4) does nothing for the overall explanatory ability of the above model, it provides us with an interesting finding.[24] Rather than having a positive effect as expected, economic freedom is found to have an unexpected *negative* impact on security rights. As observed previously, it appears that there is a linkage between economic freedom, economic development, and subsistence rights. If the argument holds

TABLE 4.4 General Security Rights Model

Independent Variable	Coefficient	Panel Corrected Standard Errors	Z
Constant	.81***	.11	6.80
Security rights$_{t-1}$	.67***	.02	31.68
Bretton Woods	.03	.03	.84
Trade openness	.001***	.0004	3.51
Financial openness	.026**	.01	2.17
Democracy	.01***	.005	3.40
Economic development	.00001***	.000003	4.28
Economic growth	−.0009	.001	−.62
International war	−.18**	.06	−2.83
Civil war	−.45***	.065	−6.898
Population growth	−.02***	.006	−3.42
Number of cases	1,089	Adjusted R^2	.74
χ^2	3,022.81***	F	310.23***
Probability $> \chi^2$	0.00	Probability $> F$	0.00

*p ≤ .05
**p ≤ .01
***p ≤ .001

that increased levels of GNP result in higher physical quality of life, then economic freedom should (at least indirectly) have an effect on basic human needs. It is assumed that this would have the same effect on security rights. From this analysis, it appears that higher levels of economic freedom have little effect on subsistence rights and could actually have a *detrimental* impact on security rights. A second important point is that globalization as measured by financial openness loses its impact here, just as it did with subsistence rights. Not surprisingly, democracy continues its trend toward better human rights across the board. Security rights$_{t-1}$ and trade openness once again provide positive effects. Also, civil war as well as population growth is consistently negative in nature. International war, though still negative, drops from being a statistically significant impediment to security rights. As before, we must be cautious in drawing strong inferences because of the reduced sample size with the inclusion of economic liberalization.

DISCUSSION AND CONCLUSION

This study has attempted to explain cross-national differences in provision of human rights (both subsistence and security) on a comprehensive data set covering 176 countries from 1980 to 1993. Pooled cross-sectional time-

TABLE 4.5 Security Rights Model with Economic Freedom

Independent Variable	Coefficient	Panel Corrected Standard Errors	Z
Constant	1.27***	.30	4.10
Security rights$_{t-1}$	.59***	.05	11.56
Bretton Woods	.01	.07	.15
Trade openness	.003**	.001	2.89
Financial openness	.23	.02	.86
Economic freedom	−.09**	.03	−2.36
Democracy	.03**	.01	3.00
Economic development	.00003**	.00001	2.89
Economic growth	−.0004	.003	−0.12
International war	−.13	.14	−.92
Civil war	−.46**	.18	−2.47
Population growth	−.02**	.007	−2.91
Number of cases	199	Adjusted R^2	.72
χ^2	488.76***	F	46.68***
Probability > χ^2	0.00	Probability > F	0.00

*p ≤ .05
**p ≤ .01
*** p ≤ .001

series (PCT) series regression models were presented to test a number of hypotheses from a variety of theoretical perspectives. While the overall models go a great distance in explaining the variation in integrity-of-the-person rights, and to a lesser extent physical quality of life, the more interesting and useful product of this effort is discerning the effects of the individual variables.

In terms of globalization, the variable of trade openness is found to be statistically and substantively significant for both dependent variables. For subsistence rights, a 100-point increase in trade openness would result in a 4-point increase in a country's Physical Quality of Life Index. While it might seem unlikely that a country could shift its trade openness (measured as exports + imports/GNP) by such a margin, a number of countries did approach this level (e.g., Guyana from 1989 to 1990). The impact appears to be uniform for both developed and developing countries alike. The effect of trade openness on security rights has an equally positive influence. For all of the variables in the security rights model, it is important for us to acknowledge the dynamic effect mediated by the lagged endogenous vari-

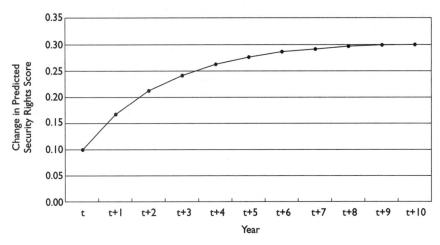

Figure 4.1. Increase in security rights due to increase in trade openness.

able. As Figure 4.1 shows, the impact of a sizable change in trade openness increases substantially over time.[25] We can see that the small initial change of .1 in the political terror scale would approach a threefold increase within eight years.

While having a strong negative effect on subsistence rights, financial openness exhibits a statistically and substantively positive effect on security rights. Assuming a move from the most restricted to the most open (e.g., Dominica from 1985 to 1986), an initial impact of .15 on the political terror scale translates into almost a .5 increase in security rights over a ten-year period. In separating the effects for OECD and non-OECD countries, it was found that this result holds for the developing countries but not for the developed countries. Not only is the impact insignificant from a statistical standpoint, but its weak coefficient is also in the opposite direction, as is the case with the general subsistence rights model. This could mean that at higher levels of economic development, further moves toward globalization (financial) are immaterial at best and indeed deleterious in the case of subsistence rights. This inconsistency calls for further research.

The findings for economic freedom also warrant additional discussion. For subsistence rights, economic freedom exhibits no statistical significance.[26] This unexpected outcome runs counter to the conventional wisdom that greater economic freedom should foster economic development, thereby enhancing the provision of basic human needs. The situation is even more striking if we turn our attention to security rights. Rather than having a positive effect or no effect at all, economic freedom is found to have an unexpected negative influence on security rights. This finding encourages us to dig deeper into the complexities of certain freedoms and integrity-of-the-person rights. One plausible explanation for this phenomenon could be the existence of substantial inequality, which is perhaps common with more extensive economic freedom. Under this development trade-off scenario, greater inequality in wealth might result in a government being less likely to guarantee basic human rights. Furthermore, an increase in inequality could result in greater social conflict, with subsequent repression by a reactionary regime. In connection with the most recent protests in Seattle and Washington concerning World Trade Organization, World Bank, and IMF policies, these findings might provide a different focus for the protestors concerned with overzealous international institutions.

While economic freedom exhibits statistical significance, it is less clear, however, that substantive significance has been obtained. The initial decline of .09 on the political terror scale as a result of a one-point annual increase (three points over three years) in economic freedom only approaches a .25 drop by the end of a decade. Though quite interesting, this effect should be regarded cautiously.[27]

The important factor of democracy achieves continued support in this study with statistical and substantive significance for both dependent variables. In terms of subsistence rights, a one-level drop in democracy (on the 0–10 Polity III scale) will result in a greater than one-point drop in the Physical Quality of Life Index. At the other end of the spectrum, if a country were to achieve the highest democratic score in one year and then abandon democracy (e.g., obtaining the lowest democratic score) in the next period, we would see a more than a ten-point decline in subsistence rights. This large degradation in physical quality of life would have dramatic impact on a country's basic human needs. These findings strongly support the previous work in this area (Moon and Dixon 1985; Rosh 1986; Spalding 1986; Moon 1991). This is especially true because the measure of democracy I use differs from that used by the previous authors.

Some may question the feasibility of this assumption of complete abandonment of democracy. Although this is unlikely, there are precedents, such as the overthrow of Chilean democracy under Salvador Allende by Augusto Pinochet in the early 1970s. As a result, after obtaining the maximum democracy score in 1973, Chile then dropped immediately to the lowest possible score. Another example might be the collapse of the Weimar Republic and the ascension of National Socialism in Germany (Poe and Tate 1994: 861).

While statistically significant, democracy's substantive impact on security rights is less pronounced. Once again assuming our complete abandonment of democracy from one period to another, a country would experience an initial decline of .1 in the political terror scale. With the utilization of the lagged endogenous variable, however, there is a combined effect as discussed above. If the cessation of democracy were to continue in our sample country, it appears that the human rights index would only decline by .3. With the security rights scale range from 1–5, this small change would be difficult to assess in terms of political prisoners held or increased torture or execution. This finding, while supporting the established literature, does not exhibit the same magnitude as previous studies (e.g., Henderson 1991, 1993; Poe and Tate 1994). This could once again call into question (as does Fein 1995) the truly linear nature of democracy and its effects on security rights.

Considering the effects of population growth rate, it appears that this study has shed some light on the diverse conclusions of previous authors. Population growth exhibits a statistically and substantively important impact on both subsistence and security rights.[28] Henderson (1993) found that population growth had an adverse effect on human rights, while level of population had no bearing. This was directly contrary to the more advanced study of Poe and Tate (1994) that argued overall population was deleterious to security rights but that growth was not significant. Future research is obviously still needed to better explain the complexities surrounding population pressures.

While this essay has contributed to the existing literature on globalization and basic human rights, it has raised a number of questions as well. Concerning policy implications, there are a number of prescriptions that can be made. First, supporting increased globalization (i.e., trade, finance) should improve (or at least not hamper) security rights provisions around the world. However, the case for subsistence rights is a bit more complicated. Though increased trade tends to improve basic human needs provision, greater financial integration could have a damaging effect. As noted above, this is probably due to the complex issue of inequality, which should be studied more extensively. Concerning efforts to democratize and develop, it would appear that the conventional wisdom holds, and that many of these initiatives can indeed promote both subsistence and security rights. Furthermore, attempts to reduce the incidence of domestic and international conflicts should be continued in order to improve both areas of human rights.

Future research will, we hope, continue on this path of discovery and help the world community better provide for its individual citizens. In addition to scrutinizing the difficult inequality issue, different measures of security rights and subsistence rights could be investigated and compared. Many of the findings from the recent literature depend as much on the ways of measuring various human rights as they do on the methodological procedures chosen.

APPENDIX.
COMPONENTS OF THE FRASER INSTITUTE INDEX OF ECONOMIC FREEDOM

I. Money and inflation (protection of money as a store of value and medium of exchange)
   A. Average annual growth rate of the money supply during the past five years minus the potential growth rate of real GDP
   B. Standard deviation of the annual inflation rate during the past five years
   C. Freedom of citizens to own a foreign currency bank account domestically
   D. Freedom of citizens to maintain a bank account abroad

II. Government operations and regulations (freedom to decide what is produced and consumed)
   A. Government general consumption expenditures as a percentage of GDP
   B. The role and presence of government-operated enterprises
   C. Price controls—the extent to which businesses are free to set their own prices
   D. Freedom of private businesses and cooperatives to compete in markets
   E. Equality of citizens under the law and access of citizens to a nondiscriminatory judiciary (this variable is included only in the 1995 index)
   F. Freedom from government regulations and policies that cause negative real interest rates

III. Takings and discriminatory taxation (freedom to keep what you earn)
   A. Transfers and subsidies as a percentage of GDP
   B. Top marginal tax rate (and income threshold at which it applies)
   C. The use of conscripts to obtain military personnel

IV. Restraints on international exchange (freedom of exchange with foreigners)
   A. Taxes on international trade as a percentage of exports plus imports
   B. Differences between the official exchange rate and the black market rate
   C. Actual size of trade sector compared to the expected size
   D. Restrictions on the freedom of citizens to engage in capital transactions with foreigners

Source: Gwartney et al., *Economic Freedom of the World: 1975–1995* (Vancouver: Fraser Institute), 16.

NOTES

1. Stohl et al. 1986; Cingranelli and Pasquarello 1985; Mitchell and McCormick 1988; Henderson 1991, 1993; Poe and Tate 1994; Fein 1995; Poe et al. 2000; Cingranelli and Richards 1997.

2. The events approach involves coding cases of repressive events from newspaper accounts. Typically, the number of these events is summed for a particular period (a month or year) and the number of events is considered a measure of repression. Some difficulties with this approach as a means to measure levels of human rights violation (e.g., Western bias) have been identified (see, e.g., Poe and Tate 1994).

3. For more on the scale, see Gibney and Dalton 1996; Milner et al. 1999. In order to be consistent with the scales of the other variables, the original five-point security rights scale has been recoded so that countries with more severe human rights violations exhibit a lower rating while nations with fewer violations are assigned a higher rating. Following the lead of Poe and Tate 1994, missing cases are filled in using similar codings gained from the U.S. State Department Reports.

4. Moon 1991: 7–9. Donnelly 1989: 163–66, provides a succinct overview of the trade-offs between development and basic needs, equality and liberty.

5. This composite is the unweighted arithmetic mean of (a) number of infant deaths per 1,000 live births, (b) life expectancy at age one, and (c) the percentage of population fifteen years of age and older who are literate.

6. In constructing his index, David Morris (1979: 20–38) lays out six criteria that all composite measures should meet: the index (1) should not assume that there is only one pattern of development, (2) should avoid standards that reflect the values of specific societies, (3) should measure results, not inputs, (4) should be able to reflect the distribution of social results, (5) should be simple to construct and easy to comprehend, and (6) should lend itself to international comparison. The PQLI meets all of these criteria.

7. See Moon and Dixon 1985; Moon 1991; and Streeten 1981: 22.

8. In addition to these three basic documents (the Universal Declaration of Human Rights; the International Covenant on Economic, Social, and Cultural Rights; and the International Covenant on Civil and Political Rights), a number of regional and secondary agreements also apply (e.g., the European Convention on Human Rights and Fundamental Freedoms, European Social Charter, American Declaration of the Rights and Duties of Man, American Convention on Human Rights, and African Charter on Human and People's Rights.

9. For a comparable measurement of international financial openness, see Quinn 1997, which unfortunately does not supply data for all the years and countries in this study.

10. Gwartney et al. 1997: 91–92. This is contingent on the fact that this economic freedom is indeed credible and potentially long-lasting.

11. It is important to note the distinction between economic freedom and political and civil liberties. Nations may indeed exhibit high levels of political rights and civil liberties while at the same time achieving a relatively low level of economic freedom. Examples include Sweden, India, and Israel.

12. Although this study concentrates on the single year of 1990, further research is being conducted that examines the entire twenty-year period.

13. Both Arat 1991 and Bollen 1990 have further expanded on their operationalization of democracy in later works.

14. Jaggers and Gurr 1995 provides an excellent comparison of Polity III with some of the most utilized constructs of democracy. These include Arat 1991; Bollen 1980, 1990; Coppedge and Reinicke 1990; Gastil 1978–94; Gassiorowski 1993; and Vanhanen 1990.

15. Studies addressing economic development include Moon and Dixon 1985; Goldstein 1985; Spalding 1986; Rosh 1986; Park 1987; Mitchell and McCormick 1988; Henderson 1991; and Poe and Tate 1994. Economic growth is included by Olson 1963; Gurr 1968; Mitchell and McCormick 1988; Poe and Tate 1994; and Duff and McCamant 1976. The issue of international war is the concern of Stohl 1975, 1976; Rasler 1986; and Poe and Tate 1994. Nieburg 1969; Tilly 1978; Skocpol 1979; and Poe and Tate 1994 utilize civil conflict in their models. Finally, population growth is addressed by Henderson 1993 and Poe and Tate 1994.

16. While GNP is considered the traditional and most popular approach, there have been several alternatives offered. These include energy consumption (Henderson 1991) and a number of basic human needs measures reviewed in the subsistence rights section above.

17. Countries included in the analysis are Afghanistan; Albania; Algeria; Angola; Argentina; Armenia; Australia; Austria; Azerbaijan; Bahamas; Bahrain; Bangladesh; Barbados; Belarus; Belgium; Belize; Benin; Bhutan; Bolivia; Bosnia-Herzegovina; Botswana; Brazil; Brunei; Bulgaria; Burundi; Cambodia (Kampuchea); Cameroon; Canada; Cape Verde; Central African Republic; Chad; Chile; China; Colombia; Comoros; Congo; Costa Rica; Côte d'Ivoire; Croatia; Cuba; Cyprus; Czech Republic; Denmark; Dijibouti; Dominican Republic; Dominica; Ecuador; Egypt; El Salvador; Equatorial Guinea; Eritrea; Estonia; Ethiopia; Fiji; Finland; France; Gabon; Gambia; Georgia; Germany; Ghana; Gibraltar; Greece; Grenada; Guatemala; Guinea; Guyana; Haiti; Honduras; Hungary; Iceland; India; Indonesia; Iran; Iraq; Ireland; Israel; Italy; Jamaica; Japan; Jordan; Kazakhstan; Kenya; Kuwait; Kyrgyzstan; Laos; Latvia; Lebanon; Lesotho; Liberia; Libya; Lithuania; Luxembourg; Macedonia; Madagascar; Malawi; Malaysia; Maldives; Mali; Malta; Mauritania; Mauritius; Mexico; Moldova; Mongolia; Morocco; Mozambique; Myanmar (Burma); Namibia; Nepal; Netherlands; New Zealand; Nicaragua; Niger; Nigeria; Norway; Oman; Pakistan; Panama; Papua New Guinea; Paraguay; Peru; Philippines; Poland; Portugal; Qatar; Romania; Rwanda; South Korea; São Tomé and Principe; Saudi Arabia; Senegal; Seychelles; Sierra Leone; Singapore; Slovenia; Solomon Islands; Somalia; South Africa; Soviet Union/Russia; Spain; Sri Lanka; St. Lucia; St. Vincent; Sudan; Suriname; Swaziland; Sweden; Switzerland; Syria; Taiwan; Tajikistan; Tanzania; Thailand; Togo; Trinidad; Tunisia; Turkey; Turkmenistan; UAE; Uganda; Ukraine; United Kingdom; United States; Upper Volta/Burkina Faso; Uruguay; Uzbekistan; Vanuatu; Venezuela; Vietnam; Western Samoa; Yemen; North Yugoslavia/Serbia; Zaire; Zambia; and Zimbabwe.

18. In order to check for the presence of multicollinearity, I employed two procedures—an ocular test that examines the Pearson's r correlation matrix and the Klein test that regresses each independent variable on all the other independent variables. For the ocular test, I take a relatively conservative stance and look for any correlations exceeding .60. For the Klein test, I look for any R2 that approaches 1.00.

19. The correlations were as follows: Bretton Woods and financial openness = .11, Bretton Woods and trade openness = -.03, financial openness and trade openness = .21.

20. The correlation between Physical Quality of Life at $_{t-1}$ and economic development was .53. The correlation between Physical Quality of Life at $_{t-1}$ and democracy was .59.

21. All regression estimation procedures were conducted with Stata 6 (software, StataCorp 1999).

22. A number of diagnostics were also performed on the various models. Ramsey RESET procedures indicate that our models are well specified and that no variables have been omitted. To guard against outliers, I employed Welsch and Kuh's (1977) DFITS statistic (Belsley et al. 1980). This measures the influence of the ith observation on the model as a whole. Among the more than 1,000 cases, I detected 22 (security rights) and 19 (subsistence rights) potentially influential cases. Furthermore, I utilized DFBETAs to determine how much each case affects each coefficient. By reestimating the models with the potential offenders excluded, I found the models to exhibit roughly the same magnitude and direction of influence over the dependent variables. With no theoretical justification for excluding these, I chose to retain all of the cases for the model estimations.

23. The significance for all variables is shown at the 95 percent, 99 percent, and 99.9 percent confidence levels.

24. As in the above model, the χ^2 and F statistic indicate an overall significant model and the amount of variance explained is a similar 72 percent. Once must also keep in mind that the number of cases is reduced from 1,087 to 192.

25. To calculate the effect of any of these variables at time$_{t+1}$, one multiplies the effect at time$_t$ by the coefficient of the lagged dependent variable and adds the direct effect of the independent variable at time$_{t+1}$. An asymptotic pattern emerges after several lags of repeating this process (Poe and Tate 1994).

26. The reader should note that the economic freedom data (for our period) are only available for 1980, 1985, 1990, and 1993.

27. The primary problem here is one of data availability. The best data come from Deininger and Squire 1997, which applies a stringent set of standards to improve the overall product (but significantly reduces the overall number of cases) .

28. Adding economic freedom to our subsistence model, however, results in negligible impact for population growth.

5

Sweatshops and International Labor Standards

Globalizing Markets, Localizing Norms

Raul C. Pangalangan

Labor and human rights advocates have attempted to improve the condition of workers in developing countries by advocating international minimum labor standards enforced by trade sanctions. They propose to link labor standards with world trade through social clauses that seal off First World markets to products made in Third World sweatshops, thus preventing social dumping and the "race to the bottom" in wages and benefits. Poor countries, on the other hand, see this as disguised protectionism by the global North that neutralizes their competitive edge in low wages. They argue that wages and standards of living will improve only as their economies develop and that sanctions will only stunt that development.

In this essay, I contrast two approaches to the problem of global sweatshops. The first calls for the incorporation of social clauses into international trade agreements, making it possible to restrict or halt the importation or preferential importation of products from "low-standard" countries. The second bypasses state-based mechanisms altogether in favor of the market, operating, for example, through social labeling, voluntary corporate codes of conduct, and NGO-led boycotts of "tainted" goods, thus enabling consumers to vote their consciences with their pocketbooks. I characterize the first as *normative/institutional*, in that it seeks to advance norms collectively through institutions, and the second as *nonnormative/noninstitutional*, in that it shifts moral judgment to the individual consumer, oblivious as it were to any communal sense of justice and independent of formal state mechanisms.

Opponents of linkage argue that labor rights are normative and local, because they are necessarily tied to domestic social arrangements.[1] Advocates of linkage argue that labor rights are both market-determined and global, because core labor rights merely accomplish the true globalization of the market—that is, the free movement of both capital and labor. The debate involves the interplay of two sets of arguments (normative and nonnormative) and two sets of institutional arrangements (international vis-à-vis domestic law), contrasting the themes of globalizing markets and localizing norms.

CONCEPTUAL FRAMEWORK

The rights implicated in these arguments are those identified in the International Covenant on Economic, Social and Cultural Rights, specifically those pertaining to the "right to work," the right to "just and favorable conditions of work," and trade unionism (including the right to bargain collectively and the right to strike).[2] Until the Covenant, these claims had scarcely been considered as part of those "human rights" that traditionally restrained state action against individuals, in contrast to workers' claims arising from the private relationship between capital and labor.

Markets: Labor as a Commodity

Advocates of international labor standards (developed countries, their trade union movements, international human rights groups) begin with the view that labor is a commodity. They characterize labor as yet another factor of production and equate it with other aspects of world trade already regulated by international rules: investments, goods, intellectual property, services, and so on. Why are intellectual property rights and environmental standards legitimate trade issues and therefore subject to international regulation, but not labor standards?[3] If public subsidies create unfair trade advantages, why not the invisible, involuntary, and state-abetted subsidy by poor workers, who toil at subsistence wages and thus absorb the true cost of production?

Linkage advocates thus protest that the trade in goods produced under substandard labor conditions merely triggers a "race to the bottom," pushing "benign" countries to lower their own standards in order to compete with low-standard countries.[4] Low labor standards lead to social dumping because they reward low-standard countries with increased trade, to the detriment of benign countries. On the other hand, linkage fosters genuine globalization by integrating national economies on the basis of higher wages, skills, and technological sophistication.[5] And indeed, higher core labor standards have been associated with increased economic growth.[6]

But, linkage opponents argue, if labor is indeed just another commodity, poor countries are right in making the most of their comparative advantage in having surplus labor, lower standards of living, and cheaper means of subsistence. The erstwhile "tiger economies" of the ASEAN, now in decline, have attacked labor rights linkage as a new form of protectionism,[7] as "illegitimate interference in the internal affairs of sovereign nations,"[8] and as neutralizing their "most valuable asset," namely, cheap labor. Malaysian representatives have asserted, for example, that social clauses are not meant to help workers but to stop foreign investment in developing countries. They conclude that the linkage is merely a "smokescreen" for protectionism by rich countries out to shield their corporate nationals and by labor unions out to secure their members' jobs—the very protectionism that the World Trade Organization (WTO) aims to extirpate.[9]

In response, linkage advocates say that the real threat to the competitiveness of a benign developing country comes from fellow developing countries capable of undercutting its labor, not from First World workers who earn 100 times more. Thus linkage "protects"—not First World economies that cannot possibly underbid the subsistence wages in the Third World—but benign developing countries determined to improve the lot of their people. The linkage debate should thus be seen, not as a campaign by First World workers to stop the job flight to Third World countries, but as an incentive for benign Third World countries to ensure that no country will "win the race [by] offer[ing] the cheapest, most exploited labor in the world."[10]

Conversely, there is no gain in competitive advantage when any of the core labor standards are reduced. Conventional wisdom assumes that capital will shift to regions where semi-skilled labor is cheap and plentiful. Yet, new conditions in modern manufacturing defy that wisdom; with declining labor costs and the rise in skills-intensive work, it is the quality of labor, not its price, that matters most.[11]

Finally, linkage opponents say, the true globalization of labor lies precisely in its freedom of movement to seek its highest price. First World governments speak of freeing capital to find the highest returns, but they would not free labor to seek its price, and they erect immigration barriers to keep out people who are "voting with their feet," for example, as migrant workers. Thus international law breaks the barriers to the free movement of capital and goods but not to the free movement of labor. Trade barriers are lowered by international law, but immigration barriers remain entrenched in national law. In other words, linkage advocates dare the First World countries to bring the "race to the bottom" closer to home. "[L]et us open our borders and let people everywhere seek the best available labor standards wherever in the world they may be found."[12]

But linkage advocates answer in kind. For as long as labor is artificially kept stationary by national laws, preventing it from finding its true market worth, the law must step in to enable the market to function as it should, that is, by enabling workers to exercise core labor rights and get the best return for their labor.

Norms: Labor and Human Dignity

In the context of international trade rules, linkage opponents delight in affirming the normative character of labor rights claims. They affirm that labor rights should be governed by principles, not by market forces, but insist that these principles be determined at the national level. First, labor rules are context- and country-specific. Though labor—like capital—is profit-seeking, the bounties of work include noneconomic factors like cultural affinity, or proximity to family and friends. Labor remains bound up with communities, groups that have embraced their own values, shaped their own collective and institutional identities, and are entitled to legal protection. If labor remains rooted in native soil, it is not simply because of legal barriers, but for sentimental, social, or other nonmarket reasons. Labor standards—being thus the legal embodiment of local sentiment and value choice—are therefore properly national rather than international.[13] Second, the social condition of labor is not "product-related"[14] in the same way as goods and property, and international trade rules should not be used to advance such noneconomic values as human dignity.[15] And third, labor standards should be reserved to domestic law because they affect only a nation's own citizens. While international law governs matters that directly affect other countries (e.g., cross-border pollution), local rules govern matters specific to sovereign countries (e.g., minimum wages, child labor, trade union rights) that affect employers and workers only within those countries.[16]

But if that is so, linkage advocates say, if indeed labor involves human beings endowed with a dignity secured by rights that stand above the market, then standard-setting in labor matters involves norms that must apply universally regardless of a country's economic development.[17] Indeed, linkage advocates have referred to the "social clause" as merely promoting "human rights at work."[18] When he signed the Convention on the Prohibition and Elimination of the Worst Forms of Child Labor of the International Labour Organization (ILO) on behalf of the United States, President Clinton declared: "Core labor standards are . . . about [human rights], not an instrument of protectionism or a vehicle to impose one nation's values on another but about our shared values, about the dignity of work, the decency of life, the fragility and importance of childhood."[19] For an overview of these debates, see table 5.1.

INSTITUTIONALIZED AND "NORMATIVIZED" LINKAGES

The Documents

Two recent international instruments serve as the high points of the "linkage" campaign: the WTO's 1996 Singapore Ministerial Declaration[20] and the ILO's 1998 Declaration on Fundamental Rights.[21]

TABLE 5.1 Standards, Markets, and Norms

	Local Standards	*International Standards*
MARKETS Labor as a commodity in the market	Labor standards are set freely between capital and labor, without the intervention of the state, according to what local workers are willing to accept in exchange for their labor.	Labor standards are set freely, but in relation to what workers in other countries are paid and taking into account the preferences of consumers abroad who may or may not wish to buy "morally tainted" goods produced in unfair or unhealthy workplaces.
NORMS Labor as a human resource governed by laws that embody moral preferences	Labor standards are embodied in national law, which are read into employment contracts and guarantee core rights (trade unionism and collective bargaining) and minimum standards (working hours, conditions of work, health benefits, etc.).	Labor standards are embodied in international instruments and enforced through sanctions or countermeasures by other governments or through intergovernmental organizations.

At its first ministerial conference in 1996, the WTO "renewed [its] commitment to the observance of internationally recognized core labor standards," while "reject[ing] the use of labor standards for protectionist purposes, and agree[ing] that the comparative advantage of . . . low-wage developing countries[] must in no way be put into question." It affirmed that it is the ILO, rather, that has the competence to deal with labor standards, and called for "continue[d] collaboration" between the two organizations.

In response, the ILO adopted a formal declaration affirming itself to be the "constitutionally mandated international organization and the competent body to set and deal with international labor standards" and proclaimed that all ILO members are obligated "from the very fact of membership" and "even if they have not ratified the [pertinent] Conventions," to uphold the following fundamental rights:

(a) freedom of association and the effective recognition of the right to collective bargaining;
(b) the elimination of all forms of forced or compulsory labor;
(c) the effective abolition of child labor; and
(d) the elimination of discrimination in respect of employment and occupation.

The ILO Declaration on Fundamental Rights closes, however, on the same note as the WTO Singapore Ministerial Declaration:

(a) "labor standards should not be used for protectionist trade purposes";
(b) "nothing in this Declaration . . . shall be . . . used for such purposes"; and
(c) "the comparative advantage of any country should in no way be called into question by this Declaration."[22]

From International Labor Standards to Core Labor Rights

Clearly, both statements are part of a compromise between the developed countries (which succeeded in getting the WTO to recognize "internationally recognized core labor standards") and developing countries, led by the ASEAN countries[23] (which succeeded in "reject[ing] the use of labor standards for protectionist purposes," affirming that their "comparative advantage . . . must in no way be put into question"). The key institutional maneuver is to deflect action away from the WTO and toward the ILO.[24]

It has been said optimistically of the Singapore Declaration that it was significant enough that labor standards were explicitly recognized in an official WTO document.[25] The declaration "leave[s] open the possibility of some general link"—for example, making WTO membership conditional upon recognition of labor standards, or recognizing the ILO's monitoring role.[26] A less sanguine reading, however, notes that it seals off any prospect for labor rights–based trade sanctions and marks the death of the social clause campaign.[27]

The ILO Declaration on Fundamental Rights, on the other hand, has been seen as "an alternative to imposing coercive trade sanctions" and as a response to the "growing pressures for linkage of workers' rights and world trade." Its effect is really to "reduce pressures on other international bodies, particularly trade organizations such as the WTO, to adopt coercive trade sanctions as the appropriate means of enhancing workers' rights and improving working conditions." "For multinational employers, the overriding importance of the Declaration is its preemptive effect on emerging 'social clauses' in trade agreements."[28]

Two shifts have thus occurred. The first is the shift from labor *standards* to labor *rights*. The ILO declaration "finesses"[29] the claim to "core labor rights," namely, collective bargaining and unionism, the ban on forced labor, the ban on child labor, and nondiscrimination.[30] These have been described as "enabling rights," which merely provide the framework conditions, in contrast to "outcomes," or cash standards (such as wages, benefits, or working conditions),[31] which are determined not by law but by bargaining in that framework. This represents a shift toward neutral *process*, rather than ideologically loaded or economically costly *substance*. While these four core claims bring back the debate to human rights terrain, they do not seek to guarantee results, but merely to achieve a level playing field. By avoiding substantive discussions about wages, hours of work, vacation leave, and other benefits, linkage advocates also avoid the claim that their goal is to erode the competitive advantage of poor countries.

The second is the shift away from "hard law" obligations, embodied in formal linkages through trade treaties, toward "soft law" obligations, now embodied in the ILO Declaration. The ILO, while declaring that core rights must be respected as a matter of "obligation arising from the very fact of [ILO] membership," does not provide for trade sanctions but merely calls upon its members "to respect, to promote and to realize . . . the fundamental [labor] rights" and directs the ILO to assist them "in response to their established and expressed needs."

The Peril of Unilateralism. The principal advantage of a proper international law approach is that it avoids the danger of unilateral action and gives the potential "victims"—that is, developing countries—the safeguards of collective enforcement: multilateral checks on powerful states, objectively verifiable tests of compliance, evenhanded and nondiscriminatory application of sanctions. Without it, the doors are opened wide for unilateral sanctions, and the failure of linkage in the Singapore Declaration is but a "precursor to yet more unilateralism in the multilateral trading system."[32]

In 1996, for example, the Commonwealth of Massachusetts adopted its so-called Burma law, a "selective purchasing" law that prohibited state agencies from buying goods or services from companies doing business with Burma (Myanmar), a country accused, among other things, of using slave labor.[33] Sanctions of this nature have been said to "undermine the President's capacity . . . for effective diplomacy."[34] Subsequently, however, President Clinton himself issued an order prohibiting executive agencies from buying goods produced "wholly or in part by forced or indentured child labor."[35]

Another prime example of a unilateral, conscience-driven measure protested by developing countries—although it is more akin to eco-labeling (discussed below) rather than social labeling—is the United States's ban on imports of shrimp harvested without turtle-excluder devices that protect sea turtles. This measure was upheld by the WTO Appellate Body, albeit with a rider to the effect that the unilateral U.S. measure had been applied in an arbitrary and discriminatory manner.[36]

The ILO, Not the WTO. The emerging consensus is that the ILO, not the WTO, is the better forum for promoting labor rights.[37] The ILO has the expertise, especially on economic and social matters, and its moral suasion has been effective.

In contrast, the WTO is ill-suited for the function. First, the inherent constraint of WTO linkage is that WTO measures are limited to the exporting sector, which limits the WTO, for instance, to child labor problems involving export-bound goods, but not those for domestic consumption. Yet studies show that child labor in South Asia is concentrated in industries (carpets, clothing and textiles, tile making, slate, and service industries such as street vendors) whose products do not enter into international trade (except for carpets and garments).[38] Moreover, these industries usually employ low-skilled labor, whereas the export trade is technologically more advanced and employs highly skilled workers, with the prominent exceptions, of course, of the garment and carpet industries (where traditional production is highly valued).[39]

Second, WTO dispute settlement procedure favors consultation and allows trade sanctions only as a last resort (when they are limited in scale and involve only the affected countries).[40] These dispute mechanisms are not geared to the "general sanctions" common to labor rights problems but to injury-specific compensation for product-based restrictions, which ultimately burden the exporter companies. There are no available standards to determine the economic injury arising from discrimination or lack of trade unionism.[41]

These arguments emphasize that the WTO has no place in essentially domestic issues, that its sanctions have only a limited effect on domestically rooted social issues, and that the proposed linkage uses trade measures to reinforce what are essentially domestic rights. These matters are outside its mandate and have traditionally been the concern of the ILO.[42] Moreover, these arguments underscore the danger of international human rights measures "crossing over" to international trade regimes. If tainted products are traded abroad, WTO-linked barriers to these products will only shift child labor to the nonexporting or the informal sector. International labor standards will not benefit the unorganized and informal sectors and are inconsistent with universal application of labor standards.[43] They protect unions, which favor the labor elite in the formal sector, ignoring unprivileged workers in the informal sector.[44]

What about a division of labor in which trading countries use the ILO for "adjudication" and the WTO for enforcement? When an ILO representative proposed that the organization exercise its competence to judge whether labor rights have been violated and leave the application of sanctions to the WTO, a representative of the group of nonaligned nations objected, saying that linkage "introduces an untenable link between labor standards and trade," since ILO standards were built on the voluntary nature of ILO conventions. Others argue that the proposed link with sanctions will fundamentally alter this and infringe upon national sovereignty.[45]

MARKET-BASED, VOLUNTARY MECHANISMS

Market-based measures rely on the power of the consumer to command the manufacturer. Consumers choose, making their own moral judgments. Each manufacturer, whether altruistic or profit-oriented, responds.

These measures rely at the threshold on a "call for corporate disclosure." To empower "consumer[s] with a conscience," they assert a "people's right to know" under "what human rights conditions and at what wages the products [he is] purchasing were made." Sweatshops thrive in production chains, involving contractors and subcontractors, such that "[e]ven the President of the United States could not find out in what factories Wal-Mart's products are made." The proponents of market-based measures urge companies to make public the list of factories producing their goods abroad and to open these factories to respected and independent local monitors.[46]

These devices directly link human rights and trade without the mediation of interstate institutions, and without waiting for collective bodies to embrace certain norms as authoritative and binding. Indeed, no such claim to authority is at all necessary in the open market. The norms are writ not in stone but in the hearts of consumers. Massachusetts was not conducting foreign policy with its Burma law; it was merely "choosing how to spend its own money, just as any private citizen may do," the legal scholar Akhil Reed Amar has noted. "If an ordinary consumer is generally 'sovereign' in the marketplace, why isn't a state consumer likewise sovereign?" The answer, it seems, lies in the motivation for the choice. It is purely commercial if the buyer rejects the product as shoddy, but political (and therefore, a matter of foreign policy) if the buyer rejects it for being "morally tainted." Yet "where does the Constitution say that states are free to be picky and selfish, but not to be altruistic and noble"?[47] Market-based measures need not analogize the state to the consumer; indeed, they assume that consumers voting their pocketbooks are no different from citizens casting their ballots.

The disadvantage of market-based linkage is the sheer proliferation of codes of conduct and social labels, the lack of reliable monitoring and inspection, and its powerlessness vis-à-vis substandard labor practices in nonexport sectors. Significantly, the proposed solutions bring us back to all the strengths of a normative and institutional response: multilateral action, codification of norms, and independent bodies to monitor and issue "goodhousekeeping seals" of approval.

Its real edge over the institutional approach, however, is that it penetrates the opaqueness of the purported will of states. Developing countries' opposition to linkage fixates excessively on the North-South tension and altogether ignores the gap between local elites and masses, including workers. Opponents embrace statist assumptions about the monolithic character of the nation. The "rhetoric of Asian values obscures the fact that Asian ruling classes are in partnership with the ruling classes of the industrialised countries, relationships which are frequently not concluded in the interests of the majority of their citizens."[48] "The rhetoric of nationalism, which works best by obscuring class and gender, is inadequate to explain the complexities of the exploitation of female labor and the expansion of international capital in Southeast Asia," Jacqueline Siapno has observed.[49]

Corporate Codes of Conduct

Corporations have voluntarily developed codes of conduct, statements that set ethical standards for themselves and others with whom they do business, including subcontractors. Individuals and private groups have already drafted such codes, including the 1977 Sullivan Principles (South Africa), the 1984 MacBride Principles (Northern Ireland), the 1987 Slepak Principles (the Soviet Union), and the 1991 Maquiladora Standards of Conduct (Mexico and Central America).[50] These codes typically cover the four core rights described above, chief among which is the prohibition on child labor, but in addition refer as well to "substantive" matters such as claims to minimum wages and payment for overtime work. They are enforced through a variety of monitoring devices, with either internal or external audit groups or, the most potent, NGO monitors.

"Right to Information" and Social Labeling

The counterpart to voluntary codes of conduct is the consumers' campaign for a "right to information," to enable buyers to know where the goods ultimately were manufactured. The operative mechanisms are "social labeling" or "child labor-free labeling" schemes.[51] The pioneering scheme devised in India in 1994 by the Rugmark Foundation, for instance, authorizes manufacturers to use its label if they agree not to employ children under fourteen in rug making, or to use subcontractors who employ children, and if they agree to spot inspections by the foundation. The manufacturer pays .3-.5 percent of the export price for the license, and the importer contributes 1 percent of the export value, the funds to be used for the rehabilitation of child workers. There are also the "child-labor-free labels" on handsewn soccer balls. It was found that 75 percent of the world's supply of handsewn soccer balls (valued at $1 billion in annual retail sales) were produced in one village in Pakistan, Sialkot, where 7,000 children from five to fourteen years of age worked full-time in football stitching. Through ILO supervision, child labor was phased out: production was centralized in registered stitching centers, grants were paid to the children, salaries were provided their teachers, and credit access was extended to the families of the former child workers.[52]

As noted, developed and less-developed countries have long tangled on the question of non-product-related PPM-based trade restrictions that would "open the door to highly coercive measures by powerful trading nations, effectively forcing less powerful nations to adopt particular production policies (including, for example, specific labor policies)."[53] Yet the 1947 GATT rules expressly allow trade restrictions for "natural conservation measures," under Article XX (g), or against products produced with prison labor, under Article XX (e). The objection persists against social labeling, which derives from the social desirability of the labor used to produce the goods,[54] despite the fact that eco-labeling is equally based on value judgments about man's relation to the earth and its resources. On this score, labor rights have a clear advantage: one, a standard-setting organization and clearly established norms (i.e., the ILO and its instruments) exist; two, labor rights help improve actual living standards and can count on the social mediation of "real parties in interest"; and, three, labor rights per se do not directly increase production costs, in contrast to environmental claims and the dangers of "green protectionism."[55]

Voluntary Social Clause Agreements

A prime example of a relatively successful "social clause" experiment, begun in 1987, is between the Swiss supermarket chain Migros and Del Monte pineapple farms in the Philippines. That clause stated: "The supplier hereby guarantees Migros that the production methods for the workers, in terms of social as well as economic conditions, are above average." Migros argued that "prices have to tell the truth and reflect the ecological and social costs incurred in production," otherwise someone else has to pay later," usually the innocent public through the insurance system, the public welfare system, and the international community.[56]

The result was that Philippine pineapples became 15–20 percent more expensive than Thai, Malaysian, or (at that time) South African pineapples (and Thailand exported two and a half times more pineapples than the Philippines). But more significantly, Migros itself had to offer a second, discounted line of pineapples without the favorable "social label" to cater to buyers who did not really care. Happily, Migros reported, shoppers continued to purchase the more expensive "labeled" goods.

CONCLUSION

The social clause debate is filled with irony. A campaign to uphold human dignity begins by equating labor with other commodities and factors of production and by relying on the logic of ensuring a fair market. The counter-campaign—justifying continued depredation by Third World elites—exalts the humanity of the worker, characterizes labor standards as a normative choice rather than a market bargain, and, assigning that choice to the nation-state, embraces the rhetoric of self-determination. The only way, they say, to remove labor standards from the sovereign domain is by invoking "international human rights," a different ballgame altogether. Thus its conceptual cousin that appears to satisfy both camps, "core labor *rights*" that merely "enable" workers to join the market more effectively (e.g., to bargain for better wages and conditions of work), and emphatically not "labor *standards*" that purport to guarantee desired outcomes or cash claims. It is strange that in the context of the trade-labor linkage debate, the language of rights becomes potent only to the extent that rights pertain to process rather than substance.

Moreover, private "social clauses"—from codes of conduct, to the "right to information," to social labeling—rely on the power of the market, and compel corporations to behave through the consumer's power to choose, regardless of whether he or she chose because a product had superior features or was produced by better-paid or freer and happier workers.

In the social clause debate, the usual lines are blurred and the usual places are reversed: between private choice made through the market and public choice made by law, between norms embraced by an international community and those embraced by sovereign nations. The contrast between the institutional and market-based strategies is that, in the first, the moral choice is made by communities and enforced through institutions; in the second, the moral choice is made by individuals oblivious to communal values.

Public choices can be expressed either through laws or through the market, and which we opt for is itself a deliberate moral choice. If public choice is expressed through law, we must distinguish which matters nations can decide for themselves (through national law) and which they must decide as members of the global village (international law). In globalizing norms through international institutions, we guard against the danger of unilateral measures. Yet in "marketizing" norms by empowering the conscienticized consumer, we explode the myth of the monolithic nation and expose the divisions and hierarchies of class, kin, and ethnicity, through which sieve we must filter every claim of a putative national good. In this light, what the trade-labor-linkage debate shows is that the real competitive advantage of sweatshops lies in a national elite's willingness to immiserize its people. That raises ethical questions that people of other nations are both entitled to judge for themselves and to respond to through international law.

NOTES

1. Historically, the normative approach has prevailed in domestic law, and with the emergence of welfare legislation, the terms of employment *cannot* in domestic law be seen as purely a contractual bargain between the employer and employee.

2. International Covenant on Economic, Social and Cultural Rights (hereinafter, the ICESCR), United Nations Treaty Series No. 14531, vol. 993 (1976), p. 3 . Under Article 6.1, "The States Parties to the present Covenant recognize the right to work, which includes the right of everyone to the opportunity to gain his living by work which he freely chooses or accepts, and will take appropriate steps to safeguard this right." Article 7 recognizes "the right of everyone to the enjoyment of just and favourable conditions of work, which ensure, in particular: (a) remuneration which provides all workers, as a minimum, with: (i) fair wages and equal remuneration for work of equal value without distinction of any kind, in particular women being guaranteed conditions of work not inferior to those enjoyed by men, with equal pay for equal work; (ii) a decent living for themselves and their families in accordance with the provisions of the present Covenant." Article 8.1 guarantees "the right of everyone to form trade unions and join the trade union of his choice." This is similarly guaranteed in the International Covenant on Civil and Political Rights, United Nations Treaty Series No. 14668, vol. 999 (1976), p. 171, Article 22. ILO Convention No. 98, Right to Organize and to Bargain Collectively (1 July 1949), guarantees the right to bargain collectively, and ICESCR, Article 8.1.d. guarantees the right to strike.

3. Haworth and Hughes 1998 (<socrates.berkeley.edu/~iir/clre/programs/death.html>).

4. National Labor Committee 1998.

5. Haworth and Hughes 1998.

6. IUED/EADI 1998; Hanami 1997. See also "ILO Governing Body to Establish Working Party on Trade and Labor," 11 *International Trade Review* 26, d13 (29 June 1994).

7. Tunsarawuth 1996.

8. Woodward 1996.

9. Bin Mohammed 1994: 176. These debates can be followed at http://www.wto.org, "Trade and Labor Standards: Subject of Intense Debate."

10. International Labor Rights Fund 1998: 3.

11. Watkins 1997.

12. Haworth and Hughes 1998, citing G. Fields 1996.

13. Eliott 1998, 2.

14. D'Andrea 1997.

15. Elliott 1998.

16. Burtless and Litan 1998: 24–25.

17. Taylor 998; Elliott 1998: 2.

18. IUED/EADI 1998.

19. 1999 Presidential Documents Online via GPO Access [frwais.access.gpo.gov] (DOCID:pdo6de99_txt-25).

20. WTO Ministerial Declaration [hereinafter, Singapore Declaration], WT/MIN(96)/DEC/W (13 December 1996), at para. 4.

21. ILO Declaration on Fundamental Principles and Rights at Work [hereinafter, the ILO Fundamental Rights Declaration], ILO Conference, 86th sess. <http://www.ilo.org/public/english/standards/relm/ilc/ilc86/com-dtxt.htm>; Follow-up action on the ILO Declaration on Fundamental Principles and Rights at Work and its Follow-up, GB.274/2 (Add. 1), 274th sess., Geneva, March 1999.

22. Swepston 1998, ILO Fundamental Rights Declaration, Preamble.

23. ASEAN Jakarta meeting, 26 July 1996; IUED/EADI 1998; Hanami 1997. See also "ILO Governing Body to Establish Working Party on Trade and Labor" (cited n. 6 above).

24. Singapore Declaration, para. 4.

25. Leary 1997.

26. Herman van Beek, "The Importance of Social and Governmental Clausing for a Sustainable Banana Industry," http://www.banafair.de/kamp/aktivitaten/rbc/5.htm.

27. Leary 1997; Haworth and Hughes 1998.

28. Coxson 1999: 504, 471.

29. Langille 1997: 15.

30. ILO Convention No. 87, Freedom of Association and Protection of the Right to Organize (1948); ILO Convention No. 98, Right to Organize and Collective Bargaining Convention (1949); ILO Convention No. 29, Forced Labor Convention (1930); ILO Convention No. 105, Abolition of Forced Labor (1957); ILO Convention No. 138, Minimum Age Convention (1973); ILO Convention No. 100, Equal Remuneration (1951); ILO Convention No. 111, Discrimination (Employment and Occupation) (1958).

31. Elliott 1998: 4.

32. Watkins 1997.

33. An Act Regulating State Contracts with Companies Doing Business with or in Burma (Myanmar), 1996 Mass. Acts 239, ch. 130 (codified at Mass. Gen. Laws §§7: 22G-7: 22M, 40 F½ (1997). The U.S. Supreme Court struck down the Massachusetts "Burma law" as interfering with the federal power over foreign affairs under the Supremacy Clause, and as having been preempted by subsequent congressional sanctions on Burma/Myanmar. In September 1996, the U.S. Congress passed a statute imposing sanctions on Burma (Myanmar); it banned all foreign, instructed U.S. representatives in international financial institutions to vote against loans to Burma, and authorized the U.S. president to ban "new investment" in Burma if it commits further human rights violations." Foreign Operations, Export Financing, and Related Programs Appropriations Act, 1997, §570, 110 Stat. 3009–121 to 3009–172. On 20 May 1997, President Clinton issued Executive Order No. 13047, 3 CFR 202 (1997 Comp.), certifying that Burma had "committed large-scale repression of the democratic opposition in Burma" and prohibiting new investment in that country.

34. *Crosby v. National Foreign Trade Council* (99–474), 181 F. 3d 38, affirmed (19 June 2000).

35. Executive Order 13126 (12 June 1999) (1999 Presidential Documents Online via GPO Access [frwais.access.gpo.gov] (DOCID:pd21jn99_txt-10).

36. WTO Appellate Body, United States–Import Prohibition of Certain Shrimp and Shrimp Products (12 October 1998), 38 I.L.M. 11 (1999).

37. "Trade and Labor Standards: Subject of Intense Debate," available at http://www.wto.org/wto/minist1/18lab_3.htm

38. R. Castle et al. 1996 (socrates.berkeley.edu/~iir/clre/programs/ilao.html).

39. Ibid.

40. IUED/EADI 1998

41. Watkins 1997.

42. Ibid.

43. Dubey, "Social Clause: The Motive Behind the Method" (Alternative Information and Development Center at aidc.org.za/archives/sc_2.html).

44. Haworth and Hughes 1998, citing J. Bhagwati, "Policy Perspectives and Future Directions: A View from Academia" (1994).

45. Taylor, "ILO Chief Comes under Fire: Developing Countries Attack Move to Link Labour Standards to Trade," *Financial Times* (London), 12 June 1997, p. 6.

46. Representative from Egypt, IUED/EADI 1998; National Labor Committee 1998.

47. Amar 2000.

48. Haworth and Hughes 1998.

49. Jacqueline Siapno, Irvine, Calif., letter to the editor, *New York Times,* 21 March 1995, on Philippine indignation over the execution of a Filipino migrant worker in Singapore.

50. U.S. Bureau of International Labor Affairs 1996: 13.

51. D'Andrea 1997.

52. "The Sialkot Story: Making Villages 'Child Labour Free,'" *World of Work,* no. 19 (1997): 14.

53. Perkins 1999.

54. D'Andrea 1997.

55. Van Beek.

56. Stuckelberger and Egger 1996: 6.

III
Communication

6

The Ironies
of Information Technology

Shayne Weyker

There is a small but extremely interesting literature on the role of new information technologies in advancing such values as human rights, democratization, and economic justice, but it has been somewhat lacking in the generalization of particular examples to larger trends.[1] This essay attempts to fill that gap, explaining why and how advances in information technology empower the human rights movement and the various ways in which the promise of technology may be neutralized or turned against human rights workers. The opportunities and pitfalls of technology are discussed below in terms of their effects on human rights organizations as self-organizing (cybernetic) entities that constantly seek both to (re)organize themselves and to receive and transmit information for the purpose of reacting to and modifying their environments.[2]

WHY DOES INFORMATION TECHNOLOGY MATTER?

The short answer is that it matters because information lies at the heart of what nongovernmental organizations (hereafter NGOs) do. If technological advances allow them to do these things better, the movements and organizations become more capable and thus, all else being equal, more effective and powerful. For other technological advances that hinder their ability to do their job or provide a relatively greater advantage to their opponents, the opposite would be true. Back in 1982, a few years before camcorders, faxes, desktop computers, and the Internet became part of many people's lives, Peter Willetts, a scholar who studied NGO's, wrote:

> [NGO] personnel, particularly at the leadership level, become professionals
> in the use of information. Generally, . . . [groups promoting a position] have

very limited financial resources . . . [or] ability to apply physical coercion [even terrorist violence is political rather than military in nature]. . . . The ability of NGOs to apply pressure is through the mobilization of legitimacy for their cause. Winning support by changing people's perception of the issues is done by presenting arguments and information . . . [NGOs] must find and transmit relevant information and once such propositions are established [as true in the minds of target audiences] they have to continue to provide information which reinforces propositions. . . . Processing of information is always a major activity of pressure groups and often it is overwhelmingly the most important activity.[3]

But, Willetts notes, this information must be perceived as invariably objective and truthful, or it will be ignored. This is because social movements lack the reputation that states do for having accurate and complete information. Moreover, they lack the coercive and legal power of states. Thus, movements' pronouncements do not carry weight simply because of who makes them. "In this unequal contest pressure groups cannot afford to make mistakes because thereafter their statements will not so readily be given credibility and references to mistakes will be continually thrown back at them," Willetts goes on. "After some time many pressure groups do get accepted as trustworthy . . . this can give them privileged access to governments [tremendously increasing the group's influence, but only as long as the trust is maintained]."[4] Well-researched, professionally presented, truthful and factual information, turned out quickly enough to be passed on to the right people at the right time, is therefore what gets results for social movements. Such movements depend on quickly and accurately doing five things: (1) collecting information from the environment; (2) processing that information; (3) making internal changes based on the acquired information where helpful; (4) preventing harmful internal changes; and (5) sending information back out to (certain people in) the environment that will cause changes in it. These things in turn imply the need for capabilities such as foresight, preventing "oversteering" (overreacting), minimizing lag times, minimizing noise that obscures the information/signal the group wants to send, and expanding the size of the audience that can be reached by the group's message.

Alison Brysk offers an updated view of what social movements do and how they do it, particularly in regards to Latin America, writing: "The state can be transformed from above and below because it may control territory, force, and resources, but it cannot monopolize information and legitimacy . . . [social movements gain power] by projecting cognitive and affective information to form international alliances."[5] Note the distinction Brysk makes between cognitive information and affective information (which are defined below). Participants in movements try to influence those in power by tapping into the potential power of bystander reference groups in other countries to achieve several benefits to their cause. These involve the reference group in supporting the movement by assisting in information gathering, processing, and distribution; applying pressure to the government the movement operates under via direct means, making the environment for the organization more hospitable and amplifying messages sent by the organization to particular persons with power); or applying indirect pressure by lobbying their own government to apply such pressure. Brysk believes that the Argentine human rights movement, for example, and many others like it:

1. Exhibit an informal division of labor between producing (a) "political theater" (affective information that elicits an emotional response) to raise public awareness and (b) "documentation" (cognitive information that gives an understanding of the extent, details, and mechanics of the problem) needed for international policy decisions[6]
2. "[A]chieve their impact through persuasion—the use of information to change behavior and institutions through changing perceptions and values"
3. "[U]se and contest factual information to reach international publics and challenge (domestic and international) institutions"
4. "[P]roject patterned symbolic information as images that mobilize legitimacy for the movement"
5. Are helped if there is "recognized a legitimate international concern by international laws, treaties, and organizations that provide a point of entry to transnational alliances" against which the conception of sovereignty is not considered applicable[7]

Before going on to discuss examples of how information technology can be helpful, it is useful to quickly consider the idea that in some ways information technology is fundamentally ambiguous, perhaps even conflicted, in its relationship to the work of human rights organizations. As James Rosenau says, "Throughout the world today . . . the sources of authority have shifted from traditional to performance criteria of legitimacy. As a result, structures of authority have entered a period [of] crisis, with the readiness of individuals to comply with governing directives being very much a function of their assessment of the performance of the authorities [at meeting goals, satisfying needs, and providing stability]."[8] Put another way, governments find themselves faced with the problems of:

1. Noise and hostile messages feeding back upon themselves and undermining the government's ability to communicate messages that build legitimacy (a friendly environment) for itself

2. The government having to act and produce results faster than before (leading to greater risk of oversteering, insufficient foresight to act in time, and acting without a coherent plan)
3. A trend toward (what to the government's leaders is) an undesirable internal reorganization of society

Rosenau writes about how this empowers sub- and supranational actors as people decide that such actors can perform better for them, leading—presumably—to people shifting their allegiances.[9] But there is also the possibility that the more demanding and more analytically competent constituencies may be more difficult to keep organized and moving toward a common goal, when times are hard and progress is painfully slow—despite the obvious importance of unity. That states suffer from this legitimacy crisis is the very reason NGOs can build the support they do. But NGOs may have to face this problem as well. Information technology can provide increased speed, as time required for gathering, processing, and distributing information is cut. But the speed "arms race" complicates all organizations' efforts to avoid overreacting and making other kinds of errors, while acting fast enough to stay ahead of what rivals are doing. More contradictions like these will appear as the same technologies, and sometimes even the very same effects created by their use, appear as both beneficial and dangerous to human rights NGOs.[10]

TECHNOLOGY TO THE RESCUE

The first of the real strengths for information technology use by human rights organizations is that computers improve the ability to marshal the facts (cognitive information) on their side into a very persuasive logical argument. Information technology speeds up, enlarges the scale, and improves the quality of information collection and processing by human rights organizations.

Dan Salcedo, then Human Rights Coordinator for the American Association for the Advancement of Science, recounted an interesting example of this from El Salvador, where human rights groups associated with the Truth Commission were trying to find out who was responsible for human rights violations by the government, so that these people could be removed from power. The human rights groups were able to acquire two separate sets of data, which separately are of little use for that purpose. One, a "military map," showed which military officers were in command in which regions of the country at which times. The other was a long list of confirmed human rights abuses that included, of course, when and where the abuses took place. Both of these sets of data were combined in a computer database and the computer was then asked questions such as: "Which officers, of those still in service, have accumulated the greatest number of human rights abuses in their jurisdiction while they were first or second in command?" This produced a list of officers who were then removed from the military based on this highly credible evidence that they either ordered abuses or allowed abuses to occur by their subordinates on a continuing basis.[11]

The next generation of such projects by human rights groups will likely involve the use of geographic information systems (GIS), geographic databases that link data to elements of a computer-generated map. This produces information-rich, easily redefined maps that can let a person viewing the map quickly and easily see where the greatest intensity of abuse is taking place based on hard data rather than have to wade through many charts and tables or trust someone else's general conclusions. This would reduce the lag time and noise associated with policymakers trying to understand and verify the full extent of the claims made by human rights advocates. It is also worth noting here that the United States's new willingness (seen in Kosovo) to use its high-resolution satellite reconnaissance capability to expose recently dug mass graves could be useful in quickly resolving disputes among countries about whether or not there are massacres of civilians taking place.[12] While having solid objective (cognitive) information does not guarantee that policies more favorable to the protection of human rights will be enacted, it is very likely to be helpful.[13]

The other main type of opportunity technology offers human rights lies in telecommunications and computer networking technology, particularly the advent of the globe-spanning Internet. These allow the creation of massive "network organizations" made up of hundreds of small organizations pooling their information and possibly their labor. This can greatly multiply each participant's access to information and ability to coordinate. Even better, people can do so without having to actually combine to form one single huge organization, with all the sacrifices that implies. A classic example of such information sharing and coordination was the Zapatistas' effort to win a public hearing of their grievances during their uprising in Mexico. This advent of this kind of network organization has several important effects.

First, the availability of new communications technology offers a better capability to draw other people into a human rights group's organizing efforts. New communications technology also allow activists to share their own experiences, information, tactics, and so on as easily as if they lived in the same country.[14] Consider the following example from the Mexican labor advocacy group Mujer a Mujer: "For our first six years [1984–1990] we depended on 'border trips': every two months, two of our members would travel 24 hours by bus to a friend's house on the U.S. side of the border, where we would take turns in a marathon of long distance calls—to organize events and keep in touch with key contacts. Now [thanks to computer networking] we are in daily coordination with our key contacts throughout the region."[15]

Second, news of crises can be spread instantly to unlimited numbers of interested people who want to help. A huge surge of moral (affective) or technical (cognitive) support for those calling for help, as well as condemnation of their enemies, creates opportunities for a global on-line cathexis (spontaneous collective action). An example of cathexis (or at least an extremely fast organized response) occurred when the Chinese government ran pictures of democracy protesters on TV and asked for tips on their location so they could be arrested. Thousands of bogus phone calls immediately flooded in from across the globe to overwhelm the government's information-gathering effort with noise. Another, somewhat more structured response, in response to a severe attack by neo-Nazis on foreigners in a German city, was sending thousands of faxes denouncing the attack to that city's local newspaper in less than twenty-four hours.[16]

The Internet also shifts activists' access to media, as seen in the Zapatistas' case. Reactions to articles written about the conflict on the Internet appeared with little or no delay and without the filtering of editorial page editors deciding which letters would see print and which would not. Beyond this, interacting through the Internet allowed activists to see their own protests against the Mexican government's actions as part of a larger movement, because they were able to read others' eyewitness accounts of protest actions. Also, on the Internet, reporters from small newspapers and activist groups received just as much attention as reporters from major newspapers. This strengthening of opposition voices relative to establishment ones was important. Reading other like-minded people's analysis and debate provided readers with a sense of collective concern necessary for taking committed forms of action.[17]

Their resilience and accessibility, combined with the frequent underestimation of their importance by governments, have made such networks tools for undermining government censorship. Thus the state's power of coercion to shut down NGOs' attacks on the government's legitimacy can be neutralized with the right combination of tools, skills, and courage.[18] For example, the Zapatistas evaded censorship by the Mexican government despite its control over the mass media in that country. Individuals sent reports out to usenet newsgroups, PeaceNet conferences, Internet mailing lists, and potentially sympathetic groups of people. Frequently, messages were forwarded by recipients. Forwarders would sometimes include translations from Spanish into other languages as well.[19]

To summarize, computers have helped human rights NGOs create impressive new kinds of hard (cognitive) information. Camcorders put the power to create powerful affective symbolic imagery into the hands of anyone with something symbolic to record, such as the famous image of a Chinese man blocking a column of tanks. Computer and fax communications networks allow for the creation of dialogue and planning of joint strategy across long distances at low cost. Those same technologies allow movements operating under hostile governments the ability to contact and mobilize a large number of people fairly quickly. Electronic communication networks also allow direct application of public opinion pressure by those tied into the network without regard for geography.

The opportunities of technology for human rights groups are only half the story, however. We now move on to a consideration of the dangers posed by technology.

THE PITFALLS OF A WIRED WORLD
FOR PROGRESSIVE SOCIAL MOVEMENTS

Several problems are discussed below that have to be avoided in a world of extensive communications and information processing if the promise information technology holds for human rights is going to be realized rather than neutralized or subverted.

The Proliferation of Voices and the Problem of "Noise"

One particularly relevant feature of social movements is their susceptibility to being harmed by "subgroupism," or internal division.[20] This is characterized by a lack of consensus on what the proper objectives are and what means should be used to achieve the group's ends. While groups must be sufficiently democratic that the membership feels they have a fair share of control, such a lack of cooperation can prevent the sufficiently quick and accurate execution of some or all the five key informational tasks an organization must carry out to be effective. "The lack of a strong bureaucratic structure for most groups and the fact that they are voluntary associations means that there is no central authority," Willetts notes. "There will usually be some central decision-making body, but it has little ability to enforce decisions. So the leadership . . . has to try and maintain a consensus within the group. Breakdown in the consensus can be more damaging to [groups promoting a cause] . . . than to other groups [(companies, unions, governments)] . . . which have economic interests to help hold them together."[21]

The enabling of more "ground-level" members of the human rights movement in the countries where rights violations are occurring to communicate directly and instantly with the outside world without working through the movement's hierarchy can potentially damage the human rights organizations' precious credibility. These "ground-level" people could speak using an international NGO's name to the media or reference public and unknowingly make false statements because they failed to do the necessary verification. Even if these people are correct, there may be a zero-sum game involved between the rank and file and the organization's headquarters for the attention of the reference group and journalists.

Steve Breyman argues that decentralizing authority in NGOs would be a good thing.[22] But advocates of centralization would argue that losing the filtering mechanism that comes with concentration of the power to release information to the world may create counterproductive "noise" in the organization's information channel to its reference public and the media. This could take the form of different statements contradicting one another, a glut of calls for action, unpredictable spacing in time of calls for action, and so on. Too many calls for action may alienate the press and demoralize reference group members. And conflicting statements may damage the group's credibility.

Organizational discipline and strong legitimacy of leaders and professional staff with those in the field might resolve the noise problem. But strong discipline and popular leadership are not always an easy combination, especially for a volunteer organization people can opt out of. As Willetts observes, volunteer organizations in which there is no economic self-interest for members to stick together and compromise are highly vulnerable to dissent and division.

The proliferation of information technology may intensify an already existing tension, between those in a movement who want rapid response and maximal results on the current case against those (usually higher up in the organization) who are more interested in protecting the movement's long-term capabilities. Amnesty International USA (hereafter referred to as AI) distributes a newsletter called *Freedom Writers*, which contains sample letters that readers can draw upon to write their own letters on behalf of people whose rights are being violated. Several years ago, a woman named Caryn Graves began to distribute the newsletter in electronic form, typing them in to her computer and posting them to a the soc.rights.human usenet newsgroup, read by thousands of people, including some critics of the human rights movement.

AI asked Ms. Graves to stop doing this. They were concerned about such a broad distribution of their message in an electronic text form, because electronic text is too easy and inexpensive to modify and redistribute. Eventually, people might begin receiving forwarded copies of these messages with non-Amnesty material added in by the forwarding person, but with Amnesty's name still in the message. It would even be possible to create a fake issue of the *Freedom Writers* newsletter that would seem genuine to the casual reader. Since malicious messages with false claims of AI authorship had appeared on the Internet before, AI felt that the instruction included in the newsletter to not modify it or redistribute it electronically would not be adequate protection against the above two dangers. Nor is this problem unique to AI. At least one individual human rights advocate once found some "bizarre and damaging" articles falsely posted under his name on the Internet.[23] And Human Rights Watch has had faxes falsely sent out under its name in India.[24] To this day, *Freedom Writers* is only distributed by e-mail mailing list and via the AIUSA web page at http://www.amnestyusa.org/group/aicasework/fw.html.[25]

Subsequently, Ms. Graves had begun to distribute *Freedom Writers* via an e-mail mailing list with AI's approval. Internet users can subscribe to such a list and have the newsletters sent directly to them via e-mail. This e-mail mailing list was unmoderated, meaning anyone could send messages that all subscribers would receive. On 30 March 1998, someone other than Ms. Graves posted a message to the *Freedom Writers* mailing list, a message that seems to have originally been written by a group called the Asian Students Association. The message was a call for action regarding someone named Andi Arief, who had been kidnapped at gunpoint. In the message, readers are told about him and some others and asked to petition the Indonesian government for his and the others' release. This message was not created or approved by AI. So readers had no way of knowing whether Arief or the others would qualify as prisoners of conscience, and whether the circumstances of Arief's capture had been verified to the extent that AI verifies such things before making calls for action.

This problem of "noise" when more people gain access to the channels of communication, which are used to speak to a human rights group's supporters, may have its origin in a related problem. Informational bottlenecks can occur in the human rights organization, making the increased information-processing capability gained in other areas useless until the bottleneck in a particular problem area is cleared. In the area of human rights for instance, there are (even for the largest organizations, with significant human resources around the world) many more cases of rights abuse being reported by the movement's rank and file than can be verified and then given sufficient publicity and international attention.[26]

Patrick Ball and his co-authors suggest why there have not been more such attempts, when the above theory suggests more should occur. Many human rights groups operating in oppressive countries make it their business to carefully document and analyze patterns in rights violations, so as to preserve the truth and identify abusers for the record, rather than try to bring individual rights violations to the world's attention. For these groups, to publicize rights violations and conduct international calls for action would have two negative effects: it would distract the groups from their original mandate, and aggravate the danger of reprisal to their members. So such groups leave it up to others like Amnesty and Human Rights Watch to do such things.[27]

Clifford Bob's chapter offers another reason for why there is less of this problem, with front-line and top-level human rights workers competing for the public's attention, than expected. He suggests that a group seeking international support is better able to do so to the extent that it possesses certain qualities: the ability to present its case abroad; knowledge of the developed world; skill in a major world language; preexisting contacts with people in the press; and universal rather than parochial goals. Given this list, it should be easy to see why reporters for major newspapers and television networks in the developed world would be more inclined to act upon information given them by international NGOs than individuals or local groups. International NGOs professional staff have all of the above qualities, while oppressed groups in developing countries will typically only have some of them.

There is mixed evidence on the extent to which the proliferation of voices and the concomitant problem of noise present a danger to human rights organizations. But such organizations should be aware of the problem and design their communication strategy to overcome it.

UNFAVORABLE ENVIRONMENTS FOR USING
TECHNOLOGY TO AID HUMAN RIGHTS WORK

The complementary social organization (infrastructure) required to effectively exploit the new information that becomes available with the spread of technology is sometimes lacking.[28] Ronnie Lipschutz notes that besides the technology, it is just as important to have, at least for people who want change, "new ways of doing things, of acting, of engaging in political and other activities." If the information produced lacks context (and is thus misleading/confusing), or is shaped by market forces, or is susceptible to the political agendas of media-owning capitalists, or is overly influenced by government "news management," then its utility for progressive political purposes is reduced.[29]

Lipschutz's criticism seems to be most valuable for reevaluating those communication technologies that must ultimately depend on the commercial mass media for their full effect. Heavily organized large demonstrations that are not covered by the press would be a stereotypical example of this. To what extent the human rights movement's efforts will continue to depend on the cooperation of commercial mass media may be an open question, however.

Moving to the global level again, it is interesting how Lipschutz's criticism confirms Brysk's observation that having a structural "point of entry" into the international regime of international law and standards of behavior is very important to a movement's effectiveness. If the international legal and media opinion "context" both in terms of reaching foreign publics and foreign elites is unfavorable to the movement's cause (lacks a "point of entry"), then NGOs' persuasive efforts will encounter more difficulty.[30]

Additionally, at the domestic level, there has to be a "point of entry" as well. People have to some extent to be psychologically ready to hear the message. Oscar Landi notes that there was an intense cynicism and tendency of the people to disbelieve the post-dictatorship Argentine press when new discoveries of the old regime's outrages were publicized for the first time.[31] This was because of the media's reputation for lying to aid the government in power and truth-obscuring sensationalism. To give a contrasting example, David Ronfeldt points out that long before the Zapatistas' uprising in Chiapas, there were both relatively more than average international contacts (with Central American guerillas, arms dealers, and drug smugglers) and more regular contacts between NGOs and the people there. That, he says is one important reason why the uprising started there and not in Guererro or Oaxaca.[32]

Second, there is another kind of domestic infrastructure, a legal one. Sheldon Annis notes that in 1992, the military in northern Guatemala was hostile to the proliferation of two-way shortwave (ham) radios and controlled their possession tightly.[33] In general, governments involved in a serious ongoing internal conflict that come to believe that the spread of a given technology (including things such as two-way radios, cryptography, and satellite maps of the country's territory) helps their enemies may tightly control and regulate that technology. Technologies the government believes are vital to economic growth might be an exception. But sometimes a government fearful of the free flow of information purposefully tries to hinder the free flow of information, even when that information is used for peaceful means.

One way of purposefully hindering the flow of information is to imprison the people who contribute to it. An example of this can be seen in the Chinese government's giving a two-year prison sentence to someone accused of selling a list of 30,000 e-mail addresses in China to a dissident Internet news service, VIP Reference News (also known as Dacankao), which reprints articles about China from major publications not available to most Chinese and e-mails them out to Chinese residents. More recently, the Chinese government arrested a citizen with dissident contacts in Hong Kong who was preparing to publish a political book on the Internet. He was charged under a law prohibiting communication with foreigners.[34]

Human rights organizations looking to use technology need to do three things here. First, avoid communicating on a channel audiences distrust. Second, plan around the presence or lack of extensive face-to-face contacts between the organization and the local people. Finally, plan around any laws that prohibit full and open use of communication technology.

New Vulnerability to Sabotage and Surveillance

A reliance on sophisticated communication technologies such as e-mail networks and the telephone/fax creates the risk of government wiretappers intercepting sensitive conversations, e-mail, and data that can reveal identities of members and group plans on a continuing basis.[35] The same databases that make it possible to carefully document patterns of human rights violations are themselves vulnerable to being copied by the authorities without the human rights organization knowing about it.[36] The advent of worldwide availability of very powerful and free encryption software (pretty good privacy, or PGP) to help prevent the interception of e-mail and other data reduces this threat, but does not eliminate it.[37] It is worth noting however that PGP is used far more often to protect stored data than to protect e-mail conversations. Because of exhaustion with resisting constant government surveillance and their low level of computer skill, many human rights workers in developing countries resist consistently carrying out the necessary extra work to use PGP with e-mail.[38] Some human rights workers who are uncomfortable with the added work of PGP are turning to the easier to use web-based encrypted e-mail service HushMail that automates the encryption and decryption process more effectively.[39] HushMail does require a relatively stable connection to the Internet, however, something not all human rights organizations in developing countries have. Also, according to Carl Ellison, a security expert, web-based encryption systems are vulnerable to being compromised by attacks where the user's connection to HushMail is redirected to a different web site on the Internet, owned by the authorities, that impersonates hushmail.com and lets the user type in his or her message. Ellison believes this is just one of a new wave of threats to private communication based on electronic impersonation. Now that it has gotten so hard, with strong encryption being used, to eavesdrop on the communication of others, it is simpler to pretend to be the intended recipient of the message.[40]

However, the safety of witnesses to rights violations who are identified in PGP-encrypted documents often depends, not on secure email, but on the security of the encrypted document file identifying witnesses and the key to decoding it staying out of the wrong hands. In one recent case, a human rights observer was arrested by the government in Kinshasa with the names of witnesses encrypted in a file on his computer. Fortunately, he resisted coercion to give up access to his secret code key until his release could be obtained. Another such researcher with encrypted data on witnesses in Kosovo had his computer confiscated from him.[41] Several other layers of security can be and are used to control access to such sensitive information, however.[42] In any event, as one human rights worker points out, sensitive human rights information about witnesses or the organization's tactical plans do not really have to remain secret very long. The secrets need only stay secret until the organization releases its report after witnesses have testified (or prepared against reprisals), or until the NGO holds its planned demonstration.[43]

Separate from the issues of interception, there is also the possibility of government sabotage of computers and phone lines. This was considered a real enough threat by the democracy movement doing vote counting in Chile in 1988 that it felt the need to have a redundant fax-based vote-reporting system simultaneously with a much more efficient (but vulnerable to sabotage) computer-based one.[44] Amnesty International recently had problems with the Tunisian government not only intercepting but also interfering with the delivery of the local section's e-mail.[45]

Another way governments can attempt to sabotage human rights groups ability to distribute or receive information is by blocking its own residents' access to web pages on the Internet containing content the government disapproves of. This is currently done in places like China where the government controls the high-capacity connections (called backbones) that most data must pass through to get into or out of the country. But while site blocking may stop the casual web surfer, people who really want to find such information will locate what are called proxy web servers, which provide the content of blocked web pages on an unblocked web page, thus bypassing the block. When access to a proxy server is blocked, usually after about two months of operation, a new one is quickly opened. So web page blocking is a rather labor-intensive and inefficient way of restricting access to information within a country's borders. Blocking certain locations on the Internet also does nothing to stop the e-mail distribution of news from sources that change the address they send from daily, as VIP Reference News does.[46]

The kinds of threats described above may eventually be reduced as networks begin to grow and gain the resiliency that comes with having many nodes and lots of communication pathways, so sabotaging those pathways of electronic communication is impractical. It is important to note, however, that many groups in poor countries depend on a very few people to send and receive messages through the Internet for them.[47] China's imprisonment of people facilitating the evasion of censorship suggests that people with Internet access and contacts with oppressed groups may become the next target of governments seeking to disrupt such groups' communication with the outside world.

Another form of sabotage can be used when a group wants to provide a forum on the Internet to let anyone speak, such as a petition or discussion hosted on a web page. The Chinese dissident Wang Dan hosts a petition on his web site calling for the Chinese government to change the official story on what happened during the protests at Tienanmen Square. Soon after he started the petition, his site was flooded with "obscene messages and insults" for all to read. It is not known whether employees of the Chinese government were involved in this campaign of electronic heckling, but it is entirely possible. Such heckling attacks on an open forum could be used to drown out the exchange of information among those interested in human rights with the "noise" of obscenities and insults and the retaliatory remarks they are likely to provoke. It is possible to address this problem by taking editorial power over what people are permitted to say in such a forum, but doing so is extra work and may run counter to the principles of those deeply dedicated to freedom of speech.[48]

Governments troubled by the work of human rights groups frequently have the means and the motive to carry out the kinds of actions described. So surveillance and sabotage could become more frequent as governments become more aware of the power of coordinated action by activist groups. Noting the success of the Zapatistas in restricting the freedom of the Mexican military to use force, the U.S. Army has conducted exercises aimed at stopping an NGO seeking to use coordinated protests and civil disobedience to prevent or delay the United States entering into a war.[49] There should be public discussion of what constitute reasonable ways of resisting pressure from activists and which ways undermine the principle of democratic decision making.

CONCLUSION

The opportunities and pitfalls of new information and communication technology for human rights NGOs are listed in table 6.1. Given the complexity of the issues discussed in this essay, it would unwise to try and predict whether these new technologies will, on balance, turn out to be a good or a bad thing for progressive social movements. If human rights groups continually fail to take steps to address the pitfalls described above, the human rights groups' prospects look considerably less rosy than some of the more optimistic scholars believe. Movements could find their ability to communicate effectively with the public hindered because there are too many spokespeople, and possibly also because of government disinformation campaigns. They could find themselves even more open to government spying into their activities. Many movements could find it legally or economically impractical to make full use of the technologies discussed here.

On the other hand, if human rights groups manage to take full advantage of the opportunities technology offers, the human rights movement will achieve more than it has in the past. Global attention will focus on humanitarian crises more quickly, longer, and with more force than in the past, no matter how physically remote those crises are from the developed world. Human rights groups will be able to coordinate strategy globally and share moral and technical support as never before. Individual and institutional perpetrators of human rights violations everywhere will find it more difficult every year to successfully deny responsibility for their deeds.

The reality will probably be some combination of the above. It seems that many NGOs are aware of the opportunities and are beginning to exploit them. The question then becomes: how well will NGOs prepare to avoid the pitfalls and how hard will their enemies work to exploit those pitfalls. The work of this essay is far from complete. There needs to be an effort to apply knowledge of these opportunities and pitfalls to a range of cases of social movements, without the selection effect of just examining cases where use

TABLE 6.1 Opportunities and Pitfalls
of New Technology for Human Rights NGOs

Opportunities	*Pitfalls*
Enhances the ability of human rights NGOs to marshal the facts to make a powerful case that rights violations are occurring and the perpetrators are known.	The proliferation of voices demanding attention for their human rights concerns might lead to a problem of too much noise interfering with effective action.
Enhances the ability of NGOs to draw other people into the group's organizing efforts and create connections through which to collaborate.	Some places are legally, socially, or economically unfavorable for the application of technology to human rights work.
Enhances the ability for NGOs to publicize events and attract global attention.	New technologies for communication and the processing of information create new vulnerabilities to surveillance and sabotage.

of technology has been fairly important or interesting. If enough such case studies are done, we would be on the way to developing a useful theory of information and communication technology's role in human rights work in a global context.

NOTES

1. See, e.g., Afonso 1990; Annis 1991; id. 1992: 591–92; Frederick 1992; Ganley 1992; Ganley and Ganley 1987; Livernash et al. 1993: 228–29, 231; "TV, VCRs Fan Fire of Revolution," *Los Angeles Times,* 18 January 1990; Don Steinberg 1988, 13; Tweedale 1988. Information technology includes everything that serves the function of creating, acquiring, searching, editing, distributing, or sharing information in whatever form it may take, including audio, video, text, computer programs, or any combination thereof. The newer information technologies discussed in this essay fall roughly into three categories; computer technology, telecommunications technology, and media technology. Computer technology (aside from computers themselves and peripherals made for use with them) includes databases, spreadsheets, geographic databases (GIS), word-processing, as well as networking together of people so that they may share data easily. Telecommunication technology is involved with making communication (and, implicitly, computer networking) at long distances quick, convenient, and affordable. Telecommunication technology includes telephone systems, fax machines, two-way radio, the Internet, and communication satellites and satellite dishes. Relevant media technology includes VCRs, camcorders, affordable video editing/production equipment, low wattage radio stations, and desktop or web publishing. Such technologies allow for the quick, cheap, and effective representation of ideas or events.

2. Deutsch 1966 was deeply influential in my conception of social movements as self-organizing informational entities, as were parts of Mulgan 1991.

3. Willetts 1982: 186–87, quoted in Brysk 1993, 264.

4. Willetts 1982 quoted in Brysk 1993.

5. Brysk 1993, 261.

6. This seems to agree with what Dieter Rucht (1993: 90, quoted in Rodger A. Payne, "Sustainable Development and Transnational Resource Mobilization" [MS, 1994], 17), has to say about environmental politics—namely, that expertise (linked to having high-quality cognitive information) is displacing moral authority (linked to having high-quality affective information) as the driving force behind policy. For an interesting alternative fourfold division of information types into media symbolism, science, (global) socioeconomic context, and (details of the) struggle, see Breyman 1993: 140.

7. Brysk 1993: 263–65; emphasis added. In the human rights case, sovereignty is thought not to be a defense, since sovereignty is itself contingent on the state being the people's defender rather than oppressor. The monopoly of force within a state's borders is limited to legitimate force (ibid., 265).

8. Rosenau 1993, 266.

9. Ibid.

10. For instance, "dataveillence" and camcorder surveillance are used both by NGOs against governments and by governments against NGOs.

11. El Rescate, "The Index to Accountability Project" (mimeo, n.d.). Dan Salcedo, interview by author, Washington, D.C., 22 December 1994. This project is also described in Ball et al. 1997: 841.

12. U.S. Department of State, Daily Press Briefing, DBP #70, 28 May 1999 (http://secretary.state.gov/www/briefings/9905/990528db.html).

13. Annis 1992: 591–92.

14. Harry Cleaver, "The Zapatistas and the Electronic Fabric of Struggle" (http://www.eco.utexas.edu:80/Homepages/Faculty/Cleaver/zaps.html).

15. Frederick 1992: 233.

16. Rosenau 1990.

17. Cleaver, "Zapatistas and the Electronic Fabric of Struggle."

18. Garrison 1989, quoted in Livernash et al. 1993: 231. Afonso 1990: 21. Cleaver, "Zapatistas and the Electronic Fabric of Struggle."

19. Cleaver, "Zapatistas and the Electronic Fabric of Struggle."

20. Rosenau 1990.

21. Willetts 1982: 188.

22. Breyman 1993.

23. Buruma 1999: 9.

24. Patrick Ball, comments at the panel titled "Analysis of Electronic Threats in a Human Rights Environment," AAAS Annual Meeting, Washington, D.C., 19 February 2000.

25. Caryn Graves, interview with author, 2 November 1999.

26. Dan Salcedo, interview by author, Washington, D.C., 22 December 1994.

27. Ball et al. 1997.

28. Lipschutz 1992: 412

29. Ibid: 413

30. For an exploration of how this works in practice, see Bob, "Globalization and the Social Construction of Human Rights Campaigns." For a different take on necessary conditions, see Rosenau 1990: 306, on when states are likely to "make room" for substantive NGO involvement.

31. Elizabeth Fox 1988: 139.

32. Ronfeldt et al. 1998:25.

33. Annis 1992: 591.

34. Buruma 1999: 10. *China News Digest–Global Newsletter,* 21 January 1999 (http://www.cnd.org/CND-Global/CND-Global.99.1st/CND-Global.99-01-21.html).

35. This risk can be large or small depending on how well funded/sophisticated the relevant internal security agencies are and how much of a threat the government thinks a given movement is. Banisar 1993: 12–15. Wayne Madsen, "The Intelligence Agency Threat to Data Privacy and Security" (MS).

36. Patrick Ball, introductory comments at the panel titled "Analysis of Electronic Threats in a Human Rights Environment," AAAS Annual Meeting, Washington, D.C., 19 February 2000.

37. Encryption software uses complicated mathematics to scramble messages and files so that only the intended recipient can decode and read them. But interception implies more than just learning what was said. There is also the opportunity to forge messages from movement members in a way that will disrupt the group's internal cohesion or operations. Alternatively, any or all e-mail or files can be prevented from being delivered or be altered in ways that may be difficult if not impossible to detect.

But depending on the circumstances, the government can take an encryption code key by force or guile to unlock all those scrambled conversations and correspondence they have saved, and, of course, hidden microphones or human spies can nullify the benefits of encryption in certain cases. For a further discussion of the limitations of encryption, see the documentation file that is included with the PGP package. Note that even those at lowest levels of poor movements for whom encryption may not be practical can always resort to the 'poor-man's encryption' of talking in oblique language and metaphor. (Dan Salcedo, interview with author, Washington, D.C., 22 December 1994)

As for the threat of voice conversations being wiretapped: Equally strong PGP-based encryption software for voice is available for those with computers with an added piece of hardware on both ends of the conversation. Some time later, phones and faxes with encryption chips built in will become widely available.

38. Patrick Ball, personal communication, 5 November 1999. Also comments made by Ken Ward, Oscar Hernandez, and Oliver Mazriegos at the panel titled "Analysis of Electronic Threats in a Human Rights Environment," AAAS Annual Meeting, Washington, D.C., 19 February 2000.

39. HushMail is available at http://www.hushmail.com.

40. Government agents in developing countries can at least get access to (if they do not already directly control) the computers of a human rights group's Internet service provider. So these agents could reprogram the ISP's computer to route connections intended for hushmail.com to a computer under government control. This called a DNS (domain name server) hijack. The user would see hushmail.com in their web browser's window showing what machine they were connected to, but they would not really be connected to that machine. To enhance the deception, government

agents might be able to buy an electronic certificate from one of the many for-profit certifying authorities. CA's are organizations that a user's web browser trusts to tell the user who really owns the web page the user is connected to. If government agents get such a certificate and associate it with their fake HushMail page, the little lock icon on the user's browser indicating an encrypted connection will light up just like with the real page. This certificate, which the user might not bother checking every time, could include identifying information about the owner of the fake Hush-Mail page that looks very similar to the identifying information for the owner of the real HushMail page. Carl Ellison, comments at "Analysis of Electronic Threats in a Human Rights Environment," AAAS Annual Meeting, Washington, D.C., 19 February 2000.

41. Human Rights Watch, "Testimony on Human Rights and Encryption before the House Subcommittee on International Economic Policy and Trade: Tuesday May 18, 1999" (http://www.hrw.org/hrw/advocacy/internet/testim-518.htm).

42. Graham Lane, personal communication, 17 November 1999.

43. Oscar Hernandez, comments at the panel titled "Analysis of Electronic Threats in a Human Rights Environment," AAAS Annual Meeting, Washington, D.C., 19 February 2000.

44. Christian 1988.

45. Amnesty International, "Tunisia: Human Rights Defenders Increasingly Targeted," October 18, 1999 (http://www.amnesty.org/news/1999/53003599.htm).

46. Buruma 1999: 11.

47. Cleaver, "Zapatistas and the Electronic Fabric of Struggle."

48. Buruma 1999: 10.

49. Cleaver, "Zapatistas and the Electronic Fabric of Struggle."

7

Globalization and the Social Construction of Human Rights Campaigns

Clifford Bob

In September and October 1999, international concern about human rights violations in East Timor mounted precipitously.[1] The global media reported daily on alleged atrocities; transnational human rights NGOs issued appeals for urgent action; foreign governments pressured Indonesia to control its paramilitaries; and a UN peacekeeping force eventually entered the territory. However briefly, East Timor took center stage on the international human rights agenda. But at the same time, from Aceh and West Papua in Indonesia to China's Xinjiang province and Senegal's Casamançe, dozens of other conflicts involving similar abuses festered with little international attention or action—just as East Timor had for most of the twenty-five years since Indonesia's invasion.

This chapter seeks to explain stark variations like these in the intensity of international activism concerning distant human rights violations. Despite rapid globalization and tremendous expansion in the contemporary human rights regime, international attention to human rights issues remains spotty. "For every voice that is amplified" by transnational advocacy networks, "many others are ignored."[2] Even abuses that arouse major human rights activism frequently include long periods in which violations go internationally unnoted.[3]

Why do some abuses leap to prominence in the international human rights regime while others languish in obscurity? Why do some individuals and certain groups arouse substantial action by human rights networks, while others do not?

This chapter argues that such variation is not random; nor does it result from a rough meritocracy of suffering in which the worst abuses attract the greatest international action; nor, finally, can it be explained by focusing only on processes, technologies, and actors at the global level. Rather, in explaining transnational activism, this chapter emphasizes strategic actions by local-level human rights victims. Such actions, conducted in interaction with home states and the human rights regime, have two primary goals: raising an oppressed group's international visibility; and fitting the group's unique grievances into a limited number of internationally recognized human rights abuses.

In these processes, globalization has important impacts. Most obviously, the rise of global communications and media affords oppressed groups better opportunities to pitch their causes to distant audiences. Globalization also furnishes symbols of oppression and repertoires of contention that some domestic movements may adopt, leading them to advocate in ways that have global and not merely local resonance. But oppressed groups do not have equal access to these opportunities or equal ability to take advantage of them. A key question therefore becomes which groups can best exploit globalization. The chapter argues that those groups with significant material resources, preexisting linkages to international actors, skill at international public relations, organizational cohesiveness, and leadership charisma will have an advantage over otherwise similar groups. These factors are in turn affected by a group's long-term interaction with global economic and political actors.

To make this argument, the chapter first defines key terms, discusses the theoretical context, and presents an alternative approach. In the next section, I present a comparative case study illustrating this approach.

CONSTRUCTING HUMAN RIGHTS ISSUES

I define human rights broadly to encompass security, social, and collective rights. In adopting this definition, I focus less on violations against individuals than against groups defined by ethnic, ideological, or other criteria. In some cases, these groups are involved in conflicts with the governments of their countries over conventional political and civil rights issues; in others, standard human rights abuses are only one of many issues in the overall conflict. I define transnational human rights activism in two ways: third party actions involving direct transfers of money, goods, and knowledge to victims of abuse; and actions that indirectly benefit the oppressed group. The latter include publicity, advocacy, and lobbying on its behalf; and opprobrium, boycotts, or other pressure against the government involved. In this analysis, I focus on support by "transnational advocacy networks" whose numbers have risen significantly in recent years.[4] In the human rights area, these networks are dominated by NGOs such as Amnesty International and Human Rights Watch. Given this chapter's expansive definition of human rights, however, I also examine nonstate actors in issue areas such as the environment and indigenous rights.

Existing research on transnational networks is rooted in the constructivist approach to international politics. One of constructivism's chief goals has been to challenge realist conceptions of a state-dominated international system. Recent studies therefore highlight ways in which nonstate actors can change the interests and identities of states and international organizations.[5] According to this work, a "boomerang" pattern has become common, with transnational advocacy networks pressuring repressive or unrepresentative governments to change policies toward their own citizens.[6]

But analysts have thus far neglected a key antecedent issue, the origins of linkages between local victims and transnational networks. Most research assumes such linkages or attributes them to contemporary technologies without showing how these general conditions produce some linkages but not others.[7] There are also a growing number of case studies analyzing successful transnational mobilizations, such as the anti-apartheid movement, but these studies have seldom aimed at broader theorizing on these linkages.[8] Most scholars also view NGOs and networks primarily as "principled" moral entrepreneurs, rather than as organizations.[9] But principles create only permissive guides for an NGO's selecting one or another needy group. Faced with a world of need, how do transnational actors choose? And what effect, if any, do the actions of local actors have in narrowing the menu of choice and enhancing their own likelihood of gaining support?

To supplement the existing literature, this chapter focuses on local actors, their strategies for arousing NGO support, and their interactions with transnational advocacy networks. To do so, the chapter roots itself in theories of social movements. Political process theories direct attention to a movement's organization, resources, and strategies, while the "new social movements" literature emphasizes identity issues and framing.[10] Recent scholarship has also begun analyzing transnational movements, but there has been no systematic attempt to understand how local movements attract transnational support.[11]

In theorizing about this issue, I assume that many victims seek international support but that NGOs have limited resources to provide it. As a result, there is loose but real competition among needy groups. Two factors then explain why some groups gain sustained NGO action while others do not: a group's international visibility; and the extent to which violations against it "fit" or "match" those recognized by international networks.

Structural factors, fixed characteristics of the arenas within which victimized groups seek to gain support, systematically favor some groups over others. Groups seeking to attract international media attention as a means of raising visibility face the reality that certain countries and world regions have far higher media profiles than others. Most of Africa, Latin America, and Asia, for instance, elicit little journalistic interest in the developed world.[12] It is therefore, harder for groups in those countries to raise their international visibility than victims of similar abuses in Yugoslavia or Russia.

Similarly, international human rights organizations have long focused their concern on basic rights rooted in the International Covenant on Civil and Political Rights. Groups suffering abuses that fit into these categories have a better chance of gaining international support than groups suffering other forms of oppression.

But oppressed groups are not powerless in the face of these structural factors. Instead, they may adopt strategies to raise their international profile and increase their chances of gaining support. Those groups best able to "pitch" themselves to international audiences and "match" their grievances to recognized abuses—often by reframing localized conflicts, parochial demands, and particularistic identities—are most likely to arouse transnational activism. The "pitch" takes two main forms: direct lobbying of potential supporters and indirect promotion through media coverage.[13]

What factors influence whether human rights victims succeed in raising visibility? For groups that lobby potential supporters directly, these factors include the group's material resources, affecting "lobbyists'" ability to present their case abroad; its leaders' knowledge of the developed world and facility in a world language; and its leaders' preexisting contacts with international journalists and NGOs. Well-connected, high profile figures such as the Dalai Lama clearly help victimized groups in their lobbying efforts. While Chinese violations against Tibetans are well known, similar violations against other Chinese minorities such as Xinjiang's Uighurs have attracted little international activism. This example also illustrates that charismatic leadership, however difficult to theorize, affects international awareness of a group's plight.

Intergroup variation in these factors strongly affects whether particular groups will gain international attention. Globalization helps create this variation, though in more subtle ways than often assumed by those who see it as a sudden, recent phenomenon. Some intergroup differences, such as leadership charisma, are largely fortuitous. But variations in material resources, organizational cohesiveness, preexisting international linkages, and skill at international public relations often result from a group's long-term contact with global institutions unrelated to human rights networks.[14] These historical interactions, rather than innate group characteristics, create a rough but real stratification among oppressed groups, enabling some groups to arouse international human rights activism more effectively than others do.

In addition to direct lobbying, many victimized groups seek attention through press coverage—and take actions calculated to attract journalists. Crucial in this regard is a group's ability to create news, often through mass protest or other actions involving surprise, unruliness, or violence.[15] Here, John Kingdon's concept of a focusing event—a "crisis or disaster that comes along to call attention to [a] problem"—is helpful.[16] While a focusing event may simply "come along," it may also result from a group's strategic mobilization or government repression. As one example, Mexico's Zapatista uprising drew the international media within hours, while less rebellious tactics by similar Mexican victims of chronic human rights violations have gone unnoticed internationally.[17]

A final factor affecting lobbying and media promotion is access; both a victim's access to potential supporters abroad and the latter's access to the group at home. In either case, the transparency of the regime involved and its capacity to block transnational contacts strongly affect the insurgency's ability to raise international awareness.[18] While transparency varies with numerous factors, a nation's integration into global economic, political, and technological processes plays an important role. Thus, in the Zapatista case, one hypothesis explaining rapid and strong international activism was Mexico's relative openness to the international media, openness that resulted from its accession to NAFTA and broader attempts to integrate into the international system.[19]

Assuming an oppressed group raises its visibility, what factors determine whether it will win support? Here it is useful to view both parties as having substantive goals and internal organizational needs. The likelihood that an oppressed group will gain NGO support should increase to the extent that there is a match between the two actors with respect to each of these attributes. With regard to substantive matching, an initial problem for some victims is that global actors may not recognize their oppression as a human rights violation. For many years, cultural rites such as clitoridectomy and social practices such as neglect of the mentally ill were not characterized as human rights violations. Where there is such an initial misfit between local and international understandings, however, a match may develop as NGOs expand their definition of "violations"—sometimes because of urging by local victims and "moral entrepreneurs." Amnesty International's recent acceptance of female genital mutilation as a rights violation exemplifies such expansion, while current attempts to establish international norms for treatment of the mentally ill may represent human rights in the making.[20]

A match may also develop due to changes involving the aggrieved group. First, even when a conflict does not involve conventional human rights abuses, repressive responses by power holders may raise such issues. The killing of Chico Mendes, for instance, turned a local Brazilian conflict over land use and the environment into an international human rights issue. Moreover, groups in conflict may unintentionally or deliberately provoke repression that amounts to an internationally recognizable rights violation. In the 1960s, the U.S. civil rights movement followed such strategies by targeting peaceful protest for southern cities known to have hotheaded police chiefs; vicious police responses served to embody chronic racial oppression in dramatic and undeniable violations of fundamental rights.[21]

Second, even if the conflict itself does not change, an aggrieved population may reframe it in terms that are internationally appealing and that match the preexisting interests of distant audiences.[22] In this regard, victims will increase their chances of attracting support if they reframe their conflict in terms that are simple and understandable to distant audiences, that involve universalistic values rather than particularistic interests, that are symbolic of broader issues, and that involve seemingly familiar "heroes" and "villains."[23] In addition, framing a conflict around institutions that operate across national boundaries increases a local movement's transnational appeal.

Here, globalization makes some difference. New communications technologies familiarize people around the world with internationally resonant events, actors, and symbols—all potentially useable as means of attracting distant supporters. The far-flung activities of multinational corporations (MNCs), while sometimes associated with rights violations, also create internationally recognized targets for mobilization. Again, however, not all groups can seize the opportunities afforded by globalization. A group's ability to do so will depend more on its own resources and knowledge than on globalization itself.

Beyond substantive matching, a fit between the organizational needs of NGOs and potential clients also appears critical. This implies that a transnational actor will carefully weigh support for an oppressed group, because it may incur high costs if its backing is found baseless. These costs, primarily loss of reputation, credibility, and prestige, are intangible but potentially severe, including reduction in the NGO's membership and contributions. Given these considerations, NGOs will carefully evaluate the legitimacy of a movement and the validity of its claims. In turn, this suggests that domestic groups may increase their likelihood of support by providing proof of their claims and constituency, building personal relationships with NGO staff, and taking other actions to increase trust among potential supporters. These considerations also suggest that groups may broaden their appeal most rapidly by cultivating relationships with "node NGOs" who have the ability to ascertain a group's bona fides and who may serve as de facto gatekeepers for other NGOs. In the human rights area, Amnesty International and Human Rights Watch are the primary organizations serving this function.

The organizational match hypothesis again suggests that globalization alone has limited analytic utility in explaining variation in international support. All else being equal, groups with greater knowledge, resources, and contacts will be better able to present their cases and provide evidence to meet NGOs' organizational needs. Globalization may help these relatively advantaged groups but by itself is unlikely to alter preexisting stratification among oppressed groups.

The foregoing approach, with its emphasis on a group's strategic pitching and matching, explains how some but not other victims gain support. As in domestic politics, however, human rights problems are typically subject to an "issue attention cycle."[24] Media interest and, to a lesser extent, NGO support wanes as the novelty of an issue begins to fade. Notwithstanding the issue attention cycle, however, gaining substantial international support is a significant accomplishment, with long-lasting impacts for human rights victims. Even if support for the group fades as repression recedes or comes to appear routine, having once achieved prominence the group will have an easier time renewing its support in the future if it again faces significant repression. Turning to the Zapatista case again, reduced international support in late 1994 rapidly changed to vocal activism in January 1995 when the Mexican government renewed its attacks on the rebels.[25] The group's newfound stature and its latent transnational linkages had long-lasting effects, which withstood vagaries in the issue attention cycle.

To illustrate this approach, the next section examines the Ogoni people, one of several Nigerian minorities that sought international support to counter state repression and neglect during the 1990s. The Ogoni gained far more international backing than the other minority groups in Nigeria. By examining the Ogoni movement in comparative perspective, I identify behavior common to groups seeking NGO action and isolate factors leading to substantial and sustained activism in a few cases.

THE OGONI, THE NIGER DELTA CONFLICTS, AND INTERNATIONAL ACTIVISM

The Ogoni are an ethnic group of 300,000–500,000 living in about 400 square miles of Nigeria's Niger River Delta region.[26] Like the other Delta minorities, who together comprise only a small fraction of Nigeria's 110 million people, the Ogoni have long demanded a greater voice in federal and state politics. Since the late 1950s, when oil drilling began in the region, these minorities have also sought more revenues from the millions of barrels of oil extracted from their land. For most of the century, however, the "oil minorities" have remained little known and politically insignificant even in Nigeria, and most have received few benefits even as the region's oil has become Nigeria's main revenue source.

In 1990, Ogoni elites led by Ken Saro-Wiwa, a journalist, television producer, and human rights advocate, formed the Movement for the Survival of the Ogoni People (MOSOP). MOSOP's primary goal was Ogoni "political autonomy within Nigeria" through which the Ogoni sought a number of subsidiary aims: political control over Ogoni affairs; control over a "fair proportion" of oil production and revenue distribution; "adequate" representation in national political institutions, preservation of Ogoni culture, religion, and languages; and protection of the Ogoni environment.[27] MOSOP hoped to achieve these momentous goals through mass protest, but mobilization efforts fizzled, and the Nigerian government ignored MOSOP's demands.[28] In late 1991, MOSOP leaders introduced an additional strategy, arousing international pressure. For one year, MOSOP failed to gain NGO support or media coverage, but in 1993, the Ogoni began winning significant external support: transnational NGOs mounted coordinated actions in support of Ogoni demands, international media carried accounts of the Ogoni struggle, foreign governments monitored Nigerian treatment of the Ogoni and their leaders, and international organizations focused unprecedented attention on southeastern Nigeria. In 1994, Saro-Wiwa was arrested and in November 1995, he and eight other Ogonis were executed, prompting international protests and diplomatic sanctions.[29]

The Ogonis' primary NGO support came from three activist networks, the environmental, human rights, and minority/indigenous rights networks. Within these networks, several NGOs played particularly prominent roles as supporters and gatekeepers for broader transnational involvement. MOSOP's earliest supporter was the Unrepresented Nations and Peoples Organization (UNPO), a small minority rights organization based in The Hague. Beginning in 1992, UNPO helped MOSOP broaden its NGO contacts and served as a clearinghouse for press releases about the Ogoni conflict.[30] The major environmental NGOs, Greenpeace International and Friends of the Earth International, initially rejected Ogoni appeals in 1991–92. Then, in early 1993, they began providing substantial support including letter-writing and media campaigns on behalf of imprisoned Ogoni leaders, widely distributed reports on environmental and health problems in the Niger Delta, and public protests against environmental abuses by Royal Dutch/Shell ("Shell"), the major oil producer in the region. In 1991–92, Amnesty International also rejected the Ogoni pleas, then, in mid 1993, took increasingly vigorous actions condemning Nigerian abuses of Ogoni activists.[31]

The Niger Delta through most of the twentieth century has therefore presented a picture of dozens of different ethnic groups facing a similar set of problems. How, then, do we explain why one of these groups—not the largest; not the most victimized; and historically not the most rebellious—gained major support from the international human rights regime? And, based on this comparative discussion, what larger conclusions can we draw about the relationship between human rights issues and globalization?

A critical initial factor was the Ogonis' ability to "pitch" their movement, to raise awareness about themselves among potential transnational supporters. Shortly after MOSOP's decision to seek international support in August 1991, Ogoni leaders began direct foreign lobbying of transnational NGOs.[32] MOSOP was able to pitch the Ogoni case for several reasons discernible by comparing MOSOP to other "oil minorities," which have sought goals similar to the Ogonis'. One factor was Ogoni resources, both money and knowledge. Ken Saro-Wiwa had considerable personal wealth and used his money to underwrite MOSOP activities, including foreign lobbying and publications promoting the Ogoni cause.[33] Other factors included the MOSOP leadership's extensive experience in Europe, preexisting linkages to transnational networks, and knowledge of basic public relations and marketing techniques. Saro-Wiwa and other Ogoni leaders had personal and professional contacts with British literary, journalistic, and human rights circles, all of which helped in guiding him to potentially interested NGO supporters.[34] The small Ogoni diaspora also had resources and professional expertise that facilitated MOSOP's international efforts.

By contrast, other "oil minorities" have not had the wealthy, dedicated, knowledgeable, and well-connected leadership that the Ogoni had, particularly in Ken Saro-Wiwa.[35] Despite political and economic grievances comparable to the Ogonis' and despite similar domestic tactics, minorities such as the far larger Ijaw people have gone unknown and unsupported abroad. In one telling incident in 1991, a British film crew working on a television documentary about multinational oil companies traveled to Nigeria to report on the state's 1990 killing of 80 ethnic Etche people peacefully protesting oil company operations near Ogoni territory. The Etche were unable to capitalize on this important contact, however, while the Ogoni, who were unknown to the film's producers before their visit to Nigeria, appeared prominently, because Saro-Wiwa was "the most articulate spokesperson for any of the ethnic groups on the Delta."[36] The documentary, broadcast nationally in Britain by Channel Four in October 1992, helped the Ogoni raise awareness among environmental NGOs, while the Etche were forgotten.[37]

One additional factor that played a substantial role in MOSOP's ability to lobby transnational NGOs becomes evident by comparing the Ogoni to similar movements outside Nigeria. MOSOP's continuing contacts with transnational NGOs were possible because the Nigerian government did not limit exit or entry to Ogoniland early in the conflict. Through mid 1993, MOSOP leaders traveled freely lobbying for assistance; until early 1995, MOSOP was also able to phone and fax news from Nigeria on a daily basis.[38] Nor did the Nigerian state limit access to Ogoniland by international journalists and NGO representatives until late in the conflict. By contrast, other political movements with grievances similar to the Ogonis' have had greater difficulties gaining international attention because their governments have limited access to conflict regions. As one example, the decade-long secessionist movement on Papua New Guinea's Bougainville Island remained "one of the world's more obscure separatist insurgencies"[39] in part because of a blockade that sharply curtailed the movement's foreign lobbying and the international media's reporting.[40]

Notably, however, MOSOP's lobbying did not lead directly to NGO support. Support arose only after MOSOP made several strategic shifts in late 1992, shifts that helped create critical "matches" between the Ogoni and potential NGO supporters. One such match concerned MOSOP's goals. In its initial lobbying efforts in 1991 and 1992, MOSOP framed its conflict around ethnic minority rights. This framing emphasized MOSOP's goals of "political autonomy within Nigeria," preservation of Ogoni culture and language, and a greater share of oil revenues—all outgrowths of long-standing Ogoni demands against the Nigerian state.[41] While appropriate to the Nigerian context, however, these demands left most of MOSOP's initial NGO contacts unmoved. Only the minority rights organization UNPO backed the Ogoni; more prominent environmental and human rights NGOs rejected Ogoni overtures.

In interviews, staff at Greenpeace International and Friends of the Earth International stated that MOSOP's demands appeared deeply enmeshed in murky and difficult issues of Nigerian politics, issues that did not match environmental agendas.[42] Beginning in late 1992, however, MOSOP took actions that led the NGOs to reverse their initial rejections. First, following the emphasis in the Channel Four documentary, MOSOP reframed its grievances to highlight environmental problems allegedly caused by a Shell subsidiary's substandard operations. Shell's misconduct, its "ecological war" against the "indigenous" Ogoni, became an increasingly prominent part of MOSOP's rhetoric both at home and abroad.[43] In November 1992, MOSOP issued a declaration demanding that Shell pay the Ogoni $10 billion in royalties and reparations within thirty days (the "Demand Notice"). This excited great interest among the Ogoni people, and in December 1992, Saro-Wiwa traveled to Europe to drum up attention and support from transnational environmental groups.[44]

In the wake of the Channel Four documentary, the MOSOP declaration, and MOSOP lobbying on environmental issues, NGOs that had long criticized multinational oil companies saw a new opportunity "to have a go at Shell—attack them."[45] In this view, the Ogonis could serve as a powerful symbol of multinationals' environmental abuses, a symbol useful in ongoing conflicts with Shell and other companies. As these NGOs gave increasing prominence to the Ogoni in their publications and domestic activities, MOSOP responded by making Shell's "devastation" of the Ogoni environment the central focus of its domestic and international campaigns. This reframing had great resonance among the Ogoni population because of long-standing resentment over Shell's failure to employ indigenes and bring prosperity to the Ogonis.[46] Moreover, there was a factual basis for complaints about Shell's environmental record.[47] Nonetheless environmental issues were not MOSOP's initial core concern and improving the Niger Delta environment would not "solve" the Ogoni conflict. Instead, reframing around the environment and Shell's misconduct was part of a successful strategy to gain support from transnational environmental NGOs. As Saro-Wiwa himself complained in a 1993 interview, the developed world seemed to care more about endangered animals than about the Ogoni people.[48] But MOSOP deftly countered this bias by reframing its conflict as one centering on the environmental abuses of a major multinational corporation.

By itself, however, MOSOP's reframing does not explain NGO responses to the Ogoni. A second set of factors relates to the NGOs' organizational needs. In their initial appeals to transnational NGOs, MOSOP leaders presented little evidence that the organization was a legitimate representative of the Ogoni people or that Ogoni grievances had a factual basis. Instead, according to several of their earliest NGO contacts, MOSOP leaders sought to persuade simply by "telling stories," many seemingly exaggerated and sensationalized. These unsubstantiated pleas formed an insufficient basis for NGO support, potentially putting NGO reputations and credibility at risk.[49] For Ogoni leaders, however, demonstrating mass support was difficult because MOSOP's 1990 attempts at popular mobilization had failed, and the grassroots movement lay moribund.[50]

When news of the Channel Four documentary reached Nigeria, however, interest among the Ogoni populace mounted.[51] MOSOP leaders capitalized on this development by organizing public meetings, issuing the demand notice, and planning a mass protest for 4 January 1993. MOSOP carefully orchestrated this "Ogoni Day March"; the organization outfitted protesters with twigs symbolizing environmental issues and signs proclaiming Ogoni solidarity with indigenous peoples worldwide. MOSOP leaders also videotaped the march and persuaded international NGO observers to travel to Nigeria.[52] For potential environmental supporters, the videotapes and eyewitness testimony offered persuasive evidence of Ogoni unity and of Shell's environmental abuses.[53]

Similar reasons explain transnational human rights NGOs' varying responses to MOSOP's appeals. In 1991, Amnesty International rejected MOSOP's claims of an Ogoni "genocide" resulting from state neglect of Ogoni economic and cultural development. Amnesty remained similarly unmoved by MOSOP's 1992 claims that Shell's "environmental degradation" had been a "lethal weapon in the war against" the Ogoni. As an Amnesty staff person told Saro-Wiwa in rejecting his pleas, "no one was dead, no one was in gaol."[54] Only when Nigerian security forces resorted to violent abuses against individuals did Amnesty take action. These changes began in spring 1993, when Nigerian security forces killed protesters, detained MOSOP leaders, and instigated bloody attacks on Ogoni villages by neighboring ethnic groups. Thus, as in the case of the environmental NGOs, support from the human rights NGOs hinged on a match between Ogoni concerns and NGO goals. Organizational matching was also important. Absent credible reports of violations against the Ogoni, Amnesty and other human rights NGOs would not have begun letter-writing campaigns, issued reports, or testified before governmental authorities in Europe and North America.[55]

While the foregoing factors help explain how the Ogoni moved from international obscurity to prominence beginning in 1993, one additional factor explains peaks of international support: a "focusing event" bringing substantial media attention.[56] Ogoni leaders sought to create such events, but their mass protests drew little coverage outside Nigeria. Far more potent were Saro-Wiwa's one-month detention in June 1993 and his execution in November 1995. In both cases, MOSOP's NGO supporters grew markedly more numerous and active.[57] While the proximate cause of these peaks was the Nigerian state's egregious behavior, attention grew because of the fertile context created by MOSOP's long-term success at building NGO support.

CONCLUSION

Globalization is often seen as a double-edged sword for human rights. On one hand, new technologies and new international norms may be a boon for victims and activists, binding the world together and making it harder for repressive regimes to act with impunity against their own citizens. On the other hand, the ideology of free trade and the spread of multinational corporations may infringe on labor rights, threaten vulnerable environments, and destroy local control.

These starkly contrasting views of globalization point most obviously to the concept's multidimensionality. "Globalization" is too big, encompasses too many contradictory trends, to have any single set of effects. Rather, its effects are multiple, contradictory, and ambiguous. The stark contrasts between "good" and "bad" globalization suggest another, more modest implication. Notwithstanding its obvious importance, globalization may have fewer consequences than one might expect. Sharp differences between haves and have-nots at the local and national levels strongly affect which among the world's many needy groups can take greatest advantage of globalization's promise—and which will suffer in isolation from its harmful consequences.

These differential impacts result in part from structural impediments at the international level. Certain states receive less attention from the global media than others, while poverty and ignorance prevent many needy groups from taking actions that would raise their international profile. For some groups, the broad doctrines of the Universal Declaration of Human Rights may also go unrealized because key international NGOs have defined human rights as a core set of civil and political rights. Oppression that falls outside this definition may not be easily cognizable in the international human rights regime.

Despite such structural impediments, oppressed groups have options—strategies aimed at raising their visibility and matching their causes to internationally resonant themes. Victimized groups will have more or less success in exercising these options depending on their underlying resources and capabilities. The differential distribution of these factors stems in part from the degree of historical interaction between local actors and global institutions, with groups like the Ogoni having significant advantages over seemingly similar groups like the Etche. In addition, contemporary globalization, particularly the presence of MNCs, may offer skillful local groups a hook for attracting international supporters, as Shell did for the Ogoni.

Moreover, the Ogoni case suggests that even as local victims reframe their struggles to attract international support, they may also reshape the "structures" of the human rights regime—a process of mutual constitution familiar to constructivists. Changing views of female genital mutilation, from cultural practice to human rights violation, exemplify such reconstitution. The Ogoni case contributed to analogous change. Human rights NGOs have now institutionalized linkages to transnational environmental NGOs and started campaigns on MNC responsibilities in the developing world.[58]

NOTES

1. As a rough indicator of heightened concern, a Nexis search for the term "East Timor" in *New York Times* articles during 1999 found 153 stories in September and 80 in October, compared to a monthly average of 14 in the eight prior months and 30 in the following two months. The same search found 69 stories for all of 1998 and a yearly average of 23 in 1988–97.

2. Keck and Sikkink 1998: x.

3. Risse et al. 1999: 22.

4. Keck and Sikkink 1998: 11. For statistics documenting recent growth of transnational NGOs, see Jackie Smith 1997.

5. See, e.g., Risse et al. 1999; Brysk 1993.

6. Keck and Sikkink 1998: 13.

7. Risse-Kappen 1995; Rosenau 1997; Lipschutz 1992.

8. Rothman and Oliver 1999; Klotz 1995b.

9. Nadelmann 1990; Wapner 1996; Keck and Sikkink 1998.

10. The seminal work on process theory is McAdam 1982. For an example of new social movements theory, see Touraine 1988. For the concept of framing, see, e.g., Snow and Benford 1992. For a synthesis, see Tarrow 1998.

11. Smith, Chatfield, and Pagnucco 1997 presents the most systematic approach to transnational movements so far.

12. Wolfsfeld 1997: 18–19.

13. Notably, globalization's effects on the pitch may be different from those often believed. New communications technologies increase the velocity and volume of interactions between local populations and transnational NGOs—but only *after* linkages between the actors have been established. Technology does not create these crucial initial ties, and it is neutral as to which oppressed groups will have access. Dozens of groups suffering various forms of oppression now have websites—but their impact is limited unless potential supporters already know of the groups. See, e.g., links at website for the Unrepresented Nations and Peoples Organization, http://www.unpo.org/.

14. Brysk 2000b.

15. Wolfsfeld 1997; McCarthy et al. 1996: 297.

16. Kingdon 1984: 99–100.

17. Bob 2000.

18. Livingston 1996.

19. See Bob 2000.

20. Amnesty International, "Why and How Amnesty International Took Up the Issue of Female Genital Mutilation," available online at http://www.amnesty.org/ailib/intcam/femgen/fgm2.htm (accessed 1 April 2000); Winerip 2000.

21. McAdam 1982: 174–79. For documentation of similar tactics in the Tienanmen Square protests, see "The Gate of Heavenly Peace," *Frontline* (GBH Educational Foundation, Boston), no. 1418 (4 June 1996).

22. For discussion of framing by transnational movements, see Keck and Sikkink 1998: 17; John D. McCarthy, "The Globalization of Social Movement Theory," in Smith, Chatfield, and Pagnucco 1997: 244–47.

23. Keck and Sikkink argue that principled NGOs form networks primarily around issues involving physical harm to individuals and legalized inequalities of opportunity. Keck and Sikkink 1998: 27.

24. Downs 1972.

25. Bob 2000.

26. Information in this and the next paragraph comes primarily from Osaghae 1995; Welch 1995; and Human Rights Watch 1995a.

27. Movement for the Survival of the Ogoni People (MOSOP), Ogoni Bill of Rights, 1990, reprinted in Welch and Sills 1996.

28. Saro-Wiwa 1995.

29. See MOSOP, Addendum to the Ogoni Bill of Rights, reprinted in Welch and Sills 1996.

30. Author's interviews with UNPO staff, The Hague, 11–12 July 1996.

31. See, e.g., Friends of the Earth International, *Earth Alarm* 10 (June 1993); Greenpeace International, "Shell-Shocked: The Environmental and Social Costs of Living with Shell in Nigeria, July 1994"; Amnesty International, *Urgent Action,* UA 268/93, 10 August 1993; Human Rights Watch 1995a.

32. Saro-Wiwa 1995. Author's interviews, Greenpeace International, Greenpeace Netherlands, Friends of the Earth International, Friends of the Earth Netherlands, Amnesty International, Survival International, and the Unrepresented Nations and Peoples Organization, May–July 1996.

33. Saro-Wiwa 1995: 89.

34. Ibid, 236.

35. Among Niger Delta minority groups that have mobilized for goals similar to the Ogonis' are the Ogbia, Ikwerre, Etche, Ijaw, Urhobos, and the Nembe Creek community. Human Rights Watch 1995a: 33.

36. Author's telephone interview with film producer, 25 June 1996.

37. Glen Ellis and Kay Bishop, "The Heat of the Moment," Channel Four (Great Britain), 8 October 1992.

38. Author's interviews with UNPO staff, 11–12 July 1996.

39. Seth Mydans, "As Election Nears, More Than Politics Divides Island," *New York Times,* 27 April 1997, sec. 1, p. 10.

40. Ease of media access has been cited as an important factor explaining varying international attention to similar African humanitarian disasters. Livingston 1996.

41. See, e.g., Saro-Wiwa 1983; United Kingdom, Colonial Office [1958] 1996: 48–50.

42. Author's interviews, Greenpeace International, Greenpeace Netherlands, Friends of the Earth International, Friends of the Earth Netherlands, May-July 1996. The Ogoni Bill of Rights focuses on political autonomy and portrays environmental issues as the Nigerian state's responsibility. See also Saro-Wiwa 1995: 88.

43. See, e.g., Bruin 1993; Saro-Wiwa 1995: 166–70.

44. Saro-Wiwa 1995: 105; *Guardian* (Lagos), 28 December 1992, 7. MOSOP to Shell, demand notice, 30 November 1992 (photocopy in author's files).

45. Author's telephone interview with consultant to Greenpeace International, 26 June 1996, and personal and telephone interviews with staff at Greenpeace Netherlands, Friends of the Earth International, and Friends of the Earth Netherlands.

46. Osaghae 1995: 325–44; author's interviews with MOSOP members, London, 21 and 23 July 1996, and St. Louis, Mo., 14 March 1998.

47. Moffat and Lindén 1995.

48. *Newsweek*, 20 September 1993, 43.

49. Author's interview with staff person at Friends of the Earth International, Amsterdam, 18 June 1996; author's interview with staff person at Survival International, London, 17 July 1996.

50. Author's interview with MOSOP official, London, 21 July 1996; Saro-Wiwa 1995: 99.

51. Saro-Wiwa 1995: 102.

52. *Newswatch* (Lagos), 25 January 1993, 9; author's interview with English environmental activist present at Ogoni Day March, Oxford, 19 July 1996; Saro-Wiwa 1995: 105.

53. Author's personal and telephone interviews with staff at Greenpeace International, Greenpeace Netherlands, Friends of the Earth International, Friends of the Earth Netherlands, May–July 1996.

54. Saro-Wiwa 1995: 88; author's interview with Amnesty International staff person, Amsterdam, 17 July 17 1996.

55. Author's interview with Amnesty International staff person, Amsterdam, 17 July 1996.

56. Kingdon 1984: 99–100.

57. Saro-Wiwa 1995: 236–7.

58. One important example is the joint Sierra Club/Amnesty International Human Rights and the Environment Campaign. See http://www.sierraclub.org/humanrights/. See generally Sachs 1995.

8

The Drama of Human Rights
in a Turbulent, Globalized World

James N. Rosenau

To facilitate an assessment of the human rights regime at the outset of the twenty-first century, this essay outlines the relevance of turbulence, of globalization, and of the drama of the most obstreperous actor as theoretical aids to understanding how human rights may—or may not—be contributing to global governance, global communication, and the global citizenship gap. Three questions drive the analysis. In what ways are turbulent conditions inhibiting and enhancing the various struggles for human rights? In what ways are the processes of globalization accelerating and undermining the struggles? In what ways do the most obstreperous actors in a system—those whose behavior is so extreme that enormous expenditures of time, energy, and resources are required to cope with and offset their conduct—help and hinder the struggles?[1]

HUMAN RIGHTS AS AN ISSUE AREA

Since the nature of the human rights regime is relevant to all three theoretical perspectives, the analysis can usefully begin with an outline of its essential foundations. Such issues revolve around the fact or potential of bodily harm to individuals or socioeconomic and political harm to their collectivities, characteristics that are so immediately imaginable that violations of the rights of persons and groups have the power to rise quickly to the top of political agendas. When people suffer bodily or collective harm imposed systematically by any organized source, such actions are bound to arouse the sensibilities of others. This ever-present intimacy that pervades human rights issues helps to explain why protest groups so readily form, why some organizations persist beyond their successful protests, why governments are sensitive to criticism of their conduct in this regard, why some governments go out of their way to hide or justify their violations of individual rights, and why people insist that their culture's conception of human rights is no less justifiable than that of any other culture. In short, however they may be defined, the rights of persons and groups are distinguished by the singular quality of striking at the heart of individual experience and, in so doing, they occupy a moral ground to which no other issue area can lay claim. And as the complexity of modern urban and transnational life deepens, the more salient this moral ground becomes.

Another distinguishing feature of the issue area is the high degree to which violations of human rights are organized and systematic. Unlike most cases of crime or corruption, those involving violated human rights do not occur as isolated events undertaken for idiosyncratic reasons.[2] Rather, whatever specific actions are engaged in by their perpetrators derive from some set of presumptions that justify depriving others of their rights. These presumptions are organized and systematic in the sense that seemingly isolated events may stem from the same deeply embedded cultural, historical, or economic premises that absolve their perpetrators of any wrongdoing (as was the case for so long with mistreatment of African Americans in the United States), or they may underlie organized campaigns to deprive whole classes of people of their rights (as was the case with the Holocaust in Germany and ethnic cleansing in Yugoslavia), or they may be the consequence of unregulated capital markets (as was the case for Indonesians during and after the Asian financial crisis).

Still another dimension of the human rights issue area is its pervasiveness and salience. The issues it encompasses can be so global in scope that it is not far-fetched to observe that wherever and whenever organized activity is undertaken with respect to them, some people are likely to be deprived of their rights. No less important, for reasons outlined below, people everywhere have become aware of such issues. While some observers argue that this awareness is universal and amounts to a "remarkable international normative consensus on the list of rights,"[3] others acknowledge the universality of the awareness but contend that it encompasses conflicting conceptions of what constitutes human rights and their violation. Despite such differences, however, there can be no gainsaying that rights issues have become a matter of widespread concern, as if the conscience of humankind has at long last found a shared focus. More than that, it is a retrospective as well as a current focus. Increasingly, the misdeeds of human rights violators no longer pass from humankind's conscience once they leave the world stage: as two former South Korean prime ministers, several members of the Argentine military, and General Pinochet painfully discovered, their retirement from office did not remove them from the danger of retribution. Indeed, an explanation of why and how past as well as present human rights issues have only lately risen to the top of local, national, transnational, and global agendas—

what one observer summarizes as the "unprecedented global diffusion of the idea of rights"[4]—is inherent in the ensuing effort to assess the impact of turbulent conditions and globalizing dynamics.

THE IMPACT OF TURBULENCE

Elsewhere I have depicted turbulence in world politics as more than extensive disarray. Rather, the turbulence model posits the transformation of three basic parameters as underlying and sustaining the course of world affairs.[5] One transformation involves a micro parameter in which the skills of people everywhere are seen as different from those of earlier generations in the sense that today individuals are more able analytically, emotionally, and imaginatively to trace the course of distant events back into their own lives.[6] A second transformation depicts a macro variable in which global structures are posited as undergoing bifurcation, with the traditional statecentric world now having a rival in a multicentric world consisting of diverse nongovernmental collectivities such as ethnic minorities, multinational corporations, professional societies, social movements, transnational advocacy networks, bureaucratic agencies, and humanitarian organizations.[7] The third transformation traces a change in a micro-macro parameter whereby the authority structures that link individuals at the micro level with collectivities at the macro level are increasingly in crisis rather than in place.[8]

The Skill Revolution

All three of these parametric transformations have a variety of major consequences for the human rights issue area, consequences that both enhance and inhibit the various ways in which rights are protected or violated. Consider first the micro parameter, or what I like to refer to as the "skill revolution," in order to emphasize the substantial degree to which this parameter has undergone transformation. Its analytic dimension has inhibited the rights violators by enabling people everywhere to more clearly assess the violations and how they affect their victims. Its emotional dimension has served to strengthen judgments about the immorality of violations. Its imaginative dimension has facilitated understanding of the implications of violations for the conduct of domestic and foreign affairs. As a result of these enlarged skills, those groups and organizations that seek to mobilize people to contest human rights violations can draw upon a degree of empathy and commitment that is widespread and intense. It is hardly a random occurrence, for example, that journalistic accounts and televised scenes of ethnic cleansing in Kosovo evoked deep, energetic, and persistent responses from numerous individuals who supported NATO's efforts to hold Yugoslavia to account for its actions.

On the other hand, the efforts of those who perpetrate human rights violations can be enhanced as well as inhibited by the skill revolution. For just as those who abhor rights violations are more easily mobilized, so are those who subscribe to value systems that justify the violations. Their newly acquired skills enable them to respond more effectively to mobilizers who appeal to their anti-rights prejudices. Put differently, a major consequence of the skill revolution is that people everywhere are increasingly able to know when, where, and how to engage in collective action, a capacity that can be just as easily put to the service of supporting as of opposing what are regarded as human rights violations. The Chilean crowds protesting and praising the detention of General Pinochet in England for human rights violations in earlier decades are illustrative of how the skill revolution can have contradictory consequences and empower both champions and violators of rights.

Bifurcated Global Structures

The transformation of the macro parameter has been especially consequential as an inhibitor of actors inclined to violate human rights. Most notably, the processes of bifurcation that culminated in the multicentric world have facilitated the formation of numerous groups and networks that coordinate their resources and energies in the struggle to contest states and other collectivities that deprive their citizens or members of their rights. The successful efforts of numerous NGOs and some states to oppose apartheid in South Africa exemplify the kind of powerful pressures that can be generated in the multicentric world to contest the actions of governments dedicated to subjugating the rights of minorities.[9] Although the form of pressure was different, a similar outcome was achieved in Argentina, led by weekly marches on the part of mothers seeking to account for their "disappeared" children.[10]

The advent of the multicentric world has also contributed to rendering violations of human rights more visible. Numerous organizations in that world—such as Amnesty International and Human Rights Watch—highlight violations by governments in ways that other states cannot readily emulate without breaking long-standing diplomatic protocols. Nor are governments the only collectivities whose practices are tracked by human rights NGOs. The work of the Southern Poverty Law Center in calling attention to the activities of private hate groups and militia organizations in the United States is illustrative of the increasing degree to which transparency has come to mark the human rights issue area. Indeed, given the diverse ways in which the bifurcation of global structures have facilitated the exposure of individuals and groups who systematically deprive others of their rights, it is difficult to identify any ways in which the transformation of the macro parameter has enhanced the efforts of the violators.

No less important, the bifurcation of global structures has tended to weaken the capacity of states to resist external pressures on behalf of human rights. The focus of numerous and unrelenting pressures from the multicentric world, those states that have long histories of assaulting the rights of their citizens are less able to hide behind the precedents of sovereignty to engage in such practices. Those states long committed to the protection of human rights experience the same pressures as bases for ignoring the sovereignty of the violating states and intervening in their affairs so as to bring violations to an end. There are a number of dynamics that account for the surge of what have come to be called "humanitarian interventions" in recent years, but the bifurcation of global structures and the relative loss of capabilities that this has meant for states is surely a prime source of such interventions.

Whatever form the pressures generated in the multicentric world may take, the channels through which they flow can vary from situation to situation. While in some instances they are brought to bear directly on the rights violators, perhaps even more frequently they are exercised indirectly through pressing sympathetic agencies of governments, which, in turn, employ their diverse resources to press the violators. Since governments still retain considerable clout, close cooperation between them and NGOs is the most effective mechanism for highlighting and rectifying human rights situations.[11]

Authority Crises

The turbulence model posits such crises as stemming from the skill revolution and the bifurcation of global structures, as well as from a number of other sources elaborated elsewhere.[12] Authority crises are conceived to be under way when public or private collectivities lack sufficient support to move toward their goals, and to be marked by fragile coalitions, divided governments, and pervasive indecision, stalemate, and paralysis in the framing, making, and implementing of policy. Put differently, traditional criteria of legitimacy have been superseded by performance criteria, with the result that as globalization renders the world increasingly complex, so are public officials and leaders in the private sector increasingly unable to generate compliance on the part of those toward whom they exercise authority. Indeed, viewed in these terms, it might well be argued that virtually all of the world's states and many of its subnational and international collectivities are undergoing some form of an authority crisis.

This transformation of the micro-macro parameter cuts both ways in terms of enhancing or inhibiting those who violate human rights. On the one hand, it enhances the violators by providing them with a line of reasoning that justifies their actions and enlarges the support proffered by their followers: such actions are defended on the grounds that challenges that move authority structures toward crisis undermine social stability and thus necessitate the curbing of rights. On the other hand, authority crises can be inhibiting in the sense that the bases of support for violation may shrink and opportunities may be created for individuals and groups to organize counteractions on behalf of those whose rights are denied such as humanitarian intervention. Under conditions of stasis or even stability, the inclination of communities to "rock the boat" by altering the prevailing formal and informal arrangements that sustain relationships and rights within them is not likely to be very intense. But when, for whatever reasons, authority is being questioned and contested, uncertainties are introduced into a community and openings to press for the rights of its members are thereby created. The amelioration of human rights is never a subdued or quiescent matter and the commotion attending authority crises thus serves to foster the conditions under which rights can be elevated to higher levels on the community's agenda.

THE DYNAMICS OF GLOBALIZATION

Human rights issues, like all the issues on the global agenda, are presently caught up in the convergence of two powerful forces, those that press for an expansion of ideas, goods, money, and people across long-standing boundaries (globalization) and those that press for a contraction of activities within existing boundaries (localization). As was vividly demonstrated during the 1999 WTO meeting in Seattle, these two dynamics are highly interactive, so much so that they amount to a singular process. More than that, they are causally linked as well as interactive, almost as if each increment of the one gives rise to an increment of the other. In order to capture the significance of these causal links, I have developed the concept of "fragmegration," a word that combines the fragmentation that often accompanies localizing reactions to globalization and the integration that is often fostered by globalizing reactions to localization.[13] The label may be awkward and grating, but that is its purpose. Its very abrasiveness is designed to continuously remind us of the complexity and reactions fostered by globalizing processes.[14] Indeed, I have become convinced that these interactive dynamics are so central to the course of events that it is more accurate to regard our era as one of fragmegration and not one of globalization.[15]

These processes are posited as having a historical starting point beyond which the pace of acceleration has shifted from a gentle upward slope to a steep incline. It could be argued that globalization is a long-term process that has been under way for millennia, ever since people began to expand their horizons across territorial space, and that thus our focus is on processes that have always been accelerating.[16] Such a line of reasoning, while surely not faulty, is misleading in the context of the perspective employed here, which posits the pace of acceleration, like human rights issues, as having quickened exponentially—even exploded—in recent decades. In what decade? A precise answer would also be misleading, as no single event can be readily cited as the birth of modern globalization. But part of the answer is that during the decades since World War II, and particularly subsequent to the 1960s, the entire dynamic discussed below took off at a rapid pace that greatly exceeded the pace of preceding decades.[17] It is estimated, for example, that today 1.4 billion e-mail messages cross national boundaries every day.[18] Quite possibly, moreover, these dynamics are poised for another step-level leap forward with the advent of the Internet (which is growing by one million web pages a day)[19] and new computer technologies, which include the prospect of a chip 100 billion (repeat: 100 billion) times faster than those available today.[20] Future generations might look back to the latter part of the 1990s and the widening scope of the Internet as the historical starting point for a new phase of modern globalization.

Microelectronic Technologies

But the Internet is only one of a number of recent microelectronic innovations that have led to the swift collapse of time and space, which, in turn, has fostered a reframing of the notion of territoriality and thereby facilitated the expansion of people, ideas, relationships,[21] goods, and money across long-standing boundaries. Global television, the fax machine, and fiber optic cable are but a few of the other technologies that are among the hallmarks of fragmegration and that have resulted in landscapes being supplemented and, in many instances, replaced by ethnoscapes, financescapes, technoscapes, ideoscapes, and mediascapes.[22]

Furthermore, and hardly less important, this communications system has contributed to processes of emulation and isomorphism that have indirectly extended the scope of the human rights regime. It is no accident, for example, that indigenous peoples have successfully begun to emulate the techniques of other human rights groups,[23] with the acquisition of their own territory in Canada by the Inuit people being perhaps a prime example of this.[24] To be sure, the success of the Inuits resulted from hard organizational work and a vigorous advocacy network, but the rapidity of their success—from an isolated minority to a full-fledged autonomous province in roughly fifteen years—can readily be interpreted as a measure of how the new microelectronic technologies have widely and quickly cascaded from one part of the world to another the bases for emulating the values, aspirations, and practices of human rights activists.

In sum, the new media of communications, and especially the Internet, are major factors underlying the transnationalization of the human rights regime. Long-standing national boundaries are no longer barriers to cooperation among like-minded people and groups devoted to exposing and contesting rights violations.

An Organizational Explosion and the Spread of Networks

Facilitated greatly by the availability of the new microelectronic technologies, but also rooted in a number of other sources, huge numbers of organizations and associations have come into being in recent decades.[25] Exact figures on the scope of this proliferation are elusive, but they are sufficiently large to justify asserting that an organizational explosion has accompanied the advent of fragmegration, and that it is no less relevant to the course of events than the population explosion. It has been calculated, for example, that Indonesia had only one independent environmental organization twenty years ago, whereas now there are more than 2,000 linked to an environmental network based in Jakarta. Likewise, registered nonprofit organizations in the Philippines grew from 18,000 to 58,000 between 1989 and 1996; in Slovakia, the figure went from a handful in the 1980s to more than 10,000 today; and in the United States, 70 percent of the nonprofit organizations—not counting religious groups and private foundations—filing tax returns with the Treasury Department are less than thirty years old and a third are less than fifteen years old.[26]

Part of the organizational explosion derives from all three of the aforementioned parametric transformations that have accompanied the onset of turbulence in world affairs: the skill revolution and the salience of new performance criteria for assessing legitimacy have encouraged people to join together in the political spaces opened up by the evolution of the multicentric world. Localizing reactions against the dynamics of globalization are another source of the explosion in the case of those people who feel threatened by change and are thus inclined to retreat to the familiar and close at hand, an inclination that brings them together into new or expanded organizations. The advent of social movements concerned with new issues on the global agenda, such as those that focus on environmental and feminist concerns, have also been a major source of the organizational explosion.

And, of course, the movement of human rights issues toward the top of the global agenda has been accompanied by a mushrooming of new organizations devoted to protecting and enhancing the rights of people. In 1999, there were said to be more than two hundred NGOs associated with human rights issues in the United States, a similar number in the United Kingdom and Europe, and increasing numbers in developing countries.[27] Indeed, between 1981 and 1990, the number of human rights groups in Latin America rose from 220 to over 550.[28] This array of organizations is not in itself the prime source of support for the human rights regime, since the latter also includes the agencies of national governments and international organizations,[29] but the regime's growth and solidification is a clear-cut indication of the large extent to which the dynamics of fragmegration have accelerated the salience of the many values that attach to the concept of human rights.

A major feature of the organizational explosion involves the evolution of a new organizational form, a horizontal network of ties both within and among NGOs. The vertical, hierarchical forms of earlier eras have neither disappeared nor been superseded, but the advent of networked organizations facilitated by the Internet and other recent technological innovations has added considerably to the number, capabilities, and effectiveness of NGOs in the multicentric world. A measure of the growth of transnational networks is readily evident in the estimate that the ranks of transnational NGOs have risen from 6,000 in 1990 to more than 26,000 in 1999.[30] Equally impressive, a measure of the capabilities and effectiveness of networked organizations is provided by the events surrounding the 1999 WTO meeting in Seattle, where some 1,500 NGOs signed an on-line anti-WTO protest, a phenomenon called an "NGO swarm," which can do great damage to international governmental organizations (IGOs) precisely because it has no "central leadership or command structure; it is a multiheaded, impossible to decapitate."[31]

In short, the explosive advent of networked organizations has enabled like-minded NGOs to reach across boundaries and pool their resources, share their information, exchange their personnel, and otherwise coordinate their efforts without undue concern for the bureaucratic rivalries that can undermine the programs of hierarchical structures.

The Mobility Upheaval

For a number of reasons—from the incentives provided by economic dislocations and political oppressions to the new transportation technologies that have provided the means, from global television that has provided close proximity to distant cultures to the cheap communications technologies that have provided immediate access to distant relatives and friends—the dynamics of fragmegration have launched and sustained a vast movement of people around the world. This mobility upheaval, which includes everyone from the tourist to the terrorist and the migrant to the jet-setter, has been so extensive that around 5 percent of the people alive today are estimated to be living in a country other than the one where they were born.[32] Indeed, to cite an equally impressive statistic, every day half a million airline passengers cross national boundaries.[33]

In important ways the mobility upheaval has had the consequence of undermining the struggle for human rights. Or at least one of its main dimensions, the migration of large numbers of people from southern countries into northern countries, has led to considerable prejudice and, in some cases, violence, on the part of natives of the host countries. Whatever the reasons for the migrations—and there are many—the migrants are seen by more than a few of the long-standing citizens of the host countries as threats, as low-wage or specialized competitors for jobs, as conveyors of alien cultures, as strangers who need to be controlled, if not removed. Right-wing politicians are especially antagonistic to the swelling number of immigrants and not unwilling to argue for policies that would violate the rights of immigrants. Indeed, politicians such as Jörg Haider in Austria, Jean-Marie Le Pen in France, Pauline Hansen in Australia, and Pat Buchanan in the United States have conducted campaigns founded on anti-immigrant appeals and generated more than trivial electoral support. And the more unemployment and other economic difficulties pervade countries that are host to large numbers of immigrants, the more are the rights of the latter likely to be jeopardized.

While the negative consequences for human rights of the mobility upheaval can hardly be understated and can seem insurmountable, there are also ways in which it has fostered positive consequences. Most notably, the vast movements of people have contributed to a worldwide preoccupation with identity, with a sense of ethnic, religious, cultural, gender, or other common roots that has enabled people to aggregate themselves into groups and press collectively for a recognition of their rights at all levels of community. Examples abound. Facilitated by the new microelectronic technologies and the organizational explosion, as well as by the mobility upheaval, women, indigenous people, the handicapped, and homosexuals are among those who have become sufficiently aware of their shared interests and identities to become transborder political movements that national governments and international organizations cannot ignore.

In sum, the worldwide surge toward identity politics has been both a boon and a detriment to the human rights movement. On the one hand, it has given many people a new or renewed sense of themselves, an uplifting integrity and dignity that had not existed before and that is consistent with the goals of those who espouse human rights. On the other hand, a keener sense of identity can mean that those who do not share in it are outsiders, strangers who may not be trustworthy, whose rights are questionable, and who can easily be redefined as threats to the insiders' way of life. For every group that has found strength in a greater sense of common identity, there is a Yugoslavian disaster waiting to happen or currently unfolding.[34]

The Globalization of National Economies

As previously indicated, some observers regard the world's shift away from Keynesian to neoliberal economic models in which trade and investment are subjected to many fewer governmental controls than heretofore—and which has thus resulted in a single global economy rather than many national ones—as such a fundamental source of fragmegration that all the others are secondary. While the premise of this essay is that such a line of reasoning is faulty, it is surely the case that the emergence of a global economy is a major stimulant of the turbulent and fragmegrative dynamics presently at work in the world. And it is equally the case that the global economy has widened and intensified the gap between the rich and poor both within and among countries. If one is inclined to view these economic deprivations generated by the global economy as an assault on human rights (as many, especially Asian, observers do), or if one is disposed to view the global economy as producing like-minded consumers who have little choice about the commodities and values they hold dear (as more than a few observers do), then clearly the corporate executives and others who initiate and sustain these economic dynamics can be treated as actors who undermine human rights in huge ways. By the same token, to the extent that the same dynamics raise standards of living, reduce the unfairness in the system, and lessen the rich-poor gap (as seemed to be the case during the several years prior to the Asian financial crisis), they brighten and accelerate the processes favoring human rights.

The Multidirectional Flows of Culture

Observers who fear that a global economy is leading the world toward a stifling uniformity underestimate the strength of local cultures and the incentives for cultural values to spread West as well as East and South as well as North. McDonald's may be thriving in Asia and thousands of other locations around the world,[35] but so are Chinese, Japanese, Vietnamese, and Korean restaurants frequented widely in the United States and Europe, and much the same can be said about the direction of intercultural flows in the fields of medicine, education, and religion. To be sure, the global economy is producing more Western consumers than Eastern ones, but there are good reasons to presume that worldwide tastes in clothing, food, and music are not overwhelming and desiccating local tastes. As indicated by McDonald's adapting its menu to the core preferences of host countries,[36] local cultures are rooted in deep-seated habits and a resilience that tend to absorb rather than emulate the lures of the global economy.

In a complicated and somewhat convoluted way, so it is with human rights. In those parts of the world where such rights are violated, people seek through the norms and practices of the human rights regime to preserve some of the basic premises of their own cultures. Michael Ignatieff notes:

> [T]he emergence of the global market has assisted the diffusion of human rights, since markets break down traditional social structures and encourage

the emergence of assertive temperaments. But while markets do create individuals, as buyers and sellers of goods and labor, these individuals often want human rights precisely to protect them from the indignities and indecencies of the market. Moreover, the dignity such a person is seeking to protect is not necessarily derived from Western models. The women in Kabul who come to Western human rights agencies seeking their protection from the Taliban militias do not want to cease being Muslim wives and mothers; they want to combine respect for their traditions with certain "universal" prerogatives, like the right to an education or professional health care provided by a woman. . . . Human rights has gone global, but it has also gone local.[37]

Weakened States and Narrowed Sovereignty

While observers may differ on the extent to which the dynamics of fragmegration have weakened states and narrowed the range of their sovereignty, few would quarrel with the proposition that the scope of the authority of states has lessened as fragmegrative processes have accelerated. Most states can no longer control the flow of ideas, money, drugs, and crime across their borders, and, given the depth and breadth of the mobility upheaval, even the flow of people has proven difficult to handle. The skill revolution, the bifurcation of global structures, and the new criteria of legitimacy that sustain turbulence in world affairs have combined with the new technologies, the organizational explosion, and the other dynamics of fragmegration to reduce the autonomy of states and to weaken their capacity to pursue innovative policies at home and influence developments abroad. States vary, of course, in the degree to which their capabilities and authority have declined: perhaps a few have managed to ward off the full range of fragmegrative dynamics, just as a few others have failed to meet the challenges and ceased to exist. The central tendency, however, is one in which most states have to struggle to retain a modicum of control over the course of events within their ever more porous borders.

As their control at home and abroad has diminished, so the sovereignty of states has eroded. If the sovereignty of a country involves having the final say over what transpires within its borders, then the discrepancy between the huge increase of transborder flows and the ability of states to control these flows is a measure of the degree to which they have lost sovereignty.

THE DRAMA OF THE MOST OBSTREPEROUS ACTOR

Several decades ago I wrote a short text organized around "drama" as a metaphor for the problems that beset political systems.[38] The difficulties systems encounter in maintaining their coherence and reconciling their tensions, while at the same time framing and moving toward their goals, were conceived to be pervaded with dramatic content. Like marriages, business firms, and communities, the text argued, polities are fragile social entities, ever susceptible to deterioration and always on the edge of collapsing into their environments. Divorce for a marriage, bankruptcy for a firm, and race riots for a community serve as extreme reminders of these potentials, and the fact that many marriages, businesses, and communities manage to survive and, indeed, to thrive and prosper was posited as remarkable, as anything but certain, and as a triumph of human will, ingenuity, and habit. The text offered twenty-seven dramas as illustrative of what any polity experiences in its effort to cohere and endure.[39]

What I called "the drama of the most obstreperous actor" always struck me as the most intriguing and telling. Its origins derived from having read somewhere that "a family is a tyranny run by its most obstreperous member." Every system can be assumed to have a most obstreperous actor, a person, group, organization, or country that says or does things that are more extreme than that of any other actors in the system and thus becomes a preoccupation for the rest of the system in its efforts to cope with its challenges. It is characteristic of the most obstreperous actor that the system needs to expend extensive energy and resources to pick up the pieces strewn about by the actor's obstreperousness. At the time of its first iteration, this drama was illustrated by the story of Joseph McCarthy in the U.S. Senate and Charles de Gaulle in the North Atlantic Treaty Organization, both of whom conducted themselves in such a way that their respective institutions invested considerable time and energy in coping with, absorbing, or otherwise adapting to the excessive demands, unexpected irregularities, and system-threatening actions of their most obstreperous actors.

Once I immersed myself for the first time in the literature on human rights, I was frequently reminded of the drama of the most obstreperous actor. The drama's extreme circumstances seem highly relevant to the moral, empirical, and historical foundations of the diverse situations in which human rights are or have been central concerns. More specifically, in the years since the adoption of the UN Charter and the Universal Declaration of Human Rights in the 1940s, any individual, group, or state that systematically violates the rights of others can be viewed as generating the kind of systemic preoccupations and consuming the kind of restless energies that mark the drama of the most obstreperous actor. Indeed, perhaps more than any other kind of issue or situation in politics today, those involving human rights are pervaded with most obstreperous actors and the energies devoted to coping with them.

Since these energies are the focus of much of the preceding analysis, the foregoing amounts, in effect, to a second iteration of the drama of the most obstreperous actor. It treats the diverse struggles to improve human rights presently under way throughout the world as dramas in which various types of systems at the subnational, national, transnational, international, and global levels seek to cope with their most obstreperous actors in the context of the pervasive turbulence and globalization that prevails at the onset of a new century.

In so doing, the drama does not deny the existence of different conceptions of human rights that rest on various ontological and epistemological foundations,[40] but neither does the drama metaphor depend on a particular set of foundations. Rather it focuses a spotlight on the efforts in any political system—local or global, southern or northern, developed or developing—undertaken to sustain systemic coherence by identifying, containing, and bringing to justice the obstreperous violators of what the system defines as human rights.

Identifying Most Obstreperous Actors and Their Opponents

Much of the literature on human rights tends to treat states as the prime culprits. But a most-obstreperous-actor approach suggests that there is a multiplicity of types of violators. Some states, especially those viewed as having rogue qualities, are surely sources of human rights deprivations, but so are leaders who arouse latent ethnic or racial hatreds, private organizations that contribute to or sustain cultures of prejudice, multinational corporations that suppress peaceful protests,[41] militia groups that derive their coherence from a loathing of foreigners, rebel movements that treat their goals as justifying any means to achieve them, military juntas that are not reluctant to suppress public demands for change when they perceive a threat to societal stability, and so on across a wide range of individual and collective actors for whom the rights of people are not a high priority.

Much the same can be said about the actors who seek to protect and expand human rights. These can include states that are committed to enhancing the well-being of individuals, nongovernmental organizations (NGOs) that contest those who violate human rights and that seek to mobilize support for their efforts; publics that are outraged by cases in which rights have been brutally negated; like-minded elites who launch advertising campaigns on behalf of groups who have been deprived of their rights; individuals with heroic pasts as victims of prejudice and injustice; public officials who are moved to isolate, undermine, or otherwise contain the most obstreperous actors who voice or act out their prejudices; and so on across a vast array of individual and collective actors for whom rights issues are especially salient. The human rights issue area, in short, has become dense with actors on the various sides of any situation in which people are regarded as having been deprived of their well being.

TABLE 8.1: The Impact of Turbulence
and Globalization on the Conduct of Most Obstreperous
Actors (MOAs) in Four Domains of Human Rights.

Aspects of global change	Security Rights	Economic Rights	Cultural Rights	Political Rights
Skill revolution	Constrains MOAs through increased sensitivity of individuals and groups to their needs and wants	Constrains corporations as MOAs by empowering individuals to oppose violations of labor rights	Constrains MOAs through greater awareness of multiple identities and threats thereto	Constrains MOAs through increased capacity of individuals to know when, where, and how to engage in collective action
Authority crises	Constrain MOAs by spotlighting rights of groups and individuals; embolden MOAs to curb rights	Constrain MOAs by heightening sensitivities to the potential of eliminated jobs	Empowers MOAs through increased consciousness of cultural differences and animosities	Undermines stability and competence of states as MOAs
Bifurcation of global structures	Allows for more effective pressures on governments and corporations as MOAs	Constrains government MOAs by weakening their control over markets	Hampers MOAs by encouraging a pre-occupation with identity on the part of sub-cultures	Facilitates activities of vigilante groups as MOAs; hampers states as MOAs through evolution and coherence of multicentric world

Organizational explosion	Constrains MOAs by facilitating proliferation of human rights organizations	Constrains corporations as MOAs through proliferation of competitors	Constrains MOAs through proliferation and strengthening of diaspora	Constrains MOAs through the disaggregation and decentralization of authority
Mobility upheaval	Empowers MOAs opposed to the presence of "foreigners"	Enables corporations as MOAs to more easily form business alliances	Undermines MOAs through dispersal of minorities or other opponents; enhances MOAs through presence of "foreigners" to target	Constrains MOAs by contributing to greater awareness of minority rights
Microelectronic technologies	Constrains MOAs by facilitating organizational networks	Empowers crime syndicates as MOAs to more easily launder and move their money	Constrains or helps MOAs by facilitating greater sense of cultural differences	Constrains MOAs by enabling opposition groups to mobilize more effectively
Weakening of states and sovereignty	Renders governments as MOAs more vulnerable to rights protests	Strengthens corporations as MOAs	Constrains MOAs by encouraging development of multicultural regimes	Strengthens prejudices of MOAs during periods of stress

THE HUMAN RIGHTS REGIME

Since NATO forces belatedly took a stand against ethnic cleansing in Kosovo, it seems clear that the most powerful consequences of a turbulent and frag-megrative world are those that have fostered greater local, national, and transnational sensitivities to human rights. In the decades since the 1948 adoption of the Universal Declaration of Human Rights, the regime that has evolved through various treaties, advocacy networks, situational outcomes, and policy pronouncements can be readily discerned, even though it encompasses contradictory and conflictual elements. To be sure, these contradictions and conflicting perspectives are serious and portend the possibility, even the expectation, that the moral consensus that has undergirded the regime since 1948 will continue to splinter as localizing definitions of rights fracture the globalizing notion that such rights are universal.[42] Nonetheless, Ignatieff observes, "[t]his does not mean the end of the human rights movement, but its belated coming of age, its recognition that we live in a plural world of cultures which have a right to equal consideration in the argument about what we can and cannot, should and should not do to other human beings."[43]

Moreover, recent years have been marked by enough evolution of the norms, principles, rules, institutions, and procedures comprising the human rights regime to suggest that some of its core will survive the splintering that lies ahead. The fall of the junta in Argentina, the detention of General Pinochet in London, and the indictment of selected persons in Bosnia and Serbia as war criminals—not to mention China's "vigorous" struggle to avoid being listed as a human rights violator by the UN Human Rights Commission[44]—are cogent indicators that the regime and the international law supporting it retain a measure of coherence. Indeed, whatever the wisdom of NATO's resort to bombing on behalf of the Kosovars, the forcefulness of the military campaign has in all likelihood permanently altered the meaning of sovereignty and the readiness of governments to assault the rights of their own people. The world's intrusion into the domestic affairs of countries that undertake such assaults may be inconsistent and variable, as a comparison of its actions in Yugoslavia, Chechnya, and several situations in Africa clearly demonstrate, but the principle that sovereignty is inviolable has been narrowed.[45] Put differently, the human rights regime has been both the victor over and the victim of its most obstreperous actors in a world of accelerating fragmegration.

SUMMARY AND A RESEARCH AGENDA

Perhaps the best way to summarize the preceding analysis is to acknowledge that it is interpretive and not empirical, that it focuses on big structures, large processes, and huge comparisons[46] and thus consists of no more than a series of broad hypotheses that can serve as an agenda for future research. Table 8.1 suggests some of these hypotheses by delineating how the most obstreperous actors who violate the rights of individuals or groups are hindered or facilitated by the dynamics of turbulence and globalization (the seven rows) in four domains (the columns).[47] The abbreviated entries in the table's twenty-eight cells outline only a few of the propositions that could usefully be explored, either through the extant literature or through the generation of new data and cases studies.

While the cell entries are crude summaries of hypotheses that need to be formulated at greater length, table 8.1 makes it clear that numerous research tasks lie ahead if the links between globalization and human rights are to be clarified and fully grasped. But, equally clearly, they are tasks well worth undertaking.

NOTES

This chapter originated in a paper prepared for presentation at the Conference on Globalization and Human Rights: Transnational Problems and Transnational Solutions? (University of California Irvine, 15–16 January 2000). An earlier version of the paper was presented at the Annual Meeting of American Political Science Association (Atlanta, 4 September 1999). I am indebted to Susan Burgerman, Alison Brysk, David Earnest, and Kathryn Sikkink for their helpful criticisms of earlier drafts.

1. Furthermore, the impacts of turbulence and globalization are mutually reinforcing. One is not a primary cause and the other a secondary cause. As will be seen, the onset of both sets of dynamics are presumed to have occurred in the same historical period, but they consist of different processes that involve different aspects of the human condition. Turbulence and globalization, in other words, are not aspects of each other. Through mutual reinforcement, however, they together constitute a powerful force for both good and bad insofar as human rights are concerned.

2. For a discussion of corruption as an issue area, see Wang and Rosenau 1999. Technically, both incidents of crime and corruption deprive their victims of human rights, but they are not normally located in the human rights issue area precisely because they tend to derive from idiosyncratic rather than systematic sources. To be sure, some crime is sustained by organizations, but a preponderance of criminal actions throughout the world is undertaken by individuals who bear no organizational relation to each other.

3. Donnelly 1989: 23.
4. McGrew 1998: 194.
5. Rosenau 1990.
6. For an effort to demonstrate empirically the transformation of this micro parameter, see Rosenau and Fagen 1997.
7. Rosenau 1990, ch. 10.
8. Rosenau 1992b.
9. Klotz 1999.

10. Brysk 1994.

11. For an elaborate and cogent discussion of the various stages through which interactions over human rights issues can unfold between the state- and multi-centric world, see Risse et al. 1999.

12. Cf. Rosenau 1990, chs. 8, 14.

13. This concept was first developed in Rosenau 1983. For a more recent and elaborate formulation, see Rosenau 1994.

14. Other single-word labels designed to suggest the contradictory tensions that pull systems toward both coherence and collapse are "chaord," a label that juxtaposes the dynamics of chaos and order, "glocalization," which points to the simultaneity of globalizing and localizing dynamics, and "regcal," a term designed to focus attention on the links between regional and local phenomena. The chaord designation is proposed in Hock 1994: 1–2; the glocalization concept is elaborately developed in Robertson 1995; and the regcal formulation can be found in Tai and Wong 1998. I prefer the term "fragmegration" because it does not imply a territorial scale and broadens the focus to include tensions at work in organizations as well as those that pervade communities.

15. Cf. Rosenau 1997, ch. 6.

16. An analysis along these lines can be found in R. P. Clark 1997.

17. For an amplification of this line of reasoning, see Rosenau 1997, chs. 2–3, and Held et al. 1999: 424–44.

18. White House, Office of the Press Secretary, "Remarks by President Clinton at University of Chicago Convocation Ceremonies," 12 June 1999, 2 (http://www.whitehouse.p-ov/WH/New/html/19990612.html).

19. Ibid., 1.

20. Markoff 1999.

21. As one analyst put it, "*The so-called 'information revolution'* . . . *is actually, and more accurately, a 'relationship revolution.'* Anyone trying to get a handle on the dazzling technologies of today and the impact they'll have tomorrow, would be well advised to re-orient their worldview around relationships. Along every conceivable dimension—from the intimate to the institutional—digital media force both individuals and organizations to redefine what kind of relationships create value." Michael Schrage, "The Relationship Revolution" (http://www.ml.com/woml/forum/relation.htm), 3 (emphasis in the original).

22. For a discussion of these "scapes," see Appadurai 1996: 33–37.

23. A compelling analysis along these lines can be found in Brysk 2000b.

24. Nunavut came into being as a territory for the Inuit people on 1 April 1999. See Martin O'Malley, "Nunavut: Canada's Nw Territory," CBC News Online—Indepth: Nunavut (http://CBCnews.CBC.CA/news/indepth/nanuvut/home.htmi).

25. Salamon 1994.

26. Bornstein 1999.

27. Held et al. 1999: 67. During a 1999 visit to Katmandu, I was informed by the president of the Human Rights Organization of Nepal, Kapil Shrestha, that the number of human rights organizations in Nepal had risen from fifteen to forty in just a few years.

28. Keck and Sikkink 1998: 92.

29. Waslin 1998.

30. *Economist*, 11 December 1999, p. 21.

31. Ibid.

32. Tharoor 1999: 7.

33. White House, Office of the Press Secretary, "Remarks by President Clinton at University of Chicago Convocation Ceremonies," 2.

34. Wittes 1997.

35. Ritzer [1993] 1996.

36. Watson 1997.

37. Ignatieff 1999a: 59, 60.

38. Rosenau 1973.

39. Ibid., ch. 3

40. For a cogent discussion of these foundations, see Chris Brown 1997: ch. 24.

41. See, e.g., Human Rights Watch 1999.

42. Ignatieff 1999a: 62.

43. Ibid.

44. Elizabeth Olson 1999.

45. Miller 1999.

46. Tilly 1984.

47. I am indebted to Kathryn Sikkink for the idea of constructing such a table.

IV

Cooperation

9

Transnational Civil Society Campaigns and the World Bank Inspection Panel

Jonathan Fox

For more than two decades, the World Bank has been a lightning rod for transnational civil society action. International environmental, human rights and indigenous rights networks have repeatedly challenged the World Bank's sustained support for repressive regimes, as well as its high profile promotion of socially and environmentally costly development strategies. These transnational campaigns can be understood as efforts to hold one of the most powerful multilateral organizations publicly accountable for investments made in the name of "socially and environmentally sustainable development." The diversity of civil society Bank campaigns across countries and issues, as well as their long-term, sustained track records, make them especially rich sources of lessons for understanding transnational advocacy coalitions more generally.

The World Bank has responded to its critics in many different ways, ranging from short-term damage control concessions and enlightened-sounding policy reforms on the one hand, to persistent gaps in meeting in its own social and environmental reform commitments on the other. From the point of view of campaigns in defense of the rights of communities directly hurt by Bank projects, the institution's official safeguard policies for mitigating the social and environmental costs of its investment decisions constitute a new set of minimum rights. Most notably, each decade, literally millions of people are forcibly evicted by Bank-funded projects, and North-South resistance coalitions have encouraged the Bank to rethink its policies for dealing with what it calls "involuntary resettlement." Across a wide range of social and environmental issues, the Bank's reform commitments have, in turn, become benchmarks that chart the terrain for subsequent struggles over rights with international organizations and nation-states more generally. While transnational campaigns have clearly led the World Bank to change its official discourse dramatically, a huge gap remains between its rhetoric and its practice.[1] This "disconnect," to use World Bank jargon, fueled campaigns for institutional changes that would go beyond specific social and environmental policy issues to focus on the problem of accountability itself. A combination of symbolic and leverage politics pressured the World Bank to create an innovative pro-accountability institution, the Inspection Panel. This relatively autonomous panel is mandated to investigate claims from directly affected people that the Bank's reform policies have been violated. In terms of both its political origins and its institutional design, the Inspection Panel is a paradigm case of transnational civil society's capacity to hold powerful international organizations more accountable. In an effort to draw broader lessons about the institutional impact of transnational civil society campaigns, this essay offers a brief assessment of the panel's first five years.

WINNING THE BATTLE WHILE LOSING THE WAR?

The World Trade Organization's recent debacle in Seattle led the *Economist* to trace the civil society trade protests in part back to the "50 Years is Enough" campaign against the World Bank and IMF in 1994. The *Economist* proceeded to congratulate the World Bank for its subsequent effort, supposedly successful, to demobilize and to co-opt its NGO critics, observing: "From environmental policy to debt relief, NGOs are at the center of World Bank policy. Often they determine it. The new World Bank is more transparent, but it is also more beholden to a new set of special interests."[2] Is it possible that NGOs have gained this much influence? Have they really demobilized? While it is true that, since 1994, the IMF, MAI and the WTO superseded the Bank on some protesters' lists of top targets, many other advocacy groups and social organizations—especially those closer to the ground and further from the global media spotlight—remain deeply involved in trying to get the World Bank to live up to its social and environmental reform commitments.

The analytical challenge implicit in the *Economist*'s assessment is how to disentangle co-optation from substantive concessions, while recognizing that the difference is often in the eye of the beholder. There is, moreover, a basic contradiction in the *Economist*'s assessment: if NGOs really did determine World Bank policy, that would suggest that they have much more influence than the term "co-optation" implies. For example, if NGOs really did determine World Bank policy, then it would be difficult to explain why more than half of the Bank's 1999 lending went to structural adjustment for the first time ever. These macroeconomic "reform" loans are inherently far removed both from civil society levers of influence, as well as largely immune from the scrutiny of the Bank's own social and environmental reform policies. Even at the level of specific infrastructural investments—which offer critics much more tangible targets—the World Bank continues to propose

new projects that directly subsidize huge transnational corporations to carry
out likely environmental disasters, as in the case of Exxon and the Chad-
Cameroon pipeline.[3] Both regimes that are to benefit from this project are
highly repressive, suggesting serious human rights implications as well.

Another World Bank/human rights case heated up in 1999 after the discovery that the Bank was planning to fund a project called "China Western Poverty Reduction," which turned out to threaten ethnic Tibetans and
Mongolians. In spite of the Bank's well-known, sophisticated NGO en-
gagement, involving extensive operational collaboration, policy consultations and enlightened discourse, in the Tibet case, the institution unknowingly stumbled over one of world's most influential indigenous rights
campaigns. The resulting mobilization was almost as intense as the previous "peak" of anti-Bank protest back in the early 1990s, leading to unusual
"no" votes by the U.S. and German representatives on the Bank's board,
high-level international diplomatic tensions with China, imprisonment and
serious injury to NGO investigators, a critical investigative report by the
Bank's official Inspection Panel, as well as widespread negative news and
editorial attention in many of the most influential English-language newspapers in the aftermath of the April 2000 World Bank/IMF street protests.
This project campaign had the broader effect of revitalizing one of the
Bank's most promising pro-accountability reforms, the Inspection Panel,
and led China to withdraw the proposed project in July 2000.[4]

THE WORLD BANK INSPECTION PANEL:
WHEN DOES TRANSNATIONAL CIVIL SOCIETY MAKE A DIFFERENCE?

In 1993, the World Bank's board of directors responded to international environmental and human rights critics by creating a precedent-setting public
accountability mechanism. Local-global civil society advocacy networks
found allies in donor governments and their message resonated with internal World Bank concerns about the need to reverse the declining effectiveness of its investments.[5] Through the Inspection Panel, citizens of developing countries can now make direct complaints about the environmental and
social costs of World Bank projects. The World Bank is the only major international organization that permits such direct citizen access. Composed
of distinguished independent development experts, the panel is a transnational entity embedded in a multilateral institution. On balance, it has been
a remarkably autonomous body, permitting people negatively affected by
Bank projects the opportunity to gain some degree of diplomatic standing,
potential transnational public interest allies, media access, and even the possibility of some tangible concessions. In spite of its limits, the World Bank's
Inspection Panel is one of its most tangible institutionwide policy changes
in response to almost two decades of environmental and human rights crit-

icism. As World Bank President James Wolfensohn put it, the Inspection Panel is a "bold experiment in transparency and accountability that has worked to the benefit of all concerned."[6]

The Inspection Panel's experience constitutes an important empirical test of the widely noted influence of nongovernmental actors in international relations. Here is an institution that all parties agree was created in response to sustained advocacy campaigns by North-South NGO/grassroots coalitions. By creating the panel, the World Bank board of directors recognized the legitimacy of the normative principle that international organizations should be publicly accountable, another powerful indicator of the influence on nongovernmental actors in international affairs. In the process, transnational advocacy networks consistently used combinations of what Margaret Keck and Kathryn Sikkink crisply frame as: "(1) *information politics,* or the ability to quickly and credibly generate politically usable information and move it to where it will have the most impact; (2) *symbolic politics,* or the ability to call upon symbols, actions or stories that make sense of a situation for an audience that is frequently far away; (3) *leverage politics,* or the ability to call upon powerful actors to affect a situation where weaker members of a network are unlikely to have an influence; and (4) *accountability politics,* or the effort to hold powerful actors to their previously state policies or principles" (1997: 16). Keck and Sikkink's agenda-setting study goes on to evaluate transnational network impact in terms of various "stages": agenda-setting, encouraging discursive policy commitments from states and other actors, causing international or national procedural change, affecting policy, and influencing actual behavioral change in target actors (1998: 201).

This study's assessment of the Inspection Panel confirms core elements of this proposition. The panel experience demonstrated the capacity of transnational advocacy networks to make World Bank accountability a legitimate international issue (agenda-setting). The panel experience also demonstrates the power of transnational advocacy networks to get the World Bank to recognize that its compliance with its own social and environmental policies has often been inadequate (accountability politics). The panel's creation is also evidence of transnational networks' capacity to promote new institutional access points for civil society (procedural change). This is the context for this study's focus on the next genre of impact in this sequence, the issue of changes in actual institutional behavior as a result of the panel. Do the World Bank and its nation-state partners actually comply more consistently with their own social and environmental reform mandates as a result of the panel? Here the findings are much more ambiguous, since transnational advocacy networks' impacts via the Inspection Panel are mainly indirect and to some degree based on counterfactual logic ("reform compliance would have been even worse in its absence . . . "). These findings raise more general questions about the relationship between international and national actors in the process of institutionalizing transnational civil society advocacy impacts. This essay is part of a broader study whose main finding is that even in this paradigm case of transnational advocacy-driven multilateral institutional innovation, nation-states retain powerful levers to block accountability politics most of the time.

Thomas Risse, Stephen Ropp, and Kathryn Sikkink have posed directly relevant questions about the relationship between changing international accountability norms and institutional behavior in their important new study of human rights norms. They start by recognizing that the growing literature on international norms "is underspecified with regard to the causal mechanisms through which these ideas spread . . . and rarely accounts for the variation in the impact of international norms."[7] Their promising framework for understanding the relationship between international norms and domestic changes is informed by extensive comparative case analysis. However, their approach is least specified at its final stage; the point after norms are nominally accepted by institutions, but before they are consistently respected by institutions in practice.

Once institutions like nation-states or the World Bank accept and make policies to respect more enlightened norms, how do international and national forces interact to determine the degree to which they actually comply with these policy commitments in practice? Risse, Ropp, and Sikkink's approach suggests continued predominance of international factors at this point. More extensive comparative case analysis may indicate, however, that at this "final" stage of making institutional behavior consistent with human rights norms, domestic political factors often become primary.[8] The Inspection Panel's first five years' experience suggests that process of interaction between international and national factors that transforms normative, discursive, and policy changes into more tangible changes in institutional behavior remains ambiguous.

The Inspection Panel case, as well as the broader experience with social and environmental reform at the World Bank, suggests that transnational advocacy network-led changes often get "stuck" between their agenda-setting, discursive, and policy impact and their influence on the actual behavior of powerful institutions.[9] The panel experience suggests that the mix of transnational and national factors that can produce agenda-setting and policy victories at the international level may be different from the constellation of forces that has the capacity to make institutional behavior consistent in practice. The relative causal weights of international and national factors in this final "institutionalizing" phase may well shift toward the national arena.

Recent studies of several World Bank social and environmental reform policies consistently found that policy reforms were driven by a mutually reinforcing interaction between external advocacy pressures on nation-states as well as the Bank, on the one hand, and the uneven presence of insider reformers on the other. These specific studies include the following policies: environmental impact assessment, poverty-targeted lending, NGO relations, energy, forests, water, indigenous peoples, resettlement, gender, agricultural pest management, and public information access policy.[10] Complementary studies of civil society campaigns to change specific projects found that influencing Bank and nation-state practice was consistently more difficult than reforming Bank policy. Because many of these project-focused Bank campaigns deliberately focused on the gap between reformed policies and practice, they are powerful tests of the limits and possibilities of "account-ability politics." A systematic assessment of almost two decades of environmental, social, and human rights campaigns to change specific Bank projects up until 1997 found little tangible impact on the projects themselves, most often limited to partial mitigation measures.[11] Indeed, project campaigns tended to have much more impact on international discourse and policy than on the projects themselves that provoked the campaigns in the first place — thus setting new benchmarks and reconstituting the terrain on which subsequent campaigns unfolded, but leading to few tangible results for the original participants.

REVIEWING THE INSPECTION PANEL'S FIRST FIVE YEARS

This study will not attempt to cover the full range of the Inspection Panel's experience so far. Its political origins are already clear. Even official Bank discourse acknowledges that the panel was created in direct response to international environmental and human rights campaigns.[12] Many of the actual claim issues have been analyzed in detail in the sources cited in the references that follow. The panel has also been analyzed in the context of international law.[13] Explanations of the panel's mandate and procedures, many of the original case materials and official panel responses, plus details regarding the recent debates over how to change the panel's mandate are publicly accessible.[14] This study builds on past research on the process of the Bank's social and environmental reforms and draws on the extensive literature specifically on the panel and on unpublished Bank policy analyses. It is also based on interviews with World Bank social and environmental specialists, panel staff and a former panel member, U.S. and developing country policymakers, Washington-based advocacy NGOs, borrowing country NGO and grassroots leaders, and researchers who follow controversial projects on the ground. The main conclusion is that the panel has had a contradictory impact on Bank-state-society relations. The panel appears to subvert nation-state sovereignty, in favor of broader notions of rights, but in practice the panel has also emboldened some nation-states to lead a backlash that seeks to block the implementation of transnational accountability reforms.

The panel's mandate regarding accountability links three core concepts: noncompliance with Bank policies, material harm (or the threat of it) and causation (establishing the link between noncompliance and harm).[15] The panel's point of departure is that the Bank has already established a wide range of social and environmental policy reforms that attempt not merely to "first do no harm" but also to actively promote poverty alleviation and sustainable development. Since the panel's creation, a core subset of these policies has come to be called within the Bank "safeguard policies." Since the panel was created, however, some of the policies have been "reformatted," a process discussed below. In short, these reform policies are the benchmark standards that permit the otherwise vague concept of "accountability" to be operationalized in practice. Table 9.1 summarizes these benchmark policies and their various stages of revision.[16] In addition, the World Bank has also issued many other important sustainable development policy mandates since the mid-late 1980s, involving gender, poverty reduction, NGO collaboration, community participation, water resources, and energy efficiency/ conservation. Many of these additional policies are remarkably detailed and enlightened, but they are not written as mandatory minimum benchmark standards (in contrast to the safeguard policies, such as the requirement to carry out environmental impact assessments or action plans to minimize and deal with large-scale "involuntary resettlement"). The Inspection Panel was not designed to encourage higher levels of compliance with essentially "good practice" recommendations, and therefore these additional reform policies do not fall within its scope of direct impact.

The Inspection Panel is extraordinary because any affected borrowing country citizen can seek recourse directly, without having to go through his or her national government. In this sense, its very existence challenges key assumptions of national sovereignty, even though its mandate is limited to examining Bank policy failures rather than those of borrowing governments. At the same time, while the panel constitutes a transnational arena for managing conflict, it does not exactly bypass nation-states, because they remain represented on the Bank's board of executive directors, which retains authority over whether the panel can investigate. Both donor and borrowing governments are represented on the Bank's board, and the panel experience has shown that the board is far from a pliable instrument of a handful of donor governments, as is widely assumed. This impression was created by the fact that the panel itself was created through the influence of Northern donor governments on the World Bank. The United States played a critical leadership role in this process and managed to induce a consensus in spite of its minority voting power (17 percent of the shares in a one-dollar, one vote system).

In the case of the creation of the Inspection Panel, the exercise of U.S. influence in favor of accountability reform was made possible by an unusual

TABLE 9.1 World Bank Safeguard Policies

Policy	Key Features	Conversion Status
OP/BP/GP 4.01 Environmental Assessment (EA)	*Potential environmental consequences of projects should be identified early in the project cycle *EAs and mitigation plans are required for projects with significant environmental impacts or involuntary resettlement *EAs should include analysis of alternative designs and sites, or consideration of no option *Requires public participation and information disclosure before board approval	Approved January 1999
OP 4.04 Natural Habitats	*Prohibits financing of projects involving "significant conversion of natural habitats unless there are no feasible alternatives" *Requires environmental cost/benefit analysis *Requires EA with mitigation measures	Approved 15 October 1995
OP 4.36 Forestry	*Prohibits financing for commercial logging operations or acquisition of equipment for use in primary moist tropical forests	Conversion incomplete
OP 4.09 Pest Management	*Supports environmentally sound pest management, including integrated pest management, but does not prohibit the use of highly hazardous pesticides *Pest management is the borrower's responsibility in the context of a project's EA	Conversion complete
OD 4.30 Involuntary Resettlement	*Implemented in projects that displace people *Requires public participation in resettlement planning as part of the EA for a project *Intended to restore or improve income-earning capacity of displaced populations	Conversion incomplete
OD 4.20 Indigenous Peoples	*Purpose is to ensure that indigenous peoples benefit from bank-financed development and to avoid or mitigate adverse affects on indigenous peoples	Has not been converted; the bank is consulting with indigenous peoples

Policy	Description	Status
	*Applies to projects that might adversely affect indigenous peoples or to projects that target indigenous peoples as beneficiaries *Requires participation of indigenous peoples in creation of "indigenous peoples development plans"	and NGOs prior to changing the policy
OPN 11.03 Cultural Property	*Purpose is to assist in the preservation of cultural property, such as sites having archeological, paleontological, historical, religious, and unique cultural values *Seeks to assist in their preservation and avoid their elimination Discourages financing of projects that will damage cultural property	To be issued as OP/BP/GP 4.11
OP/BP 4.37 Safety of Dams	*Applies to large dams (15 meters or more in height) *Requires review by independent experts throughout project cycle *Requires preparation of EA and detailed plans for construction and operation and periodic inspection by the Bank	Conversion complete
OP/BP/GP 7.50 Projects on International Waterways	*Covers riparian waterways that form a boundary between two or more states, as well as any bay, gulf, strait or channel bordered by two or more states *Applies to dams, irrigation, flood control, navigation, water, sewage, and industrial projects *Requires notification, agreement between states, detailed maps, feasibility surveys	Conversion complete
OP/BP 7.60 Projects in Disputed Areas	*Applies to projects in which there are territorial disputes *Allows the bank to proceed if governments agree to go forward without prejudice to claims *Requires early identification of territorial disputes and descriptions in all bank documentation	Approved November 1994

SOURCE: Bank Information Center, "Toolkits for Activists," http://www.bicusa.org/toolkits/policyTK/policy1.htm#recent. The full texts are accessible on www.worldbank.org).

NOTE: all policies are not yet converted are still in force in their "old" format.

confluence of events. After all, U.S. policy influence at the World Bank usually focuses on a narrower set of interests, such as private banks concerned with the repayment of their international debts or exporters of U.S. capital goods to developing countries.[17] Not only did Democrats control both the presidency and congress during a brief 1992–94 political window of opportunity, but an internationalist reformer, Congressman Barney Frank, controlled a key House banking subcommittee. For more than a decade, environmentalists and human rights activists (in a de facto alliance with Republican foreign aid critics) had been using U.S. congressional oversight over foreign aid appropriations as a critical lever to push the U.S. government to call for World Bank reform, to limited effect.[18] By 1993, however, the credibility of the World Bank's promises to change was at a dramatically low point. A media-savvy, broad-based North-South campaign against India's Narmada dam had obliged the Bank to create an independent commission to review the project, which found systematic violations of Bank social and environmental policies, thus vindicating the critics. At the same time, the Bank had also just inadvertently released a major internal report that documented a pervasive "culture of loan approval" that undermined the quality of its investments.[19] The Narmada campaign brought together the key levers posited by Keck and Sikkink: information politics, symbolic politics, accountability politics, as well as a powerful example of leverage politics. The leverage came from the political opportunity created by the U.S. House of Representatives' annual foreign aid budget debate. U.S. congressional reformers, under pressure from transnational advocacy coalitions, threatened to cut appropriations for the World Bank's soft loan window unless the Bank agreed to create a major accountability window and a new, more open information disclosure policy.[20]

BROAD PATTERNS IN PANEL CLAIMS

When reviewing the Inspection Panel's first five years, several puzzles emerge. First, why did the panel receive only eleven claims in its first five years from NGOs and grassroots movements? After all, the World Bank approves hundreds of new projects each year, and only some of them have been influenced by its enlightened new sustainable development discourse. It turns out that using the panel effectively is easier said than done, and its official mandate only applies directly to a fraction of controversial projects. Second, the World Bank's board of directors has rejected most of the panel's recommendations, followed by a recent effort by some member governments to weaken the panel's already-limited powers. Third, the panel has an ambiguous relationship with the World Bank's broader array of "safeguard policies," the institution's many social and environmental policy mandates designed to mitigate harm and to promote sustainable development. Beyond actual claims it has addressed, has the panel contributed to improved compliance with reform policies more generally? If so, how, and how would we know?

Panel claims so far have tended to focus on large infrastructure projects. Most charges of policy violations have focused on "involuntary resettlement," environmental assessment, and the indigenous peoples' policy. Three of the fourteen claims filed so far have come from domestic private sector interests, and will not be addressed here. Nine of the eleven civil society claims filed as of mid 1999 involved infrastructure projects, including five hydroelectric dams (Arun, Bíobío, Yacyretá, Itaparica, Lesotho Highlands), a major bridge (Jamuna), a power plant (Singrauli), an ostensibly pro–sustainable development project in the Amazon that involved road infrastructure (Planafloro), and urban drainage (Lagos). Resettlement was also involved in a tenth case (India Eco-Development). Most claims so far have consistently focused on resettlement, environmental impact assessment, and indigenous peoples policy violations.

This pattern is consistent with the characteristics of the most controversial Bank projects over the past two decades, including India's Narmada Dam, which provoked the creation of the panel in the first place.[21] Large-scale infrastructure projects have provoked a disproportionate share of World Bank protests, compared to their share of the portfolio as a whole. Forced mass evictions tend to bring affected people together to resist common threats, as well as to unite national and international environmental and human rights allies. Long-standing local and international controversies over how to deal with "involuntary resettlement" have led the Bank to develop one of its explicit and contentious benchmark standards. Internal Bank studies show that achieving full compliance with this policy has proven to be quite difficult, in spite of its lightning-rod effect.[22]

Table 9.2 shows that, geographically, of the fourteen claims filed during the panel's first five years, almost half of the cases involve Brazil (3) and India (3, if one includes Nepal's Arun dam, which was designed to provide power to India). Moreover, locally based international environmental/human rights protests against Bank-funded infrastructure projects have long been especially prominent in Brazil and India. Brazil was the scene of the media and popular imagery that framed the international protest campaigns in the 1980s, as Bank-funded roads accelerated the burning of the western Amazon rain forest, and India witnessed the broad-based, militant campaign against the Narmada dams, which in turn led to the creation of the Inspection Panel in the first place. Both states are led by nationalist political classes for whom such infrastructure projects are powerful symbols of national development.[23] It is not surprising, therefore, that these nation-states' financial authorities led the 1999 backlash to weaken the Inspection Panel's mandate.

So far, the tangible impacts of panel claims have been limited and uneven.

TABLE 9.2 World Bank Inspection Panel Claims Filed, 1994–1998

Country	Bank Project	Date Filed
Nepal	Arun III Hydroelectric Project	October 1994
Ethiopia	*IDA Financed Credits to Ethiopia*	*April 1995*
Tanzania	*Tanzania Power VI Project*	*May 1995*
Brazil	Rondonia Natural Resources Management ("Planafloro")	June 1995
Chile	Bíobío Hydroelectric Project	November 1995
Bangladesh	Jamuna Bridge Project	August 1996
Argentina and Paraguay	Yacyretá Hydroelectric Project	September 1996
Bangladesh	*Jute Sector Adjustment Credit*	*November 1996*
Brazil	Itaparica Resettlement and Irrigation Project	March 1997
India	NTPC Power Generation Project ("Singrauli")	April 1997
India	Eco-Development	April 1998
Nigeria	Lagos Drainage and Sanitation Project	April 1998
South Africa and Lesotho	Lesotho Highlands Water Project	April 1998
Brazil	Land Reform and Poverty Alleviation Pilot	December 1998

NOTE: Private-sector-led cases are in italics and are not addressed here.

The Bank's board has been very reluctant to permit full-scale inspections. Only the very first claim won a clear-cut major victory for claimants (see Table 9.3). The planned Arun III dam was cancelled before construction began. This was a powerful example of the mutually reinforcing convergence of sustained transnational advocacy pressure and internally embedded World Bank dissent. Arun was an exception to the dominant pattern of panel impact on the Bank, at least until the recent China/Tibet claim. In all the other cases during the panel's first five years, tangible impacts on the ground were limited to three cases of partial damage control, as in the cases of Brazil's Planafloro, Argentina/Paraguay's Yacyretá dam, and Bangladesh's Jamuna Bridge.[24]

Nevertheless, the panel campaigns have clearly established the precedent of granting affected people the right to direct access to an impartial international body. Many claimants report that this process has empowered them, even if they have not gained direct concessions on the ground. As World Bank President Wolfensohn wrote, "by giving private citizens—and especially the poor—a new means of access to the Bank, it has empowered and given voice to those we most need to hear. At the same time, it has served the Bank itself through ensuring that we really are fulfilling our mandate of improving conditions for the world's poorest people."[25] Indeed, the World Bank's executive directors even felt obliged to grant panel claimants a direct hearing,

TABLE 9.3 Official Responses to World Bank
Inspection Panel Claims Filed, 1994–1998

Inspection Panel Claims	Bank Management Response	Panel Recommends Investigation	WB Board Approves Investigation	Partial Concessions to Affected	Major Concessions
Arun III Hydro	Deny violations	Yes	Yes		Yes
IDA Ethiopia		*Not eligible*			
Tanzania Power		*Not eligible*			
Planafloro	Partial acceptance	Yes		Yes	
Bíobío Hydroelectric		Not eligible	Independent study		
Yacyretá Hydro	Deny violations	Yes	No (limited review)	Yes	
Jamuna Bridge	Deny violations	No		Yes	
Jute Sector	*Deny violations*	*No*			
Itaparica	Deny violations	Yes	No [rollcall vote]	Promised, then denied	
NTPC–Singrauli	Partial acceptance	Yes	Yes (limited to desk review)	Proposed	
India Eco-Development	Deny violations	Yes	No	Proposed	
Lesotho Highlands	Deny violations	No			
Lagos Drainage	Deny violations	No			

NOTE: Private sector claims are in italics and are not addressed here.

as a group, before making their 1999 decision to change the panel's mandate.[26] Yet it is precisely this granting of international standing that appears to have profoundly irritated the financial authorities of several major borrowing governments, as discussed below.

Even before the recent revision of the Inspection Panel's mandate, several factors inside and outside the institution constrained its potential impact. First, as noted above, the board often rejected the panel's recommendations. The panel is relatively autonomous, but remains a Bank institution that serves and acts at the board's discretion. Second, most civil society actors affected by Bank projects remain unaware of the panel and its pro-accountability potential. This is not only due to lack of information about the panel itself, but also because most Bank-funded investments appear to those affected to be exclusively nation-state projects. Even if they knew the Bank provided funding, they would still need to be aware of the Bank's social and environmental safeguard policy commitments to know that reform "compliance" was even an issue (and therefore subject to "accountability politics" strategies). Third, many possible problems with many Bank projects are not perceived as directly subject to the panel's mandate. Fourth, even in cases where affected people are informed about the panel and Bank policies, and their concerns fit the panel's mandate, the costs and risks of filing a claim can be substantial. The costs involve limited human resources needed to carry out the highly technical process of preparing, filing, and lobbying for a claim. The perceived risks also depend on whether potential claimants face the threat of violent reprisals (as happened in the Singrauli and China/Tibet cases). Finally, the motivation to use an institutional channel like the Inspection Panel cannot be taken for granted. The panel's procedures and the Bank's extremely specialized policy language require a command of English as well a high level of familiarity with and tolerance of Western-style legal culture, not to mention an implicit acceptance of the Bank's legitimacy as a reformable institution.[27]

THE INSPECTION PANEL AND SAFEGUARD POLICY COMPLIANCE: ANALYTICAL DILEMMAS

It is quite possible that the panel's most important effects on the World Bank are less direct and may well extend far beyond the scope of the small number of projects that provoked formal claims. For example, one could hypothesize that the existence of the panel as a de facto court of last resort might make Bank staff and managers more circumspect in their attention to safeguard policy compliance. However, tracing any possible causal linkages between the panel's presence and increased safeguard policy compliance implies that one can first independently document patterns of improvement in policy compliance.

Assessing Compliance

Assessing the degree to which hundreds of ongoing Bank projects actually comply with safeguard policies is not easy. Few comprehensive field-based assessments of Bank and borrowing government compliance with these reform policies exist. Many of the most reliable field-based assessments have been carried out by the Bank's own highly autonomous Operations Evaluation Department, but most of their evaluations are "desk reviews." Such studies are of limited usefulness because they are based on official project files that are created, by definition, by interested parties. Most field-based assessments of actual project implementation, moreover, cover specific projects rather than entire sectors or country portfolios. Most external critiques of the World Bank cover a wide range of projects and policies, but few isolate those projects approved *after* the reform policies were issued. This is in part due to the long lead time involved in project cycles. Most projects implemented in the mid 1990s were designed either before many of the reform policies or in the early years of their institutionalization. Most projects conceptualized since the environmental and social reform policies of the early 1990s are just beginning to be implemented. Because the social and environmental policies did not apply retroactively, the fact that disastrous pre-reform projects are still ongoing is not an adequate test of the degree to which the newer reforms are being complied with.[28] Independent assessments of the dynamics of Bank reform are continually challenged by the fact that the institution is an ever-moving target, and actual project outcomes depend on complex state-society dynamics that are often far removed from the Bank itself.[29] At the same time, the Bank's internal decision-making structures are changing. Its ongoing internal decentralization appears likely to weaken internal checks and balances that could encourage reform policy compliance. As one leading Bank environmental analyst recognized, "With the Bank's devolution of responsibility, however [to six regional operational vice-presidencies], comes the need to ensure consistent compliance with the safeguard policies across the six regions."[30]

In spite of the massive empirical challenges involved in externally assessing compliance with reform commitments, two broad patterns are clear. On the one hand, the Bank does appear to be funding fewer obviously disastrous new infrastructure mega-projects. Potential "development disasters" like the Narmada Dam receive more scrutiny and are more likely to be dropped early on in the project cycle.[31] On the other hand, the available evidence suggests that many projects continue to fall short of the Bank's own safeguard policies. For example, some high-impact projects appear to include planned safeguard provisions that high-level Bank environmental officials regard as public relations exercises designed to "buy time from our critics," according to a recently leaked internal memo.[32] Public interest groups also charge that the practice of miscategorizing projects continues to be widespread, which permits avoidance of environmental and social impact assessments, alternative approaches, and mitigation measures.[33] Indeed, many Bank social and environmental staff confide that they know of dozens of projects that fall far short of reform policies and therefore could be subject of panel claims.

The Inspection Panel's Indirect Effects

Given the relatively small number of panel claims and their uneven record in terms of actual outcomes, it is likely that the panel's greatest impact has been indirect. In its early years, the panel members spent some of their time forwarding inquiries from project-affected groups to the particular Bank staff involved.[34] The claim process requires a track record of prior contact with Bank officials, though subsequent dialogue may have avoided the need for formal claims. More generally, the panel appears to have raised the potential public relations costs to the Bank of violating at least the most clear-cut of the "safeguards," such as the (human rights-related) resettlement and environmental assessment policies.[35] Some insiders have dubbed the staff response in the project design process as "panel-proofing," as they work from their checklists to make sure that they have a paper trail to demonstrate policy compliance in the event of a challenge. "Panel-proofing" appears to be a contradictory process, in some cases leading to involving potentially important degrees of increased compliance, while in others promoting the pro forma fulfillment of administrative requirements rather than focusing on actual changes on the ground.

To assess the panel's indirect impact, one must also take into account the inherited pressures on managers and staff to lend funds to governments as quickly as possible, with as little friction as possible.[36] President Wolfensohn's emphasis on a "client focus" perpetuates these tensions (referring to borrowing governments). Wolfensohn has also highlighted the conflict between the pressure to lend and the need for quality results, and Bank management has carried out several major institutional changes in response, but the "client focus" appears to dominate so far. What is clear is the magnitude of the challenge. According to a major internal study of "unsatisfactory project performance," for example, staff continue to design projects with inadequate attention to beneficiary input. The study found that staff suffer from "institutional amnesia, the corollary of institutional optimism and, despite lessons of experience, Bank staff are overoptimistic and tend to propose overambitious operations that are beyond local implementation capacity."[37]

Even if *most* Bank managers and staff were to do their utmost to comply with reform commitments, it would not take very many noncompliers to leave many high-impact projects in their wake. As a result, some internal and external participants in the reform process stress the importance of bolstering individual accountability—an issue excluded from the scope of the panel.

Shifting Benchmarks: The Conversion of the Reform Policies

Just as the Bank as an institution is a moving target, so too are its reform policies. The Inspection Panel was based on the premise that the reforms of the 1980s and 1990s set the standards against which the Bank can now be held accountable. Management responded by arguing that these policies were too detailed and unwieldy, and staff were therefore largely unfamiliar with many of their key provisions. Management argued that the policies needed to be "reformatted," meaning separated into very brief mandatory sections (two pages) and the "recommended" good practice section would then be much more extensive. As one senior manager recognized internally, "it has been hard for staff and managers to define clearly what is policy and what is advisory or good practice. *Our experiences with the Inspection Panel are teaching us that we have to be increasingly careful in setting policy that we are able to implement in practice*" (emphasis added).[38]

Both external watchdog groups and insider Bank reformers agree that some important social and environmental policies are being diluted, as key issues are moved from mandatory to recommended status (from Operational Policies to Good Practices).One Bank official concerned with accountability also worries that the definition of what is mandatory is being blurred by the frequent "in the judgement of . . ." references in the new policy language. One could argue, therefore, that the existence of an accountability mechanism may be having a perverse effect, driving a weakening of the very policy standards initially set by the Bank itself.

Borrowing Government Backlash

The Inspection Panel's effort to follow its mandated procedures provoked a sustained backlash from borrowing governments. The resulting ongoing conflict within the World Bank's board of directors suggests a picture of North-South relations that is much more nuanced than the conventional image of U.S. imposition. The board's September 1997 vote on the Itaparica resettlement claim was a major turning point. The Brazilian government effectively turned back the perceived northern threat to its sovereignty, based on weak promises of ad hoc solutions (later broken). The U.S. executive director requested a rare roll call vote on whether or not to authorize an inspection. This was quite unusual, because the vast majority of board decisions are made by consensus, and to influence them, as one close observer, David Hunter of the Center for International Environmental Law, put it: "It helps to bring a big check, but clients have leverage too. The World Bank needs clients almost as badly as donors." More generally, he added, 'The credibility of the institution depends on not having a big split between donors and borrowers."[39]

The governments of Brazil and India led the counteroffensive to limit the panel's scope and autonomy. For example, their proposals excluded the panel from examining any social/environmental problems that were jointly caused by governments and the Bank (which account for a large fraction of policy violations). The economic structure of the Bank-state relationship may be relevant to this debate. For most of this decade, both India and Brazil have been paying much more money to the Bank than it has been lending to them. These flows are known as "net negative transfers." This implies, first, that in order to buffer the net negative transfer problem, the Bank needs India and Brazil to continue borrowing. However, if it pushes too hard in favor of economically and politically costly social and environmental requirements, those governments will be less inclined to borrow from it. Second, against the backdrop of these "net negative flows," the panel's perceived political intrusion—directly recognizing the legitimacy of claims by groups that have not been heard by the state—is likely to be seen by economic policymakers in India and Brazil as adding insult to injury. For example, when Brazil's broad civil society advocacy network dealing with international financial institutions (Rede Brasil) met with Brazil's president, Fernando Henrique Cardoso, they criticized his government for pressuring the World Bank to block a panel inspection of the land reform project. The former leftist sociologist "explained that he did that because 'in his day' it would have been unacceptable for a civil society group to ask an agent of 'imperialism' to get involved in internal issues."[40]

This is the context in which the Itaparica Board vote was called, around the same time as India's Singrauli claim was being debated. The actual board vote is quite revealing of the hidden cleavages within the World Bank's board of directors. Recall that although the board is the ultimate body of authority that governs the World Bank, executive directors have been widely assumed by outside observers to be powerless. For example, they have never rejected a loan proposed by management. Observers differ over whether it is Bank management or the U.S. government that really has the last word, but the Itaparica vote suggests that the issue of social and environmental policy compliance has turned the board into a more contested arena.

Votes taken by the World Bank's executive directors are confidential, but this case was reconstructed through interviews with former policymakers and NGO activists involved. While it is widely known that the large donors are heavily weighted because of the one-dollar-one vote system, few are aware that many of the "jurisdictions" that hold Board votes include unusual combinations of nation-states. The heterogeneity of these groupings complicates the efforts of civil society organizations to hold their countries' financial authorities accountable for the votes of their Board representatives. Most notable is the many votes that are held by representatives of blocs of countries that *combine* North and South, or North and East (referring to the former Soviet bloc). As Table 9.4 shows, in the Itaparica case, all the borrowing country blocs voted against the inspection, almost all the Northern-only votes supported the Inspection Panel's recommendation (except for France), while the many votes that combined Northern with Eastern and/or Southern countries were quite divided, often along difficult-to-predict lines.[41] For example, the Italian government voted against the inspection, in spite of Italian civil society's sophisticated Bank reform campaign, which has influence in parliament—perhaps because many of the world's dams involve Italian construction firms. Korea also voted against the inspection, though had Australia (its partner in the same voting bloc) been holding the seat that day, the whole outcome may have been different, due to the closeness of the vote (Korea, Australia and a dozen small countries hold 3.15 percent of the Board's votes). The final tally was 52.9 percent against, with 47.09 percent in favor of the Itaparica inspection. In short, the panel—supposedly a tool of the North against the South—was successfully resisted by a coalition of Bank members from the South, East and a divided North. U.S. hegemony has been overstated, at least insofar as its capacity to defend social and environmental reforms are concerned.[42] This was underscored by the mid-1999 defeat of US government opposition to China's controversial loan involving Tibet, leading to another loss of a rare roll call vote.[43]

According to both World Bank and advocacy NGO participants in the international debate over the panel's fate, the Itaparica claim vote was a turning point because it revealed the Board's tenuous support for the panel. The Itaparica vote emboldened the Brazilian and Indian governments to go beyond their ad hoc defensive moves and instead to take the offensive to weaken the panel. The Board created a working group to review the panel's procedures, including Brazil and India. They produced a set of recommendations that would have dramatically weakened it. The panel appeared to be destined to complete evisceration.[44] The panel members fought back hard to defend their mandate and credibility. In addition, an international campaign by organized claimants and their NGO allies led the Board to decide to hear claimants' views directly, and a major consultation with them was held in Washington. As a result, the Board made some important changes in the proposed revisions. The panel still appears to have been significantly weakened, though the degree of change remains to be seen.

TABLE 9.4 World Bank Board Votes
on the Itaparica Dam Resettlement Claim, September 1997

Executive Director	Alternate	Casting Votes of	IBRD % of Total	Vote
Northern Seats:				
United States	United States		17.04	Yes
Japan	Japan		6.04	Yes
Germany	Germany		4.67	Yes
France	France		4.47	No
United Kingdom	United Kingdom		4.47	Yes
Sweden	Denmark	Denmark, Estonia, Finland, Iceland, Latvia, Lithuania, Norway, Sweden	3.27	Yes
Combined North and East/South Seats:				
Belgium	Turkey	Austria, Belarus, Belgium, Czech Rep., Hungary, Kazakhstan, Luxembourg, Slovak Rep., Slovenia, Turkey	4.93	No
Netherlands	Romania	Armenia, Bosnia and Herzegovina, Bulgaria, Croatia, Cyprus, Georgia, Israel, Macedonia, Moldova, Netherlands, Romania, Ukraine	4.64	Yes
Venezuela	El Salvador	Costa Rica, El Salvador, Guatemala, Honduras, Mexico, Nicaragua, Panama, Spain, Venezuela	4.44	No
Canada	Barbados	Antigua and Barbuda, Bahamas, Barbados, Beliza, Canada, Dominica, Grenada, Guyana, Ireland, Jamaica, St. Kitts and Nevis, St. Lucia, St. Vincent and the Grenadines	4.00	Yes
Italy	Portugal	Albania, Greece, Italy, Malta, Portugal	3.54	No
Switzerland	Poland	Azerbaijan, Kyrgyz Rep., Poland, Switzerland, Tajikistan, Turkmenistan, Uzbekistan	2.96	Yes
Korea	Australia	Australia, Cambodia, Kiribati, Korea, Marshall Islands, Micronesia, Mongolia, New Zealand, Papua New Guinea, Solomon Islands, Vanuatu, Western Samoa	3.15	No

Southern Seats:

Mozambique	Namibia	Angola, Botswana, Burundi, Eritrea, Ethiopia, Gambia, Kenya, Lesotho, Liberia, Malawi, Mozambique, Namibia, Nigeria, Seychelles Sierra Leone, South Africa, Sudan, Swaziland, Tanzania, Uganda, Zambia, Zimbabwe	3.55	No
India	Bangladesh	Bangladesh, Bhutan, India, Sri Lanka	3.53	No
Algeria	Pakistan	Afghanistan, Algeria, Ghana, Iran, Iraq, Morocco, Pakistan, Tunisia	3.51	No
Philippines	Brazil	Brazil, Colombia, Dominican Rep., Ecuador, Haiti, Philippines, Suriname, Trinidad and Tobago	3.16	No
China	China		2.89	No
Saudi Arabia	Saudi Arabia		2.89	No
Russia	Russia		2.89	No
Kuwait	Egypt	Bahrain, Egypt, Jordan, Kuwait, Lebanon, Libya, Maldives, Oman, Qatar, Syrian Arab Rep., United Arab Emirates, Yemen	2.83	No
Indonesia	Thailand	Brunei, Fiji, Indonesia, Lao People's Dem. Rep., Malaysia, Myanmar, Nepal, Singapore, Thailand, Tonga, Vietnam	2.64	No
Bolivia	Argentina	Argentina, Bolivia, Chile, Paraguay, Peru, Uruguay	2.41	No
Comoros	Djibouti	Benin, Burkina Faso, Cameroon, Cape Verde, Central African Rep., Chad, Comoros, Congo (Dem. Rep.), Congo (Rep.), Côte d'Ivoire, Djibouti, Equatorial Guinea, Gabon, Guinea, Guinea-Bissau, Madagascar, Mali, Mauritania, Mauritius, Niger, Rwanda, São Tomé and Principe, Senegal, Togo	2.07	No

Final Tally (%): YES 47.09
NO 52.90

SOURCES: IBRD percentages of votes from World Bank Annual Report, 30 June 1997, appendix 2, "Executive Directors and Alternates of the World Bank and Their Voting Power," 149: confidential Itaparica Dam resettlement claim roll call votes as reported in interviews with Washington-based public interest groups and policymakers, April 1999.

CONCEPTUAL IMPLICATIONS FOR UNDERSTANDING
CIVIL SOCIETY IMPACT ON INSTITUTIONS:
UNPACKING THE BANK, STATES, AND CIVIL SOCIETIES

The World Bank's social and environmental policy reform process, including the panel experience, supports the proposition that the World Bank,
nation-states, and civil societies (local, national and international), are all
internally divided over how to deal with pressures for public accountability.
The corollary of this proposition is that patterns of transnational advocacy
effect on the actual behavior of powerful institutions will be driven by bargaining processes that cut across state, society, and international actors. For
example, the degree to which pro–sustainable development policymakers
within states will be able to carry out reforms that increase institutional accountability will depend largely on their degree of support from outside allies. In other words, such reformist policymakers rarely dominate their states
and therefore their influence rests on mutually reinforcing interaction with
pro-reform actors internationally and within their own civil society. Conversely, the degree to which reformist forces within civil societies can
influence their state's practices will depend largely on their capacity to form
broader alliances, both internationally and within their own states. Internationally, the degree to which pro-accountability World Bank officials can
comply with their own reforms will depend on their capacity to bolster pro-
reform interlocutors in both states and societies. In short, no one set of pro-
reform actors can get very far on their own.

Historically, the process of setting policy standards is driven primarily in
the two lower rectangles, as North-South NGO/grassroots coalitions begin
to put the social and environmental costs of World Bank projects on the international political agenda. Especially in the 1980s, most local movements
in borrowing countries had little leverage over their governments, but their
mobilization, "authenticity," and credible alternative information bolstered
their northern NGO partners' efforts to encourage donor governments to
pressure the World Bank for reform. Note that the shaded areas in figure
9.1 are not depicted "to scale," so to speak, but are simply intended to suggest that these transnational advocacy coalitions represent distinct sub-
groups, often at the margins within their respective societies, and that their
relationships are often rooted in linked transnational wings of largely local
or national movements.[45] These linkages are illustrated by the overlapping
ovals in the lower central part of the diagram.

The need for local roots is built into the Inspection Panel claim process,
which relies on directly affected individuals willing to make their claims on
the record. Most often, only a small part of each local movement is aware of
and engaged in the process of building transnational coalitions. The key
transnational links often take the form of a handful of individuals who share
social capital and trust with distinct movements in different countries and

social sectors.[46] The Internet and foundation-funded airplane tickets facilitate these transnational relationships, but it is the cross-cultural diplomatic skills of individuals that generate the political trust necessary to turn low-intensity networks into collaborative working coalitions.

North-South civil society coalitions combined southern mass protest and northern media coverage to put sustainable development reforms on the agendas of donor governments starting in the mid-late 1980s. At most, however, they usually manage to win over minority factions within the executive and legislative branches of their national governments—hence the shaded triangle on the left side of figure 9.1. Northern policymakers responsive to transnational advocacy coalitions managed in turn to influence the World Bank through their formal governmental representation on the board of directors, which is depicted here as a backdrop to the World Bank itself. As a multilateral organization, the Bank's board bridges representation from both donor and borrowing governments, while being organizationally distinct from both individual governments and the World Bank apparatus itself. In other words, the main avenue for transnational advocacy leverage over the World Bank is through nation-states, mediated largely by the advocacy groups' media skills and social base within their respective northern societies.[47]

Pro–sustainable development reform supporters on the board of directors rarely dominate votes, when they are called, and hence they are depicted as a minority by the shaded area on the left hand side of the horizontal bar at the top of figure 9.1. Pro–sustainable development policymakers in developing countries rarely manage to gain control over their representatives on the board of directors. This is because these positions are usually controlled by national finance ministries, which are usually highly insulated and therefore capable of resisting possible dissent from usually weak environmental protection agencies. Finance ministries often control the budgets of other government agencies that might be led by reformers who would support a different set of social and environmental priorities. National legislatures, meanwhile, rarely manage to exercise whatever nominal power they may have over Bank-state relations. This generalization holds even in societies where pro–sustainable development civil society forces are broad and deep, as in Brazil, India, and Mexico.[48] Figure 9.1 therefore does not include any "pro–World Bank policy reform" arrow coming "up" from borrowing governments on the right hand side of the chart. The pathway for pro-change leverage politics is largely limited to northern governments and their representation on the Bank's board.

When these reformist civil society-state coalitions do manage to exercise influence over the World Bank apparatus, this impact usually is expressed by bolstering the power of pro-reform policy currents within the Bank itself. In other words, external pressure influences the organization by reinforc-

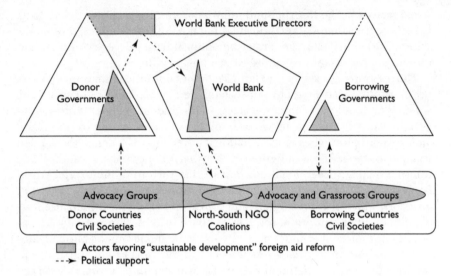

Figure 9.1. The political dynamics of the World Bank's "sustainable development" reforms.

ing insider reformists' leverage over the rest of the operational apparatus (i.e., through strengthening mandatory reform policies), as well as by increasing the small share of Bank loans targeted for potentially prosustainable development projects.[49]

The narrow triangle inside the Bank in Figure 9.1 represents insider reformists, who also often engage in mutual support relationships, overtly or implicitly, with transnational advocacy coalitions (suggested by the two-way arrows in the center). At the same time, it must be kept in mind that each arrow depicting "political support" here is accompanied, implicitly, by conflictive relationships—within civil societies, between civil societies and states, between states and the World Bank, and within the World Bank itself. The main thrust of this stylized picture is to underscore the importance of the balance of forces *within* as well as across diverse institutional arenas.

If and when Bank reformers manage to gain control over lending decisions and project design, they are well positioned to channel both legitimacy and resources to pro-reform counterparts within borrowing governments (if any). Pro-reform national policymakers, depicted by the small shaded triangle on the right in Figure 9.1, in turn often engage in mutual support relationships with grassroots movements and NGOs in their countries, as suggested by the two-way arrows. Indeed, support by World Bank reformists for southern civil society actors is often mediated by their support for more tolerant factions within borrowing states. It is this reciprocal interaction between pro-reform actors within developing countries that may have the greatest potential to promote more Bank and state practices that would be more consistent with sustainable development policy reforms.

This approach suggests that different kinds of cross-sectoral coalitions may be needed to have different kinds of impact on institutional behavior. The kinds of local/national/transnational coalitions needed to mitigate socially and environmentally costly Bank or state practices may be different from those needed to promote pro-actively positive institutional practices. Recall that most of the Bank's safeguard policies are designed primarily to mitigate negative costs, rather than to promote positive alternatives. Within the category of transnational advocacy campaign impact on institutional practices, there may be a qualitative difference between the causes of fewer "public bads" versus more "public goods." For example, international environmental or human rights NGOs may have more of the kind of leverage needed for damage control, whereas they may have much less capacity to promote truly sustainable "sustainable development" institutional behavior. In this arena, the key actors driving more consistent Bank and state practices are likely to be national/local state-society partnerships.[50] More extensive cross-sectoral and cross-national case analysis is needed to test this hypothesis.

CONCLUSIONS

The Inspection Panel is a paradigm case, both of the influence of transnational advocacy networks over international norms and policies and of their limited leverage over institutional behavior in practice. The panel has encouraged partial "damage control" within some controversial projects, but more often its impact has been quite intangible and open-ended. So far, it has produced few on-the-ground solutions—indeed, solutions were not in its mandate. Within the Bank, the panel has contributed most by increasing the internal profile of the broader package of minimum social and environmental "safeguard" policies. However, neither transnational advocacy campaigns nor insider reformers have managed to promote more systematic pro-accountability reforms, such as credible sanctions for managers or staff involved in environmental destruction or human rights violations.

Because of constraints on its mandate and its practice, at most the panel can deliver some degree of transparency, contributing only indirectly to accountability. More generally, the experience reminds us that transparency is necessary but not sufficient for accountability. While the panel's direct relationships with affected people suggest a profound questioning of national sovereignty, its future fate will be determined by representatives of nation-states—the World Bank's executive directors.

One of the most important lessons of the World Bank campaign experience for other civil society efforts to hold powerful transnational institutions accountable points to a shifting North-to-South "center of gravity." In the early years of the Bank campaigns, southern coalition partners provided the credibility, while northern NGOs had the media influence and political clout with donor governments that turned out to be critical for extracting commitments to environmental and social policy reform. These policy reforms set important benchmark standards, but have proven to be limited in terms of their capacity to change what the World Bank and its national government partners actually do in practice most of the time. Reform promises from the World Bank are no substitute for democratizing nation-state development aid strategies in both North and South.

More generally, whether the issue is World Bank reform, human rights, or corporate accountability, North-South civil society campaigns have proven to be quite successful both at "damage control" and at extracting *promises* of reform in the form of more enlightened discourses. But then what? The conditions under which North-South civil society coalitions can translate apparent campaign victories into sustained accountability remain to be seen.

NOTES

This chapter is a revised and shortened version of Jonathan Fox 2000 and also draws on Brown and Fox 2001. The background research reflects findings presented in Fox and Brown 1998b. Thanks very much to my colleagues in both the advocacy community and the World Bank for generously sharing their time and insights, both on and off the record. Kay Treakle of the Bank Information Center and John Gershman provided especially helpful feedback on an earlier draft. Thanks also to Anna Gruben for research and graphic assistance with figure 9.1.

1. The World Bank's social and environmental reform policies date from the early 1980s, and since the early 1990s, the Bank has also expanded its scope of action to include explicit support for "good governance." This concept attempts to create a "depoliticized" technocratic discourse for addressing issues of accountability, corruption, respect for the rule of law more broadly, and, therefore, increasingly explicitly, human rights. This dimension of the relationship between the Bank and human rights is beyond the scope of this chapter, but see the conference proceedings published in "Human Rights, Public Finance and the Development Process," *American University Journal of International Law and Policy* 8, no. 1 (Fall 1992); Bradlow 1996b; Cahn 1993; Gillies 1996; Lawyers Committee for Human Rights 1995; and Treakle 1999. On specific countries, see, e.g., Lawyers Committee for Human Rights and the Institute for Policy Research and Advocacy 1995; Lawyers Committee for Human Rights and the Venezuelan Program for Human Rights Education and Action 1996.

2. "Citizens' Groups: The Non-Governmental Order—Will NGOs Democratise, or Merely Disrupt, Global Governance?" *Economist*, 11 December 1999, 20.

3. In this case, embarrassing internal memos revealed that the Bank's senior environmental policymakers planned a deliberate greenwashing strategy. See Paul Brown 1999.

4. For details, see www.savetibet.org; www.ciel.org and www.bicusa.org.

5. On transnational advocacy networks, see, inter alia, Keck and Sikkink 1997; Princen and Finger 1994; Risse et al. 1999; and Smith, Chatfield, and Pagnucco 1997.

6. Umaña 1998: vii.

7. Risse et al. 1999: 4.

8. Ibid.: 31–33. Not coincidentally, as Risse et al. note, the interest and vigilance of civil society in the West often drops off once policy victories are apparently won and the problem becomes the less obvious one of translating reform commitments into consistent institutional practice. This proposition would apply to World Bank social and environmental reforms as well as to national human rights practices. However, Risse et al. 1999's definition of the last stage of impact incorporates the assumption that international factors remain primary: "socialization" is the final phase in which "international human rights norms are fully institutionalized domestically" (33). Alternative interpretations of international-national interaction would leave open the possibility that international factors may bolster the capacity of domestic actors to embed their own human rights norms into national institutions. Risse et al. recognize what they call "the primacy of domestic politics" as an alternative argument to theirs, but they define it in ways that limit it narrowly to economic and social-structural explanations. They do not address the possibility that domestic politics (actors, institutions, ideas) might constitute a different alternative explanation for institutionalization (36–37).

9. For a similar argument based on a comparison of the rather limited impacts of U.S.-Mexican labor, environmental and human rights coalitions, see Jonathan Fox 2000a.

10. For analyses of internal Bank responses to external pressures from this approach, see Wade 1997 and Jonathan Fox 1998b..

11. See the project and policy cases detailed in Fox and Brown 1998b.

12. See Umaña 1998's comprehensive compilation and Udall 1997.

13. For the viewpoint of the former director of the World Bank's Legal Department, see Shihata 1994. For assessments by international environmental law specialists, see Bradlow 1993, 1994, 1996a; Dana Clark 1999.

14. See details on the web sites of the World Bank (www.worldbank.org/inspectionpanel) and the Center for International Environmental Law (www.ciel.org).

15. This is clearly framed by Bradlow 1993, 1994, and 1996a.

16. Table 9.1 was prepared by the NGO Bank Information Center, based on official Bank policies (the full texts are accessible at http://wblnoo18.worldbank.org/Institutional/Manuals/OpManual.nsf). For another official summary, see *Environment Matters*, Fall 1998, 61.

17. Barbara Upton, a former policymaker, frames the U.S. role in the World Bank in terms of a "two-tiered" process. On the issues key to finance capital, the U.S. government is accountable mainly to Wall Street, pushing the Bank for more bailout funding, while at a secondary level, the U.S. Treasury Department's environmental and social policy agenda for the World Bank reflects the more limited influence of U.S. civil society organizations (see Upton 1999, 2000). In this context, the United States has a great deal of influence on the first level but much less on the second level—in part because the U.S. Treasury invests corresponding amounts of political capital.

18. On the history of World Bank reform campaigns in the United States, see, inter alia, Bramble and Porter 1992; Bowles and Kormos 1995; Sanford 1988; Kurian 1995; Keck and Sikkink 1997; Rich 1994; and Wade 1997.

19. World Bank 1992.

20. On the history of the Inspection Panel and the Narmada campaign, see Udall 1997 and Fisher 1995. The Morse Commission report was published as Morse and Berger 1992. See also Wade 1997.

21. See Udall 1997; Fisher 1995; Sen 1999b.

22. There is an extensive literature on the World Bank and involuntary resettlement, including the most systematic evaluation of reform policy compliance patterns ever carried out (see World Bank 1994). For an analysis of this internal review process, as well as further bibliographic references, see Fox 1998b. See also World Bank 1998.

23. For further discussion Brazil/India comparisons regarding infrastructure projects, the Inspection Panel and elite nationalism, see Sen 1999a, "Of Mushrooms That Bloom." (The title alludes to an alleged World Bank staff aphorism: "The executive directors are like mushrooms. Keep them in the dark and feed them shit.")

24. For more detailed discussion of the impact of each panel claim campaign, see Dana Clark 1999 and Fox 2000a. For further details on the Planafloro case, see Keck 1998; Millikan 1998; Feeney 1998; Hunter 1997. On the Chilean dam case, see Hair et al. 1997. Previously the IFC had commissioned an internal social impact review by the University of Arizona anthropologist Ted Downing that turned out to be quite critical. The resulting controversy led the American Anthropological Association to take up the issue publicly with the World Bank. See the documents posted at www.ameranthassn.org/pehuenc.htm. For Chilean critiques, see Opaso 1998 and Shannon 1999. On Brazil's Itaparica dam, see, inter alia, Hall 1992; Vianna 1997, 1998a, 1998b. The World Bank's Operations Evaluation Department carried out a very critical study, published as World Bank 1998. On the Lesotho Highlands dam, see Letsie and Bond 1999a, 1999b. Assessments of the other cases are based on personal communications with Kay Treakle (Bank Information Center), Dana Clark (Center for International Environmental Law), Hanna Schmuck (anthropologist, Jamuna Bridge case), Zander Navarro (sociologist, Brazil land reform case), and Aurelio Vianna (all Brazil cases).

25. Umaña 1998: vii. Panel watchers agree that without Wolfensohn's strong support, the panel would never have survived.

26. For details on this consultation, see "World Bank Approves Controversial Proposal to Change Inspection Panel," Bank Information Center & Center for International Environmental Law, Washington, D.C., 21 April 1999 (www.ciel.org).

27. For a detailed elaboration of these points, see Jonathan Fox 1998a.

28. The long lead time between changes in top-level decision-making processes and outcomes on the ground creates the "pipeline effect," where policymakers claim change at one end of the pipe—newly designed projects are better—while citizens' groups continue to experience the results of past decisions. This "pipeline effect" creates an ongoing political dissonance problem between the Bank and its critics, since reform promises can never be "definitively" assessed until an ever-moving point in the indefinite future. For further discussion of these issues and an assessment of the available literature on reform policy compliance, see Fox and Brown 1998a.

29. On civil society Bank monitoring, see Jonathan Fox 1997a.

30. As one Bank social development expert put it, "The big question is how do sanctions operate? No one ever lost their job for violating safeguard policies."

31. As the Bank's social and environmental standards have gone up, national governments increasingly turn elsewhere to fund highly controversial infrastructure projects, such as bilateral aid agencies (e.g., China's Three Gorges dam).

32. Cited in Paul Brown 1999. This news report refers to the World Bank's promotion of an oil pipeline from Chad through Cameroon that would pass through vulnerable rain forest, affect indigenous populations, and subsidize Exxon (Shell subsequently withdrew). The implementation of the proposed mitigation measures would depend on two corrupt and authoritarian regimes.

33. Kay Treakle, Bank Information Center, personal communication, June 1999. For example, the Bank clearly miscategorized the Western China Poverty Reduction Project as intermediate rather than high impact, though it turned out to have major environmental and indigenous rights implications.

34. Interview, Eduardo Abbott, World Bank Inspection Panel secretariat, April 1999.

35. Other safeguard policies are easier to violate, such as the indigenous peoples policy. For example, the World Bank's huge portfolio of anti-poverty projects in Mexico by definition affect many millions of indigenous people. The Bank's long-standing policy ostensibly requires their "informed participation" in any project that affects them. This includes projects that ostensibly help them, not only infrastructure-related "damage control." Large amounts of Bank funding reaches indigenous people in Mexico, but mainly through politicized patronage rather than informed participation, including apparent funding of the "soft" side of "low-intensity conflict" in Chiapas. This is an important example of a project risk that would not fit well with existing panel procedures, in part because of the difficulty of aggregating patterns of untold and invisible village-level "material adverse effects." For details on rural civil society monitoring efforts in Mexico, see the work of Trasparencia at www.laneta.apc.org/trasparencia. See also Jonathan Fox 1997b. The risk of authoritarian electoral manipulation of social funds became an issue in Bank-Indonesia relations, leading to the postponement of a major social loan, but has yet to enter the national debate in Mexico (Solomon 1999).

36. On the links between internal institutional priorities and social/environmental conflict, three definitive studies are Rich 1994; Rich 1999; and Wade 1997.

37. The 1997 Annual Review of Development Effectiveness found notable improvements, but at the same time found persistent problems in some areas of the Bank, including "pressure to lend; fear of offending the client . . . fear that a realistic, and thus more modest project would be dismissed as too small and inadequate" (quoted in Waldmeier and Suzman 1997). According to Robert Picciotto, director of the Bank's Operations Evaluation Department, the 1998 Annual Review of Development Effectiveness shows continued improvement, and OED's concerns led President Wolfensohn to create the Quality Assurance Group in the first place (personal communication, 12 April 1999).

38. Internal World Bank memo, Myrna Alexander, OPRDR, on "Conversion of Remaining ODs," 15 March 1996.

39. Interview, 5 April 1999.

40. Quoted in *Folha de São Paulo,* 19 July 1999, p. 3 (translation by the author).

41. Reportedly, the French government views the Inspection Panel as a U.S. creation and therefore opposes it on principle. Until recently, France also lacked a powerful civil society Bank reform campaign (in contrast to England, Germany, Scandinavia, Switzerland, and the Netherlands).

42. Recall Barbara Upton's proposed "two-tier" model of U.S. policy influence at the World Bank, noted above (Upton 1999, 2000).

43. As the *New York Times* editorialized, "approving this loan may violate the bank's own guidelines for assessing the social and environmental impacts of its projects" (23 June 1999). See also Sanger 1999 and "Tibetan Tinderbox," *Economist,* 19 June 1999. For detailed updates, see www.savetibet.org.

44. See Phillips 1999.

45. For example, most of the key U.S. environmental activists who led the campaign to reform the World Bank via their leverage over U.S. congressional aid debates were located in the small, usually low-profile and low-priority international policy departments of large membership organizations whose concerns are overwhelmingly domestic (e.g., National Wildlife Federation, Environmental Defense Fund, Sierra Club, etc.). This is not a coincidence; the large membership bases of these organizations were their main source of leverage in congress. On the southern end of these coalitions, roots are critical because the "authenticity" of the local partners in the advocacy coalitions provides critical media credibility and a response to the frequent backlash charges of "green imperialism" from both the Bank and nation-states.

46. For comparative case analysis of local/transnational distances and accountability within transnational advocacy networks dealing with the World Bank, see L. David Brown and Jonathan Fox, "Accountability within Transnational Coalitions," in Fox and Brown 1998b. On the related concepts of "intersectoral social capital" and "bridging organizations," see L. David Brown 1991; Brown and Ashman 1996.

47. For example, the German government's decision to oppose Nepal's Arun III dam was a critical turning point in the campaign against it. The original base of the German campaign was quite small, but it managed to establish a high degree of credibility with national media, as well as mobilizing the usually apolitical trekkers' associations and German-Nepal Friendship Societies. Interviews, Heffa Scheucking, Urgewald organization (http://www.urgewald.de/urgewald/index.htm), and Bruce Rich, Environmental Defense Fund, Washington, D.C., October 1995.

48. Analysis of the power relations between the World Bank and Mexican state reveals that the partnership bolsters the Finance Ministry and its leverage over the rest of the state and civil society. See Jonathan Fox forthcoming.

49. This may be one reason why civil society critics of structural adjustment have had so little influence; either possible alternative macro policy advocates within the Bank are too weak to be viable pro-change partners, external critics have not pursued strategies that could bolster insider sympathizers, or both.

50. For conceptual discussion and case analysis of state-society synergy, see the thematic section of *World Development* 24, no. 6 (June 1996), edited by Peter Evans (also published as Evans 1997).

10

Humanitarian Intervention
Global Enforcement of Human Rights?

Wayne Sandholtz

When globalization refers to the economy, people can easily anchor the conversation in well-known referents: trade, transnational investment, international currency markets. But when globalization talk turns to political values and norms, the moorings vanish and the discussion bobs around uncertainly. For whereas money offers a sort of lingua franca (at least you can count it), the sharing of norms and values across widely differing cultures seems less reducible to a common currency. Yet international society affirms basic human rights in a set of conventions and declarations that constitute what some refer to as an "International Bill of Human Rights" (Donnelly 1995: 116). If states abuse the basic security rights of their citizens, or are unable to halt abuses committed by other groups, can international society use force to compel respect for its declared norms? That is the question of humanitarian intervention.

In this chapter I argue that global society has developed a set of rules that permit, but do not require, forcible intervention to stop gross violations of basic security rights. The emergence of these norms has been shaped fundamentally by two dimensions of globalization. The first has to do with values, the second with information. A globalization of basic human rights values has occurred, such that there seems to be universal consensus that no culture or political system is justified in curtailing the essential rights of its people. Though societies differ fundamentally over the meaning and importance of principles like "free speech" and "gender equality," they converge on a set of basic security rights, those that protect people in their physical freedom and bodily integrity. Put differently, no culture or government would claim that torture, extrajudicial killings, or genocide are legitimate values, or are fundamental elements of their traditions. The globalization of information refers to the widely remarked "CNN effect": any large-scale, brutal, or systematic abuse of security rights will quickly be reported around the world via both print and electronic media, complete with appalling images. It is virtually impossible to keep massive human rights abuses secret. Even though reliable information is often scarce, the globalization of news media means that people around the globe know when a human rights tragedy is occurring, even if they cannot assess all of the relevant facts.

The globalization of human rights values and the globalization of information media have combined, especially since the end of the Cold War, to push the development of norms of humanitarian intervention. These norms, I argue, establish necessary conditions for legitimate intervention; international society has not yet attempted to fashion sufficient conditions, that is, those that would make intervention mandatory. The community of states has thus declared that forcible humanitarian intervention is justifiable in some cases but has not committed itself actually to intervene in all of those instances (see Murphy 1996: 295–96). The purpose of this chapter is to assess whether evolving rules of humanitarian intervention constitute an opportunity for international society to enforce certain human rights norms. Such an assessment must address two problems. First, under what conditions can states use armed force, as opposed to other tools, such as criminal tribunals or sanctions, to enforce human rights norms? As the analysis will show, armed intervention has been justified to halt massive violations of basic security rights (physical freedom and integrity). Second, how do norms of intervention interact with or modify sovereignty norms? The chapter will show that states engaging in gross human rights violations forfeit the protection of sovereignty rules against intervention.

The first section of this chapter briefly assesses the international political context of humanitarian intervention since 1990. The second section outlines a logic of norm change and examines how the basic rule structures of international society have shifted. The third section describes two fundamental norms of humanitarian intervention. The fourth, and largest, section analyzes in more detail the dynamic interplay between sovereignty-related rules of nonintervention and liberal rules of humanitarian intervention, distilled from the empirical record of recent cases.

THE INTERNATIONAL POLITICAL CONTEXT

The end of the Cold War decisively altered the context in which norms of humanitarian intervention were evolving. To be clear, international human rights norms did not suddenly emerge after 1990. The fundamental statements of international human rights norms (the United Nations Charter, the Universal Declaration, and the International Covenants) were all agreed before or during the Cold War. What changed after the abandonment of U.S.-

Soviet rivalry, and subsequent collapse of the Soviet Union, was the ability of governments to agree on interventions to halt human rights abuses. Prior to 1990, humanitarian intervention virtually could not be an issue for multilateral decision and action, for one or the other of the superpowers would veto any proposed intervention against one of its allies or clients. When the superpowers themselves intervened with declared humanitarian goals, like the United States in Grenada (a procedure classified as justified by Tesón 1997: 210–23) Cold War calculations and motivations so permeated the action that it had virtually no impact on shaping international norms of humanitarian intervention.

Since 1990, debates over intervention to halt human rights abuses have not automatically been slotted into Cold War categories. In more practical terms, the UN Security Council has been able to achieve consensus in cases that previously would have been deadlocked by the U.S.-Soviet rivalry. Thus, the number of interventions rose dramatically after the collapse of the Soviet Union; I identify eight instances in the decade after 1990 as compared to only three in the period from 1945 to 1990. In addition, the nature of interventions changed. Before 1990, interventions were generally unilateral (India in East Pakistan, Tanzania in Uganda, France in Central Africa). After that date, most interventions have been multilateral, another product of the increased potential for consensus in the Security Council.

A related question has to do with whether the changing status of humanitarian intervention is truly the product of international norms or the result of American hegemony. To be sure, in the early 1990s, the United States assumed an assertive, pro-intervention stance. And the participation of the United States, the preeminent military power in the world, in an intervention was usually indispensable. American advocacy of humanitarian intervention thus certainly had a major influence on the practice of intervention, and thus on the development of international norms. But the United States was not simply imposing its preferred rules on subordinate states. In UN debates, other governments, including some that could not be considered historically aligned with or dependent on the United States, made similar arguments in support of interventions. Furthermore, Security Council votes in favor of intervention had to include positive votes from a variety of Third World states that are hardly U.S. clients, not to mention agreement or abstention from Russia and China. In short, the United States clearly played a leading role, but could hardly be said to have imposed its preferences on a skeptical world. The empirical analysis demonstrates the extent to which norms of intervention received broad international support.

Finally, normative considerations are never divorced from practical factors—and practical issues have normative implications. In particular, the size and power of the states involved are the first filters in determining which cases have the potential for justified humanitarian intervention. Because armed intervention is always costly, in lives and resources, governments must take into account whether or not a proposed intervention has a reasonable chance of success. The likelihood of success depends, among other things, on the power of the intended target. A well-organized and militarily potent target implies high costs and low probability of success. Thus large and powerful states are never the objects of intervention. Notwithstanding that Russia appears to have committed numerous atrocities and gross human rights violations in Chechnya, there has never been a question of other states organizing a humanitarian intervention. Almost by definition, interventions involve those who possess the military means (large and powerful states) acting against weak or collapsed regimes. But this in no way invalidates the argument based on international norms. I argue that international norms delineate necessary conditions for justified intervention, not that they constitute the only criteria.

THE EVOLUTION OF RULES IN INTERNATIONAL SOCIETY

Debates over forcible humanitarian intervention highlight the tension between two of the primary rule structures of international society, what I call "sovereignty rules" and "liberal rules." Like all social systems, international society is constituted by rules. Rules are statements that identify standards of conduct, and they are always linked together in larger structures. The coexistence of multiple rule structures means that conflict among norms is inevitable. A given action can invoke different rules, with diverging behavioral standards. For instance, some who opposed NATO's 1999 air attacks on Serbia cited international rules that prohibit the use of force against another state except for self-defense, or as authorized by the Security Council. Other commentators justified the air campaign on the basis of international rules against genocide and, in some cases, an emerging norm of humanitarian intervention to prevent gross human rights abuses. Such discourses are at the heart of norm change.

The point is not that logical inconsistencies among or within rule structures drive international norm change. Rather, rule conflicts are part of a process of norm change when they are brought to the surface by actors who disagree about the appropriateness of specific actions. In other words, potential conflicts between rules, when activated by behaviors or events, lead to dialogues and debates over the meaning of the actions and the substance of the rules. The dialogues in turn steadily modify actors' perceptions of what kinds of conduct the community considers acceptable, or unacceptable. Acting on those understandings, actors shift patterns of behavior. Dialogues and actions are in constant, mutual transformation, and this is what changes social rules.[1]

Traditional Sovereignty Rules

Sovereignty rules constitute one of the fundamental rule structures of international society. They establish what would seem to be a general presumption against the permissibility of forcible humanitarian intervention. Armed intervention to enforce human rights norms could be proscribed by two sets of rules, one that forbids interference in the domestic affairs of another state, and one that prohibits the use of force in international relations. Sovereignty implies exclusive internal jurisdiction, which in the prevailing interpretation has meant that only the government of a given state is entitled to create laws and policies regarding its territory and population, and other countries may not exercise an uninvited role in that process. If anything, the ban on the use of violence is even clearer: no state may resort to force of arms in its interactions with other states. Either norm could be interpreted as ruling out humanitarian intervention.

The nonintervention rule is, as R. J. Vincent argues, a fundamental support of international order (Vincent 1974: ch. 9). Indeed, the complex of rules centered in the United Nations has traditionally seemed to privilege order and related values—peace and stability—over other values, including human rights (Arend and Beck 1993: 131–32). As S. D. Murphy notes, "In the context of projecting military force, the Charter is oriented to the preservation of order, not the protection of human rights" (Murphy 1996: 2). Nevertheless, the UN Charter nowhere enunciates an unambiguous prohibition of intervention, though it implies such a rule in several places (Vincent 1974: 236). Article 2 (1) grounds the United Nations in the "sovereign equality of all its Members," and Article 2 (3) obliges member states to settle their disputes by peaceful means. Article 2 (7) forbids the United Nations Organization "to intervene in matters which are essentially within the domestic jurisdiction of any State," and many observers (and member states) have interpreted this injunction as applying also to states. The lack of an explicit ban against intervention led some states to push for clarifications, which have taken the form of General Assembly resolutions. The 1950 Peace through Deeds Resolution condemned the "intervention of a State in the internal affairs of another state" (quoted in Vincent 1974: 237). A 1957 Declaration concerning the Peaceful Coexistence of States affirmed the obligation of states to practice "nonintervention in one another's internal affairs" (Vincent 1974: 238). Other declarations followed: the Declaration on Inadmissibility of Intervention in Domestic Affairs of States and Protection of their Independence and Sovereignty (1965), and the Declaration on Principles of International Law concerning Friendly Relations and Co-operation among States in Accordance with the Charter of the United Nations (1970).

UN rules against the use of force would also seem to weigh against humanitarian intervention. Article 2 (4) enunciates the famous injunction against the use or threat of force. The Charter provides only two explicit exceptions to this prohibition. The first is "individual or collective self-defense" (Art. 51), and the second is UN action, when mandated by the Security Council, to halt "threats to the peace, breaches of the peace, and acts of aggression" (Chapter VII). Though the Charter does not expressly permit the use of force to enforce human rights, many legal scholars have argued that forcible humanitarian intervention is clearly compatible with central objectives of the UN and that the absence of a prohibition makes it permissible (Tesón 1997). Still, in authorizing humanitarian intervention the Security Council has usually made a determination that gross human rights violations constituted a threat to the peace, thus enabling UN enforcement actions under Chapter VII. However, in a pair of cases (Somalia and, less clearly, Haiti) the Security Council justified forcible intervention for humanitarian purposes even when there were no obviously urgent transborder threats or problems.

Liberal Rules and the Globalization of Security Rights

Liberal values, emphasizing the autonomy and dignity of each person, undergird clusters of international rules whose purpose is to safeguard a core of basic individual rights. International human rights rules thus delineate individual entitlements, which simultaneously imply limits on state behaviors. Governments should neither violate the basic human rights of their citizens nor permit other groups (guerrillas, paramilitaries, militias) to deprive citizens of their rights.

Human rights rules find formal expression in the UN Charter and in other UN conventions and declarations. The preamble to the Charter affirms a common "faith in fundamental human rights, in the dignity and worth of the human person, in the equal rights of men and women."[2] Article 1. . in promoting and encouraging respect for human rights and for fundamental freedoms for all without distinction as to race, sex, language, or religion" (3). In addition, under Chapter IV, Article 13 (b), the General Assembly is to "initiate studies and make recommendations for the purpose of . . . assisting in the realization of human rights and fundamental freedoms for all." Article 55 (c) declares that the United Nations "shall promote . . . universal respect for, and observance of, human rights and fundamental freedoms," and in the following article "all Members pledge themselves to take joint and separate action in co-operation with the Organization for the achievement" of those purposes (Chapter IX, Article 56).

The members of the United Nations followed up with a series of declarations and conventions that spelled out a range of human rights, starting with the Convention on the Prevention and Punishment of the Crime of Genocide (1948), and the Universal Declaration of Human Rights (1948).

In Donnelly's account (Donnelly 1995: 123), formal rule making culminated with the International Covenant on Economic, Social, and Cultural Rights and the International Covenant on Civil and Political Rights (both in 1966), the latter listing (among many others) the rights that we label "security rights" in this volume. Treaties on special topics followed, including women's rights (1979), torture (1984), and the rights of children (1989).

Though rules sanctifying security rights have thus received a high degree of specificity and formality in the United Nations, enforcement mechanisms are significantly less developed. The Charter provides no means for monitoring human rights abuses or enforcing international human rights norms, but the United Nations has gradually developed organizations and procedures for addressing violations. The UN Commission on Human Rights (under the Economic and Social Council) acquired the capacity to discuss specific countries in 1967, and in 1970, it was authorized to carry out confidential inquiries into complaints that indicated "a consistent pattern of gross and reliably attested violations of human rights and fundamental freedoms." The commission later began to establish working groups on specific topics and countries. The International Covenant on Civil and Political Rights established a UN Human Rights Committee, which reviews voluntary reports from states on their human rights compliance and can investigate complaints from individuals against states that have also signed the First Optional Protocol (a minority of the world's countries) (Donnelly 1995: 125–28). Finally, the UN General Assembly in 1993 created the position of UN high commissioner for human rights (UNHCHR), an under-secretary-general, which in 1997 absorbed the Human Rights Center within the Office of the UNHCHR. Still, as Jack Donnelly sums up the situation, though "norms and the process of norm creation have been almost completely collectivized," and monitoring has moved somewhat in that direction, "implementation and enforcement remain almost exclusively national" (Donnelly 1995: 146).

Liberal Rules and the Evolution of Sovereignty

Rules define membership in any society, who counts as "in" and who as "out." Yet actors also constitute, and reconstruct, social structures, including the rules of membership. In the period after World War II, sovereignty was largely defined in terms of effective control of a territory defined by fixed borders (Barkin 1998: 243–45). Full membership in international society now appears to include a human rights dimension: gross violators can be shamed, shunned, and sometimes sanctioned, though not yet with a high degree of predictability or consistency. In J. S. Barkin's account, once the Cold War ended, human rights norms began to modify the territorial norm. Legitimate sovereignty started to depend on a state guaranteeing to its citizens certain basic civil and political rights. If a state did not adhere to human rights norms, other states would be justified in excluding it from participation in international society, and, in some cases, in intervening to enforce human rights norms (Barkin 1998: 246–47). In the post–Cold War era, there is an emerging sense that when states engage in gross, systematic, or large-scale human rights abuses, they thereby forfeit or suspend their status as sovereign equals in interstate society.[3]

PRACTICE AND THE EVOLUTION OF NORMS

Over the past decade, the international community has in several cases justified armed intervention to halt large-scale human rights abuses, but there is no consensual checklist of conditions under which it will authorize humanitarian intervention. In fact, governments are wary of creating a general right or duty of collective humanitarian intervention. Perhaps the most we can say is that the society of states has allowed forcible humanitarian intervention onto the list of potentially justified responses to massive human rights violations. In other words, though interstate society has not begun to enunciate the *sufficient* conditions that would trigger collective enforcement of global human rights norms, it has achieved some consensus on *necessary* conditions.

In this section, I distill two basic norms of justified humanitarian intervention from the actions and discourses surrounding post–World War II instances of it. I then examine the shifting, and uncertain, balance between these emerging norms of humanitarian intervention and the general rule against intervention. This will be an empirical assessment of what states do and how they justify their actions. The analysis of justifications focuses largely on the language of Security Council resolutions and on the statements made by national representatives in debates in the Security Council or the General Assembly. In such debates, because actors are aware that their statements become part of a recorded public discourse that shapes rules and precedents, talk is not always cheap and people will not just "say anything." Thus I assume that even rational, strategic actors recognize that UN discourses on intervention shape the emergence, interpretation, and application of rules of forcible intervention.

For the empirical analysis, I employ a fairly standard definition of forcible humanitarian intervention: "the threat or use of force by a state, group of states, or international organization primarily for the purpose of protecting the nationals of the target state from widespread deprivations of internationally recognized human rights" (Murphy 1996: 11–12; see also Tesón 1997: 5, 135). Analysts disagree about which events are instances of forcible humanitarian intervention. F. R. Tesón identifies four post-1945 cases of unilateral humanitarian intervention (Uganda, Central Africa, East Pakistan, Grenada) and five of collective humanitarian intervention (Iraq, Somalia,

Haiti, Rwanda, Bosnia) (1997). Murphy examines seventeen cases in all but decides that in only nine of them were humanitarian objectives central to the intervention (Pakistan, Uganda, Central Africa, Liberia, Iraq, Bosnia, Somalia, Rwanda, and Haiti). He judges that in the case of Haiti, human rights reasons were subordinate to the goal of restoring a democratically elected government (also a human right, but not a security right), and that in three of the cases (Pakistan, Uganda, and Bosnia), humanitarian motives did not clearly predominate but were mixed with political or security goals (Murphy 1996).

My criteria for case selection are as follows. The analysis is based largely on interventions taking place in the post–Cold War period (1990 or later, for reasons explained above), though I sometimes draw on evidence from pre-1990 interventions (East Pakistan, Uganda, Central Africa). The earlier cases sometimes offer useful insights into the evolving norms of justifiable intervention. The intervention must involve the threat or use of armed force. It must take place without an invitation from the target government, or in the absence of an effective government. Human rights objectives must figure among the major justifications of the intervention, but need not be the only consideration. On these grounds, I will assess evidence from interventions in Liberia (1990), Iraq (1991–92), Bosnia (1992), Somalia (1992), Haiti (1993), and Rwanda (1994). I exclude cases in which a humanitarian motive may have been advanced by some actors, but where the balance of the evidence shows that other objectives predominated (Congo, 1964; Cambodia, 1978; Grenada, 1983; Panama, 1989).[4]

For two primary norms there seems to be a general international consensus: (1) states and international organizations may intervene to halt violations of security rights, as opposed to political or socioeconomic rights; and (2) the violations at issue must be large-scale and systematic. The discussion of these norms will be relatively brief, after which I turn to an examination of the ongoing tension between norms of humanitarian intervention and rules of nonintervention. It is here, at the interface between liberal and sovereignty norms, where we can observe the processes of normative change. What we see is the enduring vigor of nonintervention norms, as states generally try to avoid carving out explicit exceptions, preferring to justify interventions that have a clear humanitarian component in more traditional sovereignty terms (self-defense; suppressing threats to peace and security).

Violation of Security Rights

The international community has been willing to contemplate and approve forcible intervention in situations where states violate the security rights of their own citizens, or when the collapse of a state enables nonstate actors (paramilitary groups, warlords, guerrillas, and so on) to commit such violations. The abuse of political and civil rights, many of which are also affirmed in global conventions, has not yet provoked interstate society to contemplate armed interventions, with one notable exception. Political rights protect a spectrum of activities through which citizens interact with governments and other social institutions: freedom of conscience and expression; freedom of the press; freedom to organize and assemble; the rights to vote and run for office; rights to nondiscrimination and equal protection of the laws. Even further removed from the possibility of international intervention is the third category, which includes social and economic rights (to own property; to work; to food, clothing, and housing; to medical care and social security; to education).

The latter two clusters of rights are not generally part of the discourse on humanitarian intervention for a number of reasons. First, as noted in the introduction to this book, many privilege security rights because "security rights are 'basic' or enabling rights that make the pursuit of other rights possible" (Shue 1980). Second, political leaders have no desire to subject domestic political and economic systems to international surveillance or sanction. Indeed, international rules (including the UN Charter) acknowledge that a range of political and economic systems are compatible with membership in interstate society, and are therefore to be considered a matter of exclusively internal jurisdiction. The only potential exception to this is what some have identified as an emerging right to democratic governance. Some legal scholars, for instance, have argued that the international community is beginning to make democratic institutions a key marker of international legitimacy (Fox 1992; Franck 1992; Fox and Roth 2000). Third, security rights are more universal in their recognition and acceptance. Margaret Keck and Kathryn Sikkink have argued that two types of human rights claims seem to find acceptance most readily across countries and cultures, those that prohibit bodily harm and those that affirm legal equality (Keck and Sikkink 1998: 204–6). That is, representatives of a wide variety of political and economic institutions and cultures can agree that no government is justified in carrying out ethnocide, or extrajudicial executions, or torture.

In two cases, however, intervention took place based on human rights claims that were not clearly, or solely, tied to security rights. The subversion of democratic norms was the principal justification (not the sole motive) for forcible intervention in one case (Haiti, where the OAS and the Security Council demanded the reinstatement of the democratically elected Aristide government). Even so, the international community seems far from ready to justify forcible intervention to restore democracy, *when extensive violations of security rights are not also at issue.* The other possible exception is Somalia. The most distressing catastrophe in Somalia was the famine, which had both natural and social causes. The civil war certainly injured, maimed, and killed far too many Somalis, but it was also responsible for preventing food supplies from reaching hundreds of thousands of people on the verge of, or succumbing to, starvation. In one sense, the right to survival is the most basic of security rights; forced starvation is clearly an assault on bodily safety and integrity. In another sense, however, the right to basic subsistence could be construed as a socioeconomic right; it is one step from guaranteeing a right to subsistence to ensuring some "minimal" level of nutrition, health, and shelter.

Massive and Sustained Violations

Governments that violate human rights on a small scale can generally be confident that they do not run the risk of external armed intervention, though they may elicit condemnations from other governments and NGOs. The occasional or intermittent torturer (for example) may become a diplomatic outcast or suffer economic sanctions, but forcible intervention is generally reserved for abuses on a larger scale. At work may be an implicit norm of proportionality; since the use of force necessarily implies violence and loss of life, it is the measure of last resort. Only the most severe human rights violations can justify the most severe international response. Thus, in general, armed interventions have been justified when the number of deaths has been at least in the thousands and accompanied by extreme suffering (torture, expulsion, starvation) on the part of even more.

For instance, in East Pakistan, civilian deaths may have reached 1,000,000 and the number of refugees (mostly fleeing to India) as high as 10,000,000. Under the rule of Idi Amin, the Ugandan government perpetrated widespread atrocities against the population, with deaths numbering as many as 300,000 (Murphy 1996: 98, 105). The civil war in Liberia produced widespread acts of extraordinary brutality—rapes, maimings, torture—with an estimated 150,000 deaths (Murphy 1996: 148); more than half of the population of 2.6 million became refugees (Wippman 1993: 163). Iraqi brutality toward the Kurds generated refugee flows numbering in the hundreds of thousands toward Iran and Turkey (Gordon 1994: 548; Tesón 1997: 237). The Serb campaign against Bosnians killed tens of thousands and created hundreds of thousands of refugees (Stiglmayer 1994; Cigar 1995; Rieff 1995). The toll in Rwanda was between 500,000 and one million killed, with hundreds of thousands displaced (Murphy 1996: 244; Tesón 1997: 259). In Somalia, the number killed in factional violence was small compared to the hundreds of thousands who died in the famine that was produced, at least in part, by the political chaos.

In two cases, however, interventions took place in countries where the recorded human rights abuses, though heinous, did not appear to be "massive." The military regime that overthrew President Jean-Bertrand Aristide in Haiti inflicted widespread human rights abuses against the supporters of the deposed president. According to Amnesty International, the junta engaged in arbitrary arrests, torture, rapes, and over 3,000 murders (Nanda et al. 1998: 842). In Central Africa, Bokassa was clearly a nasty dictator; what precipitated the intervention against him was an inquiry that found that he had participated personally in beating to death some 200 students. But in quantitative terms, the abuses in Central Africa and Haiti do not come close to matching the scale of disaster in cases mentioned previously.

NONINTERVENTION VERSUS INTERVENTION NORMS: THE ONGOING TENSION

The conflict between humanitarian intervention and norms of nonintervention is a site of contemporary normative change. A continuing presumption against intervention means that forcible actions in support of human rights must be justified. For reasons that are not hard to fathom, governments are not willing to grant automatic exceptions to the general ban against intervention. Humanitarian motives are almost always mixed with other political or strategic goals; states do not wish to make it easier for potential interveners to cloak self-interested intrusions with a mantle of humanitarianism. Besides, governments are often going to be more interested in shoring up their own security—as against external interventions—than in defending the rights of faraway noncitizens. Finally, international order remains an important value, and the nonintervention norm supports order and stability. To the extent that humanitarian exceptions might lead to further erosion of the nonintervention norm, they can be seen as potentially undermining order and stability.

Instances of humanitarian intervention always generate intense debate, precisely, I would argue, because state officials understand that they are not merely deciding a specific case but also establishing norms. An examination of the discourses surrounding humanitarian interventions in the past decade reveal that states cling to the nonintervention norm and are reluctant to authorize exceptions that might be seen as generating precedents, even in the face of appalling atrocities. Thus states frequently prefer to justify humanitarian intervention on grounds that are not humanitarian but are instead closer to traditional sovereignty norms, like self-defense and threats to peace and security. Evidence for this proposition is: (1) the reluctance of both interveners and other governments to rely principally on explicit humanitarian grounds, as opposed to self-defense or regional stability, as justifications for intervention; and, (2) the aversion of the international community to interventions in which the target is a functioning government.

Justifications for Intervention

We learn a great deal about the state of international norms by examining the justifications that intervening states offer for their actions, and the degree to which other governments accept those justifications. I assume that governments generally justify their conduct as being compatible with rules that they perceive to enjoy broad acceptance internationally. The arguments of interveners thus reveal their judgment concerning the status of various international norms. The responses of other governments are equally informative.

Uganda.   With respect to identifying legitimate grounds for intervention, the case of Tanzania's 1979 invasion of Uganda offers useful evidence. Idi Amin's notorious regime had engaged in widespread, documented repression, including torture and extrajudicial killings; an estimated 300,000 people had perished at his government's hands. In late 1978, Ugandan troops crossed the border with Tanzania and seized an area known as the Kagera Salient. Tanzanian troops subsequently expelled the invaders, then continued across the border, ultimately reaching the Ugandan capital, Kampala. Amin fled and a new government assumed control in April 1979. Tanzanian President Julius Nyerere had often expressed his revulsion for Amin and his horrendous abuses of human rights (Tesón 1997: 185). But it is interesting that during the course of the intervention, Nyerere justified it in terms other than humanitarian. He named as motives self-defense, punishment of the Ugandan regime's aggression, prevention of subsequent incursions by Amin, and assistance to groups within Uganda seeking to overthrow Amin.

The international reaction essentially tolerated the Tanzanian intervention, without explicitly condoning it, and welcomed the fall of Amin. Four countries condemned Tanzania (Kenya, Libya, Nigeria, Sudan). Neither the UN Security Council nor the General Assembly addressed the conflict. Even the Organization of African Unity, whose charter vigorously expresses a non-intervention norm, did not condemn the Tanzanian action. A wide variety of states quickly recognized the new Ugandan government.[5] In short, neither Tanzania nor the international community explicitly relied on humanitarian factors to justify an intervention that they nevertheless, implicitly at least, considered justified.

Liberia.   Civil war broke out in Liberia in 1990, unleashing a period of massive human rights abuses. Though the United Nations and the Organization of African Unity steadfastly ignored the unfolding calamity, the Economic Community of West African States (ECOWAS, with sixteen members) began monitoring events and sponsoring a series of peace initiatives. As the forces of the rebel National Patriotic Liberation Front, or NPFL, led by Charles Taylor, pushed toward the capital, Monrovia, President Samuel Doe requested that ECOWAS send in a peacekeeping force. ECOWAS decided to send an "ECOWAS Cease-fire Monitoring Group" (ECOMOG) to restore order and enforce a cease-fire, citing massive human rights violations, danger to foreign nationals, and the possibility of the conflict spreading to neighboring countries. Six countries provided troops for the mission (whose numbers eventually rose to 15,000). The decision for forcible intervention was not unanimous. Togo, Mali, Côte d'Ivoire, and Senegal suggested that the group was exceeding its legitimate functions. The president of Burkina Faso declared that ECOWAS had "no competence to interfere in member states' internal conflicts" (Wippman 1993: 167–68). Nevertheless, the intervention moved forward.

However, the broader international community steadfastly refused to contemplate intervention. The United States brushed aside suggestions that it intervene, calling the crisis an "internal affair." The Security Council also declined to take up the problem of Liberia, in part because Council members agreed with the U.S. view, but also because of opposition from Ethiopia and Zaire, both Council members, as well as Côte d'Ivoire (Wippman 1993: 165). However, once the ECOWAS intervention was under way, the international community welcomed it. In response to an ECOMOG-brokered cease-fire, the Security Council, via a "note" from its president, commended the efforts of ECOMOG, effectively endorsing the intervention (Murphy 1996: 153). After various cease-fires had broken down, the Security Council again commended ECOWAS, welcomed its continuing efforts, and adopted the arms embargo proposed by the regional organization. The justification offered was not humanitarian, but rather that "the deterioration of the situation in Liberia constitutes a threat to international peace and security, particularly in West Africa as a whole" (Resolution 788, November 1992). Statements made during debates in the Security Council and the General Assembly endorsed the ECOWAS intervention (Murphy 1996: 163). Several African leaders—including the secretary-general of the OAU as well as its chairman, President Yoweri Museveni of Uganda, and Zimbabwe's president, Robert Mugabe—explicitly approved of the intervention on human rights grounds, which is significant given the OAU's traditional opposition to intervention (Wippman 1993: 181). In sum, though human rights figured importantly in the ECOWAS justification for its intervention, international acceptance of it came in the guise of traditional peace and security language.

Iraq.   When the government of Iraq undertook a campaign of violent repression against its Kurdish minority in the north, both Iran and Turkey requested an urgent UN response. Both countries had significant Kurdish minorities of their own, and both anticipated massive flows of refugees fleeing the brutality in Iraq. Iran and Turkey justified their requests for action on the basis that the refugee movements constituted a threat to security and stability in the region, not on the basis of humanitarian concerns. In response, the Security Council passed Resolution 688 (April 1991), by a 10–3 vote with two abstentions. Resolution 688 condemned the Iraqi repression, demanded that it cease, insisted that Iraq provide immediate access for humanitarian organizations to all parts of the country, and requested that member states contribute to the humanitarian effort.

What makes this case ambiguous is that the resolution did not explicitly authorize military force, and it did not refer to Chapter VII, which provides for UN enforcement measures. On the contrary, it recalled Article 2 (7), which prohibits the United Nations from intervening in the internal affairs of states. During the Security Council debates leading up to the Resolution, three states (Cuba, Yemen, and Zimbabwe) opposed it on the grounds that it constituted intervention in purely domestic matters. A number of states emphasized the destabilizing consequences of the refugee flows (Austria, Belgium, Côte d'Ivoire, Ecuador, Italy, Romania, the United Kingdom, the United States, the USSR, and Zaire, plus non–Security Council members Denmark, Ireland, Luxembourg, and Sweden). Several states also stressed human rights abuses as a primary justification (France, UK, plus non–Security Council members Germany, the Netherlands, and Spain) (Stromseth 1993: 87–88; Gordon 1994: 548–49).

Nevertheless, American, British, and French military forces entered northern Iraq in April 1991 for the expressed purpose of creating safe conditions for the delivery of relief supplies to the Kurdish population and for the return of Kurdish refugees. The United States further declared a "no-fly zone" above the 36th parallel, to be enforced by allied aircraft. The intervention forces eventually numbered nearly 30,000 from thirteen countries (Tesón 1997: 238). The allies consistently justified the mission in humanitarian terms, both as a means of compelling the Iraqi regime to cease its brutal campaign against the Kurds and as a way to enable the delivery of food and other emergency supplies to the displaced Kurds (Stromseth 1993: 90; Murphy 1996: 172–74). The states that initially carried out the intervention (Britain, France, the United States) claimed either that Resolution 688 implied the use of force or that the larger context of previous resolutions authorizing the use of force against Iraq and the ongoing efforts to compel Iraqi compliance permitted forcible intervention.

Yugoslavia.   The complex conflict in the former Yugoslavia passed through several phases. UN intervention began with the UN Protection Force (UNPROFOR), a peacekeeping mission established in February 1992 to operate in Croatia. This essay will focus on the UN and NATO actions in Bosnia-Herzegovina, which had a clearer element of humanitarian intervention. There were two overlapping wars in Bosnia, one an internal conflict in which Bosnian Serbs and Croats inflicted large-scale human rights violations against the Bosnian Muslim population, and the other, once the international community had recognized Bosnia as an independent state (April 1992), a cross-border conflict in which Serbian forces supported the Bosnian Serb fighters. The interventions eventually carried out by NATO and the United Nations thus had three primary justifications. One, of course, was the appalling violations of human rights perpetrated largely by the Bosnian Serbs; the campaign of ethnic cleansing was reported globally, and routinely called a "holocaust" or a "genocide." A second justification for intervening in Bosnia was that the fighting might spread to neighboring countries, thus constituting a threat to regional peace and security. A third justification for intervention was to assist Bosnia in its self-defense, to the extent that Yugoslav military forces were operating inside Bosnia. In fact, the General Assembly determined by 136–1 (five abstentions) that Bosnia was the subject of international aggression, entitling it to self-defense under Article 51 (General Assembly Resolution 46/242). The self-defense rationale was clearly not primary; indeed, the UN arms embargo covered Bosnia as well as Serbia, in essence crippling Bosnia's efforts to defend itself. Thus the interventions in Bosnia were justified chiefly on humanitarian and threats-to-peace-and-security grounds (Tesón 1997: 262).

The international community, acting through the United Nations, clearly justified forcible interventions in Bosnia on both humanitarian grounds and traditional considerations of the threat to international peace.[6] The Security Council had by May 1992 imposed both an arms embargo (Resolution 713, September 1991) and a general economic embargo (Resolution 757, May 1992) on Serbia. The first of these determined that the conflict was a threat to international peace and security. The second repeats the finding of a threat to international peace and security, stressing also the inviolability of Bosnia's borders and demanding that all outside forces withdraw. But in addition it condemns "forcible expulsions" and ethnic cleansing ("attempts to change the ethnic composition of that population"), deplores obstacles to "unhindered delivery of humanitarian assistance," and affirms the need for "effective protection of human rights and fundamental freedoms." The Security Council subsequently authorized states and regional bodies (in practice, NATO and the EU) to enforce the embargoes, and to "use such measures commensurate with the specific circumstances as may be necessary." The Resolution (787, November 1992) made reference to "massive and systematic violations of human rights and grave violations of international humanitarian law" and condemns "ethnic cleansing."

When the embargoes failed to halt the fighting, the Security Council authorized states to take "nationally or through regional agencies or arrangements all measures necessary" to enable the delivery of humanitarian assistance (Resolution 770, August 1992). This, of course, is the language legitimizing the use of force. The resolution labeled the conflict a "threat to international peace and security," but it also made reference to the territorial integrity of Bosnia and to the imperative to assure the delivery of humanitarian assistance. No state or group of states undertook to organize an armed intervention, and the only action taken was to expand the UNPROFOR mission to the protection of relief convoys. In March 1993, the Security Council banned all flights over Bosnia, and authorized member states or their regional organizations (in effect, NATO) to use all necessary means to enforce the ban (Resolution 816).

The Security Council, by unanimous vote, also designated six "safe areas" and authorized UNPROFOR to deter attacks against them, to occupy tactical points toward this end, and to reply to bombardments (Resolution 819, April 1993; Resolution 824, May 1993). Both Resolutions condemn ethnic cleansing and refer to humanitarian needs; both also cite the sovereignty and territorial integrity of Bosnia. Finally, the Security Council, by a 13–0 vote with Pakistan and Venezuela abstaining, authorized member states or their regional organizations (NATO) to take "all necessary measures, through the use of air power" to support UNPROFOR in its mission to protect the safe areas. The resolution made references to ongoing violations of humanitarian law, cited the sovereignty of Bosnia, and, once again, stated that the situation constituted a "threat to international peace and security" (Resolution 836, June 1993). Under this authority NATO aircraft carried out limited bombing raids against Serb targets. In the end, however, UNPROFOR and NATO were unable to prevent Serb forces from overrunning the safe areas.

Somalia.   The intervention in Somalia, in contrast, had an almost purely humanitarian basis. Indeed, the United States, which eventually took the lead in organizing and providing troops for a multinational intervention, began its involvement in Somalia by shipping emergency food supplies to relieve the famine there, and by authorizing U.S. military aircraft to carry the shipments. When President George Bush offered in December 1992 to send 20,000 U.S. troops to Somalia, it was clearly justified in humanitarian terms: the sole American objective was to protect emergency food supplies from marauding warlords and to secure the means of distributing the food to the Somali population in desperate need (Coll 1997: 2–6). Somalia thus represents an exception to the general rule that the violation of security rights, but not political or socioeconomic rights, can justify intervention. Though numerous Somalis were being killed in the factional fighting, the larger problem was that hundreds of thousands more were being deprived of the right to survival by the disorder and were in danger of starvation.

The initial Security Council Resolution on Somalia (733, January 1992) instituted an arms embargo under Chapter VII and urged an end to the fighting in the country and cooperation in delivering relief supplies. The debates preceding the resolution made reference to a request from the government of Somalia (although whether Somalia had a government at the time was debatable), to the refugee problem, and to the humanitarian crisis (Gordon 1994: 552). The Security Council subsequently authorized a UN Operation in Somalia (UNOSOM), which could include observers and technical assistance, security personnel, and an emergency airlift. An August 1992 resolution increased UN personnel in Somalia by 4,200 (Resolution 775). As the warring clans continued to seize food and medical aid sent to Somalia, the Security Council (Resolution 794, December 1992) authorized the member states to use force to ensure the delivery of relief supplies. In the event the United States offered to provide 20,000 troops, and UNITAF came under American command. The Council, as recommended by the secretary-general, determined that the situation in Somalia was a "threat to the peace," without specifying why the problem was now international or how it threatened peace and security. The humanitarian crisis itself, apparently, was a threat to the peace, even in the absence of identified cross-border problems. The resolution referred to "the unique character of the present situation in Somalia" and "complex and extraordinary nature," which was clearly a way of trying to minimize the precedential value of the intervention. The justification for the intervention, however, was just as clearly humanitarian; the resolution notes "the human tragedy" and "widespread violations of international humanitarian law," including hindering the delivery of relief supplies. During the discussions, Austria argued that the UN was following the precedent of Resolution 688 (Iraq), and other Western countries described the action as a collective humanitarian intervention (Gordon 1994: 554).

Subsequent resolutions expanded the UNISOM mission, both in its numbers and in its mandate, which included authorization to engage in combat (Resolution 814, March 1993). Command of the international forces in the country passed from the United States to UNISOM II. After forces loyal to Aideed killed twenty-four Pakistani soldiers, the Security Council reaffirmed the authority of UNISOM II to employ all necessary means to pursue and bring to justice the perpetrators of the attack (Resolution 837, June 1993). After the fiasco with the U.S. Rangers, segments of the local population turned against the interveners, who thus found it impossible to establish order and security. The United States pulled its forces out, followed by some of the European countries. UNISOM II withdrew between January and March 1995 (Nanda et al. 1998: 836).

Rwanda.   The slaughter in Rwanda commenced the day that the airplane carrying President Juvénal Habyarimana crashed on approach to Kigali airport. Militant Hutus immediately seized control of the government, murdering the prime minister, Agathe Uwilingiyimana, and ten Belgian UN soldiers. Within hours, apparently according to prearranged plans and spurred on by Hutu radio stations, Hutu militias began the slaughter of innocent Tutsis as well as moderate Hutus. There were in Rwanda at the time 2,700 UN personnel, whose mission (UNAMIR) was to monitor a peace agreement between the government and the Rwandan Patriotic Front (RPF), a Tutsi rebel force. In response to reports of widespread massacres, the Security Council decided to reduce its presence in Rwanda to 270 (Tesón 1997: 258–59). Shortly thereafter, Secretary-General Boutros-Ghali proposed a UN force of 5,500 troops. With the United States resisting (probably still stung by the experience in Somalia), the Security Council equivocated. The Council in mid-May finally agreed to increase the UNAMIR force to 5,500 and to expand its mandate to the protection of refugees and of relief supplies, and imposed an arms embargo. In its Resolution 918, the Security Council referred to the deaths and displacement of thousands of innocent civilians, called the situation a "humanitarian crisis of enormous proportions," and even made reference to genocide as punishable under international law. However, the resolution also labeled the crisis in Rwanda "a threat to peace and security in the region." In June, the Security Council agreed to the full 5,500 force (Resolution 925); fourteen African countries had volunteered troops for the mission, but countries with the logistical capabilities to put them in place (especially the United States) were not forthcoming (Murphy 1996: 246; Nanda et al. 1998: 850).

Finally, the French government offered to spearhead a multinational force that would be under member-state command (as the UNITAF had been in Somalia) (Nanda et al. 1998: 850). Top French officials, including Foreign Minister Alain Juppé and Defense Minister François Léotard, stressed that the French mission was strictly humanitarian, that it aimed to stop the massacres and protect refugees, and would remain politically neutral (Murphy 1996: 248–49). The Security Council agreed (Resolution 929, June 1994), authorizing the use of "all necessary means" to achieve the humanitarian objectives of the United Nations. The justification stated was that "the magnitude of the humanitarian crisis in Rwanda constitutes a threat to peace and security in the region." In other words, the Security Council declared that the human rights crisis within Rwanda was itself a danger to peace, without citing any cross-border threats. However, again hoping to limit the precedential significance of its actions, the Council noted that "the current situation in Rwanda constitutes a unique case." There were, however, international misgivings about the French offer. Neither the United States nor any of France's partners in the European Union offered to supply troops. Burundi, Tanzania, and Uganda declined to permit France access to their territories for staging purposes (Nanda et al. 1998: 249). The vote authorizing the French mission was 10–0, with Brazil, China, New Zealand, Nigeria, and Pakistan abstaining.

Haiti. A coup in September 1991 deposed the elected president of Haiti, Jean-Bertrand Aristide. The Organization of American States promptly condemned the coup and recommended that its member states impose economic and political sanctions on Haiti (Tesón 1997: 250). Though the UN General Assembly condemned the coup and called for the protection of human rights, the Security Council initially declined to act, as a majority of its members considered the affair an internal matter (Tesón 1997: 249). After the OAS responded, all members of the Security Council criticized the coup and approved of the OAS action, the Council passed no formal resolution to that effect. China and some of the nonaligned states were wary about UN involvement in domestic problems (Tesón 1997: 250). The General Assembly condemned the coup and called for the protection of human rights. Some states justified UN attention in terms of the growing international refugee problem (France, Guyana, the United States, Venezuela), though Mexico urged caution with respect to the domestic affairs of Haiti (Gordon 1994: 557).

When regional (OAS) sanctions failed to produce any changes in Haiti, and as the military government continued to perpetrate human rights abuses against supporters of Aristide, the Security Council (Resolution 841, June 1993) instituted an economic embargo against Haiti, basing it in Chapter VII as a response to a threat to the peace. The purpose of the embargo was to force the military government to begin negotiations with the UN for the return of the legitimately elected Aristide government. By insisting on the reestablishment of a specific government, the United Nations was breaking new ground. (Gordon 1994: 558). However, Resolution 841 also stressed that Haiti was a "unique and exceptional situation," justifying "extraordinary measures"—again the concern with solidifying general norms. After the junta failed to comply with the terms of the Governors Island Agreement, and turned back a ship carrying UN personnel, the Security Council authorized states to enforce the economic sanctions by military means.

Finally, in July 1994, the Security Council authorized member states to form a multinational force and "to use all necessary means to facilitate the departure from Haiti of the military leadership . . . [and] the prompt return of the legitimately elected President" (Resolution 940). The resolution passed by a 12–0 vote, with China and Brazil abstaining. China argued that military intervention would set a "dangerous precedent," and Cuba, Mexico, and Uruguay (not members of the Security Council) participated in the debate and voiced reservations. The countries that supported intervention referred in the debates both to extensive human rights abuses in Haiti and the need to restore the democratic government (Murphy 1996: 269). The resolution, as had become Security Council custom, referred to the "unique character of the present situation in Haiti and its deteriorating, complex, and extraordinary nature, requiring an exceptional response." The Clinton administration committed 10,000—20,000 American troops; a dozen other countries contributed token numbers. With U.S. troop ships visible off the coast and military aircraft literally in the air, Haitian military leaders agreed to step down and to cooperate with the U.S. military mission, which in the event entered the country unopposed (Murphy 1996: 271). International reaction to the U.S. insertion of troops to supervise the transition was generally favorable; Venezuela was the only Latin American country to criticize the U.S. action (Tesón 1997: 252).

Intervention and Status of the Target Government

Governments are able at least partially to skirt the sensitive sovereignty issue in cases where intervention was carried out in states without a functioning government in control of its territory (Somalia, Liberia, Bosnia, possibly Rwanda after the RPF renewed its insurgency), or without a recognized government (Haiti). The international community was reluctant to provide explicit assent for interventions against functioning governments (Pakistan, Uganda, Iraq), though many states condoned or even welcomed the interventions.

The intervention in northern Iraq was complicated by the presence in Baghdad of a functioning government. In fact, the debate preceding the resolution showed that even the states that favored it were keenly sensitive to the norm of nonintervention in the affairs of a sovereign state. After all, Iraq did possess a single government in effective (perhaps excessive) control of its territory, and states were reluctant to authorize intervention without the prior consent of the affected sovereign government (Gordon 1996). Without direct authorization, some argued, the United Nations could not act within Iraq without the regime's permission. Resolution 688 did not explicitly authorize military intervention. Nevertheless, the allies moved military forces into Iraq immediately after the passage of the resolution. The United Nations eventually signed a memorandum of understanding with the Iraqi government, but this came after allied troops were already in place (Gordon 1994: 174). In short, this does seem to be a case in which UN member states intervened militarily for humanitarian purposes, without the prior consent of the target country.

The case of Liberia is less ambiguous with respect to the presence of a functioning government with some claim to sovereignty. By the time of the intervention, Charles Taylor's NPFL controlled the majority of Liberia's territory, including parts of the capital. The government of Samuel Doe was embroiled in a three-way battle for the capital with the NPFL and the INPFL (a rival rebel faction). The ECOWAS committee that decided for intervention, in its report, cited "a state of anarchy and the total breakdown of law and order in Liberia" and declared, "Presently, there is a government in

Liberia which cannot govern" (quoted in Wippman 1993: 176). In short, the intervention was based in part on the premise that there was no effective government whose sovereignty could be compromised.

The case of Somalia is similar to that of Liberia. After the departure of Siad Barre, there was no central government in the country, and none of the warring factions was able to impose itself as a government. Thus, in the Security Council debates leading up to the authorization to use force, some states emphasized the collapse of government in Somalia as creating a unique situation, that is, one that would not establish a precedent of intervening in a country against the wishes of a functioning government (China, Ecuador, Zimbabwe) (Gordon 1994: 553).

In Rwanda, the case was made that the country was without order; the generalized terror and slaughter having displaced the rule of law. The militant Hutu government in Kigali soon found itself struggling against RPF forces, which eventually won control of Rwanda by military victory. Even so, the resolution authorizing the French-led intervention reminded the interveners of their obligation to remain neutral and impartial as between the warring sides, thus indicating the international community's unwillingness to countenance actions that could be seen as interfering in domestic affairs, namely, the contest between a government and its opposition.

The issue of intervening against an effective government did not arise in the case of Haiti. The international community did not recognize the military junta as a legitimate government; the intervention was therefore not really against a government at all. The "true" government of Haiti was that of Aristide, a virtual government-in-exile.

CONCLUSIONS

The impassioned controversies surrounding humanitarian intervention are evidence that human rights norms have not yet displaced other principles of legitimate sovereignty, in particular the territorial norm. Human rights principles coexist, and remain in tension, with the principle of territorial control. Though the society of states has on several occasions been willing to suspend the territorial sovereignty of governments involved in massive human rights abuses, it has done so while making clear that each such intervention must be justified as an exception to the norm of nonintervention.

From the actions and discourses surrounding recent instances of humanitarian intervention, we can discern some basic norms. First, the international community has shown itself prepared to countenance intervention to halt abuses of security rights, that is, in cases where citizens are subjected to physical harm, murder, and expulsions. The violation of political or socioeconomic rights does not in general trigger international responses. However, there are two recent, if partial, exceptions to this norm, in Somalia and

Haiti. The intervention in Somalia aimed largely to relieve the catastrophic famine, implying a basic socioeconomic right to adequate nutrition. In Haiti, the intervention sought to restore democracy and the elected president, Aristide, thus enforcing a political right.

A second general norm is that intervention is justified only when the violations of security rights are gross, massive, and sustained. The interventions in Pakistan, Uganda, Liberia, Iraq, Bosnia, Somalia, and Rwanda clearly fit this criterion; in each case, civilians subjected to human rights abuses numbered in the hundreds of thousands, or even the millions. However, human rights violations in Central Africa and Haiti were smaller in scale. The violation of security rights in these cases, however, was either especially heinous (Bokassa was himself involved in at least one documented mass murder) or combined with broad and brutal political repression (Central Africa and Haiti).

Governments are careful in every instance to shore up sovereignty and exclusive internal jurisdiction. We saw this in the reluctance of states, both when they intervene themselves and when they authorize interventions, to justify the actions in straight human rights terms. Even when human rights considerations were central, the Security Council tended to justify intervention as a response to a threat to international peace and security. However, we also notice a shift in the use of the term "threat to international peace and security." In Somalia most clearly, the Security Council labeled the internal disaster a threat to regional peace and stability, without identifying any actual cross-border dangers. That is, the domestic abuse of human rights can in itself be a threat to international peace. The international community also reveals its reticence to compromise nonintervention norms in the way it considers the target government. There is greater opposition to, and criticism of, intervention when the target state has a functioning government (East Pakistan, Uganda, Iraq, Serbia, Kosovo). In contrast, it seems easier to justify intervention when the target country is either without an effective government (Liberia, Somalia) or lacking a legitimate government (Haiti). Finally, I have noted the regularity with which the Security Council labeled a situation "unique" or "extraordinary," and an intervention "exceptional" or "special." These locutions are an attempt to prevent the accretion of precedents. But after a series of unique exceptions, precedents do take hold, and norms emerge.

More difficult, in some ways, is the task of judging the effectiveness of humanitarian interventions. Do emerging norms of humanitarian intervention constitute an effective opportunity for expanding respect for human rights in a globalizing world? The challenge in making any such assessment stems in part from the lack of clear criteria. Most militarized humanitarian missions have multiple objectives, in addition to the halting of human rights abuses. In Iraq, for instance, the Western powers wanted to relieve the besieged Kurds, but they also wanted to keep the pressure on the regime of Saddam Hussein. The international missions in Somalia evolved over time, from an initial objective of protecting relief supplies from warlords to resolving the factional violence and rebuilding society.

Developing appropriate criteria and measures of effective intervention would probably require a chapter of its own. Nevertheless, some preliminary judgments are possible with respect to the specific goal of reducing or halting violations of basic security rights. Three categories seem to cover the range of outcomes offered by the cases examined here: cases in which intervention did appear to reduce the extent or intensity of human rights violations; cases in which it did not; and cases in which the results are mixed or ambiguous. The first category could plausibly include all three of the pre-1990 cases (East Pakistan, Uganda, and Central Africa), plus Iraq and possibly Liberia. Intervention did not reduce human rights violations in Rwanda (where it came too late). The ambiguous cases include Bosnia, Somalia, and Haiti. In Bosnia, the UN forces were not able to halt the slaughter of Bosnians by Serbs, as evidenced by the catastrophe at Srebrenica. However, subsequent use of NATO air power may have driven Serbia to negotiate, and the Dayton accords, for all their problems, did at least stop the fighting. In Somalia, the UN forces were initially successful in securing the delivery of relief supplies to many of the regions where starvation was occurring or imminent. But the subsequent shift in the mission (especially the American campaign to arrest Aideed) led to U.S. and UN casualties and the eventual withdrawal of the interveners, abandoning the country to the sordid status quo ante. In Haiti, the intervention did succeed in dislodging the junta and the return of an elected government. But in the period since, systematic political violence has been on the rise, placing in doubt the restoration of democracy and human rights.

Still, the poor overall record of interventions in terms of stopping human rights violations should not blind us to the important role they have played in some instances, and even where interventions have failed to stop human rights abuses, they have not demonstrably made bad situations worse. In any case, the existence of norms of humanitarian intervention is in itself an outcome of some value. Norms of intervention reaffirm and reinforce the underlying human rights norms. It is better to have the tool of intervention than not, even if governments use it inconsistently and with mixed success. Saving some lives is better than saving none.

NOTES

1. When legal scholars attempt to identify international legal rules, they examine two primary sources of law, convention (formal treaties) and custom (practices that states both regularly engage in and believe to be obligatory). This study employs

analogous methods, locating international rules in treaty law and in state practice. With respect to custom, however, I am less interested in *opinio juris* than in how states justify interventions and to what extent their actions are condemned or approved by other states.

2. All quotations from the UN Charter come from the text published in Brownlie 1995.

3. Tesón 1997: 86–87, 98, for example, makes a powerful argument to this effect.

4. In these cases, my assessment agrees with that of Murphy 1996.

5. This paragraph relies largely on the more detailed accounts of Arend and Beck 1993: 123–25; Murphy 1996: 105–7; and Tesón 1997: 179–95.

6. The following paragraphs draw on Murphy 1996: 198–217; Steinberg 1993; and Nanda et al. 1998: 839–41.

11

Human Rights, Globalizing Flows, and State Power

Jack Donnelly

In this essay, I reflect on the effect of globalization on human rights through the exercise or replacement of state power: globalization through the middle. As Alison Brysk's introduction suggests, the role and type of state are critical mediating variables in this relationship. In my discussion, the themes and patterns of this relationship follow the organization of the volume through five globalizing flows—commodities, people, information, norms, and political sanctions. My own analysis shows that the impact of globalizing flows depends on relations of power, which are still largely shaped by states.

GLOBALIZATION

Brysk offers a "consensus" definition of globalization: the growing interpenetration of states, markets, people, and ideas across territorial boundaries. Thus defined, globalization is very ancient indeed.[1] Within the academic discipline of international studies, the contemporary concern for globalization has clear parallels with earlier literatures on "integration" (Haas 1964; Nye 1971), "interdependence" (Keohane and Nye 1977), and "sovereignty at bay" (Vernon 1971). The literatures on "dependency" (Cardoso and Faletto 1979; Palma 1977) and "world systems theory" (Wallerstein 1974) developed analogous themes from more Marxist perspectives.

Globalization, however, appears in most of the preceding chapters as something fundamentally new. And it certainly is plausible to suggest that, whatever the historical parallels or antecedents, at least the pace of change is accelerating, with important qualitative differences. I therefore treat globalization as a characteristic of the decades on either side of the year 2000. In fact, "globalization" often seems a label for whatever is characteristic of the post–Cold War era. It refers, for example, not to all cross-national or even global markets but to the recent interpenetration of national labor markets and the communication-mediated creation of a single global capital market. "Globalization" is connected, not with telegraph, radio, telephone, or television, but with "telecommunications," high-speed digital networks with ever-growing bandwidth. The "third wave" of electoral democracy and the spread of human rights ideas is usually thought to merit the label "globalization," but not the historically far more important global spread of sovereign territorial states.

As a step beyond such strangely solipsistic "globalization is now" accounts, I suggest a simple two-dimensional typology. Globalization can be seen either as a process or as an end state. And it can be seen as a comprehensive whole or as a contingent clustering of largely separable "things." We can further refine our analysis by specifying the substantive domains within which globalization operates. Most of the authors in this volume understand globalization more as a process than as an outcome and see it more as an integrated whole than as a concatenation of largely independent pieces. Furthermore, given that we are primarily political scientists, the implicit focus is on the state and the challenges to its privileged place in national and international politics.

In effect, we take the 1960s, the high point of the sovereign, territorial state, as a baseline for comparison. This was a time when faith in the capacity of the state—which typically had more control over the economy than at any previous point in history—generated widespread optimism about the prospects for prosperity and economic development. Decolonization reflected the unquestioned predominance of the state as a political ordering principle. Even the threat of nuclear war seemed to subside after the Cuban Missile Crisis, moderating talk about nuclear weapons having made states obsolescent. Today, states more often provoke dissatisfaction, even disillusionment.

The state increasingly appears too small a unit for organizing relations and transactions. Faced with ever larger and stronger business enterprises that are adopting a truly global perspective, even powerful states are losing control over aspects of their economies that they had grown accustomed to dominating. Regional and international organizations increasingly influence, and sometimes even make, decisions that once were unquestionably the province of states. Transnational nongovernmental organizations exert increasingly sophisticated and effective pressures against states (and businesses) on issues such as human rights and the environment. And ordinary citizens—at least those with access to the latest communications and transportation technologies—increasingly interact with one another without regard to state boundaries and interests.

The state also appears to have become too large. Regionalism, devolution, and autonomy are increasingly common themes not just in Europe but across the globe. New communities forged in the wake of globalization are as likely to be subnational as transnational. Localization is increasingly another dimension of globalization, rather than a primordial condition.

In fact, the local and the global are increasingly linked without the intermediation of the state. Multinational business provides the most obvious example. But new information and transportation technologies increasingly allow the weak as well to leap over their own (usually hostile or indifferent) states, as Alison Brysk (2000) has shown in the case of indigenous peoples in the Americas. This is a striking example of what Margaret Keck and Kathryn Sikkink (1998) call the "boomerang" model of transnational advocacy: local actors direct information and appeals to transnational colleagues, foreign states, and regional and international organizations, which respond by mobilizing external pressure on the resistant state.

There are, of course, more frightening scenarios. Global markets, led by multinational banks and corporations, may provide forms of reintegration that reduce the enjoyment of economic and social rights in developed and developing countries alike. Fragmentation *without* reintegration is possible. And even empowering forms of subnational and transnational (re)integration may prove problematic. Consider ethnic chauvinism and religious fundamentalism. Amalia Cabezas's chapter presents a particularly striking example of the complex, and often surprising, mixture of the threats to and opportunities for human rights presented by globalization. The predatory inflow of sex tourists into the Dominican Republic has provoked creative and self-empowering responses by Dominican women that have made them more than simply victims of globalization.

HUMAN RIGHTS

Let us turn now to the other side of our topic, human rights. They are, literally, the rights that one has simply as a human being. As such, human rights are equal rights, because we are all equally human beings. They are also inalienable rights, because no matter how inhumanely we act or are treated, we cannot become other than human beings.

The 1948 Universal Declaration of Human Rights has been endorsed by virtually all states, having arguably acquired the status of customary international law (Meron 1989: ch. 2; Simma and Alston 1992). The 1966 International Covenant on Civil and Political Rights currently has 144 parties and the International Covenant on Economic, Social, and Cultural Rights has 142 parties.[2] The Vienna Declaration and Programme of Action was adopted by consensus by the 171 states that participated in the 1993 World Conference on Human Rights. These documents, which reflect a thin but nonetheless real consensus, largely set the meaning of "human rights" in contemporary international society. And the legitimacy of a state, from within this perspective, is a function of the extent to which it respects, protects, and realizes the human rights of its citizens. The Vienna Declaration is unusually forthright, claiming in its first operative paragraph that "human rights and fundamental freedoms are the birthright of all human beings; their protection and promotion is the first responsibility of Governments."

The Universal Declaration, however, explicitly presented itself as a standard of achievement for nations and peoples. And through the 1970s, states and analysts continued to devote considerable attention to the question of *whether* human rights are a legitimate subject of international action. Today, although international implementation machinery remains weak, our focus instead is on when, where, and how we ought to act in response to gross, persistent, or systematic human rights violations. And the most common complaint heard today is that verbal condemnations, the outer limit of the permissible even thirty years ago, are no longer enough.

There is also a (thin but real) consensus on the substance of internationally recognized human rights. Both governments and leading movements of political opposition now typically take the Universal Declaration and the Covenants as authoritative statements of international norms, in word if not deed. Cold War ideological debates about priorities between civil and political and economic, social, and cultural rights have lost most of their force.[3] For example, it was agreed at Vienna that "lack of development may not be invoked to justify the abridgement of internationally recognized human rights." And the motto of the office of the High Commissioner for Human Rights in 1998, the year of the fiftieth anniversary of the Universal Declaration, was "All human rights for all."

We should not overestimate the depth, or even the breadth, of this consensus. Every major geographical region contains at least one striking exception. There is also great variation within and across regions, with Africa and Asia trailing Europe and the Americas, and the Middle East still largely outside this consensus. Individual states still do regularly insist that exceptional circumstances free them from the obligation to implement rights, at least in the short run. Nonetheless, today the Universal Declaration and the Covenants are accepted as (at least in principle) something very much like a *minimum* standard by which the human rights performance of *all* states may be judged. But blind reliance on the Universal Declaration and Covenants poses at least three major dangers.

First, important questions have been raised about what is *not* included in these and other international instruments. In recent years, this has perhaps been most evident in calls to recognize ethnic, cultural, and religious minorities as rights holders, rather than simply as collections of individuals holding individual rights to nondiscrimination, freedom of association, and so on.[4] We also regularly encounter arguments that "new issues," such as the environment, require new rights. Many of these issues are precisely those that cross state boundaries or challenge state control.

Second, the implicit "liberal" justificatory theory of the Universal Declaration is frequently contested. Even where "liberal democratic" values have no serious challenger, they often are more a "default option"[5] than anything else; that is, they are accepted largely because the obvious alternatives have been delegitimated. To the extent that this is true, the penetration of the contemporary international human rights norms into the practices of states and the consciousness of citizens is likely to be extremely limited. Thus human rights often prove more valuable for condemning or resisting old practices than for building new social and political orders. For example, many who shared "Western" assessments of what was wrong with the totalitarian regimes will not share "Western" views about what should be created in their place, or how to get there.

Third, there is a "hegemonic" dimension to the current international human rights consensus. Human rights are *not* politically or morally neutral. Quite the contrary, they privilege certain social groups, practices, and values, while marginalizing others. Whatever their moral or legal justifications, human rights are *also* part of (national and international) political, economic, and cultural struggles. And they are specially associated with the self-understandings and foreign policies of "the West" in general and the United States in particular.

Many of the preceding chapters in this volume raise or acknowledge these and other concerns about international human rights norms. Nonetheless, they focus not on inadequacies in international human rights norms but rather on how globalization influences and is shaped by internationally recognized human rights. I strongly endorse this perspective. The human rights project implicit in the Universal Declaration, for all its limitations, deserves priority over expanding or redefining that project. In most places in the world, including (very prominently) the United States, much more work needs to be done before we meet current international human rights standards. And very difficult work will be required to protect current achievements from being undermined, by forces ranging from globalization to vicious leaders to complacent citizens. Let us turn, then, to an overview of each of these forms of globalization, conceived in terms of five flows: flows of people, commodities, information, values, and sanctions.

FLOWS OF PEOPLE

Migration challenges a foundational assumption of international human rights law, namely, that the primary, and often exclusive, responsibility for protecting and implementing "universal" human rights lies with the state of which one is a national. As Kristen Maher emphasizes, nationality or citizenship provides a right to rights.

International human rights law permit states to deny noncitizen residents many rights, including rights of political participation and some economic and social rights. Decisions on citizenship are left largely to the discretion of states, which typically place roadblocks in the way of migrants becoming full participants in the social and political communities of their new home. States are also largely free to prohibit entry in the first place. But the permeability of borders and the demands of labor markets often lead to the creation of a further class of even more marginalized "illegal" immigrants and temporary workers without rights of residence.[6]

The "obvious" solution is to link the enjoyment of internationally recognized human rights to some other institution(s)—although exactly what such institutions might be, and how the transition might be achieved, is anything but obvious. The possible contribution of globalization may lie in its encouragement of practices that foster multiple political identities. If the problems of migrants arise from fusing nation, state, citizenship, and territory into a single dominant, and dominating, identity, multiple citizenships may be the remedy (cf. Davidson 2000). Consider, for example, the Maastricht Treaty, which creates citizenship in the European Union for every national of a member state, and extends to EU citizens the right to vote and stand for election in their place of residence, irrespective of nationality.[7]

In a world of sovereign, territorial nation-states, political identity has largely been a function of where one was born. Migrants either remained aliens or were naturalized as citizens, renouncing prior allegiances. This stark choice seems increasingly inappropriate to a growing number of migrants and communities. By struggling against the problems of global migration in a world of state and territorial identities, migrants may help to develop new practices and identities that allow (or force) us to free ourselves from "traditional forms of imposed identity" (Franck 1999: ch. 1).

As political realists correctly, if rather monotonously, remind us, states remain central actors, not just in international relations but in the daily lives of most people in most parts of the globe. The resilience of states in response to immigration should not be underestimated (Joppke 1999). Even the new powers of the EU over citizenship and migration do "not entail a decisive weakening of individual states;" states "remain critical players rather than diminishing entities" (Bhabha 1998a: 721, 697).

MARKET FLOWS

Market flows are at the heart of most contemporary discussions of globalization, including the chapters by Wesley Milner, Richard Falk, and Raul Pangalangan in this book. My focus here will be on the threats economic globalization poses to one of the great human rights triumphs of the past century, the taming of capitalist markets by welfare states. As the separation between locales of production and consumption continues to grow, firms are increasingly free to move "offshore" to escape the costs imposed by welfare state guarantees of economic and social goals. The resulting market pressures to constrain national social welfare policies are increasingly supplemented by pressures from international financial institutions.

The transfer of production to less developed countries might allow people there to better realize *their* economic and social conditions. But without strong welfare states, there is no guarantee that the fate of economic and social *rights* is likely to improve, especially in the short and medium run, even if overall national prosperity increases. For example, firms fleeing health and safety regulations relocate dangerous production that at least partly cancels any income and investment benefits they bring.[8]

Economic globalization tends to shift the balance of power toward business, which is becoming increasingly global and mobile, and away from workers and the state, which remain much more national. Or, even more ominously, welfare states may be giving way to new state forms as capitalism globalizes. "Capitalism has not escaped the state, but rather . . . the state has, as always, been a fundamental constitutive element in the very process of extension of capitalism in our time" (Panitch 1994: 87). "The capitalist state, precisely because it is capitalist, is a site for the development of internationalizing tendencies. Thus at least certain states should be seen not as nation-states in the narrow sense . . . but as internationalized states whose apparatus is geared in important ways to the promotion not of national but international accumulation" (Glassman 1999: 691). Old affinities and compacts that linked states, firms, and citizens in support of nationally redistributive policies are being eroded by the increasingly global perspective of *both* firms and states.[9]

Markets are geared to aggregate efficiency and increased total production, and they thus base distributions on the share of (market) value added. Economic and social rights, by contrast, are concerned with fair distributions, defined as assuring certain minimums for all.[10] Without welfare states (or other comparable redistributive mechanisms) there is no necessary connection between market-led growth and development and the enjoyment of economic and social rights for all. In fact, Robert Goodin and others show in *The Real Worlds of Welfare Capitalism* (1999) that even among contemporary capitalist welfare states, institutional design is important to outcomes with respect to growth, poverty, and social integration.

We have not been able to create effective alternatives to the welfare state, our principal institution for mediating the competing claims of efficiency and equity. Quite the contrary, globalization is not only forcing the retreat of welfare states, it is reorienting international organizations to market forces.

Consider the changing character of the International Monetary Fund. It was created to supervise a global financial regime based on fixed exchange rates, which were intended to *increase* national economic control in order to better realize welfare state policies. Today, however, it enforces the ever widening penetration of market mechanisms with little if any concern for social welfare and economic and social rights.

States and citizens have tried in various ways to resist a purely market logic. The European Union might be seen as a multilateral effort to protect the European welfare state by limiting the regional "race to the bottom." Jonathan Fox's discussion of the World Bank Inspection Panel addresses an interesting, if marginal, mechanism by which national and transnational civil society may participate directly in multilateral economic decision making. Seattle has rapidly become a symbol of revolt. Consumer boycotts have had some modest successes. The defeat of the Multilateral Agreement on Investment was in significant measure a joint endeavor of transnational activists and Third World states. These and other counterhegemonic forces, however, are dwarfed by those of global corporations and the economic chiropractic of structural adjustment.

INFORMATION FLOWS

If markets are the most familiar aspect of globalization, a strong case can be made that information flows are the most distinctive. Earlier transportation and communications technologies shrank the globe. The current "information age" holds out the prospect of rendering space, at least on this planet, increasingly irrelevant to economic, political, and even cultural interactions. And information itself is increasingly what is at stake, rather than a means to something else. While information may diminish the monopoly of *state* power, it does not eliminate the state. Furthermore, information flows show that globalization does not transcend power—rather, globalization of information requires us to examine different kinds of power relationships.

Shayne Weyker has looked directly at the impact of new information technologies on human rights NGOs, which have been empowered with new ways to marshal evidence, reach out to and organize people, and draw attention to human rights violations. Clifford Bob's discussion of the Ogoni illustrates how these technologies can draw attention to a previously obscure and ignored struggle. But the Saro-Wiwa story does not have a happy ending, instead, it culminated in martyrdom. And these same technologies create new opportunities for surveillance and state intervention.

From a human rights perspective, two issues seem central today. First, will new information technologies alter the balance of power between corporate and individual actors? Individuals certainly have been empowered to make choices and develop relationships that were not previously available to

them. But these same information technologies have been central to the globalization of production and finance and the resulting increase in corporate
power. Who controls which of the new networks and communities that are
being created will be crucial to the consequences of these technologies.

The battle over Napster provides a glimpse, in an admittedly minor issue
area, of the basic struggle. But to the extent that new communities deal with
issues such as pop music and copyrights, the human rights benefits would
seem nil. And the increasingly central place of e-commerce in discussions
of the Internet suggests that commercial power is asserting itself with a
vengeance. Will the era in which the Internet was an open and anarchic realm
prove to be just a quaint interlude between its roots in the American military-
industrial complex and a future dominated by global corporate oligopolists?
If the forces of global commerce do not yet have the upper hand, they certainly are not in retreat.

Second is the problem of unequal access, the so-called digital divide. Even
if these new technologies do not end up subject to corporate domination,
will they simply increase the range of options available to an already privileged elite? Will they allow new individuals and groups to enter that elite?
Will they create a substantially new elite? Or will they erode elite privileges,
which at least in the past have rested in part on proximity to economic and
political power? In the short and medium run, we cannot be very sanguine
about the likelihood of "the people" empowered by these new technologies
including very many in the bottom third, or even the bottom two-thirds, of
the global distribution of income. But if including "a few" who would otherwise have remained outside the economic, political, and cultural mainstream means millions, or even tens of millions, of people, isn't this a valuable achievement?

FLOWS OF VALUES AND NORMS

Contemporary discussions of globalization are distinguished from most earlier work by a greater attention to norms, values, and institutions. In Marx-
ian terms, the analysis is more Gramscian.[11] Within the field of international
studies, the approach is more constructivist.[12] These analytical frameworks
suggest that power is increasingly based on (or constructed by) norms and
ideas.

Consider the four major parts of this volume. In the domain of commodities, globalization concerns not just the transnational consolidation of
capitalist markets, but also the spread of neoliberal market ideology and its
enforcement by formal and informal multilateral agencies and mechanisms.
In the domain of citizenship, globalization involves not just the rise of new
actors but also the emergence of new local, transnational, and supranational
identities. In the domain of communications as well, we are witnessing the

emergence of new ways of understanding ourselves and the communities in which our lives are embedded. And in the domain of cooperation, globalization involves not just the spread of American or Western economic and political power, but also the spread of Western economic and political ideas and models—including human rights.

The spread of international human rights norms, often in association with norms of democracy,[13] have altered national and international definitions of legitimacy and political possibilities. Even more striking than the demise of most totalitarian party-state regimes has been the spread of electoral democracies in all regions of the world. Even where this has been largely a cover for military or civilian dictatorship—for example, in Venezuela, Belarus, Benin, and Indonesia—the demand to observe democratic formalities does constrain state behavior. National, transnational, and international human rights advocacy, based on the international normative consensus discussed above, has further limited the options of even repressive regimes. It has also helped to consolidate progress and limit backsliding.

Norms and values certainly do not operate divorced from power. As in the case of market norms, the spread of human rights and democratic values is connected to the West in general and the United States in particular. But the progress of those norms cannot be reduced to the power of their leading sponsors. In many countries, both human rights and markets were powerful lures; they did not need to be imposed on very many of those who had been forced to endure decades of political repression and economic mismanagement.

With human rights in particular, very few ordinary citizens needed to be pressured by the West to appreciate not being repressed or impoverished by their governments. Force is most evident instead in countries such as China, Syria, and Zimbabwe, where governments deny internationally recognized human rights to their citizens. The lesson of the past two decades is that pretty much every place where people have been given a free choice, they have chosen human rights. The current hegemony of human rights has more to do with the moral appeal of the values than with their support by leading powers. One might even suggest that international human rights norms attract power more than they depend on it.[14]

Even norms that are hegemonic in a more strictly Gramscian sense of the term—that is, a mechanism of class domination—often can be used by subordinated groups. This has regularly been the case with human rights. Even where initially implemented for a privileged elite—for example, a propertied, white, male, Christian elite in Locke's world—the inherent universality of appeals to human rights is readily turned against those who would deny some human beings rights that are represented as universal. Over and over again, human rights have been used—by workers, women, religious and racial minorities, colonial peoples, and, today, migrants, homosexuals, and the disabled—to achieve particular advantages or remedies, systematic improvements in their treatment and status, and, ultimately, full political incorporation into the body of citizens.

The spread of international human rights norms thus may be the one dimension of globalization with opportunities that are not substantially counterbalanced by threats. But other global flows of norms do threaten human rights. Consider the spread of neoliberal economic ideology, which I think all the contributors to this volume agree is on balance a serious threat to human rights.[15] The spread of a homogenized Western "consumer culture" is often presented as a negative normative and cultural consequence of globalization—although often in a distressingly paternalistic way by those who are deeply enmeshed within that culture. Flows of norms, like the other globalizing flows, present both threats and opportunities.

FLOWS OF SANCTIONS

One of the most striking human rights developments during the post–Cold War era has been the emergence of an international practice of humanitarian intervention in response to genocide.[16] This practice can in significant measure be attributed to global flows of norms, as well as new information flows that have brought mass suffering abroad much closer to home. Here, however, I want to consider it in the context of new flows of political decisions and sanctions. Intervention is practiced by states upon states, often via interstate organizations. Thus, I begin by drawing attention to four important limitations, building on Wayne Sandholtz's discussion.

First, armed humanitarian intervention has been restricted to instances of genocide[17] with no hint of spillover into coercive international responses to other human rights violations. Even North Korea, a weak state in the throes of state-induced mass starvation, has provoked no significant calls for intervention. Somalia does suggest that "failed" states facing a massive humanitarian crisis may provoke intervention. But so long as a state remains "in business" and refrains from killing large quantities of citizens directly, it has little to fear from international action.

Second, the armed interventions that we have seen typically have been tragically tardy. Rwanda is the classic case: international assistance arrived only after most of the killing had stopped. But Kosovo, the one case where armed humanitarian intervention *preceded* genocide, provoked considerable criticism. One must wonder whether in the future we will revert to waiting until after the killing has reached a fever pitch.

Kosovo also raises a third problem, authorization. Should we let people die when there is no consensus in the Security Council? A norm of great power self-authorization certainly is far too subject to abuse to be acceptable. But is convincing a substantial group of regional partners with a genuine capacity enough to provide multilateral legitimacy? And if tens of thousands of people have been massacred, are we really willing to say that a great power should not act alone? We are only beginning to grapple with the political, legal, and moral issues involved in such questions.

Selectivity is a fourth issue often raised in recent discussions. Although a legitimate concern—why *did* the international community do more in Bosnia than in Rwanda?—I find it much less troublesome. Until human rights trump all other national interests, which is not even remotely close to the case in any current state, motives in addition to humanitarian ones often are essential to mustering adequate political support. Where additional motives are lacking, humanitarian intervention is less likely—not to mention when nonhumanitarian motives counsel nonintervention. Selective intervention, so long as it always has a central humanitarian purpose, is better than no intervention.

Similar progressive developments are evident in the area of individual international criminal responsibility for war crimes and certain gross and systematic violations of security rights, as illustrated by the creation of an International Criminal Court and the nearly successful effort to prosecute Augusto Pinochet. Even if largely symbolic and generally peripheral to most national and international human rights struggles, these new institutions and practices point to emerging flows of international sanctions that, if not entirely without precedent, certainly are qualitatively different from anything we have previously witnessed.

Much more problematic, however, has been the post–Cold War experience with *economic* sanctions, which simply don't work very well (Cortright and Lopez 2000). On reflection, it probably is not surprising that rulers who are willing and able to massively abuse their own citizens can use their power to protect their own privileges and show little concern for whatever additional sufferings their citizens endure. And rather than their triggering a liberating revolution, the principal effect of economic sanctions, as Iraq shows most clearly, often is that the victims of national oppression are further burdened by internationally imposed suffering. Cases such as Cuba and Serbia even seem to suggest that clever nationalist dictators can turn sanctions into a political tool of their own.

We must also remember that multilateral decision making is not always good for human rights. We have already referred to the negative human rights impact of international financial institutions. States sometimes are the good guys—or at least not the worst of the bad guys—a point to which we shall return below.

We see a similar mixed picture when we turn from these new flows of international or multilateral decisions and sanctions to the transnational level. We must not forget that MNCs are the most powerful transnational actors in the contemporary world. *Private Authority and International Affairs*, edited by Claire Cutler, Virginia Haufler, and Tony Porter (1999), documents the rise of private and quasi-public regulatory regimes in which firms are authorized by states to set national and international standards and rules that previously were the unquestioned prerogative of states, either directly or indirectly through international organizations. Although few direct negative human rights consequences are apparent at the moment, there would seem to be nothing favorable to human rights in governance structures in which firms hold regulatory powers. Interesting human rights opportunities might be comparable were governance extended to representatives of NGOs and social movements. Fox's discussion of the World Bank, however, suggests that such initiatives today are, at best, underdeveloped and marginalized.

HUMAN RIGHTS, GLOBALIZATION, AND THE STATE

I want to close this essay on what is something of a discordant note in discussions of international human rights, namely, one, perhaps even two, cheers for the state. We all know the horrible things that states can do, have done, and will continue to do. During the Cold War era, national, transnational, and international human rights advocacy was largely focused, rightly I believe, on the state as violator. I want to suggest, however, that today we might do well to focus more on the essential role that states play in implementing and protecting human rights.

Even today—as the idea of citizenship as a right to rights underscores—most people enjoy their internationally recognized human rights almost exclusively through the agency or mediation of the states of which they are nationals. Even Europe's strong and effective regional human rights regime remains a relatively minor, although important, supplement and spur to national action. Only in the case of genocide has international action become a systematically crucial factor in determining whether internationally recognized human rights are violated. And—without in any way diminishing the immense significance of killing or keeping alive hundreds of thousands, even millions, of people—it has to be conceded that genocide is only a tiny part of the overall picture of international human rights violations.

Until we develop institutional mechanisms to implement and protect internationally recognized human rights, an active positive role for states will remain essential. As Brysk's introduction suggests, even "negative" civil and political rights usually require much more than simple state restraint.[18] An active state is even more essential for economic and social rights. The fate of human rights in the coming decades is likely to depend, as it has in the past, on who controls the state.

Transnational business is using globalization to press, with considerable success, for more (neo)classically liberal states that give greater emphasis to markets—the domain of social action where business's power and skills are greatest. Human rights advocates and allied elements of civil society are seeking to use their electoral power, as well as their organizational and moral power—which has been significantly enhanced by globalization—to establish, strengthen, maintain, and protect states committed to economic and social rights. And they often share a common interest with government elites who, whether because of a genuine commitment to human rights or for selfish reasons, have an interest in controlling transnational business. An alliance between human rights advocates and state elites, who so often are the enemy of human rights, may prove the best way to maintain or (re)establish social control over markets necessary to assure economic and social rights for all.

Some might suggest that this is thinking too small and in ways too constrained by a rapidly fading past. Certainly, there is an important place for creative efforts to develop new institutions, norms, and practices. But there is an immense amount of work that needs to be done now. And that requires the active support of states, especially in the case of economic and social rights, the domain in which globalization poses the greatest immediate threats.

Humane, redistributive states, even in the decades on either side of the 1960s, were hardly the statistical norm. But neither were they a rarity. If liberal democratic welfare states become dinosaurs, the short- and medium-term prospects for human rights are likely to be bleak. The task, then, is to keep them from becoming an endangered species—or better yet, to support their spread. A central purpose of human rights advocacy has always been to empower people to force "their" state to treat them as they deserve to be treated. Today, beyond the intrinsic attractions of such a project, this may also be the best way to counter some of the most important threats to human rights posed by globalization.

NOTES

1. The creation of the Persian empire in the sixth century B.C., spreading from India to Egypt and southeastern Europe; the spread of Greek peoples and culture, from the colonizations of the late eighth century B.C. through the conquests and rule of Alexander the Great and his successors; and the even wider spread of the Roman world involved interpenetrations of states, markets, people, and ideas that produced transformations at least as significant as anything we have experienced in recent years. Even if we insist on the global dimension of globalization, current processes can be readily traced back to the fifteenth and sixteenth century, when European adventurers and traders crossed the Atlantic, sailed around Africa, circumnavigated the globe, and then, more slowly, joined by soldiers, settlers, missionaries, and bureaucrats, penetrated the inland areas of Asia, Africa, and the Americas. Marx, of course, provided a classic analysis of this phase of globalization (Avineri 1968).

2. See http://untreaty.un.org/English/sample/EnglishInternetBible/partI/ chapterIV/treaty5.asp and . . . /treaty4.asp.

3. The principal exception, which proves the rule, is the reluctance of the United States to accept economic, social, and cultural rights on the same footing as civil and political rights. The other leading exception is China, whose position is largely a mirror image of that of the United States.

4. The only collective right recognized in the Covenants is the right of peoples to self-determination. (The Universal Declaration recognizes none.) Even "minority rights," in the language of Article 27 of the International Covenant on Civil and Political Rights, as seen as rights of "persons [individuals] belonging to" religious, ethnic, or linguistic minorities.

5. I take this term from Claus Offe, who used it in an oral presentation at a conference at Yale University in the spring of 1999.

6. Here perhaps is an appropriate place to raise concerns about Brysk's categorization of human rights, particularly her implicit (although certainly not intentional) denigration of civil and political rights other than security rights. Political participation is centrally at stake for migrants. More generally, the issues of citizenship addressed in Part II are concerned more with political participation than security. One might even argue that political participation is essential to security. We can also note that many economic and social rights are centrally about security.

7. Schmitter 2000: ch. 2 discusses Euro-citizenship in the context of regional democratization. Castles 1998b discusses multiculturalism and citizenship with a European focus. These improvements in the treatment of migrants from member states, however, have occurred alongside substantial efforts in most EU countries to exclude other migrants more effectively and to limit the access and options of asylum seekers. And there is little evidence of similar changes in other regions. See Sutcliffe 1998.

8. In part for such reasons, Ramesh Mishra (1998) argues—provocatively, but (to me at least) unconvincingly—that the most effective response would be social standards rather than social rights.

9. The preceding should not be read as a blanket attack on national and international markets. The international community, and most states as well, have become well aware of—and often quite aggressive in asserting—the costs of command economies, which almost always swamp any equity benefits, especially in the medium and long run. There are indeed wondrous aspects to global markets, and the vast array of goods, services, and opportunities that they have created. But the wealth and opportunities of globalization seem to be flowing disproportionately to the already privileged. In addition to any transfer of resources from relatively privileged Western workers and giving to less privileged workers elsewhere, even more privileged capitalists, managers, bureaucrats, and investors are leading beneficiaries of globalization.

10. I pursue this contrast in more depth in Donnelly 1999a: 626–30. For complementary but very different perspectives on links between markets, rights, and welfare, see Levine 1988 and DeMartino 2000: pt. 1.

11. See Gramsci 1971 and Cox 1983, reprinted in Cox and Sinclair 1996.

12. Ruggie 1999; Katzenstein et al. 1999; Wendt 1999.

13. On the differences between the logics of human rights and democracy, see Donnelly 1999: 619–22.

14. The international campaign against apartheid provides a particularly striking example. On the way in which international norms led to the redefinition of American interests in relations with South Africa, see Klotz 1995. On norms in international relations more generally, see Katzenstein 1996 and Finnemore and Sikkink 1999.

15. For a wide-ranging set of essays by heterodox economists making this basic argument, with often interesting attempts to suggest policy alternatives, see Baker et al. 1998.

16. I use "genocide" broadly to include what technically may be better called "politicide," mass killings for political reasons not centrally connected with race or ethnicity.

17. Haiti is an exception that increasingly appears to be an anomaly rather than a precedent.

18. For example, to assure that the police "merely refrain" from treating suspects brutally requires that those inclined to brutality must, if possible, be screened out, and in any case restrained, typically through extensive and expensive systems of training, monitoring, and (administrative, legislative, and judicial) oversight. "Classic" liberties such as free elections and fair trials require not simple restraint, but extensive state action. And as the language of affirmative action makes clear, effective enjoyment of equal rights for all often is impossible with policies that seek only passive legal and political neutrality.

Conclusion

From Rights to Realities

Alison Brysk

This volume has applied a variety of analytical and academic tools to map the impact of globalization on human rights conditions. How can these multiple perspectives make globalization more responsive to human rights concerns? This essay will review the general findings of the volume, situate this analysis in terms of international relations theory, and suggest some initial policy prescriptions.

NEW (AND OLD) THREATS TO HUMAN RIGHTS

What are the leading patterns of threats to human rights today? Our findings suggest that the key determinants are the type of globalization, the level of analysis, and the type of state. In these essays, the new threats can be grouped by those emanating from globalized states, markets, and civil societies. Future work should also examine the threat of transnational violence, such as terror and crime. Meanwhile, new opportunities derive mainly from above, across, and below the state.

States and the illegitimate exercise of state power are still the outstanding problem for many of the world's inhabitants, as Jack Donnelly's essay reminds us. But some of the forms of state repression have evolved along with globalization and transnational flows (see Kristen Hill Maher's chapter). Even global governance itself can threaten human rights (for example, West African regional peacekeeping forces have been accused of human rights violations). While states still murder their citizens, and allow or encourage different communities to murder each other, they are now more often weak states seeking to consolidate power rather than totalitarian hegemons. And interstate military engagements that violate human rights are inspired increasingly by *international* interest: from abusive interventions to combat South American failure to control international flows of drugs to inhumane sanctions to counter Iraq's failure to comply with UN weapons inspections.

International markets have long presented direct threats to social rights and indirect ones to security rights, through subsidizing or even subcontracting repressive states (as in Burma). Some of the abuses of labor rights committed by MNCs backed by pliable governments differ little from traditional imperialism; strikers and dissidents are simply killed by state or paramilitary forces in places like Guatemala and Nigeria.[1] Globalization as an increase in transnational investment, commodity networks, and export dependency has certainly increased opportunities for this kind of abuse, although global communications and civic networks have also increased monitoring. But other aspects of globalized markets may pose less direct but more pervasive threats. International economic adjustment mandated by multilateral economic organizations and attendant economic crises are systematically correlated with increases in social inequality and crime, coupled with declines in social safety nets and rights-protective government services such as judiciaries (Brysk 2000c; Loker 1999; Ghai 1991). Crisis-ridden regimes are also ill equipped to consolidate democracy by incorporating former repressive forces, which often fosters the growth of mafias and paramilitary groups, further threatening the security of citizens and at the same time "justifying" curtailments of civil liberties. Even the most decentralized, potentially beneficial forms of exchange, such as tourism, can produce threats to human rights through their structural distortions (see chapter 2 by Amalia Lucia Cabezas). Thus, security forces in Southeast Asia can hardly be expected to protect young women from kidnapping, assault, rape, and slavery for the prostitution trade, when police and militaries are not only bribed by but actually investors in the brothels (Lim 1998).

Global civil society is generally seen as the "great white hope" of international relations, and a counterbalance to state, market, and organizational threats. But the growth of transnational civic links can also distort and even threaten human rights. First of all, groups whose goals directly contradict human rights are also forming transnational links (mercenaries, terrorists, religious cults, neo-Nazis). Second, even the rights-supportive channels of information campaigns and NGO appeals are highly uneven in access and responsiveness, in ways that may distort the plight of certain kinds of victims, particularly women, illiterates, the rural poor, and lumpen urban informal sectors (see chapter 7 by Clifford Bob). Third, local civil societies, in variable relationships to global forces, may become a threat to human rights, as when neighborhood vigilantes in painfully globalizing societies lynch suspected criminals in Latin America (or suspiciously prosperous accused "witches" in southern Africa or Indonesia). Finally, some agents of global civil society have mobilized around distinctive goals that may challenge human rights in particular situations—especially when civic agents substitute for weak states—such as the well-documented conflicts between indigenous rights groups and transnational environmentalists (Brysk 2000a).

Persisting threats come mainly from states, while emerging threats are often generated (directly or indirectly) by markets. This means that states must be simultaneously limited in their ability to violate security rights and strengthened in their ability to provide social rights. Opportunities for human rights protection that rely on global governance must therefore grapple with the broader question of how and whether legitimate but nonauthoritative collectivities and consciousness can regulate sovereign coercion and invisible interests.

NEW GLOBAL OPPORTUNITIES

Alongside the new threats to human rights, the growth of a global system also offers significant new opportunities. The key characteristics of globalization—connection, cosmopolitanism, communication, and even commodification—are precisely those that open new avenues for human rights accountability. But most of these forces go above or across states, less often below and rarely through them.

In terms of connection, human rights norms articulated in international law and treaties assert growing levels of transnational accountability (Falk 1998). These norms are implemented by an "international human rights regime," which not only connects perpetrators and victims to global institutions that cross borders, but also connects international organizations and networks to each other. Furthermore, states enforce human rights connectedness through fostering bilateral legal accountability, economic sanctions, and, in the last instance, through humanitarian intervention (see chapter 10 by Wayne Sandholtz). Connectedness has also been useful in mobilizing consumer boycotts of multinationals, citizen protest against multilateral economic institutions, and transnational debate regarding neoliberalism and structural adjustment (such as those discussed by Fox and Falk). Connectedness has also strengthened domestic human rights NGOs, through participation in international campaigns, infusions of external resources, and cross-border learning (Aguayo 1996).

Cosmopolitanism means that the exchange of power across borders occurs increasingly through individuals and transnational entities. In this sense, human rights opportunities flow from the growing number of organizations above, below, and beside the state that can conceivably check human rights abuses (see James Rosenau's chapter). These include not just the international human rights regime and movement but a broader range of international and nongovernmental organizations which monitor states, empower citizens, and aid victims: from anti-corruption (Transparency International) to election monitors to development organizations to transnational ethnic associations. New international organizations and mechanisms for human rights—like the International Criminal Court and multilateral sanctions—foster both accountability and enforcement of global human rights standards. Individuals also have greater access to transnational human rights campaigns: from organizing against land mines to establishing a foundation (Price 1998). While this limited diffusion of power and responsibility has had some impact on some states, it has been less effective in addressing broader claims against markets and civil society. And transnational entities like the World Bank are often the targets as well as the source of human rights claims (see chapter 9 by Jonathan Fox).

Even commodification can present new opportunities for human rights, despite markets' systematic production of inequality and exploitation. The modernization of markets can diminish "inefficient" forms of subjugation such as totalitarianism, gender oppression, or feudal local production relationships (see chapter 2 by Amalia Lucia Cabezas and chapter 5 by Raul Pangalangan). Since stable markets ultimately depend on a certain measure of transparency and the rule of law, commodification may in the long run also contribute to state reforms that create a climate conducive to improvements in security and political rights, as Wesley Milner's work suggests. Beyond these liberal spillovers, economic globalization can increase accountability for labor rights and social conditions, and even transfer some resources to victims. As Raul Pangalangan's chapter points out, transnational labor exploitation generates more monitoring and challenge than local ownership. New market mechanisms based in civil society, such as socially responsible investment and green marketing, seek to harness commodification to improve social conditions and promote empowerment. But, as Jack Donnelly reminds us, liberal spillovers ultimately depend on a liberal state.

Communication, like its associated base in civil society, has been granted a privileged status by scholars as both a hallmark of globalization and a promoter of human rights. It is also a form of globalization that flows above, across, below, and (often) through the state. Campaigns against World Bank projects (chapter 9), appeals by indigenous peoples in Africa (chapter 7), and mobilization against sweatshops in Asia (chapter 5) have all relied heavily on media diffusion and electronic networking. In these cases and others, communication carries information that challenges the expertise and legitimacy of state and global institutions, images that connect marginalized human rights victims to global publics, and new agendas that orient local discontent and galvanize global organizations. Media appeals have also been important precursors of humanitarian intervention, while information flows of legal standards and factual data have supported transnational legal accountability.

But while communication is clearly increasing, and communication does create new potential for the pursuit of human rights goals, the character and impact of communication must be analyzed more carefully. First, communication has not simply increased in volume, but shifted in structure from centrally controlled print media to a mix of centrally produced but widely received electronic media ("the CNN effect") and diffusely produced electronic communication received by a "new class" of knowledge processors and (some) activists. While access to wider information and low-cost channels of communication facilitates human rights monitoring and appeals for connection, both of these features are selectively available to different sectors of civil society, creating a grassroots "digital divide." Even among the transnational elites, global media may distort responses in various ways (Shaw 1999). In addition, the social effects of new communications technologies change over time; there may even be a life cycle of innovation, adaptation, and institutionalization. Thus, just as the printing press that enabled Protestantism is now an indistinguishable tool of principled protesters and paramilitary death squads, the Worldwide Web may soon be overtaken by multilevel marketing schemes and the exchange of recipes. In chapter 6, Shane Weyker explores other contradictory effects of the new communications technologies, especially their intersection with state power.

The obvious conclusion of human rights analysts is that these new opportunities are promising but insufficient. However, beyond the need for more and better IGOs, NGOs, information, and learning, what is to be done? As Donnelly's essay reminds us, beyond its persistence as a source of threat, the globalized state matters as a declining source of opportunity and citizenship. All of this means that the challenge for human rights in the global era is threefold: restraining newly or increasingly threatening states, empowering weak democratizing states, and crafting alternative mechanisms of citizenship above and below the state to substitute for its declining functions.

INTERNATIONAL RELATIONS THEORY AND THE CITIZENSHIP GAP

In the introduction to this book, I introduced the concept of a "citizenship gap"—a lack of political mechanisms to ensure individual membership, power holders' accountability, and respect for human rights in a globalizing world system. Each of the regnant perspectives on international relations (and by extension, globalization) contributes something to the analysis of this problem, but each also fails to address some critical component of the problem of human rights and global governance.

Traditional realism, associated with a skeptical view of globalization, can remind us of the persistence of traditional human rights threats through power-seeking states and the limits of new transnational opportunities when they confront sovereignty. Realism can also show how—contrary to the conventional wisdom of liberalism on state limitation—weak states can be the most deleterious to human rights. States still set the baseline for global governance as they maintain territorial order, create social space for NGOs and civil society, and participate in intergovernmental "international society" (Latham 1999; Reus-Smit 1997).

A modified, more structural realism influenced by theories of international regimes might acknowledge the ways in which human rights norms and institutions have already transformed the goals and capabilities of global governance. International regimes can help to restrain abusive states and provide new levels of accountability for international flows (see Sandholtz's chapter 10). However, in hard cases such as those requiring humanitarian intervention or extradition, governance will ultimately be enforced by states (or coalitions of states) (Hurrell 1999). States are still critical actors in global governance, blocking international reform in some cases (see Fox's chapter 9 on the World Bank) while spearheading reform coalitions in others (like the Landmines Treaty and the International Criminal Court). The problem, then, is how to translate new norms, identities, and transnational connectedness into the political will of strong states (Lumsdaine 1993). This also implies a linkage between citizenship rights, which empower members of those states, and the improvement of global conditions (Nadelmann 1990).

Turning to the other half of the "first debate," human rights represent perhaps the "highest stage of liberalism," as freely chosen governments protect individual liberty as a condition of their monopoly of coercion. The social contract of citizenship provides accountability for state power, which was traditionally the prime determinant of security. The spread of liberal states and transnational action may restrain state-based abuse, but does not address power vacuums at the state or global levels. Global governance may restrain abusive states, but it is plagued by coordination problems, and does not address abuses generated by other actors or levels (Rosenau and Czempiel 1992; Paolini et al. 1998).

Liberalism can envision a withering away of state power in favor of cosmopolitan decentralization (globalist optimism), but it cannot comprehend the rise of new threats to security from the very forces that claim to limit the state and promote individual liberty and greater global welfare: markets, technology, and civil society. Yet in this sense, liberalism is like its prescribed "emerging markets": international and domestic promissory notes of increased political rights cannot be honored without the economic and social resources to back them. As Richard Falk argues in chapter 3, global governance has no mechanism or claim either to regulate markets or to provide a mode of production, consumption, and exchange that is responsive to the citizenship claims of human dignity and universal membership. David Held's normative model of "cosmopolitan democracy," with multi-level mechanisms for a democratic legal order, is the most developed response to this dilemma (Held 1995), but much remains to be done in theory as well as practice.

This brings us to the "third debate": the challenges to state-centric and positivist views posed by critical theory, postmodernism, feminism, constructivism, and "the cultural turn," including sociological institutionalism (Lapid 1996). All of these views see state power as the result of something else and go beyond liberal "transnationalism" to depict globalization as an autonomous and constitutive force (Crawford 1998: 122). Critical and postmodern perspectives also take globalization and human rights for granted as background conditions of international relations. Because the third debate shares an emphasis on discourse and a skepticism about progress, each of these approaches attempts to deconstruct and interrogate both "rights talk" and narratives of globalization.

Both postmodernism and sociological institutionalism see human rights as an arbitrary modernist conceit, which cannot provide voice to identity or authentic local development. "World culture is a factory of social problems that are both products of theorization and occasions for further cultural growth. In addition, these problems foster diverse forms of moral entrepreneurship that collide with one another" (John M. Meyer et al. 1997: 170). Sociological institutionalists also associate the growth of human rights with state expansion (Boli 1987). They elucidate a new level of sources of the "citizenship gap," but offer only pessimism or irony as a response.

Critical theory, constructivism, world order models, and some forms of feminism go beyond this critique to attempt an affirmative project based on the relocation of authority and value. For critical theory, democratization of the life-world, transnational social movements, and global governance of the market can expand human rights and rescue globalization (Ray 1993; Cox and Sinclair 1996; Cox and Sjolander 1997; Devetak 1996). Constructivism will focus on the transformative potential of reconstructing international norms; "how our arguments can change the world" (Crawford 1998:139). Those feminist theorists seeking to globalize an "ethic of care" focus on relational needs rather than individual rights (Robinson 1999), which ends up broadening conceptions of human rights and strengthening global responsibility. For these theorists, the citizenship gap can be decreased through democratization of markets and civil society, as well as greater grassroots participation in global governance.

For this family of theory, the response to state abuse and weakness is similar to liberal transnationalism, but with a stronger focus on norms. Norms and ideas are shown to affect political behavior directly through constituting actors' identities and preferences, and indirectly by constructing institutions that both constrain and create interests (Onuf 1997; for an application to global governance, see Vayrynen 1999). If the core idea is that universal human dignity sets limits on the use of coercion (instructive rule), its corollary mandates global responsibility (directive rule), and a set of new or evolving mechanisms to institute it (commitment rule) (Onuf and Klink 1989). One small indicator of the power of norms in this type of transnational transformation is the observation that U.S. congressional sponsors of bans on child labor come from the *least* trade-displaced districts, flouting arguments that campaigns for international labor rights are a kind of surrogate protectionism (Rodrik 1997: 33).

On the other hand, both constructivist analysis and James Rosenau's turbulence model highlight the central irony of globalization: while it spreads human rights norms, global responsibility, and political and communications technologies that empower potential victims, globalization simultaneously promotes competing norms, nationalist backlash, and access to the same technologies for potential violators. As Pangalangan reflects, global human rights norms conflict not just with state power but with legitimate norms of sovereignty as self-determination. Global responsibility is counterposed to globalization's competing neoliberal doctrine of free markets. The emergence of transnational communities as human rights advocates competes with local identities preexisting and responding to globalization, alternative transnational identities (ethnic, religious), and state citizenship (Ian Clark 1999:128).

And theorists of globalization point to problems with each democratizing project in its own terms. Democratic deficits within the state cannot be fixed by democratizing global institutions (Ian Clark 1999). Putting civic actors on a par with states in international organizations may exacerbate the gap, since they are in many ways less accountable and inclusive than governments (Schmidt and Take 2000). The sectors of "global citizens" who are emerging are more often narrow sectors of old-style idealists, transnational capitalist elites, or intergovernmental managers than harbingers of new identities (Falk 1994). And international organizations have their own democratic deficits (Gruhn 1999).

CONSTRUCTING GLOBAL CITIZENSHIP?

In different ways, these theoretical perspectives each point to a greater challenge for global governance to close the citizenship gap. Transnational and intergovernmental mechanisms are needed to restrain repressive globalized states. New venues and forms of participation must be constructed to broaden accountability and citizenship above, below, and through the state. And, somehow, norms and identities must be transformed to foster universal membership, reconstructions of sovereignty, and evolving conceptions of human dignity.

World society scholars offer the beginning of a framework for response in distinguishing (constructed) world society from (organic) world community (Albert et al. 2000). Thus, global governance and evolutions of sovereignty would be based on a constructed world society, mindful of each of the dilemmas outlined above. The next step in constructing such a world society is experiential, not theoretical; world citizens are made, not born. Just as state identities have been crafted over long periods through repeated participation in complex social processes, their successors and supplements will require a kind of *normative* functionalism. Within one generation, it has become normal and typical for groups of individuals participating in international NGOs to mobilize their national civil societies to lobby their own states to pressure foreign governments or international organizations (Deacon 1999). The accretion and spread of such forms of political action will eventually build diffuse but meaningful global citizenship. This will empower some people faster than others, and it will broaden opportunities sooner than it will halt state threats. But slow or partial citizenship is better than none at all.

POLICY POSSIBILITIES

What does this analysis of new threats and opportunities for human rights in an era of globalization tell us about how to achieve them? How does international relations theory help us to increase the influence of human rights on globalization? Following the analysis of the volume, the discussion of policy possibilities will be organized by the type of globalization, crosscut with considerations of the level of analysis and type of state.

As a conceptual foundation, the new global patterns and potentials for abuse must be matched by the agendas of transnational advocates and policymakers. A system that developed to defend and enhance the rights of citizens within states must now recognize that the greatest unmet need is *the rights of noncitizens,* whether women in the home, ethnic minorities or diasporas, refugees across borders, or workers in denationalized sweatshops. Above and below the state, the NGOs and international organizations that established the benchmark norms of international human rights must now work to define and defend a new level of transferability of rights, from any individual to any locus of authority. Thus, human rights reporting must supplement its country focus with more systematic attention to unrepresented populations, while existing institutions for noncitizens such as the UN High Commission on Refugees must be more systematically incorporated into the human rights machinery (perhaps even changing its name to the Commission on the *Rights* of Refugees). In addition, new mechanisms may be necessary to compensate for the silences of the state system: councils of unrepresented people should be created in regional and international institutions (Bruin 1993), in an expanded version of the direct transnational representation of the European Parliament. This also means that potential victims should be identified by this noncitizen status rather than ascriptive identity—which can lead to fragmented campaigns and offices for an endless (and competitive) series of special groups.

Across states, mobility creates specific challenges for accountability in sending and receiving areas. Increased international deliberation and standard setting on the rights of migrants is one potential source of leverage over liberal but lagging host states and a counterweight to local prejudice and protectionism. Regional trade arrangements could easily provide adjustment funds to buffer the effect of concentrated migration on local employment and infrastructure, mitigating the social costs in host areas. Delinkage of civil and social rights from legal national citizenship is another important step. National laws must guarantee the human rights of all residents subject to the authority of that state, independent of the lawful regulation of borders. One small step in this direction is the United States's recent adoption of standardized regulations for the humane treatment of detained migrants, formerly subject to an unaccountable patchwork of often abusive federal, state, local, and even private imprisonment. Monitoring and reform of asylum policies in receiving states is also critical (Keely and Russell 1996). Defensive retrenchment of immigration policies in response to terrorism must distinguish legitimate improvements in policing from blanket—and ultimately ineffective—denials of rights.

On the other side of the equation, sending states can attempt to exercise more accountability for their citizens. Here, the type of state is a critical intervening factor, as many sending states are by definition weak at home as well as abroad. Nevertheless, some transitional states, such as Mexico, are trying to increase accountability to and for their diasporic populations, including increased voting rights at home and advocacy abroad. And stronger liberal states who send citizens abroad as tourists and investors can and should increase their accountability for extraterritorial abuses. Pioneering efforts in this area include Australian, German, and French legislation penalizing the sexual abuse of children overseas by "sex tourists," as well as U.S. codes forbidding bribery by officers of multinational corporations.

In the realm of global markets, the current mode of citizenship offers exit but no voice (Hirschman 1970). Migrants vote with their feet, consumers and investors vote with their dollars, but invisible hands set the agenda and calculate the trade-offs. Global market citizenship can be expanded in two directions, to improve the scope and breadth of economic governance. First, new actors can be brought to the table. This expands the existing check on global markets, discussed in Jonathan Fox's chapter 9, in which protestors translate the power to disrupt narrowly based global economic institutions into mechanisms for expanded accountability. This type of campaign has recently produced a World Bank–IMF program of debt relief for twenty-two severely impoverished nations. But "globalization with a human face" must go beyond ad hoc reforms to give particular human faces seats at particular tables. This will involve some sort of extension of the "ILO model" of labor representation to the trade and finance troika of the World Bank, IMF, and World Trade Organization. The World Bank already consults more systematically with nongovernmental advocates, but not always with direct representatives of affected parties.

In terms of the breadth of economic governance, an increasing range of issues must be subject to human rights standards and accountability. Model efforts to extend the range of accountability include the recent adoption by the United Nations of a code of conduct for multinational corporations, as well as efforts to license diamonds from conflict zones, lest their export subsidize abuse. Financial investment and speculation, one of the fastest growing and most globalized forms of exchange, is also ripe for greater control. The growing trend of "socially responsible investment" represents one consumer-based mode of human rights accountability, with some attempts to expand sanctions, disinvestment, and shareholder campaigns directed at institutional and governmental actors. Measures such as state and local disinvestment from Burma and state purchasing boycotts of products manufactured by prison labor in China show promise, although such initiatives have faced increasing legal challenge in the U.S. Distinct but related pressures for greater financial transparency and corporate governance serve a variety of goals; they also lay the groundwork for the further development of market citizenship.

Global governance of information for human rights presents greater opportunities but murkier issues of membership and accountability; unlike markets, it is all voice and no exit. Our analysis highlights the importance of various proposals to address the "digital divide" of uneven access to information—but it suggests that programs of technical assistance within and among states are not enough. A true communications policy for human rights requires more than wiring the global village; it means fostering the translation of various levels of language. At the literal level, rights-relevant information must be made available to speakers of local and minority languages—who are often the very noncitizens most at risk of human rights abuse. Private and intergovernmental aid programs that are beginning to make this connection for select populations must be expanded and broadened to foster a universal right to information. At the symbolic level, global policy must promote the translation of human rights challenges into the language recognized by NGOs and global institutions. This involves a dual movement: an effort by transnational actors to broaden their understanding and appreciation of the interdependence of globalizing human rights challenges, along with increased education for victims—so that recognition of their rights does not depend on charismatic leaders or lucky connections with information processors (like sympathetic journalists). Academics can play a positive role at both ends of this educational process, with particular attention to challenging the ways in which legal discourse has thus far hegemonized the concept and language of "rights."

Along with language, governance of information involves a reexamination of representation. From the bottom up, information is channeled by self-appointed representatives of civil society. From the top down, even weak states attempt to control and restrict information access. The latter problem merely requires an updated version of earlier waves of transnational campaigns against censorship. Technological solidarity can be fostered by more sophisticated forms of technical assistance from transnational advocates, such as encryption of e-mail, "swarming" state surveillance channels, or remote hosting of forbidden Web sites. Meanwhile, liberal states and international organizations must add electronic freedom of information to more traditional monitoring and pressure on repressive states, and recognize that such freedom can sometimes leapfrog blockages in conventional access. However, the channeling and legitimacy of voice from the bottom up is intertwined with the more complex problem of grassroots representation and the democratization of civil society. The promotion of grassroots accountability for the global representation of information will require a broader transnational set of mechanisms for assessing the legitimacy of civic groups, going beyond UN certification of NGO status (Brysk 2000b). As an interim measure, civic groups and transnational media should strive to better identify the nature of human rights representatives and advocates.

Policy prescriptions for global governance focus above, across, and through the state (which also involves the type of state). To illustrate the range of mechanisms that can now be brought to bear, even in a "hard case" of labor rights in a globalizing weak state, consider the criticism of a Taiwanese-owned Chentex textile assembly plant located in Nicaragua's Las Mercedes Free Trade Zone for poor working conditions, impeding labor association, and suppressing free speech. In response, a loose coalition of Nicaraguan unions, U.S. labor, and transnational human rights groups have launched a campaign of information, lobbying, and economic pressure. Activists have lobbied three states. The Taiwanese government has expressed concern and recommended that the private owner rehire fired Nicaraguan union activists. Activists have organized monitoring tours and meetings with Nicaraguan state agencies, leading to intermittent enhanced enforcement of Nicaraguan labor codes and recent favorable court rulings. Because the U.S. military is a major buyer from the overseas apparel plant, activists have appealed to the U.S. trade representative and received a letter of support from 67 U.S. congressional representatives. Above the state, the campaign has appealed to international organizations such as the ILO and OAS. Across states, U.S. unions have filed a class action suit on behalf of Nicaraguan workers under the U.S. Alien Torts Act, a human rights measure that allows foreign nationals resident in the United States to sue or be sued in U.S. courts (the Taiwanese owner has an outlet in Los Angeles). Below the state, activists have also organized consumer pressure on Chentex's principal buyer, the Kohl's department store chain. Finally, the cause celèbre and resultant transnational network have helped to catalyze the formation of a regional coordinating committee for *maquila* (export assembly) unions, with representatives from throughout Central America and the Caribbean.

While a focus on global governance *through* the state goes against the grain of much of the globalization literature, realist theory and our findings suggest that some aspects and stages of cooperation may depend on the political will of strong states (also see chapter 11 by Jack Donnelly). However, as constructivism would observe, such political will does not necessarily derive from conventional understandings of "national interest," but may evolve from state identities, internalization of international norms, grassroots or transnational campaigns, or simply changes in knowledge and belief (on "endogenous enforcement" of norms, see Vayrynen 1999). Thus, a powerful state may commit troops to a humanitarian intervention that does not enhance that state's economic or strategic position: (1) because it is an ex-colonial power which feels historical responsibility for the affected area, (2) because an international organization supports the intervention and the state values its international standing, (3) because domestic humanitarians or co-ethnics pressure policymakers, (4) because experts foresee undesirable effects of inaction, or (5) because policymakers have become persuaded that it is the right thing to do. Human rights advocates, then, can seek to systematically increase states' availability for global governance by measures that promote these motivating factors of identity, norms, knowledge, and participation.

While human rights advocates already engage in efforts in each of these areas, this analysis shows that such efforts could be more profitably tailored for different types of states and venues. Rather than broad appeals to "world public opinion," advocates should distinguish strategies by types of states. It is still important to mobilize states with established humanitarian or internationalist identities to lead or initiate global governance for human rights, but in states that lack such understandings—such as the United States—transnational activists should focus more narrowly on lobbying, linkage, and expertise. In these settings, globalists should strategically deemphasize principled internationalism in favor of functional management of rights-related areas with strong domestic constituencies—such as freedom of religion in the United States. Finally, within leading states, advocates must emphasize symbolically appealing issues and victims where the tenets of liberalism are clearly violated (i.e., child labor), as a stepping stone for the establishment of broader understandings of rights and mechanisms of global responsibility.

Above and across states, human rights require cosmopolitan democracy—but what does this mean in practice? First, cosmopolitan democracy means going beyond the interstate model of global governance, with greater representation of diverse social sectors in global organizations and negotiations. The thematic U.N. conferences on the environment (1992), women (1995), and human rights (1993), with substantial participation by NGOs, represent a model for this type of interaction—but the interactions must be routinized and made more receptive to participation by civic groups and unrepresented sectors. Second, cosmopolitan democracy means shifting interstate interactions to more multilateral mechanisms. Within the current trend toward global governance, decision making is increasingly concentrated in the narrower international organizations and forums. Yet broader participation makes international law more universal, sanctions more effective, and intervention more humane. The danger here is that multilateralism may bring human rights standards down to the lowest common denominator, but this is an argument for stronger international norms and linkage, not less participation. A liberal constitutional analogy also suggests that international norms and precedents become embedded in international legal institutions, such as the recently created International Criminal Court.

Finally, the nascent experience of global governance shows the need for greater coordination among global human rights policies. The current system attempts to govern "most obstreperous actors" through a shifting blend of aid, standards, education, tribunals, sanctions, and intervention. Newly democratizing states generally receive the first set of incentives, recalcitrant hard states get sanctions, and extremely weak states are subject to intervention. There are a number of well-documented problems with this "system": nonstate violators are not affected, sanctions are effective under limited conditions and produce substantial side effects (Weiss et al. 1997), intervention cannot fill power vacuums, and combinations of these measures may produce unintended consequences. Even the most rudimentary coordination, such as the crisis consultations convened by state and private creditors with international institutions when states fall into debt crisis, would be an improvement. Long-term strategic planning under the aegis of the U.N. High Commission on Human Rights would maximize the effectiveness of these policies.

Constructing global citizenship means reconstructing accountability, when globalization has eroded institutional membership and shifted patterns of authority. Globalization can become more responsive to human rights, by harnessing global governance to different streams of globalization and different types of states. Transnational campaigns for greater accountability should balance policymaking insiders with grassroots outsiders and provide both positive incentives and negative sanctions. Like domestic democracy, mechanisms for global human rights depend on broadening representation, fostering transparency, providing and accessing multiple venues, and building common foundational norms.

In the era of globalization, we must reconceive the political vocabulary created by the French, American, and UN "rights revolutions," so that the "rights of man and the citizen" become both universal and cosmopolitan. Future scholarship, political theory, and global practice can integrate rights discourse into the legitimacy of all forms of authority—from sovereignty to development to identity. Rewriting the ancient idea of "citizens of the world"—so that it is universal but diverse, and linked to real solidarities and political consequences—is the central theoretical and ethical challenge of our age.

NOTE

1. For details of various violations associated with the operations of multinationals, see the newsletter *Multinational Monitor*. And see also Gai 1999.

Acosta Vargas, Gladys.
1996. "La prostitución forzada como fenómeno global desde una perspectiva de los derechos humanos: Caso Colombia." International Report Project for the U.N. Special Rapporteur on Violence against Women, San Juan, Puerto Rico.

Adkins, Lisa.
1995. *Gendered Work: Sexuality, Family, and the Labor Market.* Philadelphia: Open University Program.

Afonso, Carlos Alberto.
1990. "NGO Networking: The Telematic Way." *Development* 2.

Aguayo Quezada, Sergio.
1996. "Displaced Central Americans: Mexican NGOs and the International Response." In *International Migration, Refugee Flows and Human Rights in North America: The Impact of Free Trade and Restructuring,* edited by Alan B. Simmons, 290–308. New York: Center for Migration Studies.

Albert, Mathias, Lothar Brock, and Klaus Dieter Wolf, eds.
2000. *Civilizing World Politics: Society and Community beyond the State.* Lanham, Md.: Rowman & Littlefield.

Alesina, Alberto, Bittorio Gilli, and Gian Maria Milesi-Ferretti.
1994. "The Political Economy of Capital Controls." In *Capital Mobility: The Impact on Consumption, Investment, and Growth,* edited by Leonardo Leidermand and Assaf Razin. Cambridge: Cambridge University Press.

Alston, Philip, and Henry Steiner, eds.
1996. *International Human Rights in Context: Law, Politics, and Morals.* New York: Oxford University Press.

Amar, Akhil Reed.
  2000. "A State's Right, a Government's Wrong." *Washington Post,* 27 March,
    B01.

Anderson, Benedict. [1983]
  1991. *Imagined Communities: Reflections on the Origin and Spread of Nationalism.* Rev.
    ed. New York: Verso.

An-Na'im, Abdullahi A., ed.
  1992. *Human Rights in Cross-Cultural Perspectives.* Philadelphia: University of Penn-
    sylvania Press.

Annis, Sheldon.
  1991. "Giving Voice to the Poor." *Foreign Policy* 84 (Fall): 93–106.

  1992. "Evolving Connectedness among Environmental Groups and Grassroots
    Organizations in Protected Areas of Central America." *World Development* 20,
    no. 4 (April): 587–95.

Appadurai, Arjun.
  1990. "Disjuncture and Difference in Global Cultural Economy." *Public Culture*
    2, no. 2: 1–24.

  1996. *Modernity at Large: Cultural Dimensions of Globalization.* Minneapolis: Uni-
    versity of Minnesota Press.

Arat, Zehra.
  1991. *Democracy and Human Rights in Developing Countries.* Boulder, Colo.: Lynne
    Rienner.

Archibugi, Daniele, David Held, and Martin Köhler, eds.
  1998. *Re-Imagining Political Community: Studies in Cosmopolitan Democracy.* Stan-
    ford, Calif.: Stanford University Press.

Arend, A. C., and R. J. Beck.
  1993. *International Law and the Use of Force.* New York: Routledge.

Arregui, Eduardo Velasco.
  1996. "The Rights of Mexican Workers in the Context of NAFTA." In *Interna-
    tional Migration, Refugee Flows and Human Rights in North America: The Impact of
    Trade and Restructuring,* edited by Alan B. Simmons, 65–80. New York: Center
    for Migration Studies.

Avineri, Shlomo, ed.
  1968. *Karl Marx on Colonialism and Modernization.* Garden City, N.Y.: Doubleday.

Azize Vargas, Yamila.
  1996. "Tráfico de mujeres para prostitución, trabajo doméstico y matrimonio:
    América Latina y el Caribe." Informe Preliminar, Encuentro Regional. Domi-
    nican Republic.

Bacon, David.
  1999. "For an Immigration Policy Based on Human Rights." In *Immigration: A
    Civil Rights Issue for the Americas,* edited by Susanne Jonas and Suzanne Dod
    Thomas, 157–74. Wilmington, Del.: Scholarly Resources.

Baker, Dean, Gerald Epstein, and Robert Pollin, eds.
    1998.   *Globalization and Progressive Economic Policy.* Cambridge: Cambridge University Press.

Balibar, Etienne.
    1991.   "Racism and Nationalism." In *Race, Nation, Class: Ambiguous Identities,* edited by Etienne Balibar and Immanuel Wallerstein, 37–68. New York: Verso.

Ball, Patrick, Mark Girourard, and Audrey Chapman.
    1997.   "Information Technology, Information Management, and Human Rights: A Response to Metzl." *Human Rights Quarterly* 19, no. 4 (November): 836–58.

Banisar, David.
    1993.   "A Primer on Electronic Surveillance for Human Rights Organizations." *International Privacy Bulletin* 1, no. 3.

Barkin, J. S.
    1998.   "The Evolution of the Constitution of Sovereignty and the Emergence of Human Rights Norms." *Millenium: Journal of International Studies* 27, no. 2: 229–52.

Barnet, Richard, and John Cavanagh.
    1994.   *Global Dreams: Imperial Corporations and the New World Order.* New York: Simon & Schuster.

Barrera, Mario.
    1979.   *Race and Class in the Southwest: A Theory of Racial Inequality.* Notre Dame, Ind.: University of Notre Dame Press.

Barry, Tom, Beth Wood, and Deb Preusch.
    1984.   *The Other Side of Paradise.* New York: Grove Press.

Basch, Linda, Nina Glick Schiller, and Cristina Szanton Blanc.
    1994.   *Nations Unbound: Transnational Projects, Postcolonial Predicaments, and Deterritorialized Nation-States.* Amsterdam: Gordon & Breach.

Bauböck, Rainer.
    1991.   "Migration and Citizenship." *New Community* 18, no. 1: 27–48.

    1994.   *Transnational Citizenship: Membership and Rights in International Migration.* Brookfield, Vt.: Edward Elgar.

Baudot, Jacques.
    1999.   "Criteria and Values for Assessing the Quality of Economic Systems." In *The Democratic Process and the Market: Challenges of the Transition,* edited by Mihály Simai, 27–36. Tokyo: United Nations University Press.

Bauer, Joanne R., and Daniel A. Bell, eds.
    1999.   *The East Asian Challenge for Human Rights.* New York: Cambridge University Press.

Bell, Laurie, ed.
    1987.   *Good Girls/Bad Girls: Feminists and Sex Trade Workers Face to Face.* Seattle: Seal Press.

Belsley, David A., Edwin Kuh, and Roy E. Welsch.
1980. *Regression Diagnostics*. New York: Wiley.

Bhabha, Jacqueline.
1998a. "Enforcing the Human Rights of Citizens and Non-Citizens in the Era of Maastricht: Some Reflections on the Importance of States." *Development and Social Change* 29: 697–724.

1998b. "'Get Back to Where You Once Belonged': Identity, Citizenship, and Exclusion in Europe." *Human Rights Quarterly* 20, no. 3: 592–627.

1999. "Belonging in Europe: Citizenship and Post-National Rights." *International Social Science Journal* 159: 11–24.

Bhaghwati, Jagdish.
1994. "Free Trade: Old and New Challenges?" *Economics Journal* 104, no. 423 (March): 231.

Bin Mohammed, Mahathir.
1994. "Workers' Rights in Developing Countries." In International Labour Organization, *Vision of the Future of Social Justice —Essays on the Occasion of the ILO's 75th Anniversary,* 176. Geneva: ILO.

Bindman, Jo.
1997. *Redefining Prostitution as Sex Work on the International Agenda*. London: Anti-Slavery International.

Bob, Clifford.
2000. "Beyond Transparency: Visibility and Fit in the Internationalization of Internal Conflict." In *Power and Conflict in the Age of Transparency,* edited by Bernard I. Finel and Kristin M. Lord. New York: Palgrave.

Boli, John.
1987. "Human Rights or State Expansion? Cross-National Definitions of Constitutional Rights, 1870–1970." In *Institutional Structure Constituting State, Society, and the Individual,* edited by George M. Thomas et al., 133–49. Newbury Park, Calif.: Sage Publications.

1999. "Conclusion: World Authority Structures and Legitimations." In *Constructing World Culture,* edited by John Boli and George M. Thomas, 267–302. Stanford, Calif.: Stanford University Press.

Boli, John, Thomas A. Loya, and Teresa Loftin.
1999. "National Participation in World-Polity Organization." In *Constructing World Culture,* edited by John Boli and George M. Thomas, 50–80. Stanford, Calif.: Stanford University Press.

Boli, John, and George M. Thomas.
1997. "World Culture in the World Polity: A Century of International Non-Governmental Organization." *American Sociological Review* 62 (April): 171–90.

1999. "INGOs and the Organization of World Culture International Non-governmental Organizations Since 1875." In *Constructing World Culture,* edited by John and Thomas Boli, George M., 13–49. Stanford, Calif.: Stanford University Press.

Bollen, Kenneth A.
    1990.   "Political Democracy: Conceptual and Measurement Traps." *Studies in Comparative International Development* 25: 7–24.

Bonilla, Juan.
    1997.   "Jefe de turismo estudiará formulas para control de la prostitución." *Periodico Hoy* (Santo Domingo, Dominican Republic), 23 June.

Bornstein, David.
    1999.   "A Force Now in the World, Citizens Flex Social Muscle." *New York Times,* 10 July, B7.

Bowles, Ian, and Cyril Kormos.
    1995.   "Environmental Reform at the World Bank: The Role of the U.S. Congress." *Virginia Journal of International Law* 35, no. 4 (Summer).

Bradlow, Daniel.
    1993.   "The Case for a World Bank Ombudsman." Statement submitted to the Subcommittee on International Development, Finance, Trade and Monetary Policy of the Banking, Finance and Urban Affairs Committee, U.S. House of Representatives.

    1994.   "International Organizations and Private Complaints: The Case of the World Bank Inspection Panel." *Virginia Journal of International Law* 34.

    1996a.   "A Test Case for the World Bank." *American University Journal of International Law and Policy* 247.

    1996b.   "The World Bank, the IMF, and Human Rights." *Transnational Law and Contemporary Problems* 6, no. 1 (Spring).

Bramble, Barbara, and Gareth Porter.
    1992.   "NGO Influence on the United States Environmental Politics Abroad." In *The International Politics of the Environment,* edited by Andrew Hurrell and Benedict Kingsbury, 313–53. New York: Oxford University Press.

Brecher, Jeremy, and Tim Costello.
    1994.   *Global Village or Global Pillage: Economic Reconstruction from the Bottom Up.* Boston: South End Press.

Breyman, Steve.
    1993.   "Knowledge as Power: Ecology Movements and Global Environmental Problems." In *The State and Social Power in Global Environmental Politics,* edited by Ronnie Lipschutz and Ken Conca. New York: Columbia University Press.

Brown, Chris.
    1997.   "Globalization and Human Rights." In *The Globalization of World Politics: An Introduction to International Relations,* edited by John Baylis and Steve Smith, 469–82. Oxford: Oxford University Press.

Brown, L. David.
    1991.   "Bridging Organizations and Sustainable Development." *Human Relations* 44, no. 8 (August): 807–31.

Brown, L. David, and Darcy Ashman.
    1996.   "Participation, Social Capital and Intersectoral Problem-Solving." *World Development* 24, no. 9 (September): 1467–79.

Brown, L. David, and Jonathan Fox.
2001.   "Transnational Civil Society Coalitions and the World Bank: Lessons From Project and Policy Influence Campaigns." In *Global Citizen Action,* edited by Michael Edwards and John Gaventa. Boulder, Colo.: Lynne Rienner.

Brown, Lester, Christopher Flavin, Hilary French, et al.
2000.   *State of the World 2000: A Worldwatch Institute Report on Progress Toward a Sustainable Society.* New York: Norton.

Brown, Paul.
1999.   "World Bank Pushes Chad Pipeline." *Guardian,* 11 October.

Brownlie, I.
1995.   *Basic Documents in International Law.* Oxford: Clarendon Press.

Brubaker, William Rogers.
1989.   "Introduction." In *Immigration and the Politics of Citizenship in Europe and North America,* edited by William Rogers Brubaker. Lanham, Md.: University Press of America/German Marshall Fund of the United States.

1998.   "Immigration, Citizenship, and the Nation-State in France and Germany." In *The Citizenship Debates,* edited by Gershon Shafir, 131–66. Minneapolis: University of Minnesota Press.

Bruin, Guido de.
1993.   "Human Rights: Unrepresented Peoples' Forum 'Coming of Age.'" *Inter Press Service,* 5 February. Available from NEXIS, news library, wires file.

Brysk, Alison.
1993.   "From Above and Below: Social Movements, the International System, and Human Rights in Argentina." *Comparative Political Studies* 26, no. 3: 259–85.

1994.   *The Politics of Human Rights in Argentina: Protest, Change and Democratization.* Stanford, Calif.: Stanford University Press.

2000a.   "Democratizing Civil Society in Latin America." *Journal of Democracy* 11, no. 3 (July): 151–165.

2000b.   *From Tribal Village to Global Village: Indian Rights and International Relations in Latin America.* Stanford, Calif.: Stanford University Press.

2000c.   "Globalization: A Double-Edged Sword." *NACLA Report on the Americas* 34, no. 1 (July–August): 29–33.

Bunch, Charlotte, and Susana Fried.
1996.   "Beijing '95: Moving Women's Human Rights from Margin to Center." *Signs* 22, no. 1 (Autumn): 200–204.

Burbach, Roger, Orlando Núñez, and Boris Kagarlitsky.
1997.   *Globalization and Its Discontents: The Rise of Postmodern Socialisms.* Chicago: Pluto Press.

Burbidge, John.
1997.   *Beyond Prince and Merchant: Citizen Participation and the Rise of Civil Society.* New York: Pact Publications.

Burgerman, Susan D.
   1998.   "Mobilizing Principles: The Role of Transnational Activists in Promoting
      Human Rights Principles." Human Rights Quarterly 20, no. 4 (November):
      905–24.

Burtless, Gary, and Robert Litan.
   1998.   "These Ties Will Bind: The Trouble with Tying Trade to Labor and En-
      vironmental Standards." *New Democrat,* May–June, 24–25.

Buruma, Ian.
   1999.   "China in Cyberspace." *New York Review of Books,* 4 November.

Cabezas, Amalia Lucia.
   1998.   "Discourses of Prostitution: The Case of Cuba." In *Global Sex Workers: Rights,
      Resistance, and Redefinition,* edited by Kamala Kempadoo and Joe Doezema. New
      York: Routledge.

   1999.   "Women's Work Is Never Done: Sex Tourism in Sosua, the Domini-
      can Republic." In *Sun, Sex, and Gold: Tourism and Sex Work in the Caribbean,*
      edited by Kamala Kempadoo, 93–123. Lanham, Md.: Rowman & Littlefield,
      1999.

Cahn, Jonathan.
   1993.   "Challenging the New Imperial Authority: The World Bank and the De-
      mocratization of Development." *Harvard Human Rights Journal* 6 (Spring).

Calavita, Kitty.
   1992.   *Inside the State: The Bracero Program, Immigration, and the I.N.S.* New York:
      Routledge.

Caldwell, Gillian, Steven Galster, and Nadia Steinzor.
   1998.   "Crime and Servitude: Traffic in Women from Newly Independent States."
      WIN News 24, no. 2 (Spring): 50.

Cardoso, Fernando Henrique, and Enzo Faletto.
   1979.   *Dependency and Development in Latin America.* Berkeley and Los Angeles:
      University of California Press, 1979.

Carens, Joseph H.
   1989.   "Membership and Morality: Admission to Citizenship in Liberal Demo-
      cratic States." In *Immigration and the Politics of Citizenship in Europe and North Amer-
      ica,* edited by William Rogers Brubaker, 31–49. Lanham, Md.: University Press
      of America/German Marshall Fund of the United States.

Castells, Manuel.
   1997.   *The Power of Identity.* Malden, Mass.: Blackwell.

Castle, R., et al.
   1996.   *A New Province for International Law And Order? The Social Clauses of the WTO
      Agreement and Child Labour in South Asia.* Wollongong, Australia: International
      Business Institute, University of Wollongong.

Castles, Stephen.
   1998a.   "Globalization and Migration: Some Pressing Contradictions." *Interna-
      tional Social Science Journal* 50, no. 2 (June): 179–87.

1998b.   "The Spaces of Multiculturalism and Citizenship." *International Social Science Journal* 50, no. 2 (June): 201–13.

Castles, Stephen, and Mark J. Miller.
1998.   *The Age of Migration: International Population Movements in the Modern World.* 2d ed. New York: Guilford Press, 1998.

CEPROSH [Centro de Estudios Sociales y Demográficos].
1996.   *Proyecto hotelero.* Puerto Plata, Dominican Republic.

CESDEM [Centro de Estudios Sociales y Demográficos].
1996.   "Encuesta sobre conocimientos, creencias, actitudes y prácticas acerca del SIDA/ETS en trabajadoras sexuales y hombres involucrados en la industria del sexo en las localidades de Puerto Plata, Sosu y Monte Llano." Mimeo. COVICOSIDA, Puerto Plata, Dominican Republic.

Chavez, Leo.
1997.   "Immigration Reform and Nativism: The Nationalist Response to the Transnationalist Challenge." In *Immigrants Out! The New Nativism and the Anti-Immigrant Impulse in the United States,* edited by Juan F. Perea, 61–77. New York: New York University Press.

Chin, Christine B. N.
1998.   *In Service and Servitude: Foreign Female Domestic Workers and the Malaysian "Modernity" Project.* New York: Columbia University Press.

Chinkin, Christine.
1999.   "Gender Inequality and International Human Rights Law." In *Inequality, Globalization, and World Politics,* edited by Andrew Hurrell and Ngaire Woods, 95–121. New York: Oxford University Press.

Chomsky, Noam, and Edward S. Herman.
1979.   *The Political Economy of Human Rights.* 2 vols. Boston: South End Press.

Chossudovsky, Michel.
1997.   *The Globalization of Poverty: Impacts of IMF and World Bank Reforms.* London: Zed Books.

Christian, Shirley.
1988.   "Pinochet Foes Guard against Fraud." *New York Times,* 13 September, A3.

Cigar, N. L.
1995.   *Genocide in Bosnia: The Policy of "Ethnic Cleansing."* College Station: Texas A&M University Press, 1995.

Cingranelli, David, and Louis Pasquarello.
1985.   "Human Rights Practices and Distribution of U.S. Foreign Aid to Latin American Countries." *American Journal of Political Science* 29, no. 3 (August).

Cingranelli, David, and David Richards.
1999.   "Measuring the Level, Pattern, and Sequence of Government Respect for Physical Integrity Rights." *International Studies Quarterly* 43, no. 2 (June).

"Citizens' Groups: The Non-Governmental Order—Will NGOs Democratise, or Merely Disrupt, Global Governance?"
1999.   *Economist,* 11 December, 20.

Clark, Dana.
    1999.   *A Citizen's Guide to the World Bank Inspection Panel.* 2d ed. Washington, D.C.:
    Center for International Environmental Law (www.ciel.org).
Clark, Ian.
    1999.   *Globalization and International Relations Theory.* New York: Oxford Univer-
    sity Press.
Clark, R. P.
    1997.   *The Global Imperative: An Interpretive History of the Spread of Mankind.* Boul-
    der, Colo.: Westview Press.
Cohen, Robin.
    1998.   "Transnational Social Movements: An Assessment." Department of Soci-
    ology, University of Warwick, UK.
Coll, A. R.
    1997.   *The Problems of Doing Good: Somalia as a Case Study in Humanitarian Inter-
    vention.* New York: Carnegie Council on Ethics and International Affairs.
Commission on Global Governance.
    1995.   *Our Global Neighborhood: The Report of the Commission on Global Governance.*
    New York: Oxford University Press.
"Conferencia acusa a países complicidad tráfico mujeres."
    1996.   *El Mundo,* 14 December, 22.
Constable, Nicole.
    1997.   *Maid to Order in Hong Kong: Stories of Filipina Workers.* Ithaca, N.Y.: Cornell
    University Press.
Coppedge, Michael, and Wolfgang Reinecke.
    1990.   "Measuring Polyarchy." *Studies in Comparative International Development*
    25: 51.
Cornelius, Wayne.
    1998.   *The Role of Immigrant Labor in the U.S. and Japanese Economies.* San Diego:
    Center for U.S.-Mexico Studies, UCSD, 1998.
Cortright, David, and George A. Lopez, eds.
    2000.   *The Sanctions Decade: Assessing UN Strategies in the 1990s.* Boulder, Colo.:
    Lynne Rienner.
Covey, Jane.
    1998.   "Critical Cooperation? Influencing the World Bank Through Policy Dia-
    logue and Operational Collaboration." In *The Struggle for Accountability: The
    World Bank, NGOs and Grassroots Movements,* edited by Jonathan Fox and L. David
    Brown, 81–119. Cambridge, Mass.: MIT Press.
Cox, Robert W.
    1983.   "Gramsci, Hegemony, and International Relations: Beyond International
    Relations Theory." *Millennium* 10 (Summer): 162–75.
Cox, Robert W., and Timothy J. Sinclair.
    1996.   *Approaches to World Order.* Cambridge: Cambridge University Press.

Cox, Wayne S., and Claire Turenne Sjolander.
    1997. "The Global Village and The Global Ghetto: Realism, Structural Material-
    ism, and Agency in Globalization." In *Constituting International Political Economy,*
    edited by Kurt Burch and Robert A. Denemark. Boulder, Colo.: Lynne Rienner.

Coxson, Charles.
    1999. "The 1998 ILO Declaration on Fundamental Principles and Rights at
    Work: Promoting Labor Law Reforms through the ILO as an Alternative to
    Imposing Coercive Trade Sanctions." *Dickeson Journal of International Law* 17,
    no. 469.

Crawford, Neta.
    1998. "Postmodern Ethical Conditions and a Critical Response." *Ethics and In-
    ternational Affairs* 12: 121–40.

Crossette, Barbara.
    2000. "Making Room for the Poor in a Global Economy." *New York Times,* 16
    April, 1, 4.

Cutler, A. Claire, Virginia Haufler, and Tony Porter.
    1999. *Private Authority and International Affairs.* Albany: State University of New
    York Press.

D'Andrea, Barbara.
    1997. "Social Labelling Schemes and the WTO Agreement on Technical Bar-
    riers to Trade." Conference paper. Workshop on Trade Liberalization and
    Labour Markets and Standards: Practical Experiences, Issues and Avenues for
    Action. Quaker House: 6–8 October.

Danielsen, Dan, and Karen Engle.
    1995. "Introduction to Sexuality." In *After Identity: A Reader in Law and Culture,*
    edited by Dan Danielsen and Karen Engle, 3–5. New York: Routledge.

Davidson, Alastair.
    2000. "Fractured Identities: Citizenship in a Global World." In *Citizenship, Com-
    munity and Democracy,* edited by Ellie Vasta. New York: St. Martin's Press.

Deacon, Bob.
    1999. "Social Policy in a Global Context." In *Inequality, Globalization, and World
    Politics,* edited by Andrew Hurrell and Ngaire Woods, 211–47. New York: Ox-
    ford University Press.

Deere, Carmen Diana, Peggy Antrobus, et al.
    1990. *In the Shadows of the Sun: Caribbean Development Alternatives and U.S. Policy.*
    Boulder, Colo.: Westview Press.

Deibert, Ronald J.
    1997. *Parchment, Printing and Hypermedia Communication in World Order Transfor-
    mation.* New York: Columbia University Press.

Deininger, Klaus, and Lyn Squire.
    1997. "Economic Growth and Income Inequality: Reexamining the Links." *Fi-
    nance and Development* 34, no. 1 (March).

Delacoste, Frederique, and Priscilla Alexander, eds.
    1987. *Sex Work: Writings by Women in the Sex Industry.* Pittsburgh: Cleis Press.

DeMartino, George F.

    2000.   *Global Economy, Global Justice: Theoretical and Policy Alternatives to Neoliberalism.* New York: Routledge.

Deutsch, Karl W.

    1966.   *The Nerves of Government: Models of Political Communication and Social Control.* New York: Free Press.

Devetak, Richard.

    1996.   "Critical Theory." In *Theories of International Relations,* edited by Scott Burchill and Andrew Linklater, 145–78. New York: St. Martin's Press.

Dixon, William J.

    1994.   "Democracy: The Peaceful Settlement of International Conflict." *American Political Science Review* 88, no. 1 (March).

Dixon, William J., and Bruce E. Moon.

    1987.   "The Military Burden and Basic Human Needs." *Journal of Conflict Resolution* 30: 660–84.

Donnelly, Jack.

    1986.   "International Human Rights: A Regime Analysis." *International Organization* 40, no. 3 (Summer): 599–642.

    1989.   *Universal Human Rights in Theory and Practice.* Ithaca, N.Y.: Cornell University Press.

    1995.   "State Sovereignty and International Intervention: The Case of Human Rights." In *Beyond Westphalia? State Sovereignty and International Intervention,* edited by G. M. Lyons and M. Mastanduno, 115–46. Baltimore: Johns Hopkins University Press.

    1998a.   "Human Rights: A New Standard of Civilization?" *International Affairs* 74, no. 1: 1–24.

    1998b.   *International Human Rights.* Boulder, Colo.: Westview Press.

    1999a.   "Human Rights, Democracy, and Development." *Human Rights Quarterly* 21, no. 3 (August): 608–32.

    1999b.   "The Social Construction of International Human Rights." In *Human Rights in Global Politics,* edited by Tim Dunne and Nicholas J. Wheeler, 71–102. Cambridge: Cambridge University Press.

Dooley M., and P. Isard.

    1980.   "Capital Controls: Political Risk, and Deviations from Interest Rate Parity." *Journal of Political Economy* 88: 370–384.

Downs, Anthony.

    1972.   "Up and Down with Ecology: The Issue Attention Cycle." *Public Interest* 28: 38–50.

Duarte, Isis.

    1989.   "Household Workers in the Dominican Republic: A Question for the Feminist Movement." In *Muchachas No More: Household Workers in Latin America and the Caribbean,* edited by Elsa M. Chaney and Mary Garcia Castro, 197–219. Philadelphia: Temple University Press.

Duff, Ernest, and John McCamant.
1976. *Violence and Repression in Latin America.* New York: Free Press.
"Easter March Protests Border Deaths."
2000. *Immigration News Briefs,* April 1.
Ebstein, Gerald A., and Juliet B. Schor.
1992. "Structural Determinants and Economic Effects of Capital Controls." In *Financial Openness and National Autonomy,* edited by Tariq Banuri and Juliet B. Schor, 136–61. Oxford: Clarendon Press.
Eliott, Kimberley Ann.
1998. *International Labor Standards and Trade: What Should Be Done?* Washington, D.C.: Institute for International Economics.
Enloe, Cynthia.
1989. *Bananas, Beaches, and Bases: Making Feminist Sense of International Politics.* Berkeley and Los Angeles: University of California Press.
Epstein, Steven.
1996. *Impure Science: AIDS, Activism, and the Politics of Knowledge.* Berkeley and Los Angeles: University of California Press.
Eschbach, Karl, Jacqueline Hagan, Nestor Rodriguez, and Ruben Hernandez-Leon.
1999. "Death at the Border," *International Migration Review* 33, no. 2 (Summer): 430.
Evans, Peter, ed.
1997. *State-Society Synergy: Government and Social Capital in Development.* Berkeley, Calif.: Research Series/International and Area Studies, University of California at Berkeley. Also in *World Development* 24, no. 6 (June 1996).
Evans, Peter, Harold Jacobson, and Robert Putnam, eds.
1993. *Double-Edged Diplomacy: International Bargaining and Domestic Politics.* Berkeley and Los Angeles: University of California.
Falk, Richard.
1981. *Human Rights and State Sovereignty.* New York: Holmes & Meier.
1994. "The Making of Global Citizenship." In *The Condition of Citizenship,* edited by Bart van Steenbergen, 127–40. Thousand Oaks, Calif.: Sage.
1995. *On Humane Governance: Toward a New Global Politics. The World Order Models Project Report of the Global Civilization Initiative.* University Park: Pennsylvania State University Press, 1995.
1997. "False Universalism and the Geopolitics of Exclusion: The Case of Islam." *Third World Quarterly* 18, no. 1 (March): 7–23.
1998. *Law in an Emerging Global Village: A Post-Westphalian Perspective.* Ardsley, N.Y.: Transnational Publishers.
1999a. "The Challenge of Genocide and Genocidal Politics in an Era of Globalization." In *Human Rights in Global Politics,* edited by Tim Dunne and Nicholas J. Wheeler, 177–94. Cambridge: Cambridge University Press.
1999b. *Predatory Globalization: A Critique.* Malden, Mass.: Polity Press.

Falk, Richard, and Richard Strauss.
    2001.   "Towards Global Parliament." *Foreign Affairs* 80, no. 1 (January–February):
    212.

Falk, Richard, Burns H. Weston, and Hillary Charlesworth.
    1997.   *International Law and World Order: A Problem-Oriented Coursebook.* St. Paul,
    Minn.: West Group.

Feeney, Patricia.
    1998.   *Accountable Aid: Local Participation in Major Projects.* Oxford: Oxfam.

Fein, Helen.
    1995.   "More Murder in the Middle: Life Integrity Violations and Democracy in
    the World." *Human Rights Quarterly* 17: 170–91.

Ferreira, Francisca.
    1996.   "Prostitución y tráfico de mujeres en la República Dominicana." Traffic
    in Women and Forced Prostitution, Latin America and the Caribbean. San Juan,
    Puerto Rico, May.

Fields, G.
    1996.   *Trade and Labour Standards: A Review of Issues.* OECD Working Papers 4,
    no. 7. Paris: Organisation for Economic Co-operation and Development.

Fields, Rona M.
    1998.   "Refugees: Human Rights in Economic Globalization." *Migrationworld* 26,
    no. 4: 23–25.

Finnemore, Martha.
    1996.   "Norms, Culture, and World Politics: Insights from Sociology's Institu-
    tionalism." *International Organization* 50, no. 2 (Spring): 325–47.

Finnemore, Martha, and Kathryn Sikkink.
    1999.   "International Norms Dynamics and Political Change." In *Exploration and
    Contestation in the Study of World Politics,* edited by Peter J. Katzenstein, Robert O.
    Keohane, and Stephen D. Krasner. Cambridge, Mass.: MIT Press.

Fisher, William, ed.
    1995.   *Toward Sustainable Development? Struggling over India's Narmada River.* Ar-
    monk, N.Y.: M. E. Sharpe, 1995.

Fiss, Owen.
    1998.   "The Immigrant as Pariah." *Boston Review,* October/November, 4–7.

Fiss, Owen.
    1999.   *A Community of Equals: The Constitutional Protection of New Americans.* Edited
    by Joshua Cohen and Joel Rogers. Boston: Beacon Press.

Flores, William V., and Rina Benmayor, eds.
    1997.   *Latino Cultural Citizenship: Claiming Identity, Space, and Rights.* Boston: Bea-
    con Press.

Foucault, Michel.
    1977.   *Discipline and Punish: The Birth of the Prison.* Translated by Alan Sheridan.
    New York: Pantheon Books.

Fox, Elizabeth, ed.

1988.   *Media and Politics in Latin America: The Struggle for Democracy.* Newbury Park, Calif.: Sage.

Fox, G. H.

1992.   "The Right to Political Participation in International Law." *Yale Journal of International Law* 17, no. 2: 539–607.

Fox, G. H., and B. R. Roth, eds.

2000.   *Democratic Governance and International Law.* Cambridge: Cambridge University Press.

Fox, Jonathan A.

1997a.   "Transparency for Accountability: Civil Society Monitoring of Multilateral Development Bank Anti-Poverty Projects." *Development in Practice* 7, no. 2 (May).

1997b.   "The World Bank and Social Capital: Contesting the Concept in Practice." *Journal of International Development* 9, no. 7 (November–December).

1998a.   "Thinking Locally, Acting Globally: Bringing the Grassroots into Transnational Advocacy." Regional Worlds-Latin America: Cultural Environments and Development Debates. Center for Latin American Studies and the Globalization Project, University of Chicago, 21–23 May.

1998b.   "When Does Reform Policy Influence Practice? Lessons from the Bankwide Resettlement Review." In *The Struggle for Accountability: The World Bank, NGOs and Grassroots Movements,* edited by Jonathan Fox and L. David Brown, 303–44. Cambridge, Mass.: MIT Press.

2000a,   "Assessing Binational Civil Society Coalitions: Lessons from the Mexico-U.S. Experience." *Chicano-Latino Research Center Working Paper,* no. 26 (online at www.irc-online.org/bios/).

2000b.   "The World Bank Inspection Panel: Lessons from the First Five Years." *Global Governance* 6, no. 3 (July–September).

Forthcoming.   "Los flujos y reflujos de préstamos sociales y ambientales del Banco Mundial en México." In *Las nuevas fonteras del siglo xxi: Dimensiones culturales, políticas y socioeconómicas de las relaciones México–Estados Unidos,* edited by Alejandro Alvarez et al. Mexico City: UNAM.

Fox, Jonathan A., and David L. Brown.

1998a.   "Assessing the Impact of NGO Advocacy Coalitions on World Bank Projects and Policies." In *The Struggle for Accountability: The World Bank, NGOs and Grassroots Movements,* 485–551. Cambridge, Mass.: MIT Press.

eds. 1998b.   *The Struggle for Accountability: Grassroots Movements, NGOs and the World Bank.* Cambridge, Mass.: MIT Press.

Franck, Thomas M.

1992.   "The Emerging Right to Democratic Governance."*American Journal of International Law* 86: 46.

1999.   *The Empowered Self: Law and Society in the Age of Individualism.* Oxford: Oxford University Press.

Frankel, Jeffrey, and Alan MacArthur.
    1998.   "Political vs. Currency Premia in International Real Interest Differentials."
    European Economic Review 32, no. 5 (June).

Frederick, Howard.
    1992.   "Computer Communications in Cross-Border Coalition Building: North
    American NGO Networking against NAFTA." *Gazette: The International Journal
    of Mass Communications Studies* 50, nos. 2–3: 217–41.

Friedman, Thomas.
    1999.   *The Lexus and the Olive Tree: Understanding Globalization.* New York: Farrar,
    Straus & Giroux.

Frug, Mary Joe.
    1995.   "A Postmodern Feminist Legal Manifesto." In *After Identity: A Reader in
    Law and Culture,* edited by Dan Danielsen and Karen Engle, 7–23. New York:
    Routledge.

Gai, Yash.
    1999.   "Rights, Social Justice, and Globalization in East Asia." In *The East Asian
    Challenge for Human Rights,* edited by Joanne R. Bauer and Daniel A. Bell,
    241–63. New York: Cambridge University Press.

Ganley, Gladys D.
    1992.   *The Exploding Political Power of Personal Media.* Norwood, N.J.: Ablex,
    1992.

Ganley, Gladys D., and Oswald H. Ganley.
    1987.   *Global Political Fallout. The VCR's First Decade, 1976–1985.* Norwood, N.J.:
    Ablex.

Garrison, John.
    1989.   "Computers Link NGOs Worldwide." *Grassroots Development,* Fall.

Gassiorowski, Mark.
    1993.   *The Political Regime Change Dataset.* Baton Rouge: Louisiana Population
    Data Center, Louisiana State University.

Gastil, Raymond.
    1990.   "The Comparative Survey of Freedom: Experiences and Suggestions."
    Studies in Comparative International Development 25: 25–50.

    1978–94.   *Freedom in the World.* Annual. Washington, D.C.: Freedom House.

Ghai, Dharam, ed.
    1991.   *The IMF and the South: The Social Impact of Crisis and Adjustment.* London:
    Zed Books.

Gibney, Mark, and Matthew Dalton.
    1996.   "The Political Terror Scale." In *Human Rights and Developing Countries,*
    edited by David Cingranelli, 73–84. Greenwich, Conn.: JAI Press.

Gillies, David.
    1996.   "Human Rights, Democracy and Good Governance: Stretching the World
    Bank's Policy Frontiers." In *The World Bank: Lending on a Global Scale,* edited by
    Jo Marie Griesgraber and Bernhard Gunter. London: Pluto Press.

Gilpin, Robert.
   2000.   *The Challenge of Global Capitalism: The World Economy in the Twenty-First Century.* Princeton, N.J.: Princeton University Press, 2000.

Glassman, Jim.
   1999.   "State Power beyond the 'Territorial Trap': The Internationalization of the State." *Political Geography* 18: 669–96.

Glick Schiller, Nina.
   1999.   "Transmigrants and Nation-States: Something Old and Something New in the U.S. Immigrant Experience." In *The Handbook of International Migration: The American Experience,* edited by Charles Hirschman, Philip Kasinitz, and Josh DeWind, 94–111. New York: Russell Sage Foundation.

"A Global Disaster: The Debacle in Seattle Was a Setback for Freer Trade and a Boost for Critics of Globalisation."
   1999.   *Economist,* 11 December, 19–22.

Goldstein, Joshua.
   1985.   "Basic Human Needs: The Plateau Curve." *World Development* 13: 595–609.

Goldstein, Robert Justin.
   1987.   "The United States." In *The International Handbook of Human Rights,* edited by Jack Donnelly and Rhoda E. Howard, 429–56. New York: Greenwood Press.

Gonzalez, Gilbert G.
   1990.   *Chicano Education in the Era of Segregation.* Philadelphia: Balch Institute Press.

Goodin, Robert E., et al.
   1999.   *The Real Worlds of Welfare Capitalism.* New York: Cambridge University Press.

Gordon, R. E.
   1994.   "United Nations Intervention in Internal Conflicts: Iraq, Somalia, and Beyond." *Michigan Journal of International Law* 15: 519–89.

   1996.   "Humanitarian Intervention by the United Nations: Iraq, Somalia, and Haiti." *Texas International Law Journal* 31: 43–56.

Gramsci, Antonio.
   1971.   *Selections From the Prison Notebooks.* Translated by Quintin Hoare and Geoffrey Nowell Smith. New York: International Publishers.

Gray, Andrew.
   1998.   "Development Policy—Development Protest: The World Bank, Indigenous Peoples and NGOs." In *The Struggle for Accountability: The World Bank, NGOs and Grassroots Movements,* edited by Jonathan Fox and L. David Brown, 267–301. Cambridge, Mass.: MIT Press, 1998.

Gray, John.
   1998.   *False Dawn: The Delusions of Global Capitalism.* New York: New Press.

Grieder, William.
   1997.   *One World, Ready or Not: The Manic Logic of Global Capitalism.* New York: Simon & Schuster.

Gruhn, Isebill.
  1999.   "The Problematic of Democratic Governance at the International Level:
          Does NGO Growth and Expansion Address the Democratic Deficit in IGOs."
          Annual Convention of the International Studies Association. Washington, D.C.,
          16–20 February.

Guha, Ranajit, and Gayatri Chakravorty Spivak, eds.
  1988.   *Selected Subaltern Studies.* New Delhi: Oxford University Press.

Gurr, Ted Robert.
  1986.   "The Political Origins of State Violence and Terror: A Theoretical Analy-
          sis." In *Government Violence and Repression: An Agenda for Research,* edited by
          Michael Stohl and George A. Lopez, 45–71. Westport, Conn.: Greenwood Press.

Guruswamy, Lakshman D., Sir Geoffrey W. R. Palmer, and Burns H. Weston, eds.
  1994.   *Supplement of Basic Documents to International Law and World Order: A Problem-
          Oriented Coursebook.* St. Paul, Minn.: West.

Guy, Donna J.
  1990.   *Sex and Danger in Buenos Aires: Prostitution, Family, and Nation in Argentina.*
          Lincoln: University of Nebraska Press.

Gwartney, James, Robert Lawson, and Walter Block.
  1997.   *Economic Freedom of the World: 1975–1995.* Vancouver: Frasier Institute.

Haas, Ernst B.
  1964.   *Beyond the Nation State: Functionalism and International Organization.* Stan-
          ford, Calif.: Stanford University Press.

Haas, Michael.
  1994.   *Improving Human Rights.* Westport, Conn.: Praeger.

Hair, Jay, et al.
  1997.   "Pangue Hydroelectric Project: An Independent Review of the Inter-
          national Finance Corporation's Compliance with Applicable World Bank
          Group Environmental and Social Requirements." Unpublished conference
          paper.

Hall, Anthony.
  1992.   "From Victims to Victors: NGOs and the Politics of Empowerment at Ita-
          parica." In *Making a Difference: NGOs and Development in a Changing World,* edited
          by Michael Edwards and David Hulme, 148–58. London: Earthscan.

Hall, Rodney Bruce.
  1997.   "Moral Authority as a Power Resource." *International Organization* 51, no.
          4 (Autumn): 591–622.

Hall, Stuart, and David Held.
  1989.   "Citizens and Citizenship." In *New Times: The Changing Face of Politics in
          the 1990s,* edited by Stuart Hall and Martin Jacques, 173–88. London: Lawrence
          & Wishart.

Hammar, Tomas.
  1990.   *Democracy and the Nation State: Aliens, Denizens, and Citizens in a World of In-
          ternational Migration.* Brookfield, Vt.: Gower Publishing.

Hanami, T.

1997.   "Globalization of Employment and Social Clauses." *BULLETIN* 36.

Hannum, Hurst, ed.

1999.   *Guide to International Human Rights Practice.* Ardsley, N.Y.: Transnational Publishers, 1999.

Harden, Blaine.

2000.   "Angolan Paradox: Oil Wealth Only Adds to Misery." *New York Times,* 9 April, 3.

Hartz, Louis.

1955.   *The Liberal Tradition in America: An Interpretation of American Political Thought since the Revolution.* New York: Harcourt, Brace.

Harvey, David.

1989.   *The Condition of Postmodernity: An Enquiry into the Origins of Cultural Change.* Cambridge, Mass.: Blackwell.

Haworth, N., and S. Hughes.

1998.   "Death of a Social Clause? Reconstructing the Trade and Labour Standards Debate in the Asia-Pacific." Proceedings, International Conference on Labour Standards and Human Rights, University of California, Berkeley. Conference paper posted at socrates.berkeley.edu/~iir/clre/programs/death.html.

Heinisch, Reinhard.

1994.   "The Status of Basic Human Rights in the World: Political and Economic Explanations of Cross-National Differences in Government Basic Human Rights Performance and Effort." Ph.D. diss., Michigan State University.

Held, David.

1995.   *Democracy and the Global Order: From the Modern State to Cosmopolitan Governance.* Stanford, Calif.: Stanford University Press.

2000.   *The Global Transformations Reader: An Introduction to the Globalization Debate.* Malden, Mass.: Blackwell.

Held, David, et al.

1999.   *Global Transformations: Politics, Economics, and Culture.* Stanford, Calif.: Stanford University Press.

Henderson, Conway.

1991.   "Conditions Affecting the Use of Political Repression." *Journal of Conflict Resolution* 35: 120–42.

1993.   "Population Pressures and Political Repression." *Social Science Quarterly* 74: 322–33.

Heston, Alan, and Robert Summers.

1991.   "The Penn World Table (Mark 5): An Expanded Set of International Comparisons, 1950–1988." *Quarterly Journal of Economics* 106: 327–68.

Hewson, Martin, and Timothy J. Sinclair.

1999.   "The Emergence of Global Governance Theory." In *Approaches to Global Governance Theory,* edited by Martin Hewson and Timothy J. Sinclair, 3–22. Albany, N.Y.: State University of New York Press.

Heyzer, Noeleen, Geertje Lycklama à Nijeholt, and Nedra Weerakoon.
　　1994. *The Trade in Domestic Workers: Causes, Mechanisms and Consequences of International Migration.* Atlantic Highlands, N.J.: Zed Books.

Hicks, Norman, and Paul Streeten.
　　1979. "Indicators of Development: The Search for a Basic Needs Yardstick." *World Development* 7: 567–80.

Higham, John.
　　1988. *Strangers in the Land: Patterns of American Nativism, 1860–1925.* New Brunswick, N.J.: Rutgers University Press, 1988.

Hirschman, Albert.
　　1970. *Exit, Voice and Loyalty.* Cambridge, Mass.: Harvard University Press.

Hirst, Paul, and Grahame Thompson.
　　1996. *Globalization in Question: The International Economy and the Possibilities of Governance.* Cambridge, Mass.: Blackwell.

Ho, Laura, Catherine Powell, and Leti Volpp.
　　1996. "(Dis)Assembling the Rights of Women Workers along the Global Assembly Line: Human Rights and the Garment Industry." *Harvard Civil Rights—Civil Liberties Law Review* 31, no. 2 (Summer): 383–414.

Hock, Dee W.
　　1994. "Institutions in the Age of Mindcrafting." Paper presented at the Bionomics Annual Conference, San Francisco, 22 October. Photocopy.

Hollifield, James F.
　　1992. *Immigrants, Markets, and States.* Cambridge, Mass.: Harvard University Press.

Holm, Hans-Hendrik, and Georg Sorensen.
　　1995. *Whose World Order? Uneven Globalization and the End of the Cold War.* Boulder, Colo.: Westview Press.

Holsti, K. J.
　　1985. *The Dividing Discipline: Hegemony and Diversity in International Theory.* Boston: Allen & Unwin.

Hondagneu-Sotelo, Pierrette.
　　1995. "Women and Children First: New Directions in Anti-Immigrant Politics." *Socialist Review* 25, no. 1: 169–90.

Hossfeld, Karen.
　　1988. "Divisions of Labor, Divisions of Lives: Immigrant Women Workers in Silicon Valley." Ph.D. Diss., University of California, Santa Cruz.

Human Rights Watch.
　　1992. *Brutality Unchecked: The Human Rights Abuses along the U.S. Border with Mexico.* An Americas Watch report. New York: Human Rights Watch.

　　1995a. "Nigeria: The Ogoni Crisis: A Case-Study of Military Repression in Southeastern Nigeria." *Human Rights Watch Africa Report* 7, no. 5 (July).

　　1995b. *Slaughter among Neighbors: The Political Origins of Communal Violence.* New Haven, Conn.: Yale University Press.

1996.   *Mexico, Labor Rights, and NAFTA: A Case Study.* New York: Human Rights Watch/Americas.

1999.   *The Enron Corporation: Complicity in Human Rights Violations.* New York: Human Rights Watch.

"Human Rights, Public Finance and the Development Process."
1992.   Special issue. *American University Journal of International Law and Policy* 8, no. 1 (Fall).

Hunter, Allen.
1995.   "Globalization from Below? Promises and Perils of the New Internationalism." *Social Policy,* Summer, 6–13.

Hunter, David.
1997.   "The Planafloro Claim: Lessons from the Second World Bank Inspection Panel Claim." Washington, D.C.: Center for International Environmental Law (www.ciel.org). Unpublished paper.

1998.   "The World Bank Inspection Panel: A Forum for Accountability within a Resistant Institution." Latin American Studies Association. Chicago, September. Conference paper.

Huntington, Samuel P.
1981.   *American Politics: The Promise of Disharmony.* Cambridge, Mass.: Harvard University Press, Belknap Press.

Hurrell, Andrew.
1999.   "Power, Principles and Prudence: Protecting Human Rights in a Deeply Divided World." In *Human Rights in Global Politics,* edited by Tim Dunne and Nicholas J. Wheeler, 277–302. Cambridge: Cambridge University Press.

Hurrell, Andrew, and Ngaire Woods.
1999.   "Introduction." In *Inequality, Globalization, and World Politics,* edited by Andrew Hurrell and Ngaire Woods, 1–7. New York: Oxford University Press.

Huspek, Michael, Roberto Martinez, and Leticia Jimenez.
1998.   "Violations of Human and Civil Rights on the U.S-Mexican Border, 1995–1997: A Report." *Social Justice* 25, no. 2: 110–30.

Ignatieff, Michael.
1998.   *The Warrior's Honor: Ethnic War and the Modern Conscience.* London: Chatto & Windus.

1999a.   "The Evolution of International Human Rights: Visions Seen." Review essay. *New York Review of Books* 46, no. 9 (20 May).

1999b.   *Whose Universal Values? The Crisis in Human Rights.* The Hague: Praemium Erasmianum Foundation.

Ignatiev, Noel.
1995.   *How the Irish Became White.* New York: Routledge.

Ingram, Helen, and Anne Schneider.
1993.   "The Social Construction of Target Populations: Implication for Politics and Policy." *American Political Science Review* 87, no. 2 (June): 334–47.

1997.   *Policy Design for Democracy.* Lawrence: University Press of Kansas.

Institut universitaire d'études du développement [IUED] and European Association of Development Research and Training Institutes [EADI].
   1998.   Trade Policies and Labour Standards. Roundtable Seminar. Cited as IUED/ EADI 1998.

International Labor Rights Fund.
   1998.   *Developing Effective Mechanisms for Implementing Labor Rights in the Global Economy.* Washington, D.C.

International Organization for Migration.
   1996.   "Trafficking in Women from the Dominican Republic for Sexual Exploitation." Budapest, June.

Ito, T.
   1986.   "Capital Controls and Covered Interest Parity between the Yen and the Dollar." *Economic Studies Quarterly* 37: 223–41.

Iwersen, Albrecht, and Susanne Iwersen-Sioltsidis.
   1996.   "Tourism and Developing Countries." *Intereconomics,* November–December, 301–6.

Jabine, Thomas, and Richard Claude, eds.
   1992.   *Human Rights and Statistics: Getting the Record Straight.* Philadelphia: University of Pennsylvania Press.

Jacobson, David.
   1997.   *Rights Across Borders: Immigration and the Decline of Citizenship.* Baltimore: Johns Hopkins University Press.

Jaggers, Keith, and Ted Robert Gurr.
   1995.   "Tracking Democracy's Third Wave with the Polity III Data." *Journal of Peace Research* 32: 469–82.

Jonas, Susanne.
   1999.   "Rethinking Immigration Policy and Citizenship in the Americas: A Regional Framework." In *Immigration: A Civil Rights Issue for the Americas,* edited by Susanne Jonas and Suzanne Dod Thomas, 99–118. Wilmington, Del.: Scholarly Resources.

Jonas, Susanne, Suzie Dod Thomas, and John Isbister.
   1999.   "Introduction." In *Immigration: A Civil Rights Issue for the Americas,* edited by Susanne Jonas and Suzanne Dod Thomas. Wilmington, Del.: Scholarly Resources.

Jones, Ronald W., and Alan C. Stockman.
   1992.   "On the Concept of Economic Freedom." In *Rating Economic Freedom,* edited by Stephen T. Easton and Michael A. Walker. Vancouver: Fraser Institute.

Joppke, Christian.
   1999.   *Immigration and the Nation-State.* Oxford: Oxford University Press.

Kaldor, Mary.
   1999.   "Transnational Civil Society." In *Human Rights in Global Politics,* edited by Tim Dunne and Nicholas J. Wheeler, 195–213. Cambridge: Cambridge University Press.

Kasman, B., and C. Pigott.
1988.   "Interest Rate Divergences among the Major Industrial Nations." *Federal Reserve Bank of New York Quarterly Review,* Autumn, 28–44.

Katzenstein, Peter, ed.
1996.   *The Culture of National Security: Norms and Identity in World Politics.* New York: Columbia University Press.

Katzenstein, Peter J., Robert O. Keohane, and Stephen D. Krasner.
1999.   "International Organization and the Study of World Politics." In *Exploration and Contestation in the Study of World Politics,* edited by Peter J. Katzenstein, Robert O. Keohane and Stephen D. Krasner. Cambridge, Mass.: MIT Press.

Kearney, Michael.
1995.   "The Local and the Global: The Anthropology of Globalization and Transnationalism." *Annual Review of Anthropology* 24: 547–66.

Keck, Margaret.
1998.   "Planafloro in Rondonia: The Limits of Leverage." In *The Struggle for Accountability: The World Bank, NGOs and Grassroots Movements,* edited by Jonathan Fox and L. David Brown, 181–218. Cambridge, Mass.: MIT Press.

Keck, Margaret, and Kathryn Sikkink.
1998.   *Activists beyond Borders: Transnational Advocacy Networks in International Politics.* Ithaca, N.Y.: Cornell University Press.

Keely, Charles B., and Sharon Stanton Russell.
1996.   "Asylum Policies in Developed Countries: National Security Concerns and Regional Issues." In *International Migration, Refugee Flows and Human Rights in North America: The Impact of Trade and Restructuring,* edited by Alan B. Simmons, 229–44. New York: Center for Migration Studies.

Kempadoo, Kamala, ed.
1999.   *Sun, Sex, and Gold: Tourism and Sex Work in the Caribbean.* Boulder, Colo.: Rowman & Littlefield.

Kempadoo, Kamala, and Jo Doezema, eds.
1998.   *Global Sex Workers: Rights, Resistance, and Redefinition.* New York: Routledge.

Kempadoo, Kamala, and Ranya Ghuma.
1999.   "For the Children: Trends in International Policies and Law on Sex Tourism." In *Sun, Sex, and Gold: Tourism and Sex Work in the Caribbean,* edited by Kamala Kempadoo, 291–308. Boulder, Colo.: Rowman & Littlefield.

Keohane, Robert O., and Helen V. Milner, eds.
1996.   *Internationalization and Domestic Politics.* Cambridge: Cambridge University Press.

Keohane, Robert O., and Joseph S. Nye.
1977.   *Power and Interdependence: World Politics in Transition.* Boston: Little, Brown.

Khor, Martin.
1999.   "Developing Countries Decry WTO's Secretive Talks." *Third World Network Features,* November.

King, Russell.
    1997.   "Racism and Migration in Western Europe." *West European Politics* 19, no. 1: 176.

Kingdon, John W.
    1984.   *Agendas, Alternatives, and Public Policies.* 1984. 2d ed. New York: Harper-Collins.

Klotz, Audie.
    1995a.   *Norms in International Relations: The Struggle against Apartheid.* Ithaca, N.Y.: Cornell University Press.

    1995b.   "Norms Reconstituting Interests: Global Racial Equality and U.S. Sanctions against South Africa." *International Organization* 49, no. 3 (Summer): 451–78.

Kofman, Eleonore.
    1995.   "Citizenship for Some but Not for Others: Spaces of Citizenship in Contemporary Europe." *Political Geography* 14, no. 2: 121–38.

    1999.   "Gender, Migrants and Rights in the European Union." In *Gender, Planning and Human Rights,* edited by Tovi Fenster, 125–39. New York: Routledge.

Kofman, Eleonore, and Gillian Youngs, eds.
    1996.   *Globalization: Theory and Practice.* New York: Pinter.

König, Ilse, ed.
    1998.   *Traffick in Women.* Vienna, Austria: LEFO [Lateinamerikanische Emigrierte Frauen in Österreich].

Korten, David C.
    1995.   *When Corporations Rule the World.* West Hartford, Conn.: Kumarian Press; New York: Berrett-Koehler Publishers.

Kothari, Smita, and Harsh Sethi, eds.
    1989.   *Rethinking Human Rights: Challenges for Theory and Action.* New York: New Horizons Press.

Krause, Jill, and Neil Renwick, eds.
    1996.   *Identities in International Relations.* New York: St. Martin's Press.

Krugman, Paul.
    1999.   *The Return of Depression Economics.* New York: Norton.

    2000.   "Once and Again." *New York Times,* 2 January, sec. 5, 9.

Kudrle, Robert T.
    1999.   "Three Types of Globalization: Communication, Market, and Direct." In *Globalization and Global Governance,* edited by Raimo Vayrynen, 3–24. Lanham, Md.: Rowman & Littlefield, 1999.

Kurian, Priya.
    1995.   "The U.S. Congress and the World Bank: Impact of News Media on International Environmental Policy." In *International Organizations and Environmental Policy,* edited by Robert V. Bartlett, Priya Kurian and Madhu Malik, 103–19. Westport, Conn.: Greenwood Press.

Langenfeld, Amy.
    1999.   "Living in Limbo: Mandatory Detention of Immigrants under the Illegal Immigration Reform and Responsibility Act of 1996." *Arizona State Law Journal* 31.
Langille, Brian.
    1997.   "Eight Ways to Think about International Labor Standards." *Journal of World Trade* 31: 27–53.
Lapid, Yosef.
    1996.   "The Third Debate: On the Prospects of International Theory in a Post-Positivist Era." In *Classics of International Relations,* edited by John A. Vasquez. 3d ed. Upper Saddle River, N.J.: Prentice-Hall.
Latham, Robert.
    1999.   "Politics in a Floating World: Toward a Critique of Global Governance." In *Approaches to Global Governance Theory,* edited by Martin Hewson and Timothy J. Sinclair, 23–53. Albany, N.Y.: State University of New York Press.
Lawyers Committee for Human Rights.
    1995.   *The World Bank: Governance and Human Rights.* New York: Lawyers Committee for Human Rights.
Lawyers Committee for Human Rights and Institute for Policy Research and Advocacy.
    1995.   *In the Name of Development: Human Rights and the World Bank in Indonesia.* New York: Lawyers Committee for Human Rights.
Lawyers Committee for Human Rights and Venezuelan Program for Human Rights Education and Action.
    1996.   *Halfway to Reform: The World Bank and the Venezuelan Justice System.* New York: Lawyers Committee for Human Rights.
Lea, John.
    1988.   *Tourism and Development in the Third World.* New York: Routledge.
Leary, Virginia.
    1997.   "The WTO and the Social Clause: Post-Singapore." *European Journal of International Law* 18, no. 118.
Lenin [Vladimir Ilych Ulyanov].
    1975.   *The Lenin Anthology.* Edited by Robert C.Tucker. New York: Norton.
Letsie, David and Patrick Bond.
    1999a.   "Lesotho Highlands Water Project as seen from Johannesburg." Presented to the World Commission on Dams.
    1999b.   "Social, Ecological and Economic Characteristics of Bulk Water Infrastructure: Debating the Financial and Service Delivery Implications of the Lesotho Highlands Water Project." MS.
Levine, David P.
    1988.   *Needs, Rights, and the Market.* Boulder, Colo.: Lynne Rienner.
Li, Quan, and Rafael Reuveny.
    2000.   "Does Economic Globalization Hinder or Promote Democracy?" Annual Meeting of the International Studies Association, Los Angeles, 14–18 March.

Lim, Lin Lean, ed.
　1998.　*The Sex Sector: The Economic and Social Bases of Prostitution in Southeast Asia.* Geneva: International Labour Office.

Lipschutz, Ronnie D.
　1992.　"Reconstructing World Politics: The Emergence of a Global Civil Society." *Millennium: Journal of International Studies* 21, no. 3.

　1996.　*Global Civil Society and Global Environmental Governance.* New York: State University of New York Press.

Livernash, Robert, et al.
　1993.　"Policies and Institutions: Nongovernmental Organizations: A Driving Force in the Developing World." In *World Resources, 1992–93.* Washington, D.C.: World Resources Institute.

Livingston, Steven.
　1996.　"Suffering in Silence: Media Coverage of War and Famine in Sudan." In *From Massacres to Genocide: The Media, Public Policy, and Humanitarian Crises,* edited by Robert I. Rotberg and Thomas G. Weiss, 68–89. Cambridge, Mass.: World Peace Foundation.

Lladó, Juan.
　1996.　"El plan nacional de desarrollo turístico." X Convención Nacional y Exposición Comercial, Santo Domingo, 25–28 September.

Loker, William M.
　1999.　"Grit in the Prosperity Machine: Globalization and the Rural Poor in Latin America." In *Globalization and the Rural Poor in Latin America,* edited by William M. Loker, 9–39. Boulder, Colo.: Lynne Rienner.

Lopez, George A., and Michael Stohl.
　1989.　*Dependence, Development and State Repression.* Westport, Conn.: Greenwood Press.

　1992.　"Problems of Concept and Measurement in the Study of Human Rights." In *Human Rights and Statistics: Getting the Record Straight,* edited by Thomas B. Jabine and Richard P. Claude, 216–34. Philadelphia: University of Pennsylvania Press.

Lumsdaine, D. H.
　1993.　*Moral Vision in International Politics.* Princeton, N.J.: Princeton University Press.

Lutz, Helma.
　1997.　"The Limits of European-Ness: Immigrant Women in Fortress Europe." *Feminist Review* 57.

Macpherson, C. B.
　1962.　*The Political Theory of Possessive Individualism: Hobbes to Locke.* New York: Oxford University Press.

Maher, Kristen Hill.
　1999.　"A Stranger in the House: American Ambivalence about Immigrant Labor." Ph.D. Diss., University of California, Irvine.

2000.   "Space, Race, Class, and Immigrant Labor: Latino Workers in Fortressing Suburban Communities." MS.

Malkki, Liisa.
1994.   "Citizens of Humanity: Internationalism and the Imagined Community of Nations." *Diaspora* 3, no. 1 (Spring): 41–68.

Mander, Jerry, and Edward Goldsmith, eds.
1996.   *The Case against the Global Economy: And for a Turn toward the Local.* San Francisco: Sierra Club Books.

Marchevsky, Alejandra.
1996.   "The Empire Strikes Back: Globalization, Nationalism, and California's Proposition 187." *Critical Sense* 4, no. 1: 8–51.

Markoff, John.
1999.   "Tiniest Circuits Hold Prospect of Explosive Computer Speeds." *New York Times,* 16 July, AL.

Marshall, T. H.
1998.   "Citizenship and Social Class." In *The Citizenship Debates,* edited by Gershon Shafir, 93–112. Minneapolis: University of Minnesota Press.

Martin, Philip L.
1994.   "The United States: Benign Neglect toward Immigration." In *Controlling Immigration? A Global Perspective,* edited by Wayne A. Cornelius, Philip A. Martin, and James F. Hollifield, 83–100. Stanford, Calif.: Stanford University Press.

Massey, Douglas S.
1999.   "Why Does Immigration Occur? A Theoretical Synthesis." In *The Handbook of International Migration: The American Experience,* edited by Charles Hirschman, Philip Kasinitz, and Josh DeWind, 34–52. New York: Russell Sage Foundation.

McAdam, Doug.
1982.   *Political Process and the Development of Black Insurgency, 1930–1970.* Chicago: University of Chicago Press.

McAfee, Kathy.
1991.   *Storm Signals: Structural Adjustment and Development Alternatives in the Caribbean.* London: Zed Books.

McCarthy, John D., Jackie Smith, and Mayer N. Zald.
1996.   "Accessing Public, Media, Electoral, and Governmental Agendas." In *Comparative Perspectives on Social Movements: Political Opportunities, Mobilizing Structures, and Cultural Framings,* edited by Doug McAdam, John D. McCarthy and Mayer N. Zald. Cambridge: Cambridge University Press.

McCorquodale, Robert, with Richard Fairbrother.
1999.   "Globalization and Human Rights." *Human Rights Quarterly* 21: 735.

McGrew, Anthony G.
1998.   "Human Rights in a Global Age: Coming to Terms with Globalization." In *Human Rights Fifty Years On: A Reappraisal,* edited by Tony Evans, 188–210. Manchester: Manchester University Press.

McKenzie, Evan.
  1994. *Privatopia: Homeowner Associations and the Rise of Residential Private Government.* New Haven, Conn.: Yale University Press.

McKinlay, R. D. and A. S. Cohen.
  1975. "A Comparative Analysis of the Political and Economic Performance of Military and Civilian Regimes." *Comparative Politics* 8: 1–30.
  1976. "Performance and Instability in Military and Nonmilitary Regimes." *American Political Science Review* 70: 850–64.

Mcluhan, Marshall.
  1960. *Explorations in Communication.* Boston: Beacon Press.

McWilliams, Carey.
  1939. *Factories in the Field: The Story of Migratory Farm Labor in California.* Boston: Little, Brown.

Mellon, Cynthia.
  1999. "A Human Rights Perspective on the Sex Trade in the Caribbean and Beyond." In *Sun, Sex, and Gold: Tourism and Sex Work in the Caribbean,* edited by Kamala Kempadoo, 309–22. Boulder, Colo.: Rowman & Littlefield.

Meron, Theodor.
  1989. *Human Rights and Humanitarian Norms as Customary Law.* Oxford: Clarendon Press.

Metzl, Jamie F.
  1996. "Information Technology and Human Rights." *Human Rights Quarterly* 18, no. 4 (November): 705–46.

Meyer, John M., et al.
  1997. "World Society and the Nation-State." *American Journal of Sociology* 103, no. 1 (July): 144–81.

Meyer, William H.
  1998. *Human Rights and International Political Economy in Third World Nations: Multinational Corporations, Foreign Aid, and Repression.* Westport, Conn.: Praeger.

Miller, Judith.
  1999. "Sovereignty Isn't So Sacred Anymore." *New York Times,* 18 April, sec. 4, 4.

Millikan, Brent.
  1998. "Planafloro: Modelo de Projeto Participativo." In *Bancos multilaterais desenvolvimento participativo no Brasil: Dilemas e desafios,* edited by Jean-Pierre Leroy and Maria Clara Couto Soares. Rio de Janeiro: FASE/IBASE.

Mills, Kurt.
  1998. *Human Rights in the Emerging Global Order: A New Sovereignty?* New York: St. Martin's Press.

Milner, Wesley T.
  1998. "Globalization, Economic Freedom and Human Rights: Can We Have It All?" 39th Annual Convention of the International Studies Association. Minneapolis, 17–21 March.

Milner, Wesley T., Steven C. Poe, and David Leblang.
  1999. "Security Rights, Subsistence Rights, and Liberties: A Theoretical Survey of the Empirical Landscape." *Human Rights Quarterly* 21, no. 2 (May):
  403–43.

Miloan, Angel.
  1994. *Turismo: Nuestro industria sin chimeneas.* Santo Domingo: Editorial Letras
  de Quisqueya.

Mirkinson, Judith.
  1997. "The Global Trade in Women." *Earth Island Journal* 13, no. 1 (Winter):
  30–31.

Mishra, Ramesh.
  1998. "Beyond the Nation State: Social Policy in an Age of Globalization." *Social Policy and Administration* 32 (December): 481–500.

Mitchell, Neil J., and James M. McCormick.
  1988. "Economic and Political Explanations of Human Rights Violations."
  World Politics 40 (July): 476–98.

Mittelman, James H., ed.
  1996. *Globalization: Critical Reflections.* Boulder, Colo.: Lynne Rienner.

Moffat, David, and Olof Lindén.
  1995. "Perception and Reality: Assessing Priorities for Sustainable Development
  in the Niger River Delta." *Ambio* 24: 536–37.

Mohanty, Chandra Talpade.
  1991. "Under Western Eyes." In *Third World Women and the Politics of Feminism,*
  edited by Chandra Talpade Mohanty, Ann Russo, and Lourdes Torres, 51–80.
  Indianapolis: Indiana University Press.

Montejano, David.
  1987. *Anglos and Mexicans in the Making of Texas, 1836–1986.* Austin: University
  of Texas Press.

Montgomery, John D., ed.
  1998. *Human Rights: Positive Policies in Asia and the Pacific Rim.* Hollis, N.H.:
  Hollis Pub.

Moon, Bruce E.
  1991. *The Political Economy of Basic Human Needs.* Ithaca, N.Y.: Cornell University Press.

Moon, Bruce E., and William J. Dixon.
  1985. "Politics, the State, and Basic Human Needs: A Cross-National Study."
  American Journal of Political Science 29: 661–94.

  1992. "Basic Needs and Growth-Welfare Trade-Offs." *International Studies Quarterly* 36: 191–212.

Morokvasic, Mirjana.
  1984. "Birds of Passage Are Also Women." *International Migration Review* 18, no.
  4: 886–907.

Morris, David.
1979.   *Measuring the Condition of the World's Poor: The Physical Quality of Life Index.* New York: Pergamon Press.

1996.   *Market Power and Business Strategies.* Westport, Conn.: Quorum Books.

Morse, Bradford, and Thomas Berger.
1992.   *Sardar Sarovar: Report of the Independent Review.* Ottawa: Resource for the Future International.

Moya, E. Antonio de, et al.
1992.   "Sosua Sanky-Pankies and Female Sex Workers." Instituto de Sexualidad Humana, Universidad Autonoma de Santo Domingo.

Mulgan, G. J.
1991.   *Communication and Control: Networks and the New Economies of Communication.* New York: Guilford Press.

Muller, Thomas, and Thomas Espenshade.
1985.   *The Fourth Wave: California's Newest Immigrants.* Washington, D.C.: Urban Institute Press.

Mullings, Beverly.
1999.   "Globalization, Tourism and the International Sex Trade." In *Sun, Sex and Gold: Tourism and Sex Work in the Caribbean,* edited by Kamala Kempadoo. Boulder, Colo.: Rowman & Littlefield.

Murphy, S. D.
1996.   *Humanitarian Intervention: The United Nations in an Evolving World Order.* Philadelphia: University of Pennsylvania Press.

Muzaffar, Chandra.
1993.   *Human Rights and World Order.* Penang, Malaysia: Just World Trust.

Myrdal, Gunnar.
1944.   *An American Dilemma: The Negro Problem and Modern Democracy.* New York: Harper & Bros.

Nadelman, Ethan.
1990.   "Global Prohibition Regimes: The Evolution of Norms in International Society." *International Organization* 44, no. 4 (Autumn): 479–526.

Nader, Ralph, and Lori Wallach.
1996.   "GATT, NAFTA, and the Subversion of the Democratic Process." In *The Case against the Global Economy and for a Turn toward the Local,* edited by Jerry Mander and Edward Goldsmith, 92–107. San Francisco: Sierra Club, 1996.

Nakano Glenn, Evelyn.
2000.   "Citizenship and Inequality: Historical and Global Perspectives." *Social Problems* 47, no. 1 (February): 1–20.

Nanda, V. P., et al.
1998.   "Tragedies in Somalia, Yugoslavia, Haiti, Rwanda and Liberia: Revisiting the Validity of Humanitarian Intervention Under International Law, Part II." *Denver Journal of International Law and Policy* 26, no. 5: 827–68.

National Labor Committee.
    1998.   *The People's Right to Know.* Brochure.

Nieburg, H. L.
    1969.   *Political Violence: The Behavioral Process.* New York: St. Martin's Press.

Nosotras tambien tenemos derechos.
    1997.   Santo Domingo, Dominican Republic: Centro de Orientación e Investigación Integral (COIN).

Nye, Joseph S.
    1971.   *Peace in Parts: Integration and Conflict in Regional Organization.* Boston: Little, Brown.

Nye, Joseph S., Jr., and Robert O. Keohane.
    1970.   *Transnational Relations and World Politics.* Boston: Harvard University Press.

O'Connell Davidson, Julia, and Jacqueline Sánchez Taylor.
    1996.   *Child Prostitution and Sex Tourism in the Dominican Republic.* Bangkok: ECPAT International.

O'Donnell, Guillermo.
    1994.   "Delegative Democracy." *Journal of Democracy* 5, no. 1 (January): 155.

Olson, Elizabeth.
    1999.   "China Tries to Fend Off U.N. Censure over Rights." *New York Times,* 21 March, 9.

Olson, Mancur.
    1965.   *The Logic of Collective Action.* Cambridge, Mass.: Harvard University Press.

Ong, Aihwa.
    1999.   *Flexible Citizenship: The Cultural Logics of Transnationality.* Durham, N.C.: Duke University Press.

Onuf, Nicholas.
    1997.   "A Constructivist Manifesto." In *Constituting International Political Economy,* edited by Kurt Burch and Robert A. Denemark, 7–17. Boulder, Colo.: Lynne Rienner.

Onuf, Nicholas, and Frank Klink.
    1989.   "Anarchy, Authority, Rule." *International Studies Quarterly* 33, no. 2 (June): 149.

Opaso, Christian.
    1998.   "The Bío-Bío Hydroelectric Project: Statement by Elías Díaz Peña to the World Bank Board of Executive Directors, Washington, D.C., February 3, 1998." Accessible at www.igc.apc.org/ciel.

Ortiz, Vilma.
    1996.   "The Mexican-Origin Population: Permanent Working Class or Emerging Middle Class?" In *Ethnic Los Angeles,* edited by Roger Waldinger and Mehdi Bozorgmehr. New York: Russell Sage Foundation.

Osaghae, Eghosa E.
    1995.   "The Ogoni Uprising: Oil Politics, Minority Agitation and the Future of the Nigerian State." *African Affairs* 94: 325–44.

Palma, Gabriel.
1977.   "Dependency: A Formal Theory of Underdevelopment or a Methodology for the Analysis of Concrete Situations of Underdevelopment?" *World Development* 6 (July–August): 881–924.

Panitch, Leo.
1994.   "Globalisation and the State." In *Between Globalism and Nationalism: Socialist Register, 1994,* edited by Ralph Miliband and Leo Panitch. London: Merlin Press.

Paolini, A. J., A. P. Jarvis, and C. Reus-Smith.
1998.   *Between Sovereignty and Global Governance: The United Nations, States and Civil Society.* New York: St. Martin's Press.

Park, Han S.
1987.   "Correlates of Human Rights: Global Tendencies." *Human Rights Quarterly* 9: 405–13.

Pateman, Carole.
1988.   *The Sexual Contract.* Stanford, Calif.: Stanford University Press.

Perkins, Nancy L.
1999.   "Introductory Note, World Trade Organization Appellate Body, United States—Import Prohibition of Certain Shrimp and Shrimp Products (12 October 1998)." 38 International Legal Materials 118.

Perry, Michael J.
1997.   "Are Human Rights Universal? The Relativist Challenge and Related Matters." *Human Rights Quarterly* 19, no. 3 (August): 461–509.

1998.   *The Idea of Human Rights: Four Inquiries.* New York: Oxford University Press.

Peters, Julie, and Andrea Wolper, eds.
1995.   *Women's Rights, Human Rights.* New York: Routledge.

Pheterson, Gayle, ed.
1989.   *A Vindication of the Rights of Whores: The International Struggle for Prostitutes' Rights.* Seattle: Seal Press.

Phillips, Michael.
1999.   "The World Bank May Curb Power of Its Watchdog." *Wall Street Journal,* 12 January, A2.

Pincetl, S.
1994.   "Challenges to Citizenship: Latino Immigrants and Political Organizing in the Los Angeles Area." *Environment and Planning A* 26: 895–914.

Placencia, Luchy.
1997.   "Estima fracasaría plan zonas de tolerancia." *Ultima Hora* (Santo Domingo, Dominican Republic), 13 July, 51.

Poe, Steven C., and C. Neal Tate.
1994.   "Repression of Human Rights to Personal Integrity in the 1980s: A Global Analysis." *American Political Science Review* 88: 853–72.

Poe, Steven, Neal Tate, Linda Camp Keith, and Drew Lanier.
2000.   "Domestic Threats: The Abuse of Personal Integrity." In *Paths to State*

Repression: Human Rights Violations and Contentious Politics, edited by Christian Davenport. Lanham, Md.: Rowman & Littlefield.

Poon, Auliana.
1990. "Flexible Specialization and Small Size: The Case of Caribbean Tourism." *World Development* 18, no. 1: 109–23.

Portes, Alejandro, and Richard Schauffler.
1993. "Competing Perspectives on the Latin American Informal Sector." *Population and Development Review* 19, no. 1 (March): 33–60.

Price, Richard.
1998. "Reversing the Gun Sights: Transnational Civil Society Targets Land Mines." *International Organization* 52, no. 3 (Summer): 613–44.

Princen, Thomas, and Matthias Finger.
1994. *Environmental NGOs in World Politics: Linking the Local and the Global.* New York: Routledge.

1996. "Prostitutas piden mayor participación social." *Nuevo El Diario,* 18 December, 12.

Quinn, Dennis.
1997. "The Correlates of Change in International Financial Regulation." *American Political Science Review* 91: 531–51.

Rasler, Karen.
1986. "War, Accommodation and Violence in the United States, 1890–1970." *American Political Science Review* 80, no. 3 (September).

Ray, Larry J.
1993. *Rethinking Critical Theory: Emancipation in the Age of Global Social Movements.* London: Sage.

Raynolds, Laura T.
1998. "Harnessing Women's Work: Restructuring Agricultural and Industrial Labor Forces in the Dominican Republic." *Economic Geography* 74, no. 2 (April): 149–69.

1999. "The Real Losers [at the World Trade Organization Meeting in Seattle]." *Economist,* 11 December, 15.

Reich, Robert B.
1991a. "Secession of the Successful." *New York Times,* 20 January, sec. 6, 16, 42.

1991b. *The Work of Nations: Preparing Ourselves for 21st-Century Capitalism.* New York: Knopf.

Reimers, David.
1998. "The Immigration Debate." *Journal of American Ethnic History* 17, no. 3 (Spring): 87.

Reus-Smit, Christian.
1997. "The Constitutional Structure of International Society and the Nature of Fundamental Institutions." *International Organization* 51, no. 4 (Autumn): 555–89.

Rich, Bruce.
  1994. *Mortgaging the Earth: The World Bank, Environmental Impoverishment, and the Crisis of Development.* Boston: Beacon Press.

  1999. "The Smile on a Child's Face: From the Culture of Loan Approval to the Culture of Development Effectiveness? The World Bank under James Wolfensohn." Paper presented at Northwestern University.

Richard, Amy O'Neill.
  1999. *International Trafficking in Women to the United States: A Contemporary Manifestation of Slavery and Organized Crime.* Center for the Study of Intelligence.

Rickard, Stephen.
  1998. "Religion and Global Affairs: Repression and Response." *SAIS Review,* Summer, 52–58.

Rieff, David.
  1995. *Slaughterhouse: Bosnia and the Failure of the West.* New York: Simon & Schuster.

Risse, Thomas, Stephen C. Ropp, and Kathryn Sikkink, eds.
  1999. *The Power of Human Rights: International Norms and Domestic Change.* Cambridge: Cambridge University Press.

Risse-Kappen, Thomas, ed.
  1995. *Bringing Transnational Relations Back In: Non-State Actors, Domestic Structures, and International Institutions.* Cambridge: Cambridge University Press.

Ritzer, George. [1993]
  1996. *The McDonaldization of Society: An Investigation into the Changing Character of Contemporary Social Life.* Rev. ed. Thousand Oaks, Calif.: Pine Forge Press.

Rivera-Salgado, Gaspar.
  1999. "Comparative Analysis of Migration and Political Activism Among Mexican Indigenous Communities: The Experience of Mixtecs, Zapotecs, and Purepechas across the U.S.-Mexican Border." Ph.D. Diss., University of California, Santa Cruz.

Robertson, Roland.
  1992. *Globalization: Social Theory and Global Culture.* London: Sage.

  1995. "Glocalization: Time-Space and Homogeneity/Heterogeneity." In *Global Modernities,* edited by Mike Featherstone, Scott Lash, and Roland Robertson, 25–44. Thousand Oaks, Calif.: Sage Publications.

Robinson, Fiona.
  1999. *Globalizing Care: Ethics, Feminist Theory, and International Relations.* Boulder, Colo., Colorado: Westview Press.

Rodman, Kenneth.
  1998. "'Think Globally, Punish Locally': Nonstate Actors, Multinational Corporations, and Human Rights Sanctions." *Ethics and International Affairs* 12: 19–42.

Rodrik, Dani.
  1997. *Has Globalization Gone Too Far?* Washington, D.C.: Institute for International Economics.

Romero, Mary.
    1992.   *Maid in the U.S.A.* New York: Routledge, 1992.

Ronfeldt, David, John Arquilla, Graham E. Fuller, and Melissa Fuller.
    1998.   *The Zapatista "Social Netwar" in Mexico.* R AND MR-994-A. Available at http://www.rand.org. Santa Monica, Calif.: R AND.

Rosenau, James N.
    1973.   *The Drama of Politics: An Introduction to the Joys of Inquiry.* Boston: Little, Brown.
    1983.   "'Fragmegrative' Challenges to National Security." In *Understanding U.S. Strategy: A Reader,* edited by Terry Heyns, 65–82. Washington, D.C.: National Defense University.
    1990.   *Turbulence in World Politics: A Theory of Change and Continuity.* Princeton, N.J.: Princeton University Press.
    1992.   "The Relocation of Authority in a Shrinking World." *Comparative Politics* 24 (April): 253–72.
    1993.   "Environmental Challenges in a Global Context." In *Environmental Politics in the International Arena: Movements, Parties, Organizations, and Policy,* edited by Sheldon Kamieniecki, 257–74. Albany, N.Y.: State University of New York Press.
    1994.   "New Dimensions of Security: The Interaction of Globalizing and Localizing Dynamics." *Security Dialogue* 25 (September): 255–82.
    1997.   *Along the Domestic-Foreign Frontier: Exploring Governance in a Turbulent World.* Cambridge: Cambridge University Press.

Rosenau, James N., and W. Michael G. Fagen.
    1997.   "Increasingly Skillful Citizens: A New Dynamism in World Affairs?" *International Studies Quarterly* 41 (December): 655–86.

Rosenau, James N., and Ernst Otto-Czempiel, eds.
    1992.   *Governance without Government: Order and Change in World Politics.* Cambridge: Cambridge University Press.

Rosh, Robert.
    1986.   "The Impact of Third World Defense Burdens on Basic Human Needs." *Policy Studies Journal* 15: 135–46.

Rothman, Franklin Daniel, and Pamela E. Oliver.
    1999.   "From Local to Global: The Anti-Dam Movement in Southern Brazil, 1979–1992." *Mobilization: An International Journal* 4, no. 1: 41–57.

Rouse, Roger.
    1995.   "Questions of Identity: Personhood and Collectivity in Transnational Migration to the United States." *Critique of Anthropology* 15, no. 4: 351–80.

Rucht, Dieter.
    1993.   "Think Globally, Act Locally? Needs, Forms and Problems of Cross-National Cooperation among Environmental Groups." In *European Integration and Environmental Policy,* edited by J. D. Liefferink, P. D. Lowe, and A. P. J. Mol, 75–95. New York: Belhaven Press.

Ruggie, John Gerard.

1998.   *Constructing the World Polity: Essays on International Institutionalization.* New York: Routledge.

1999.   "What Makes the World Hang Together? Neo-Utilitarianism and the Social Constructivist Challenge." In *Exploration and Contestation in the Study of World Politics,* edited by Peter J. Katzenstein, Robert O. Keohane, and Stephen D. Krasner. Cambridge, Mass.: MIT Press.

Sachs, Aaron.

1995.   *Eco-Justice: Linking Human Rights and the Environment.* Worldwatch Paper no. 127. Washington, D.C.: Worldwatch Institute.

Sadasivam, Bharati.

1997.   "The Impact of Structural Adjustment on Women: A Governance and Human Rights Agenda." *Human Rights Quarterly* 19: 630–65.

Safa, Helen.

1995.   *The Myth of the Male Breadwinner: Women and Industrialization in the Caribbean.* Boulder, Colo.: Westview Press.

Salamon, Lester M.

1994.   "The Global Associational Revolution: The Rise of the Third Sector on the World Scene." *Foreign Affairs* 73 (July–August): 109–22.

Salas, Sonia.

1996.   "Definición de conceptos." In *Memorias: 1er. Congreso Democrático de las Trabajadores Sexuales.* Dominican Republic: Imprenta La Union.

Sanchez, George J.

1997.   "Face the Nation: Race, Immigration, and the Rise of Nationalism in Late Twentieth Century America." *International Migration Review* 31, no. 4: 1009–30.

Sanford, Jonathan.

1988.   "U.S. Policy towards the MDBs: The Role of Congress." *George Washington Journal of International Law and Economics* 1.

Sanger, David.

1999.   "China to Get World Bank Loans Despite US Objections." *New York Times,* 25 June.

Saro-Wiwa, Ken.

1983.   *First Letter to Ogoni Youth.* Port Harcourt, Nigeria: Saros International.

1995.   *A Month and a Day: A Detention Diary.* New York: Penguin Books.

Sassen, Saskia.

1988.   *The Mobility of Labor and Capital.* Cambridge: Cambridge University Press.

1996.   *Losing Control?: Sovereignty in an Age of Globalization.* New York: Columbia University Press.

1998.   *Globalization and Its Discontents.* New York: New Press.

1999.   *Guests and Aliens.* New York: New Press.

Schmidt, Hilmar.

2000.   "Time to Change: States as Problems or Problem-Solvers in World Society?" In *Civilizing World Politics: Society and Community Beyond the State,* edited by Albert Mathias, Lothar Brock, and Klaus Dieter Wolf, 167–78. Lanham, Md.: Rowman & Littlefield.

Schmidt, Hilmar, and Ingo Take.
    2000.   "Democratization without Representation." In *Civilizing World Politics: Society and Community Beyond the State,* edited by Mathias Albert, Lothar Brock, and Klaus Dieter Wolf, 169–78. Lanham, Md.: Rowman & Littlefield.

Schmitter, Philippe C.
    2000.   *How to Democratize the European Union . . . and Why Bother?* Lanham, Md.: Rowman & Littlefield.

Scholte, Jan Aart.
    1996a.   "Beyond the Buzzword: Towards a Critical Theory of Globalization." In *Globalization: Theory and Practice,* edited by Eleonore Kofman and Gillian Youngs, 43–57. London: Pinter.

    1996b.   "Globalization and Collective Identities." In *Identities in International Relations,* edited by Jill Krause and Neil Renwick, 38–78. New York: St. Martin's Press.

    1997.   "The Globalization of World Politics." In *The Globalization of World Politics: An Introduction to International Relations,* edited by John Baylis and Steve Smith, 13–30. New York: Oxford University Press.

Schuck, Peter H., and Rogers M. Smith.
    1985.   *Citizenship without Consent: Illegal Aliens in the American Polity.* New Haven, Conn.: Yale University Press.

Scully, Gerald.
    1988.   "The Institutional Framework and Economic Growth." *Journal of Political Economy* 96: 652–62.

Sen, Amartya.
    1999.   "Human Rights and Economic Achievement." In *The East Asian Challenge for Human Rights,* edited by Joanne R. Bauer and Daniel A. Bell, 88–99. New York: Cambridge University Press.

Sen, Jai.
    1999a.   "Of Mushrooms That Bloom: Critical Intersections in Washington D.C.—or, Why the World Bank's Inspection Panel Is Important to All of Us." MS.

    1999b.   "A World to Win—But Whose World Is It, Anyway?" In *Civil Society, the United Nations, and the Multilateral Future,* edited by John Foster and Anita Anand. Ottawa: United Nations Association in Canada.

Señor, Luis.
    1989.   *Codigo penal dominicano anotado, 1865–1985.* Santo Domingo: Empresion Editoria Union.

Shannon, Amy.
    1999.   "Reform of International Finance and Trade: Investing in a Sustainable Future." *In Focus* 2, no. 2 (May).

Shaw, Martin.
　1994.　*Global Society and International Relations.* Cambridge: Polity Press.
　1999.　"Global Voices: Civil Society and the Media in Global Crises." In *Human Rights in Global Politics,* edited by Tim Dunne and Nicholas J. Wheeler, 214–32. Cambridge: Cambridge University Press.

Shihata, Ibrahim F. I.
　1994.　*The World Bank Inspection Panel.* Oxford: Oxford University Press for the World Bank.

Shklar, Judith.
　1991.　*American Citizenship: The Quest for Inclusion.* Cambridge, Mass.: Harvard University Press.

Shue, Henry.
　1980.　*Basic Rights: Subsistence, Affluence, and U.S. Foreign Policy.* Princeton, N.J.: Princeton University Press.

Sikkink, Kathryn.
　1993.　"Human Rights, Principled Issue–Networks, and Sovereignty in Latin America." *International Organization* 47, no. 3 (Summer): 411–41.

Silvestre, Emmanuel, Jaime Rijo, and Huberto Bogaert.
　1994.　*La neo-prostitución infantil en República Dominicana.* Santo Domingo: UNICEP/ONOPLAN.

Simma, Bruno, and Philip Alston.
　1992.　"The Sources of Human Rights Law: Custom, Jus Cogens, and General Principles." *Australian Year Book of International Law* 12: 82–108.

Skocpol, Theda.
　1979.　*States and Social Revolutions.* New York: Cambridge University Press.

Small, Melvin, and J. David Singer.
　1982.　*Resort to Arms: International and Civil Wars, 1816–1980.* Beverly Hills, Calif.: Sage Publications.

Smith, Jackie.
　1997.　"Characteristics of the Modern Transnational Social Movement Sector." In *Transnational Social Movements and Global Politics: Solidarity beyond the State,* edited by Jackie Smith, Charles Chatfield, and Ron Pagnucco. Syracuse, N.Y.: Syracuse University Press.

Smith, Jackie, Charles Chatfield, and Ron Pagnucco, eds.
　1997.　*Transnational Social Movements and Global Politics: Solidarity beyond the State.* Syracuse, N.Y.: Syracuse University Press, 1997.

Smith, Jackie, Ron Pagnucco, and George A. Lopez.
　1998.　"Globalizing Human Rights: The Work of Transnational Human Rights NGOs in the 1990s." *Human Rights Quarterly* 20, no. 2 (May): 379–412.

Smith, Michael Peter, and Luis Eduardo Guarnizo, eds.
　1998.　*Transnationalism from Below.* New Brunswick, N.J.: Transaction Publishers.

Smith, Rogers M.
　1993.　"Beyond Tocqueville, Myrdal, and Hartz: The Multiple Traditions in America." *American Political Science Review* 87, no. 3: 549–67.

1997.   *Civic Ideals: Conflicting Visions of Citizenship in U.S. History.* New Haven, Conn.: Yale University Press.

Snow, David A., and Robert D. Benford.
   1992.   "Master Frames and Cycles of Protest." In *Frontiers in Social Movement Theory,* edited by Aldon D. Morris and Carol McClurg Mueller. New Haven, Conn.: Yale University Press.

Solinger, Dorothy J.
   1995.   "China's Urban Transients in the Transition from Socialism." *Comparative Politics* 27, no. 2 (January): 127–46.

Solomon, Jay.
   1999.   "Fearing Misuse, World Bank Delays Funds for Indonesia." *Wall Street Journal,* 13 April.

Sorensen, Georg.
   2000.   "States Are Not 'Like Units': Types of State and Forms of Anarchy in the Present International System." In *Civilizing World Politics: Society and Community Beyond the State,* edited by Mathias Albert, Lothar Brock, and Klaus Dieter Wolf, 103–18. Lanham, Md.: Rowman & Littlefield, 2000.

Soysal, Yasemin.
   1994.   *Limits of Citizenship: Migrants and Postnational Membership in Europe.* Chicago: University of Chicago Press.

Spalding, Nancy L.
   1985.   "Providing for Economic Human Rights: The Case of the Third World." *Policy Studies Journal* 15: 123–34.

Spar, Debora L.
   1998.   "The Spotlight on the Bottom Line: How Multinationals Export Human Rights (Child Labor and Sweatshop Abuses by Foreign Contractors of American Corporations)." *Foreign Affairs* 77, no. 2 (March–April): 7–12.

   1999.   "Foreign Investment and Human Rights (International Lessons)." *Challenge,* January–February, 55–56.

Spivak, Gayatri Chakravorty.
   1999.   *A Critique of Postcolonial Reason: Toward a History of the Vanishing Present.* Cambridge, Mass.: Harvard University Press.

Stahler-Sholk, Richard.
   1994.   "El Salvador's Negotiated Transition: From Low-Intensity Conflict to Low-Intensity Democracy." *Journal of Interamerican Studies and World Affairs* 36, no. 4 (Winter): 1–59.

Steinberg, Don.
   1988.   "Panamanians Use Technology to Balk Censor." *New York Times,* 14 February, 13.

Steinberg, J. B.
   1993.   "International Involvement in the Yugoslavia Conflict." In *Enforcing Restraint: Collective Intervention in Internal Conflicts,* edited by L. F. Damrosch, 27–75. New York: Council on Foreign Relations Press.

Stephens, Beth, and Michael Ratner.
　1996.　*International Human Rights Litigation in U.S. Courts.* Irvington-on-Hudson, N.Y.: Transnational Publishers.

Stewart, Frances, and Albert Berry.
　1999.　"Globalization, Liberalization, and Inequality: Expectations and Experience." In *Inequality, Globalization, and World Politics,* edited by Andrew Hurrell and Ngaire Woods, 150–86. New York: Oxford University Press.

Stiglmayer, A., ed.
　1994.　*Mass Rape: The War against Women in Bosnia-Herzegovina.* Lincoln: University of Nebraska Press.

Stohl, Michael.
　1987.　"Outside of a Small Circle of Friends: States, Genocide, Mass Killing and the Role of Bystanders." *Journal of Peace Research* 24, no. 2 (June): 151–66.

Stohl, Michael, et al.
　1986.　"State Violation of Human Rights: Issues and Problems of Measurement." *Human Rights Quarterly* 8: 592–606.

Stohl, Michael, and George A. Lopez, eds.
　1986.　*Government Violence and Repression: An Agenda for Research.* Westport, Conn.: Greenwood Press.

Stolcke, Verena.
　1999.　"New Rhetorics of Exclusion in Europe." *International Social Science Journal* 159: 25–36.

Stone, Deborah.
　1997.　*Policy Paradox: The Art of Political Decision Making.* New York: Norton.

Strange, Susan.
　1998.　*The Retreat of the State: The Diffusion of Power in the World Economy.* Cambridge: Cambridge Studies in International Relations.

Streeten, Paul.
　1981.　*First Things First: Meeting Basic Human Needs in Developing Countries.* New York: Oxford University Press.

Stromseth, J. E.
　1993.　"Iraq's Repression of Its Civilian Population: Collective Responses and Continuing Challenges." In *Enforcing Restraint: Collective Intervention in Internal Conflicts,* edited by L. F. Damrosch, 77–117. New York: Council on Foreign Relations Press.

Stuckelberger, C., and Egger.
　1996.　"A Social Clause with a TNC: The Migros–Del Monte Case." *Focal Point,* March.

Sullivan, Donna.
　1995.　"The Public/Private Distinction in International Human Rights Law." In *Women's Rights, Human Rights: International Feminist Perspectives,* edited by Julie Peters and Andrea Wolper, 126–34. New York: Routledge.

Sutcliffe, Bob.
　1998.　"Freedom to Move in the Age of Globalization." In *Globalization and Pro-*

gressive Economic Policy, edited by Dean Baker, Gerald Epstein, and Robert Pollin, 325–36. Cambridge: Cambridge University Press.

Swepston, Lee.
    1998. "International Labour Conference: ILO Declaration on Fundamental Principles and Rights at Work and Annex, Introductory Note." 37 International Legal Materials 1233.

Tai, Susan H. C., and Y. H. Wong.
    1998. "Advertising Decision Making in Asia: "Glocal" Versus "Regcal" Approach." *Journal of Managerial Issues* 10 (Fall): 318–39.

Tamayo, Juan O. T.
    1997. "Turistas viajan a Dominicana en busca de prostitución." *El Nuevo Herald* (Miami), 24 June.

Tan, Kevin Y. L.
    1999. "Economic Development, Legal Reform, and Rights in Singapore and Taiwan." In *The East Asian Challenge for Human Rights,* edited by Joanne R. Bauer and Daniel A. Bell, 264–84. New York: Cambridge University Press.

Tarrow, Sidney.
    1998. *Power in Movement: Social Movements and Contentious Politics.* 2d ed. Cambridge: Cambridge University Press.

Taylor, Co.
    1998. "Linkage and Rule-Making: Observations on Trade and Investment and Trade and Labor." *University of Pennsylvania Journal of International Economics* 19, no. 639.

Tesón, F. R.
    1997. *Humanitarian Intervention: An Inquiry into Law and Morality.* Irvington-on-Hudson, N.Y.: Transnational Publishers.

Tharoor, Shashi.
    1999. "The Future of Civil Conflict." *World Policy Journal* 16 (Spring).

Tilly, Charles.
    1978. *From Mobilization to Revolution.* Reading, Mass.: Addison-Wesley.

    1984. *Big Structures, Large Processes, and Huge Comparisons.* New York: Russell Sage Foundation.

Touraine, Alain.
    1988. *Return of the Actor: Social Theory in Postindustrial Society.* Minneapolis: University of Minnesota Press.

Treakle, Kay.
    1998a. "Accountability at the World Bank: What Does It Take? Lessons from the Yacyreta Hydroelectric Project, Argentina/Paraguay." Annual Meeting of the Latin American Studies Association, Chicago.

    1998b. "Ecuador: Structural Adjustment and Indigenous and Environmentalist Resistance." In *The Struggle for Accountability: The World Bank, NGOs and Grassroots Movements,* edited by Jonathan Fox and L. David Brown, 219–64. Cambridge, Mass.: MIT Press.

1999.   "The World Bank and Human Rights: Obligations, Impacts and Rhetoric."
Paper prepared for the International Human Rights Internship Program.

Truong, Than Dam.
1990.   *Sex, Money, and Morality*. London: Zed Books.

Tunsarawuth, Sirfah.
1996.   "ASEAN to Block Linking Social Clauses to Trade." *Straits Times* (Singapore), 24 April, 17.

Tweedale, Douglas.
1988.   "Noriega Faced with High Tech Opposition." *UPI* 3 (March).

Udall, Lori.
1997.   *The World Bank Inspection Panel: A Three Year Review*. Washington, D.C.: Bank Information Center.

1998.   "The World Bank and Public Accountability: Has Anything Changed?" In *The Struggle for Accountability: The World Bank, NGOs and Grassroots Movements*, edited by Jonathan Fox and L. David Brown, 391–436. Cambridge, Mass.: MIT Press.

Umaña, Alvaro.
1998.   "Foreword." In *The World Bank Inspection Panel: The First Four Years (1994–1998)*, edited by Alvaro Umaña. Washington, D.C.: World Bank.

United Kingdom. Colonial Office. [1958]
1996.   *Nigeria: Report of the Commission Appointed to Enquire into the Fears of Minorities and the Means of Allaying Them* [Willink Commission Report]. Reprint. London: HMSO; Port Harcourt, Nigeria: Southern Minorities Movement.

United States. Bureau of International Labor Affairs.
1996.   *The Apparel Industry and Codes of Conduct: A Solution to The International Child Labor Problem?* Washington, D.C.: U.S. Dept. of Labor, Bureau of International Labor Affairs.

Upton, Barbara.
1999.   "Formulating U.S. Policy toward the World Bank: Meeting the Challenges of the Twenty-First Century." Paper presented at Northwestern University.

2000.   *The Multilateral Development Banks: Improving U.S. Leadership*. Westport, Conn.: Praeger; Washington, D.C.: Center for Strategic and International Studies.

Vanderpool, Tim.
1995.   "The Borderless Bordello." *UTNE Reader*, no. 72 (November–December): 30–34.

Vanhanen, Tatu.
1990.   *The Process of Democratization: A Comparative Study of 147 States, 1980–88*. New York: Crane Russak.

Vayrynen, Raimo, ed.
1999.   *Globalization and Global Governance*. Lanham, Md.: Rowman & Littlefields.

Velásquez, Kelly.
1997.   "Campaña contra turismo sexual de menores." *El Nacional*, 9 July.

Vernon, Raymond.
  1971.   *Sovereignty at Bay: The Multinational Spread of U.S. Enterprises.* New York: Basic Books.

Vianna, Aurelio.
  1997.   "The Process of Request of Inspection Panel of World Bank for the Itaparica Project (Brazil), A Preliminary Evaluation." Forum '97: New Linkages in Conservation and Development, Istanbul.

  1998a.   "The Panel Inspection Request as a Process and Not a Result: A Preliminary Evaluation from the Itaparica (Brazil) Case." Annual Meeting of the Latin American Studies Association, Chicago.

  1998b.   "Statement by Aurelio Vianna (Rede Brasil) to the World Bank Board of Executive Directors, Washington, D.C., February 3, 1998." Accessible at www.ciel.org.

Vincent, R. J.
  1974.   *Nonintervention and International Order.* Princeton, N.J.: Princeton University Press.

Wade, Robert.
  1997.   "Greening the World Bank: The Struggle Over the Environment, 1970–1995." In *The World Bank: Its First Half-Century,* edited by Devesh Kapur, John P. Lewis, and Richard Webb. Washington, D.C.: Brookings Institution.

Waldmeier, Patti, and Mark Suzman.
  1997.   "World Bank 'Fails to Learn from Past Mistakes.'" *Financial Times,* 14 December.

Wallace, Rebecca.
  1997.   *International Human Rights: Text and Materials.* London: Sweet & Maxwell.

Wallerstein, Immanuel.
  1974.   "The Rise and Future Demise of the World Capitalist System." *Comparative Studies in Society and History* 16 (September): 387–415.

Walzer, Michael.
  1983.   *Spheres of Justice: A Defense of Pluralism and Equality.* New York: Basic Books.

Wang, Hongying, and James N. Rosenau.
  1999.   "Combating Corruption Globally." International Institutions: Global Processes–Domestic Consequences Conference sponsored by the Center for International Studies. Duke University, Durham, N.C., 9 April.

Wapner, Paul.
  1995.   "Politics beyond the State: Environmental Activism and World Politics." *World Politics* 47, no. 3 (April): 311–40.

  1996.   *Environmental Activism and World Civic Politics.* Albany: State University of New York Press.

Waslin, Michele.
  1998.   "Who Are the Regime Takers? An Analysis of the International Human Rights Regime." Annual Meeting of the American Political Science Association, Boston, 3–6 September.

Watkins, Kevin.
   1997.   "Globalisation and Liberalisation: Implications for Poverty, Distribution and Inequality." In *Human Development Report.* United Nations Development Programme Occasional Paper 32.

Watson, J. L., ed.
   1997.   *Golden Arches East: McDonald's in East Asia.* Stanford, Calif.: Stanford University Press.

Webster, Craig.
   1994.   "Human Rights Practices and International Relations Theory." Ph.D. diss., State University of New York at Binghampton.

Weiss, Thomas, et al.
   1997.   *Civilian Pain and Political Gain: Assessing the Humanitarian Impact of Economic Sanctions.* Lanham, Md.: Rowman & Littlefield.

Welch, Claude E., Jr.
   1995.   "The Ogoni and Self-Determination: Increasing Violence in Nigeria." *Journal of Modern African Studies* 33, no. 4: 635–50.

Welch, Claude E., Jr., and Marc Sills.
   1996.   "The Martyrdom of Ken Saro-Wiwa and the Future of Ogoni Self-Determination." *Fourth World Bulletin* 5, no. 1–2: 5–21.

Wendt, Alexander.
   1999.   *Social Theory of International Politics.* Cambridge: Cambridge University Press.

Weston, Burns H., Richard A. Falk, and Hilary Charlesworth, eds.
   1997.   *Supplement of Basic Documents to International Law and World Order.* 3d ed. St. Paul, Minn.: West Pub.

Weyker, Shayne.
   1996.   "Kayapo Spin Doctors and Truth Commission Computer Programmers: New Information Technology and Progressive Social Movements." Working Paper, Harrison Program on the Future Global Agenda.

   1997.   "New Information Technology and the Third World: The Major Debates." Postmodern Culture, Global Capitalism, and Democratic Action: The Couch-Stone Symposium. University of Maryland, College Park, 11 April.

Wijers, Marjan, and Lap-Chew Lin.
   1997.   "Trafficking in Women," *WIN News* 23, no. 4 (Autumn): 27.

Willetts, Peter, ed.
   1982.   *Pressure Groups in the Global System.* New York: St. Martin's Press.

   1996.   *The Conscience of the World: The Influence of Non-Governmental Organizations in the UN System.* London: Hurst.

Williams, Patrick, and Laura Chrisman, eds.
   1994.   *Colonial Discourse and Post-Colonial Theory: A Reader.* New York: Columbia University Press.

Winerip, Michael.
   2000.   "The Global Willowbrook." *New York Times Magazine,* 16 January, 58.

Wippman, D.

    1993. "Enforcing the Peace: ECOWAS and the Liberian Civil War." In *Enforcing Restraint: Collective Intervention in Internal Conflicts,* edited by L. F. Damrosch, 157–203. New York: Council on Foreign Relations Press.

Wittes, Tamara Coffnan.

    1997. "Mass Refugee Flows: What Challenges for State Sovereignty and Human Rights?" Paper presented at the Annual Meeting of the International Studies Association, Toronto, 18–23 March.

Wolfsfeld, Gadi.

    1997. *Media and Political Conflict: News from the Middle East.* Cambridge: Cambridge University Press.

Woodward, K.

    1996. "Neo-Colonialism, Labor Rights, and the 'Growth Triangle' of Indonesia, Malaysia and Singapore: Who Will Protect the 'Hinterland' and Indonesia's Workers?" *Dickeson Journal of International Law* 15, no. 171.

World Bank.

    1992. *Effective Implementation: Key to Development Impact.* Washington, D.C.: World Bank, Portfolio Management Task Force. Widely known as the Wapenhans report, after its principal author, the World Bank's Vice President Willi Wapenhans.

    1994. *Resettlement and Development: The Bankwide Review of Projects Involving Involuntary Resettlement, 1986–1993.* Washington, D.C.: World Bank, Environment Department.

    1998. *Recent Experience with Involuntary Resettlement, Brazil—Itaparica.* Report No. 17538. Washington, D.C.: World Bank, Operations Evaluation Department.

    2000. *World Development Report, 2000/2001: Attacking Poverty.* New York: Oxford University Press for the World Bank.

CONTRIBUTORS

Clifford Bob is Assistant Professor of Political Science, Duquesne University.

Alison Brysk is Associate Professor of Politics at the University of California, Irvine.

Amalia Lucia Cabezas is Assistant Professor of Women's Studies at the University of California, Riverside.

Jack Donnelly is Andrew W. Mellon Professor, Graduate School of International Studies, University of Denver.

Richard Falk is Albert G. Milbank Professor of International Law and Practice and Professor of Politics and International Affairs at Princeton University.

Jonathan Fox is Professor and Chair of Latin American and Latino Studies, University of California, Santa Cruz.

Kristen Hill Maher is Assistant Professor of Political Science at San Diego State University.

Wesley T. Milner is Assistant Professor of Political Science, University of Evansville.

Raul C. Pangalangan is Professor and Dean of the School of Law, University of the Philippines.

James N. Rosenau is University Professor of International Affairs, George Washington University.

Wayne Sandholtz is Associate Professor of Political Science, University of California, Irvine.

Shane Weyker is a doctoral candidate at the University of Maryland.

INDEX

accountability: legal, 2, 15, 149, 150, 244, 251; and MNCs, 66; of the World Bank, 172, 173–91; of the WTO, 62
AFL-CIO: and migrant workers, 34, 37
Africa, 135, 229; Central, 203, 208, 209, 211, 224; effects of globalization in, 5, 11, 14, 70, 164, 243, 245; West, 213–14
African Americans, 149
AIDS pandemic, 51, 57n16
Albania, 80
"aliens": and citizenship, 27, 31–32, 36; migrants as, 21, 22, 29–30, 39n14
Allende, Salvador, 92
Amar, Akhil Reed, 106
Amazon, 181, 182
American Association for the Advancement of Science, 118–19
American Friends Service Committee, 38n2
Americas Watch, 38n2
Amin, Idi, 211, 213
Amnesty International, 2, 70, 78, 83, 127, 134, 138, 143, 146n20, 151, 211
Amnesty International USA: Freedom Writers, 122–23
Angola: civil war in, 5
Annan, Kofi, 75n18
Annis, Sheldon, 125
Anti-Slavery International, 50–51
Anti-Terrorism Act, 20

apartheid: anti-apartheid movement, 135, 151
Argentina, 50, 124–25, 149, 164, 182; human rights movement, 117, 151
Arief, Andi, 123
Aristide, Jean-Bertrand, 211, 220, 222
armed intervention, 204; norms of, 202, 208–24, 236
ASEAN, 100
Asia, 135, 158, 229, 235
Asia, South: child labor in, 105
Asian Students Association, 123
Asociación de Mujeres por el Bienestar y Asistencia Recíproca (AMBAR), 50, 51–52
Asociación Pro-Derechos de la Mujer (APRODEM, "Angela Lina"), 50
assistance, humanitarian, 13
asylum: rights to, 24
Australia, 157, 189; and immigration, 23
Austria, 157, 215

Balibar, 42n32
Ball, Patrick, 123
Bangladesh, 182
Barkin, J. S., 207
Belarus, 235
Belgium, 215, 218

Benin, 235
Berlin Wall: crossings, deaths during, 2
Bhabha, Jacqueline, 25–26, 40n22
Block, Walter, 81
Bob, Clifford, 7, 9, 123–24
Bokassa, 211
Bosnia, 164, 209, 211; armed intervention
  in, 215–17, 221, 223, 224, 237
Boutros-Ghali, Boutros, 219
boycotts, 134
Bracero Program, 33–34
Brazil, 50, 137, 219, 220; and World Bank,
  182, 187–89, 194
Breyman, Steve, 121–22
British Broadcasting Corporation (BBC), 54
Buchanan, Pat, 30–31, 157
Burundi, 219
Bush, George, president, 217

California: citizen identity in, 27; immigrant
  labor in, 22, 35, 36; Proposition 187, 21,
  22
Cambodia, 209; human rights reform in, 2;
  state terrorism in, 80
Canada, 49; and immigration, 23; Inuit in,
  154
capital, international, 77, 80, 99, 100, 101
capitalism: and globalization, 7, 9–10, 77–
  97; and human rights, 64–74
Cardoso, Fernando Henrique, 188
Caribbean, 41n31, 44, 70; prostitution in, 3,
  48, 49, 54; sex worker organizations in,
  50–55
Center for Economic and Social Rights,
  75n21
Center for International Environmental
  Law, 188
Central America, 107
Centro de Orientación e Investigación
  Integral (COIN), 54–55
Chad-Cameroon pipeline, 173
Chechnya, 164, 204
Chentex, 253–54
Chiapas, 125. See also Zapatistas
Chile, 50, 64, 151; democracy in, 92,
  126–27
China, 203, 219, 220, 222, 252; democracy
  protests, 120; and the Internet, 120, 127;
  and market forces, 5, 12; migrant workers
  in, 10; rights violations, 68, 133, 136,
  235; and the World Bank, 182, 184, 189

Chinese Exclusion Act, 32, 42n35
Chirac, Jacques, 67
CIA, 64
citizenship, 14; accountability, 12; in the
  EU, 25–26; as exclusion, 26–32; "gap,"
  10–12, 14, 148, 246–47, 248, 249–50;
  global, 249–56; of migrants, 19–38; and
  rights, 229, 230–31, 238
class: and immigration, 23; and labor rights,
  106–07
Clinton, William, president, 101; and Haiti,
  221
"CNN effect," 201–02, 246
Coalition against Trafficking in Women,
  50, 52
Coalition for Humane Immigrant Rights
  of Los Angeles (CHIRLA), 43n42
Cold War, 13–14, 64–65, 66–67, 80, 226,
  229; and humanitarian intervention,
  202–03, 207–08, 209, 236, 237, 238
colonialism, 227; and migration, 22; and
  racial ideology, 32
Columbia, 50; civil conflict in, 9–10
commodification: and globalization, 7,
  12, 14
communication: and globalization, 12, 14–
  15, 16, 138, 145n13, 154–56, 226–28,
  233–35; and human rights, 77, 79–80,
  115–29, 139–46, 245
Congo, 209; civil war in, 5, 9–10
connection: and globalization, 6–7, 12
consensualism, 27–30
Constitution (U.S.): Fourteenth Amendment, 21; and John Locke, 28
corporations, multinational. See multinational corporations
cosmopolitan: dimension, and globalization,
  7, 13
Costa Rica, 50
Côte d'Ivoire, 214, 215
crime: and global markets, 4–5; and
  tourism, 45
Croatia: armed intervention in, 215–17
Cuba, 46, 64, 215, 220, 237; "aliens"
  from, 20
Cuban Missile Crisis, 227
Cutler, Claire, 238

Dalai Lama, 136
Dalton, 95n3
dam projects: and the World Bank, 180–82

Dan, Wang, 127
Danielson, Dan, 45
de Gaulle, Charles, 160
Del Monte, 108
democracy: and control of markets, 62; and
    globalization, 1, 4–5, 7, 62–63, 69, 71–
    74, 227; and human rights, 83–84, 88,
    92–93, 119, 126–27, 235, 255; and
    intervention, 210, 223, 224; "low-
    intensity," 12
Denmark, 215
deportation, 20
developing countries: foreign investment
    in, 100; labor rights in, 98, 104
development, economic, 84, 88, 227
"digital divide," 246, 252
dignity, human, 1
Doctors Without Borders, 2
Doe, Samuel, 213, 221
Dominican Republic: prostitution in, 14,
    44–50, 54, 56n2; tourism in, 46–50, 228
Donnelly, Jack, 8, 40n20, 207
drug trafficking: and repression, 9

East Timor, 2, 133, 145n1
Economic Community of West African States
    (ECOWAS): intervention in Liberia, 213–
    14, 221–22
Economist, 172
economy, international: and human rights,
    79–94; open vs. closed, 79–80; and
    prostitution and trafficking, 2–3; and
    state repression, 9–10
ECOWAS Cease-fire Monitoring Group
    (ECOMOG), 213–14
Ecuador, 215, 222
Ellison, Carl, 126
El Salvador, 118–19
encryption software, 126, 131n37. *See also*
    Internet; surveillance
England, 151
Engle, Karen, 45
environment, 108, 227, 229, 255; abuses
    against, 139–45, 244; NGOs, 145, 155;
    and World Bank, 171, 173, 175–76,
    181–82, 186, 187–89
Epstein, Steve, 57n16
Equal Economic Opportunity Commission
    (EEOC): and migrant workers, 34, 37
Etche people, 141, 145
Ethiopia, 214

ethnic cleansing, 149, 164, 216
Europe, 49, 77, 83, 227–28; immigration
    laws, 57n15; rights norms in, 25, 229,
    238; "social," 67
European Union, 233; citizenship
    in, 231
exploitation, economic: and global
    markets, 8
Exxon, 173

Falk, Richard, 8
famine, 210–11, 223
Foucault, Michel, 40n21
"fragmegration," 153–59
France, 203, 215, 219, 220, 222, 256
Frank, Barney: and the World Bank, 180
Fraser Institute, 82, 94
freedom, economic, 81–82, 87, 88–89,
    91–92, 93, 94, 95n11
Freedom House, 82
Freedom Writers, 122–23
Friedman, Thomas, 61
Friends of the Earth International, 140, 142
fundamentalism, Islamic, 13

Gap, the: and sweatshops, 67
GATT, 81, 108
Geneva Convention, 3
genocide, 236, 238, 241n16; in Bosnia,
    216; and international tribunals, 2;
    and Ogoni people, 143
geographic information systems (GIS),
    119
Germany, 215; Berlin Wall, 2; guest workers
    in, 24; Holocaust, 149; human rights
    focus in, 13; National Socialism, 92; neo-
    Nazis, 119; Weimar Republic, 92; and
    the World Bank, 173
globalization: and NGO advocacy, 133–45;
    defined, 1, 5–7, 81, 226–28; economic,
    77–94; "from above" vs. "from below,"
    7, 8, 61–74; and human rights, 1, 2, 3–
    16, 77–78, 80–94; and inequality, 5,
    139–45; and labor rights, 98–109; and
    migrants' rights, 19–38; streams of, 6–
    9; "through the middle," 226–39; and
    turbulence, 148–65; and women's rights,
    44–56; and the World Bank, 171–96
Gibney, 95n3
Goodin, Robert, 232
government, authoritarian, 4

Gramsci, Antonio, 234, 235
Graves, Caryn, 122–23
Greenpeace International, 140, 142
Grenada, 203, 208, 209
Group of Seven (G-7): 71, 77
Guadalupe Hidalgo, Treaty of, 33
Guatemala: CIA activity in, 64; control
    of radios in, 125; rights violations in,
    10, 243
Guererro, 125
Gurr, Ted Robert, 80, 84
Guy, Donna, 57n16
Guyana, 90, 220
Gwartney, James, 81

Habyarimana, Juvénal, 218
Haider, Jörg, 157
Haiti: human rights reform in, 2; inter-
    vention in, 206, 209, 210, 211, 220–
    21, 222, 223, 224, 241; state-sponsored
    abuses in, 10
Hansen, Pauline, 157
Hartz, Louis, 39n15
Haufler, Virginia, 238
hegemony: critique of, 73–74; of dominant
    group, 5, 13
Henderson, Conway, 83, 93
Heritage Foundation, 82
Hirst, Paul, 77
Hollifield, James, 25
Holocaust, 149
Holsti, K. J., 79
Hong Kong, 125
humanitarian intervention: norms of, 202–
    24, 236–38
humanity, crimes against, 12
Human Rights Watch, 69–70, 122, 134, 138,
    151
Hunter, David, 188
HushMail, 126
Hussein, Saddam, 224
Hutus, 218–19, 222

identity: ethnic, 29–36; and rights, 24–25
identity, national, 6
identity politics, 12
ideology, 12; racial ("neocolonial"), 32,
    35–36
Ignatiev, Michael, 158–59, 164
Ignatiev, Noel, 42n34

Ijaw people, 141
Illegal Immigration Reform and Immigrant
    Responsibility Act, 20
immigrants: rights of, 19–38
immigration: growth in, 22–26; and labor,
    100; and trafficking, 52; U. S. policy, 14,
    19–38
Immigration and Naturalization Service
    (INS): abuses of, 19–20, 29–30, 36
India, 95n11, 107, 122, 188, 189, 194;
    Narmada dam, 180, 181, 182, 185; and
    Pakistan, 203, 211; and the WTO, 68
indigenous peoples, 154; and citizenship,
    10; threats to, 4, 244; and World Bank,
    171, 176, 181
Indonesia, 66, 67, 155, 235; rights violations
    in, 10, 133, 149, 243
inequality: and citizenship, 24; with eco-
    nomic freedom, 92, 93; and globaliza-
    tion, 5, 10, 47, 134, 139–45, 158; labor,
    35, 106–07; social, 12; between states,
    22, 63
information: flow of, 5, 7–8, 9, 77, 201–
    02, 226, 233–34, 245–46; right to,
    107–08; technologies, 14; 115–29
International Bill of Human Rights, 3,
    80, 201
International Covenant on Civil and
    Political Rights, 3, 136, 207, 228
International Covenant on Economic, Social
    and Cultural Rights (ICESCR), 110n2,
    207, 228
International Covenant on Social and
    Economic Rights, 3, 99
International Criminal Court, 237, 245,
    247, 255
international human rights regime: emer-
    gent, 8; norms, 25–26, 28, 30, 37, 77–
    78, 133, 145, 148, 158–59, 201–12, 222,
    229–30, 235–36; scope of, 154, 155–56,
    244–46
International Labor Organization (ILO), 24,
    50–51, 107, 108, 252, 253; Convention
    on the Prohibition and Elimination of
    the Worst Forms of Child Labor, 101;
    Declaration on Fundamental Rights,
    101–05
International Monetary Fund (IMF), 55, 66,
    67–68, 81, 92, 233; and the World Bank,
    172, 251

International Organization for Migration, 57n11
Internet, 3, 154, 193, 234; and human rights, 119–20; 122–23, 125–27, 156, 253; and rights conflicts, 4
intolerance, cultures of, 2
investment, foreign, 66, 77, 100, 157–58, 252
Iran, 64, 211
Iraq, 208, 209, 211, 237, 243; armed intervention in, 214–15, 221, 223, 224
Ireland, 215
Israel, 95n11
Italy, 215
Itaparica resettlement claim, 187–89
Iwersen, Albrecht, 56
Iwersen-Sioltsidis, 56

Jacobson, David, 25, 26
Jaggers, Keith, 84
Japan, 77; and immigration, 23
Jiménez, Félix, 54
Jones, Ronald, 82
Juppé, Alain, 219

Katz, 85
Keck, 146n23, 174, 180, 210, 228
Kenya, 213
Keohane, Robert, 80
Kingdon, John, 136–37
Kinshasa, 126
Kofman, Eleonore, 57n15
Kosovo, 12, 119, 126, 150, 164, 223, 236
Krugman, Paul, 62, 75n14
Kudrle, 16
Kurds, 211, 214–15, 224

labor: abuses, 49, 50; cheap, 100; child, 76n30, 101, 103, 105, 107, 249, 254; as commodity, 99–100; exploitation of, 14; division of, 21; migrant, 23, 32–38, 52; movement of, 99; slave, 104. *See also* rights, labor
labor, free, 4. *See also* labor, forced; slavery
labor, forced, 3, 103. *See also* labor, free; slavery
Landi, Oscar, 124–25
Landmines Treaty, 247
Latin America, 12, 14, 41n31, 135, 243; and information, 116–17; labor practices in,

48; NGOs in, 155; and prostitution, 49, 54; sex worker organizations in, 50–52
Latinos: seen as aliens, 30–36
law: and citizenship, 27–30; international, 24, 100, 109
Lawson, Robert, 81
Lebanon: rights violations in, 10
Lenin, V. I., 64
Léotard, François, 219
Le Pen, Jean-Marie, 157
liberalism: and definition of citizenship, 27–30
Liberia, 209, 211; armed intervention in, 213–14, 221–22, 223, 224
liberty: right to, 4
Libya, 213
Lipschutz, Ronnie, 124
literacy, 55, 79
lobbying: and advocacy for victims, 134, 136, 140, 141–42
localization: and globalization, 228
Locke, John, 235; on consent, 28; and inequality, 41n29
Luxembourg, 215

Maastricht Treaty, 231
McBride Principles (1984), 107
McCarthy, Joseph, 160
McDonald's, 158
Maher, Kristen, 9
Malaysia, 100, 108
Mali, 214
malnutrition, 77
Maquiladora Standards of Conduct (1991), 107
markets: and globalization, 2, 4–5, 7–8, 12, 14, 226–28, 231–33, 238–39, 243, 251–52; and information, 124; monitoring of, 15; and human rights, 63–74, 82, 98, 100, 101, 106–09, 158–59, 243, 245
marriage: sex workers and, 49, 55, 57n13
Martin, Phil, 34
Marxism, 64, 226, 234
Massachusetts, Commonwealth of: Burma law, 104, 106, 111n33
match, organizational: of NGOs and oppressed groups, 137–45
media: and oppressed groups, 139–40, 144, 147n40, 245
Mendes, Chico, 137

Mexico, 220, 251; border crossings, 2; labor rights in, 2, 107; and market forces, 5; migrant workers from, 33–34; sex worker organizations in, 50; U.S. annexation of territory, 33; and World Bank, 194; Zapatista uprising, 119, 120, 125, 128, 137, 139

migrants: economic, 10, 15; labor, rights of, 19–38, 52, 235, 251. *See also* citizenship

migration: and globalization, 2, 9, 11, 13; patterns, 22–23; and repression, 9; and threats to human rights, 19–38, 48, 52, 156–57, 230–31

Meyer, William, 64, 67, 69, 75n15

Middle East: rights norms in, 229

Milner, Helen, 80

Milner, Wesley, 9

minorities: Muslim, 13, ethnic, 150

Mishra, Ramesh, 240n8

mobility, 5, 8, 9, 156–57; of status, 24

Mongolia, 173

Moon, Bruce, 79, 83

mortality, infant, 79

Morris, David, 79, 95n6

Movement for the Survival of the Ogoni People (MOSOP), 139–44; "Ogoni Day March," 143

Movimento de Mujeres Unidas (MODEMU), 53–55

Mugabe, Robert, 214

Mujer a Mujer, 119

multinational corporations (MNCs): and human rights, 64, 66, 67, 75n18, 138, 150; and labor rights, 2, 107–09; and security rights, 5–6; state regulation of, 10, 228, 237–38

Murphy, S. D., 205

Museveni, Yoweri, 214

Muslims: Bosnian, 215–17; tolerance for, 13

Myanmar (Burma), 104, 243, 252

Nader, Ralph, 62

NAFTA, 137

Napster, 234

nationalism: rhetoric of, and labor rights, 106–07

National Network for Immigrant and Refugee Rights (NNIRR), 43n42

National Patriotic Liberation Front (NPFL), 213–14, 221

Native Americans, 41n31

NATO, 150, 160, 164; in Bosnia, 215–17; in Serbia, 204, 224

nature, human: and human rights values, 4

Nepal: dam projects, 182, 200n47

Netherlands, 215

New York: attacks on, 12

New Zealand, 219

Nicaragua, 50, 253

Nigeria, 15, 213, 219, 243; Ogoni people, 139–45

Nike: and sweatshops, 67

"noise": and information, 122–28

non-governmental organizations (NGOs): campaigns of, 5–6, 161; credibility of, 121–24, 135; and governments, 152; growth of, 155–56; influence of, 3, 12, 15, 67, 133, 134, 151, 211, 227, 238, 243–44, 250; and information technologies, 115–29, 233–34; monitoring of, 4; and organizational match, 139–40, 144; and prostitution, 51, 53–55; and sweatshops, 98, 107; and the World Bank, 172–73, 174, 176–77, 189, 195

nonintervention, norms of, 221–22

North America, 77

Northern Ireland, 107

North Korea, 80, 189, 236

Nuevo Herald, El, (Miami), 54

Nuremberg, 2

Nyerere, Julius, 213

Oaxaca, 125

Offe, Klaus, 240n5

Ogoni people, 139–45, 233; and "genocide," 143

Operation Gatekeeper (San Diego), 20

Operation Wetback, 34

Organization for Security and Cooperation in Europe, 83

Organization of African Unity, 213

Organization of American States, 46–47, 210, 220, 253

Pakistan, 203, 208, 209, 211, 219, 221, 223, 224

Panama, 209

Pangalangan, Raul, 9

Papua New Guinea: Bougainville Island, 141

paramilitaries: and human rights violations, 2, 10

personhood, universal, 21, 24–25, 30
PGP (pretty good privacy): encryption
    software, 126
Philip Morris, 75n16
Philippines, 41n31, 108, 155
Physical Quality of Life Index, 86, 90, 92
Pinochet, Augusto, 92, 149, 151, 164, 237
Poe, Steven, 83, 88, 93, 95n3
police: brutality, 4, 44, 45; and migration,
    9; monitoring of, 51–52
political terror scale (PTS), 78, 86, 93
politics: international, 134–35; world,
    streams of, 7–8
Pol Pot, 80
poor, rural: and globalization, 2
population growth, 84, 86, 88, 89, 93
Porter, Tony, 238
poverty: and capitalism, 64, 76n25; and
    Universal Declaration, 71
Proposition 187 (California), 21, 22, 28–29,
    36, 38n6
prostitution: child, 54, 251; forced, 19, 45,
    51, 52, 54; and police brutality, 4, 243;
    and rights violations, 44–56; rise of, 2–3;
    and tourism, 14. See also trafficking
protectionism: and labor rights, 98, 100,
    249

race, 25; and citizenship, 29–30; and "sex
    tourism," 46, 49; and stratification, 32–
    33, 35–36. See also colonialism; ideology;
    inequality
rape, 211; and prostitutes' rights, 45, 52,
    243
refugees, 24; and armed intervention, 214–
    15, 218; and globalization, 2, 13; rights
    of, 28–29; and rights violations, 10, 211
repression: and civil war, 9; state sponsored,
    1–2, 10
resettlement: and the World Bank, 181, 186,
    187–89
rights, "basic," 4; defined, 78–79
rights, children's, 207
rights, civil: violations of, 10
rights, collective, 134; defined, 3
rights, ethnic minority, 142
rights, human, 1; abuse of, 1; and armed
    intervention, 208–24; for citizens,
    21, 24–38; defined, 3, 78–79, 134; in
    developing countries, 98; and eco-
    nomic development, 5, 89–93, 95n3;

and globalization, 2, 3–16, 63–74, 77,
    226–7, 228–39; and information, 115–
    29; and international tribunals, 2; as
    issue area, 148–50; prostitution as vio-
    lation of, 50–51; "rights talk," 6; surveil-
    lance and, 125–28, 131n37; and trade,
    106–08
rights, intellectual property, 62
rights, labor, 100, 101–09; advocates, 98;
    violations of, 10, 14
rights, political, 210, 222; denial of, 13, 20
rights, security, 4, 14, 134, 201–02, 209–11,
    222, 223; defined, 3, 78, 85, 87–89, 90,
    91–93
rights, social and economic, 210, 222;
    defined, 3; of migrants, 29–30; threats
    to, and globalization, 5, 8, 10, 13, 20,
    134, 232
rights, subsistence, 78–79, 85, 86–87, 92, 93
rights, women's, 44–56, 107, 137, 207
Risse, Thomas, 175
Riverside: beating of immigrants in, 36, 38n1
Romania, 215
Ronfeldt, David, 125
Ropp, Stephen, 175
Rosenau, James N., 7, 8, 117–18
Rosh, 83
Rucht, Dieter, 130n6
Rugmark Foundation, 107
Russia, 135, 203–04
Rwanda, 209, 211; armed intervention
    in, 218–19, 221, 222, 223, 224, 236,
    237; and genocide tribunals, 2; state-
    sponsored abuses in, 10
Rwandan Patriotic Front (RPF), 219, 221,
    222

sabotage: of technology, 126–28
Salcedo, Dan, 118–19
sanctions, trade: and human rights norms,
    202, 210, 211, 236–38; and labor rights,
    98
Sandholtz, Wayne, 9
San Diego, 20, 23
Saro-Wiwa, Ken, 139–44, 233
Scholte, Jan Aart, 6, 16
Scully, Gerald, 82
Seattle: "Battle of," 61–62, 68, 71–72, 92,
    153, 156, 172
Senegal, 133, 214
Serbia, 164, 204, 211, 223, 224, 237

sex workers: organizations, 50–52, 53–55; rights of, 14, 44–56. *See also* prostitution

Shell: abuses of, 140, 142–43, 145; advertising campaigns of, 64–65, 75n16

Shklar, Judith: on citizenship, 27, 31

Shuck, Peter: on citizenship, 28, 39n17

Siad Barre, 222

Siapno, Jacqueline, 107

Sierra Club, 2

Sierra Leone: civil war in, 5, 9–10

Sikkink, Kathryn, 146n23, 167n47, 174, 175, 180, 210, 228

slavery, 84, 104; "modern day," 3; prostitution as, 50–51, 52, 243; and tourism, 48

Slepack Principles (1987), 107

Slovakia, 155

Smith, Rogers: on citizenship, 28, 31, 39n17

Somalia, 206, 208, 209, 210, 211; armed intervention in, 217–18, 219, 221, 222, 223, 224, 236

Soros, George, 68

Sosúa, 49, 55, 57n12

South Africa, 107, 108, 151

Southeast Asia: labor rights in, 2; prostitution in, 3, 243

Southern Poverty Law Center, 151

South Korea, 149

sovereignty norms, 202, 205–06, 221–22, 223, 227, 246–47

Soviet Union, 64, 107, 202, 203

Soysal, Yasmin: on migration, 24–25

Spain, 215

Spar, Debra, 67

Srebrenica, 224

standards, labor, 98, 99–100, 101–05, 107–09

starvation, 211, 217, 224, 236

state, the: "above" and "below," 8, 9; coercion of, 5; "globalized," 9–10, 226–39; legitimacy of, 4, 228–29, 238–39, 242–44, 246–47

Stockman, Alan, 82

stratification: among oppressed groups, 136–45

subaltern discourse, 71–74

Sudan, 213

Sullivan Principles (1977), 107

Surinam, 50

surveillance, 12, 210; technology and, 125–28, 131n37

sweatshops, 67, 98, 106, 107, 245. *See also* labor: child; rights, labor; standards, labor

Sweden, 95n11, 215

Switzerland, 49; Migros chain, 108

Syria, 235

Taiwan, 253

Tanzania, 203, 211, 219

Tate, C. Neal, 83, 88, 93, 95n3

Taylor, Charles, 213, 221

technology: information, 115–29, 154–55

terror, 12; political, 78

terrorism: attacks, 12; response, 13; state, 80

Tesón, F. R., 208–09

Thailand, 108

Thompson, Grahame, 77

Tiananmen Square, 127

Tibet, 2, 136, 173, 182, 184, 189

"Tobin tax," 73

Togo, 214

torture, 84, 201–02, 207, 211

tourism, 243; and prostitution, 14, 44–50, 54, 55, 228, 251

tourists, 11

trade, 157–68; export, 105; free, as "unfair trade," 62–63

trade agreements, international: and sweatshops, 98

traditions, religious: and human rights values, 4

trafficking, 45, 50, 52, 54; and migrants, 19; rise of, 2–3. *See also* prostitution

Transparency International, 244–45

Tunisia, 127

turbulence, 148–65

Turkey, 211; and the Kurds, 214

Tutsis, 219

Uganda, 203, 208, 211, 213, 214, 219, 221, 223, 224

Uighurs, 136

unions: and state control, 10

United Kingdom, 215; NGOs in, 155–56

United Nations, 46–47, 63; Charter, 160, 202, 205, 207; Commission on Human Rights, 207; Convention on the Elimination of Discrimination Against Women, 3; Convention on the Prevention and Punishment of the Crime of Genocide, 206; Convention on the Protection of Rights of All Migrant Workers and Their Families, 24; Convention on the Rights of the Child, 3; Human Rights Commission, 164; and human rights reform, 2; peacekeeping forces, 133; on prostitution, 50–51, 54–55; Resolution 688, 215, 218, 221; Security Council, 203, 204–06, 208, 210, 213, 214–20, 222, 223, 236; Social Summit of 1995, 71; sovereignty declarations, 205; UNESCO Declaration on Race and Racial Prejudice, 24

United Network of Immigrant and Refugee Rights (UNIRR), 43n42

United States, 14, 23; African Americans in, 149; Army, 127; border crossings, deaths during, 2, 20, 38n3; civil rights movement, 137; and "consensualism," 27–30; forced labor in, 3; foreign policy of, 64–65, 66–67, 69, 79, 214, 220; hegemony of, 6; immigration policy, 14, 28–30; imperialism of, 41n31; and international rights standards, 230; labor unions, 76n30; militias in, 151; noncitizens in, 19–38; nonprofit organizations in, 155; response to terrorism, 13; satellite reconnaissance, 119; in Somalia, 218; and the World Bank, 173, 180; and the WTO, 62

Universal Declaration of Human Rights, 3, 4, 19, 39n8, 70–71, 74, 160, 164, 202, 206, 228–30

UN Operation in Somalia (UNISOM), 218

UN Protection Force (UNPROFOR), 215–17

Unrepresented Nations and Peoples Organization (UNPO), 140

Upton, Barbara, 197n17

Uruguay, 220

Uwilingiyimana, Agathe, 218

Venezuela, 50, 51–52, 220, 221, 235

Vienna Declaration and Program of Action, 228

Vietnam: "aliens" from, 20

Vincent, R.J., 205

violence: against migrants, 157; political, 13;

racial, 25; against women, 44–45, 51, 52, 53

VIP Reference News (Dacankao), 125, 127

Walzer, Michael, 40n20

war, civil, 4, 84, 86, 89; abuses during, 5, 211; and intervention, 210–11; in Liberia, 213–14; and repression, 9

war, international, 84, 86

Washington, D.C.: attacks on, 12; protests in, 92

Webster, Craig, 80, 81

Weyker, Shane, 7, 9

Willetts, Peter, 115–16, 121, 122

Wolfensohn, Peter: World Bank President, 174, 182, 186

women: feminism, 155; genital mutilation, 137, 145; rights of, 3, 4, 10, 11, 12, 44–56, 107, 201, 207, 235, 243, 255; violence against, 44–45, 51, 52, 53

workers: conditions for, 98

Working Group On Contemporary Forms of Slavery, 50

World Bank, 3, 46–47, 55, 66, 68, 75n25, 81, 92, 245, 251; and dam projects, 180–82; and the environment, 171, 173, 175–76, 186, 187–89; and human rights, 171–96, 238; Inspection Panel, 172, 173–91, 192, 195–96, 233; Operations Evaluation Department, 185

World Economic Forum, 62, 68, 71

World Trade Organization (WTO), 61–63, 68, 71, 72–73, 92, 100, 105, 153, 156; Appellate Body, 104; Singapore Ministerial Declaration, 101–05; and the World Bank, 172, 252

World War II, 24, 154, 208

xenophobia, 49

Yemen, 215

Yugoslavia, 135, 149, 150, 164; armed intervention in, 215–17; and genocide tribunals, 2

Zaire, 66, 214

Zapatistas: use of information technology, 119, 120, 125, 128, 137

Zimbabwe, 214, 215, 222, 235

Text:	10/12 Baskerville
Display:	Baskerville
Compositor:	Integrated Composition Systems
Printer:	Malloy Lithographing, Inc.